# AIRGUN FIELDCRAFT
## A lifetime's hunting advice

### IAN BARNETT

**AUTHOR**
*Ian Barnett*

**EDITOR**
*Nigel Allen*

**DESIGN**
*Lynne Stephens*

**COVER PHOTOGRAPHY**
*WildAnglia www.wildanglia.co.uk*

**PHOTOGRAPHY**
*WildAnglia, Nigel Allen, archive*

**Printed in England by Polestar Wheatons - a division of Polestar UK Print Ltd**

**Blaze Publishing Ltd**
Lawrence House, Morell Street, Leamington Spa,
Warwickshire, CV32 5SZ
**Tel:** +44 (0) 1926 339 808
**Fax:** +44 (0) 1926 470 400
**Email:** info@blazepublishing.co.uk
**Website:** www.blazepublishing.co.uk

# CONTENTS

# FOREWORD

While I'm proud to be this book's editor, I'm more honoured to be the one who provides its foreword, as I am a huge fan of Ian Barnett's airgun writings, having been the first publisher to convince him to succumb to the scribe. However, I preface this, his second airgun hunting tome, not in any editorial capacity, but entirely as a keen airgunner and air rifle hunter of 40 years.

Down those years, I shouldn't think there's a single book on airgun hunting that I haven't enthusiastically read from cover to cover. A few have been poor, some mediocre, but most have been retained in my own shooting library, to be frequently referenced and occasionally re-read. This book falls firmly into the category of 'keeper' – but I may as well prune much of my bookcase, given the sheer wealth of knowledge that *Airgun Fieldcraft* contains. If ever there is a claim for a book to be 'the only one you'll ever need to read' on a particular subject, this is it as far as airgun hunting is concerned.

Having shot – and hunted with – air rifles for 80 per cent of my life (not to mention working with them on a full-time basis for over three decades), I'd consider myself quite knowledgeable when it comes to all things airgun. I've pursued all manner of quarry through all the seasons, at dawn and dusk, with all types of air rifle, in all calibres and would, consequently, also consider myself an adept fieldsman. Therefore, it's not too arrogant of me to say that aside of them being entertaining reads, few of the airgun hunting books I've read in recent years have taught me anything new.

However, as intimately involved as I have been with this book, a stark truth has emerged.

By comparison with its author, I am a mere novice at the airgun hunting game. While I have loved every second of all those countless hours spent in the field with my air rifles, in pursuit of quarry for pest control and the pot, it appears I have wasted much of my time by missing the bigger picture. The bigger picture as seen through the eyes of a master airgun hunter, whose observational skills serve to highlight that I have been nothing more than a mere extra in my hunting scenarios.

What this book unequivocally affirms is that Ian Barnett has played a lead role in much of his airgun hunting life and its by-line – *A lifetime's hunting advice* – bears testimony to the extraordinary value of what lies, so comprehensively, within its pages. A vat of knowledge that will humble, as it did me, even the most experienced of airgun hunters.

If you have acquired Airgun Fieldcraft because you know of Ian Barnett, then your opinion of his brilliance as a hunter (and documenter) will only be confirmed – and you will, I'm sure, learn countless more golden nuggets of countryside lore that will help improve your own hunting experiences. And if you are new to the author? Then, in my opinion, you are starting with the very best mentor of all.

Either way, sit back and prepare to marvel at what I (with all due respect to existing authors in this arena) consider is the most authoritative, most entertaining and most influential writing on airgun hunting that's ever been put down on paper. ○

**NIGEL ALLEN**
**Bristol, England. Summer 2012**

# INTRODUCTION

Do you, like me, gauge your everyday life via a watch or clock, with either GMT or BST applied? A wild creature won't. It will follow the angle of the sun, the rise of the moon, the direction of the breeze, the temperature of the day or night. It will note the budding and the fall of the leaf, the height of the crop and the ripeness of the fruit. It will sense the breeding cycle of its mate, the primeval need to mate and consequently the feeding and protection of its young. It will rely on its knowledge of the prominence of its prey and the existence of its own predators. It will live and breathe with a cautious eye, at all times, fixed simply on surviving each day.

To be a hunter, you need to do the same. When I put aside the clock to ignore time pressures; when I pick up the camera to record a wild creature; when I sit in deep cover watching quarry with a gun; when I shoot a wild pest species, I put aside my 'normal' life. I am now in a different life, with different nominal values and different priorities. It is a life I often prefer over that normal life, for it's deep, pure, precarious, colourful, exhilarating, unpredictable, non-committal and forgiving. When I'm out there with an air rifle, there's no-one to criticise me, other than me. The only expectation is mine…

Throughout this book, I frequently use an archaic, endearing term 'Mother Nature'. For I can think of no other term to describe the Zen – that intangible soul that wraps itself around both man and beast in the countryside. She influences birth and death, season and weather, dominance and subservience. All in equal measure. What she gives, she also takes away in fair balance. She? I use the term deliberately – for only a female could be so devastatingly beautiful and bountiful, yet at times, so viciously cruel.

This book isn't just for the air rifle hunter. It is for anyone who roams the countryside attending to vermin in the interest of crop protection and conservation. It is for the boy with the catapult (for that's where I started) and for the mature adult stepping onto the hunting trail late in life. It doesn't matter what tool you carry; the fieldcraft needed is the same. But if I convince you, by the time you reach the end of this book, that the air rifle is a wonderful tool and capable of many a task, then it's been well worth writing.

Hunt safely, hunt responsibly – and shoot accurately. ○

*Hunt responsibly and shoot accurately*

# THE RESPONSIBLE HUNTER

## PRIDE AND PREJUDICE

As a man who spends much of his time cooped up in tedious meetings and bound to a desk, the lure of the countryside – that rich environment where I mis-spent so much of my youth and now enjoy most of my free time – courses through my very blood. To walk, watch and listen is not enough, though. I feel naked without a gun hitched over my shoulder, or a camera around my neck. Even when I shoot nothing, I will always photograph something. The camera is much more than a surrogate gun, however. It captures the essence and mood of a moment which will never return. It's much harder to explain those moments through the written medium, though this second book (like my first) is an attempt to do so. But it isn't just another book about the mechanics of handling an air rifle. Nor is it a coffee-table collection of photographs. It is a pot-pourri of quarry knowledge, anecdotes, thoughts, recollections, advice, recipes and images reflecting time spent in the British

*Vermin control is a necessary and important factor in both crop protection and conservation of vulnerable species*

countryside. It is rarely about people, for I am a deliberately reclusive man except where family is concerned.

The modern air rifle is a wonderful, but much-maligned tool. Although I have ample opportunity to carry a shotgun or a firearm, this silent, simple gun has gained me the trust and respect necessary to walk thousands of acres of Norfolk. It is efficient enough to let me cull hundreds of pest species every year. It is secretive enough to allow silent passage through wood and field. Even the best airgun ammunition is ridiculously cheap by comparison with other shooting disciplines. Yet its employment requires an element of skill and cunning, otherwise defined as fieldcraft. This book imparts some of the tactics, techniques and trickery I use to make such a feeble weapon effective.

Likewise, the modern digital camera takes the art of photography to an almost idiot-proof level. No more trips to the darkroom to wait and see if that much sought-after snap is correctly exposed. No more posting the roll of celluloid to some remote processor and waiting weeks for the results. You point, you shoot... and you immediately see the result. A bit like the air-rifle, actually. I make no claim to being a professional photographer; I just snap what I see and, usually, I get the result I want.

The privilege of walking wood and field with a gun and a trustworthy dog at your side is being threatened constantly by the bias and prejudice of folk who would be well advised to read the dictionary term for 'cruelty'. Folk who also conveniently forget that the meat on their dinner table once lived and breathed. I wonder if our critics would use the word 'cruel' if they watched (as I have) a chaffinch fledging being ripped apart, limb by limb, by a magpie? If they watched the hen pheasant fussing up and down in distress as the stoat sucks the embryos from her clutch of eggs? Were they to pick up a book like this, they might come to appreciate that those of us who choose to spend our precious free time deep in country with a gun, usually do so because of an inherent love of all wild things.

Vermin control is a necessary and important factor in both crop protection and conservation of vulnerable species. This book is dedicated not just to the like-minded souls who shoot to protect and conserve, but also to the generation who will hopefully follow us. I just pray that they still have the freedom of choice and opportunity that I have enjoyed.

One final point that's worth making: the entire content of this book refers to British quarry, British wildlife and British law at the time of writing. Parochial though this may seem, I know nothing else, for I have never hunted with an air rifle abroad. Nonetheless, the principles of successful hunting and fieldcraft are, I'm sure, universal.

## MORALS AND ETHICS

Where better to tackle this tricky subject than right at the beginning of a book about shooting? Over the years, I have been constantly concerned – though never surprised – at my activities being challenged on moral grounds. I have, thankfully, maintained many friendships with folk, mainly urbanites, who view the death of a wild creature at my hands with displeasure. Let's just say we have agreed to differ. Such people find it too difficult to understand that I take more pleasure in the tracking, stalking and getting near to vermin than the actual execution of a shot. I take no real pleasure in gazing down on a shot animal or bird, but I fully confess to enjoying the knowledge of the effect it will bring, whether that's saving a nest full of fledglings, the continued growth of a crop or the elimination of spoilage and disease. For that is the purpose of vermin control.

The argument that we are interfering with nature is not one that I can tolerate. Homosapiens have been hunting, trapping and killing since they first stood on two legs. That we have become the dominant species on this earth is no coincidence. As the creature at the top of the food chain, we have an irrevocable responsibility to manage that chain, both for the good of our species and for the threatened species around us. I would wholly agree that, at times, we have abused that status (and often still continue to). But thankfully, in modern times, a common sense approach has been taken toward the conservation of habitat and threatened species. We hunters have played an important part in that, though unfortunately, often in reparation for the sins of our parents and grandparents.

In more recent times, the sensibility of the 1981 Wildlife and Countryside Act, and the advent of the General Licences to legislate vermin control and the species allowed, have been welcomed by all responsible shooters. No longer could we raid wild birds' nests for their eggs, or shoot indiscriminately at anything. Sadly, the 2004 Hunting Act and the recent repeal of the rarely-enforced Pests Act of 1954 were steps in the wrong direction. The former pressed through by the uninformed with nothing but crass political posturing as a motive. The latter? Victim to a lack of application by a rural community reluctant to challenge its neighbours. Rather than upset an adjoining landowner, most farmers preferred to instruct someone like yours truly to take care of business on their own side of the fence, rather than bring the power of the Crown to bear on the other side of it. Such is the tolerance of the true countryman or woman.

In an age of processed, factory-reared food, I also take great pleasure in putting natural food on the table. Those friends who debate against the simple act of going out with a gun and potting a rabbit for dinner have forgotten that mankind, for all of its machines, industry and internet, is part of nature, too. The ecological damage we do, without conscience, is unbelievable – so please let me wander in my countryside (while it's still there to enjoy) with my gun and my dog, doing what comes naturally to me.

Consider this, too. For some of us, the hunting gene remains pure. For others, it's transferred into mimicry of those primeval urges. Most sport is simply an extension of the basic instinct to prove accuracy, speed, endurance and concentration. As we migrate as a species from countryside to city, other basic traits are transformed in a deep-rooted, unconscious attempt to show dominance. Violence – domestic or gang-related; mob mentality and riot; professional competitiveness in climbing the corporate ladder – can be an uncompromising and vicious journey. As a consequence, many urban dwellers now seek solace in the countryside, mostly by way of recreation – but many also choose to now escape there permanently. In both cases, they sometimes seek to challenge the traditions and lifestyles of their new neighbours – but how dare they! Consider also the hypocrisy of accepting that a new road, a new golf course or a new factory is acceptable before criticising my shot magpie or culled coney. Which will upset nature's balance the more?

The only debates I consider have merit on the subject of controlling vermin or pot-hunting are around the many methods employed: traps, snares, nets, ferrets, shotguns, air rifles, rimfire rifles, lamps, dogs. I have no axe to grind with any of them. I just prefer the challenge of 'getting up close and personal' with a silenced air rifle. It's discreet, specific… and requires a certain level of skill. I happen to be, through many years of practice, quite good at it. Yet even I don't profess to despatch cleanly with every shot. Please don't ever believe a shooter who claims they do. If I've covered the morality of shooting from my perspective, let me please expand on the 'ethic'. Very simply, it's this:

that we owe our target quarry the dignity of as quick a despatch as we can possibly achieve. To this end, we need to be accurate and need to practise precise shooting *ad infinitum* on static targets before having the audacity to shoot at a live creature. We need to check that our equipment is functioning properly and that the rifle is perfectly zeroed before shooting vermin. Most of all, we need to know how to deal with the eventuality of wounded quarry, for eventual it is. Faced with such trauma, many an air rifle shooter has abandoned the gun for good. Sadly, this is because they have neither expected it, nor received advice on how to handle such a situation. There is absolutely nothing wrong in finding the plight of a wounded creature distressing. You should; I still do even after 30-plus years of vermin control – and it's why I chose to cover morals and ethics in the very first chapter of this book. Hunting vermin does not mean you have a disdain for wildlife. It's a dirty job, and someone has to do it for the sake of protecting crops or food stores, and for vulnerable bird conservation.

## HEALTH AND SAFETY

It would be totally remiss of me, a seasoned shooter of air rifles, to go any further with this book without underlining the importance of safety with regard to ownership of a gun. Not just your own safety, but the safety of people around you while it's in your possession, either in use or stored. Sure, we're talking airguns here. Yet we are reminded, time and time again, that even the feeble airgun can kill a human in tragic or irresponsible circumstances.

If you are reading this book, it's probably because you either already own an airgun or purport to own one. So I'm going to set out my own '10 commandments' around my personal views on basic safety, and then refer you to the experts.

● Never buy or own a gun without a safety

catch, which prevents accidental firing of a loaded gun. And then never rely on that safety catch; it might fail.

● Never point a rifle, loaded or unloaded, at anyone or anything you don't intend, or have legitimate reason, to shoot.

● Never climb or cross an obstacle with your air rifle. Put it carefully on the opposite side at a safe distance, safety catch on, cross the obstacle and recover the rifle.

● Always travel to and from your shoot with the rifle cased, unloaded and with pellets distinctly separate from the gun. (Any magazine should always be transported in an unloaded state.)

● Never load your air rifle until just before hunting. After loading, engage the safety catch before moving on. Make the safety catch a habit. If you raise the gun to shoot vermin and the safety is off, you've failed as a responsible shooter.

● If, during hunting, you unexpectedly encounter someone (even if they are trespassing), immediately disarm the rifle and explain what you've just done. Never stand and converse with someone with your rifle loaded.

● Never leave your air rifle unattended while hunting. Even if searching for shot quarry, carry the gun.

● When you've finished hunting, before stowing the rifle (in the car or at home), cock and fire your rifle into the ground, remove the magazine then recock and fire again to make absolutely sure your barrel is clear.

● At home, ensure the rifle is immediately secured away (important under current legislation). Don't stop for a coffee or other drink; put away your gun.

● Whenever you have an air rifle in your arms, be aware of its capacity for harm. That's why you're carrying it. Respect it – but more importantly, respect the privilege of being deemed a person responsible enough to carry it. For when you do, you represent me and the

everyone else who reads this book – airgun hunters.

I mentioned referral to the experts and if you want a complete, up-to-date code of safety for the air rifle, I can do no better than point you in the direction of the British Association for Shooting and Conservation (BASC). Their down-loadable guides and codes of practice are available on their excellent website. Further, I would highly recommend membership of the BASC, which will also give you shooting insurance cover and access to legal advice should anything go wrong.

On a more emotive subject – which adds a one-off cost to air rifle ownership – I would always advocate a gunsafe in your house, even for sub-12 ft/lb rifles which don't legally require such high-level security. Children are eternally curious and masters of deception, and under the Crime & Security Act 2010, it is a legal requirement to have your airguns stored in a way that prevents access by minors.

## WHAT IS FIELDCRAFT?

There is no single ingredient to achieving success as an air rifle hunter; there are many. A reliable gun, robust pellets, constant shooting practice, subtle clothing, suitably placed hides and fieldcraft. All of these elements contribute to the role of an efficient shooter . Over the years, I've communicated with many air rifle hunters who, having mixed the above ingredients, still can't engage with quarry. I don't mean they miss their quarry with their shots; I mean they're unable to find, or get near to quarry on their land. The vital constituent, the spice that flavours the hunting dish, is observation. A strange word, indeed, for it doesn't just mean simply watching; it means employing every sense you have in order to understand what's going on around you.

One thing you learn very quickly in the hunting field is that even when you can't see them, wild creatures – who survive on their natural senses – will certainly see, hear or

smell you and will consequently react. That doesn't necessarily mean that they'll flee. Most small mammals, for instance, have a natural proclivity to freeze to avoid exposure. Their congenital instincts seem to tell them that movement means detection, so they cower down to lower their profile. A stalking hunter soon learns to do the same. Most birds, conversely, do the opposite – they'll remove from danger as swiftly as possible as they have the advantage of flight. Even so, many birds will hop swiftly into cover to watch any perceived threat first. Some notable exceptions are ground-nesting species – pheasant, partridge, rails, bitterns and the like – which fly poorly. They will freeze and cower, only taking flight if menace presses hard.

The huge advantage that many quarry species employ to aid survival is their own natural camouflage. What the apprentice shooter needs to develop is the 'hunter's eye' – the knack of scanning a tree-line, a hedgerow, a crop border, or any scene, and spotting the abnormal; the 'out-of-place'. This art is something that only comes with practice and learning from mistakes. If you first learn to spot departing quarry, rather than expect quarry to walk or fly right up to you, you will learn the art very fast, albeit simply out of frustration!

Most British mammals are silent when facing threat except, perhaps, some deer species which bark like a dog. The stoat and weasel may stand and scold, but only when cornered. Many birds are vociferous when threatened, particularly corvids. Learn the sounds and what they mean. Is it you they have seen, or is it some other predator? Learn the alarm sounds of other creatures and birds, too, not just your quarry. The drumming of the rabbit with its back paw means you've been rumbled; they would actually flee a fox. The harsh, machine-gun rattle of the magpie is you, too. Keep deathly still and you may still have your chance, though. The roebuck's

## CROSSING BARRIERS

The air rifle hunter will have to negotiate many barriers during the course of an average hunt. The first hurdle they will always have to cross is their own impatience! When you are in pursuit of quarry, never neglect safety.

It's often easier to climb a gate silently, than to open it and risk noise. When going over, disarm the rifle and leave it by the post at the catched end of the gate, or if the ground is dry, underneath it. Climb over the hinged end of the gate, where it's strongest, then recover your rifle and re-arm it. You've lost nothing, but time.

I have to cross many barbed-wire fences on my permissions – which is why I buy cheap, camouflaged trousers! Trust me, never 'climb' a barbed-wire fence; pass through it, or walk to the nearest gate. If you want to pass through it, disarm the rifle and lay it under the bottom wire, at one post. Walk to the next one, then on to the middle of the strands, where there is less tension. Use one hand to push the middle strand down, the other to push the top strand up, and step carefully through, keeping your head and back horizontal. When through, recover your gun and re-arm it. If you're a guy, check your wedding tackle; if anything is missing, you did it wrong!

Never cross a stream or ditch carrying an armed rifle. Again, disarm the gun, shoulder it using its sling (all my guns have slings for reasons just like this) and negotiate the obstacle. Do the same on narrow, slippery bridges or planks.

bark means he has scented you or your dog – he has no other natural threat. The scream of the jay, however, should alert you. If it's close by, or circling, it's seen you – but if it's static, manic and distant, stalk-in carefully. For the jay's mortal enemy is the grey squirrel… and such calls are marking its presence. The blackbird cock's frantic 'pip, pip, pip' has nothing to do with man; it's watching a ground-based predator such as fox, stoat or cat. When it spots man too close, it will flash horizontally through the shrubs with a continuous jarring, loud alarm call. Hear that on the far side of the wood and you know you have company – human company. (So be careful with that gun!)

The carrion crow can both amuse and

*The only person who can make sure of safety… is you*

disclose. They are a bombastic bird anyway, loving the sound of their own ugly shout. Walk out in their vision with a rifle and they will tell the whole world with a staccato "*guuun, guuun, guuun!*" At least that's what it sounds like to me! I am in no doubt that many wild creatures can detect malice. We humans certainly don't have the patent on body-language interpretation and I have been able to check this theory many times. The grey squirrel will sit on its bough watching you for an eternity, until you raise your scope in its direction – and only then will it flee.

Recently, I stepped from cover to see a hare staring back at me. My rifle was slung over my shoulder. I backed into cover and drew the camera from my bag. I stepped out and this normally wary beast allowed me to photograph it at leisure. I stepped back into cover and exchanged camera for rifle. Not that I intended to shoot a hare with an air rifle, it was simply because I wanted to move on. As soon as I emerged with the unslung rifle, the hare bolted.

Similarly, I watched a magpie perched on the roof of my neighbour's house. I knew that although it had most of its attention on their bird-table, it had half an eye on me. I moved about, preparing a barbecue and it still perched there, obviously not feeling threatened. Then I turned to the bird and slowly raised my empty arms in a mock shooting stance. The magpie immediately chattered away in alarm. Perhaps it's the profile of a man's arms, raised horizontally, that registers a 'danger' signal in the wild psyche?

Crows and jays are not the only birds that will expose you to your quarry. Tiny songbirds, such as the robin and wren, can blow your cover with their very similar '*tac, tac, tac*' alarm call. Now the jay, should she show her plumage, can be silenced with a pellet. Don't dare silence those songbirds, however. Learn to appreciate their vigilance and stalk more carefully. Shoot one and you don't only face

a stretch in one of Her Majesty's hotels, but you lose me as a friend and mentor, too. The reason we're out there is to protect such as them.

Corvids and pigeons will gravitate to high branches, using 'sitty' trees where they can alight and scan for food or threat. You will see the birds from a distance. Note the time of day that you saw them. More importantly, note the position of the sun, if there is one. Learn where the greatest cover is in relation to these vantage points. Learn, too, how to move toward them on a path that will keep you hidden. Even the smallest copse can be a stop-over for a myriad of wildlife, if not a haven. Pass it by and it will be at your loss. Small coverts are often superb for roost-shooting and pigeon decoying.

You would be wise not to neglect the farmyard itself. Explore the farm buildings, sheds, grain stores and waste piles carefully and find the clues as to its raiders. Rat spoor; pigeon droppings; the cast feather of the magpie or crow; the paw and claw prints of bird and beast. All these signs will decide when, where and how you target your quarry.

Quarry habit is the weakness of every type of pest which will render it vulnerable to its own 'predation' by the hunter. Returning repeatedly to an abundant food source; perching at the same watching point; roosting overnight in the same tree; drinking from the same water source; following the same trail from a den or a burrow. When you see the gnawed kernel lying on the margin near the maize crop, hide away for a while and wait. That grey squirrel is either in the crop stealing more, or will come back from the wood to raid again soon. It will bring a juicy yellow cob to the margin again, where it's then able to turn it freely between its paws. This is your chance...

Look for where vermin take on water. Every living creature needs water. Ponds, troughs, streams, becks, pools – they all attract passing vermin. Even scavengers like the magpie can't resist the occasional bath in a shallow puddle. Rats, of course, are rarely far from water and spread the *leptospira* bacteria they carry to water sources. Some of your quarry, though, will dislike getting its feet wet. Similarly, the squirrel will drink at the well that's formed in the cleft of a tree or amongst its roots. They'll come back to the pool – habit!

Another thing to learn is outline. As you get to know your permission more intimately, it becomes easier to spot the unusual. Yet to understand what is 'odd', you first need to learn how to identify quarry (or even parts of quarry) at a mere glance. From a legal viewpoint alone, it's a wise shooter who reads up on how to recognise their quarry's silhouette – even its flight or movement – before venturing a shot. It's this instantaneous recognition that can transform your bag considerably.

It's not something that can be easily taught; it's something that needs to be gradually learned, often the hard way. How can I describe it? Take the shady, motionless form on a tree trunk, conspicuous against a grey sky. Should it be there? The magnification and light-capture of the riflescope shows more detail… and the grey squirrel, frozen still to avoid detection, plummets into the leaf mulch with a splash.

The flicker of a familiar, iridescent pink that catches my eye against the green canopy of a summer beech wood. The sight picture in the scope, gently raised so as not to return the glint, marks the woodpigeon's plumage – and the shot is on.

The bobbing flight of a bird into the stark branches of a winter oak. With the lowering sun blinding my eyes, an instant decision is made before it lands: if it perches horizontally, head in line with tail, it risks death as a legitimate pest species. But the bird lands upright, head high above tail, so I place the shot on 'hold' –

it's probably a green woodpecker. As I move forward, a harsh shriek rips through the wood… and it is, in fact, a jay that departs, for I was wrong. At least, though, I didn't make a mistake – and never have in 30 years of hunting. Had it landed with its head in line with its tail, I would definitely have known it was a jay… and it would be despatched.

Fieldcraft isn't just about watching, though. It's about everything in the woodsman's very demeanour. Veteran hunters learn to move lightly and stealthily through the countryside, merging with the form and shadow of the landscape, staying in harmony with the scene around them. They will pause often, for long periods, knowing that haste and sudden, erratic movement will drive back the alert creatures before them. In the forest, they will check the floor before them for a soundless path, devoid of twigs and dry leaf litter. They will take three, four, five steps… then pause to study the panorama around them, listening for movement, alert to disturbance. Then they will move on again, slowly. This calculated progress will bring them silently to their destination. They will settle under cover, arrange their gear and wait; wait for as long as it may take. Within just 15 minutes of retreating into cover, the forest will forget their existence. Birds and mammals will return to their industry – the sombre tasks of finding food, breeding, raising young. The hunter's moment will come, with patience.

Habitual intelligence is another trend that fascinates me as a hunter. The ability of bird and beast to memorise incident and consequence, the way they can associate activity with outcome. Sometimes, it works to their advantage. Often, it can be their downfall. An example of this is the baiting of corvids. Regular baiting (shoot a rabbit, paunch the rabbit, leave the paunch in the same spot) will get results. The crows or magpies will associate the spot with food and revisit regularly. Once the routine is established, you can hide up and be certain of a shot or two. Shoot the spot too often, however, and they will steer clear. That little memory chip in that tiny brain will now associate the location with danger. Incident and consequence.

Perhaps more impressive (or sinister) are the foxes that follow me when I'm lamping rabbits at night. Not only do they know that they are guaranteed rabbit paunches before I leave (activity and outcome), but they also seem to be sure that my air rifle is not a weapon which would threaten them. In fact, one vixen that often followed me was so intelligent (or reckless), she ran down my beam from behind me one night to try and snatch a rabbit I had cowering in the light! She damn near got a pellet in the rear end, but I managed to pull the shot in time. She missed, for the rabbit bolted, then stood in my beam looking forlornly at the empty spot where the rabbit had squatted. I held the beam on her and she trotted back up the light, eyes like tiny moons, to position herself behind me

*If you can get this close to wildlife, you're on the right road!*

again. Her demeanour spoke volumes: "Let's try that again, can we?" I've never seen the like since.

There are many more tips in this book which may help the hunting newcomer gain their feet, or the experienced hunter to rethink their approach to certain creatures. They relate to several things that every hunter should learn very intimately if they're going to make a mark. The natural history, the habits, the habitat and, also, the behaviour of the creatures that we hunt.

## CHAINSAWS AND SCYTHES

The modern airgun hunter has an absurd range of rifles from which to choose. Pick up any shooting publication and you'll drool at the various combinations, calibres and styles available. You can read the latest rifle reviews and speculate on how a particular rifle may improve your shooting skill. You can read the many instructional pieces telling you how to shoot, where to shoot and what to shoot.

If you've read them, I probably have, too. Hopefully, I wrote some of them! One of my 'golden rules' in life is based on Mahatma Ghandi's famous quote "Live as if you were to die tomorrow. Learn as if you were to live forever". For life is no challenge if you think you already know everything. This applies strongly in the ambiguous natural arena that combines both shooting and wildlife conservation. There are no experts, very few artisans… yet a whole host of practitioners. Just as there are numerous 'right' ways to shoot and hunt, so there are also many 'wrong' ways. As an obsessive scholar of everything pertaining to country sports, I always focus on new hunting articles and new contributors in these magazines, hoping to learn more, and I'm happy to admit this. The shooting press in the UK (and its editorial teams) are second to none. I rarely see an article slip through that gives bad advice. Sure, there is sometimes disagreement and debate about methods, but that makes the reading all the more interesting.

If I spot an imaginative piece of kit, I'll explore it. Sometimes, I'll get excited about a review of a new rifle, but it has been a long time since one drew my hard-earned cash. There are very few substandard air rifles around these days, only substandard or impatient shooters – the type that expect their gun to all the work for them and to attain a level for which the rifle was never designed. Shooters need to realise that you can't cut a reed-bed efficiently with a chainsaw, nor will you topple an oak tree using a scythe. I'm sure you grasp the analogy; you need to pick the right tool for the job.

I make no apology for being a 'one-gun' hunter. Though I'm well placed to trial and field-test other rifles, I generally decline. Time spent changing scopes, zeroing, finding the right pellet for the barrel and the like is hunting time wasted a far as I'm concerned – and I'm precious about my hunting time.

Not to mention collecting guns from RFDs (Registered Firearms Dealers), packaging them up to go back and delivering them back again!

To me, the air rifle is a tool. Having carefully selected, bought and mastered the rifle (and scope and pellets) which best serve my purpose – currently the Weihrauch HW100K-S – it would be illogical to keep changing. You can't keep searching for the 'best' when you believe that you already have it. You just need to learn to shoot consistently and accurately. Unless you have a serious technical fault on the gun, it's usually the shooter to blame if results decline. Don't rush out to buy a new gun, revisit your shooting technique first. I've done this many times, often to find that I'm getting too cocky or too relaxed in the approach to the shot. Not getting the right stance; not breathing properly; not getting eye-relief right on the scope and therefore tilting or canting the rifle. Shooting technique should be natural, but certainly not slapdash. If your technique declines to that level, the most expensive gun in the world won't cure the problem.

I have found, though, that no two rifles of the same brand and model are necessarily the same. I have stuck religiously to my brand, yet have had to change pellets in a newer version of the same rifle simply because barrels can be 'pellet-fussy'. Even the scope I use now is the one I fitted five years ago.

Show me a freezer full of rabbit meat and I'll bet that the owner uses the same rifle, hunt after hunt. Show me a shooter who has enough air rifles to supply a gun shop and I'll bet that I could show you his empty freezer! For this will usually be a shooter who expects the rifle to do all the work and who still hasn't found a 'decent' gun. Workmen, tools and blame spring to mind…

At a recent game fair, a guy who had recognised me from the magazines stepped forward, introduced himself and shook my hand, saying how much he enjoyed reading my articles. Flattered, I asked him what it was about my writing that attracted him. He said it was because I don't just write about guns, but about fieldcraft, wildlife, the scenery and the sounds. He could see that I clearly love 'being out there', despite the shooting. He was absolutely right. The rifle is the tool that both fills the pot and gives me right of entry to an abundant, secret wilderness that very few people enjoy. This guy felt the same about his shooting. He owned only one air rifle and we talked for a while about how much pleasure we get from from being out in the wood or the field. Surrounded by the milling throng of the game fair, we both confessed to each other that we'd much rather be out there now than in this madhouse!

So in this book, you won't find any complex advice about selecting a gun, though you will find advice about power levels or calibres. I stand by my choice: a legal limit (12ft/lb), silenced, multishot, precharged pneumatic (PCP) carbine in .22 calibre.

**Legal limit** – as I can use it in any situation with minimum risk.

**Silenced** – as I don't like to advertise my activities to man or beast.

**Multishot** – as I get maximum opportunity for minimum effort.

**PCP** – as I don't have to break the barrel and disturb wildlife.

**Carbine** – as it can be used comfortably in hides and outbuildings.

**.22 calibre** – because I intimately know the trajectory.

There are several components which come together to make a mediocre shooter an exemplary one. Random behaviour isn't one of them. You cannot pick up any rifle at whim, feed it with different ammunition or use the scope at a different magnifications and expect to get consistent results. Find one gun, scope, magnification range and pellet combination that suits your purpose, practise with it constantly, learn its competencies and limitations, and hunt with it regularly. What will evolve is a knowledge of your rifle and its capability which becomes second nature and consistent. Very simple, but very precious advice. ◯

# THE RABBIT

## A NIGHT IN THE WARREN

*You wake from your semi-slumber, aware that your kits are scrabbling up to the surface. It's too early yet for you to go 'up'. The shafts of light penetrating the tunnels tell you that dusk is yet an hour away. Let the youngsters frolic, such is the exuberance of youth. You doze again, but a distant, dull vibration brings you alert. Your whiskers touch the side of the nesting stop, and you can feel the danger. Footfall. You raise a back paw and start to slowly thump the floor of the nest, drumming an alert to your young. Too late. The double thunder-crack above the ground sends a deafening echo reverberating through the buries.*

*Two of your kits come tumbling down into the nest, panting heavily. The scent of fresh urine*

*follows them. Together, you huddle, terrified, as the stomping above continues for some time, then finally recedes.*

*Your other two young fail to return.*

*Only after darkness do you venture out, driven by the need to feed, followed by your kits. Outside the bury, you hesitate and scent the breeze. The sweet smell of kale is tainted with the visceral stench of death, blood and guts. The musk of fox still hangs in the air. It has passed recently to clean up what remained of your kits. Up and down the warren, other coneys emerge, giving a sense of communal security. You tentatively lope toward the crop and sustenance, sensing the fading acrid smell of gunpowder. You stop to sniff at the spent cartridges on the margin, then bolt for the cover of the kale.*

*The rabbit has changed the landscape across Britain, figuratively and literally*

*Your kits follow, equally nervous, sensing your fear.*

*A sweeping white ghost makes you cower as it glides over, wings wide. But you need not fear the barn owl. She is searching for much smaller prey. Tonight, it is man and fox you must fear. Beneath the silver orb of the moon, you feast on the succulent kale leaves with one eye on every movement and your ears turning like radar dishes. Your whiskers and nose work overtime. Twice you move your family deeper into cover: once at the passing of a badger, its lumbering stroll too noisy to surprise you; the second time when the two monstrous white eyes of a noisy machine pass down the margin, leaving a trail of choking smoke. You lead your kits carefully to the margin when they've passed.*

*Another scent hangs in the air now, and you're reluctant to cross to safety. A scent with which you are far too familiar. The kits both bolt across the grass and their white scuts disappear below ground. You hop out onto the ride and a sudden shaft of yellow light breaks over you. Familiar with this danger, you instantly sprint for the bury as a lithe, panting beast bears down on you. You feel its hot breath on your scut as you jink and turn into the hole… and safety. A close call. Below ground, you listen to the hot, frustrated snorts of the beast at the tunnel entrance. The man-shout, the slap and the whimper of the chasing beast are the last you hear before the danger passes. You settle, ready to sleep. It's been a good night. It's always a good night when you live to enjoy another.*

## A NATURAL HISTORY

The thought of a British countryside without the humble, yet abundant rabbit (*Oryctolagus cuniculus*) doesn't bear thinking about. Depending on which side of the farmer's fence you sit, its introduction by our Roman or Norman ancestors (the jury is still out on that debate) was a stroke of sheer genius. Throughout our history, it's provided nourishment, sport, even clothing for the common man. Hunted with bow, crossbow, dog, gun, ferret, snare and trap, it has beaten them all. Farmed (in warrens) for a few hundred years, its meat was a staple in the market place and its pelt was used for hats and clothing in bygone days. It has changed the landscape across Britain, both figuratively and literally.

The rabbit has become iconic, too. The subject of children's books, a symbol of Easter and spring. Folk used to carry its paw, believing it to be a harbinger of good luck – though probably not for the rabbit from whence it came!

With the British rabbit population estimated at something like 45 million as I write (and slightly less by the time you read this, courtesy of my rifle!), we airgun hunters plainly have a

role to play. Not least because climate change means that the rabbit is now breeding in many areas during every month of the year, rather than its traditional February to October cycle. I have culled rabbit kits in every month of the year for the past three years.

While it has been prey for the hunter, it has been a huge pest for the farmer. A passive animal, it has long vied with the woodpigeon as Britain's most prolific agricultural pest. Lately, its ranking has dropped in Britain's 'most wanted' list, while the country focuses on another non-native pest, the grey squirrel. For the air rifle hunter, though, the rabbit is an important quarry. It is the key reason for landowners granting permission to shoot on their land. Its sheer fecundity makes it hard to eradicate. Put simply, it procreates faster than we can clear it – and long may that remain the case. The principle is straightforward: no rabbits, no shooting permission. You're not needed.

The coney itself has a low life expectancy, and many will invariably end up in the food chain. But it will probably already have guaranteed survival of the species! A female can – and does – breed within 16 weeks of birth, and will produce four or five litters of around five kits each per year. Now, imagine that three kits in every litter are female and breed to this cycle… and the maths show why they need constant attention.

Rabbits live for most of their lives in a warren, a maze of burrows and subterranean tunnels with several entrances and exits. Females will delve nursery 'stops' (so called because they are dead-ends), in which to rear young. Warrens can be found in some of the most extraordinary places, not just in hedgerows or embankments. Wood warrens are common and on open heathland, rabbits will dig out in the open. Don't overlook spoil tips or rubble piles, either – the coney will dig in anywhere. In high summer, when the burrows are beseiged by fleas, it is also common to find rabbits lying out beneath gorse, broom or similar low, dense shrubs.

The average life expectancy of a coney is two to four years, unless they're on shooting permission, when it's significantly shorter! Yet, perhaps, the most important point is that with an average body weight of two kilograms, there's around 90,000 tons of prime, organically-fed, cost-free meat chasing around our fields for the taking. I have written many times that this is possibly Britain's 'most neglected harvest'.

Poisoned, gassed and subject to biological warfare in the form of myxomatosis and more recently VHD (Viral Hemorrhagic Disease), the rabbit continues to thrive. The biggest ever deliberate pogrom on rabbits was the introduction of myxomatosis, in 1954, which killed 95 per cent of the population. DEFRA (the UK government Department for Environment, Food and Rural Affairs) claim that rabbit numbers are already back up to 40 percent of the pre-myxy population (112 million) and now increasing two per cent annually as resistance to the disease increases in every new litter. There is absolutely no doubt that rabbits have built a resistance. I regularly pick up scarred rabbits who have clearly had this awful disease, yet have survived.

Colour variation in rabbits is rare and localised. Jet black rabbits are frequently seen out in the Anglian fens and having seen a shot one, I can confirm that this wasn't a domestic pet. It was definitely a melanistic wild rabbit. In fact, history tells us that these were prized by warreners of old, who called them 'parson' rabbits. They were encouraged in the warrens, much like the gamekeeper's black pheasants of latter years, for they stood out easily. If they disappeared (this holds for pheasants, too), poaching or a predatory fox would be suspected and dealt with. White (albino) rabbits occur, too. I've recently seen two feeding on a busy roadside verge locally – true albinos, with pink eyes and noses.

Unfortunately, it's illegal to shoot within 50 feet of the centre of a highway if your activity could endanger or distract its users – and this one's a busy one!

## FOOD AND PREDATORS

Rabbits cause an estimated £100 million worth of crop damage every year in Britain. That has a heck of a lot of farmers and agricultural growers gnashing their teeth. Remember that earlier population figure of 45 million? That equates to about £2 of damage per rabbit per year.

Feeding activity produces herb and crop damage. An adult rabbit eats about half-a-kilo of vegetation per day. That's 22,500 tons of pasture or crop, daily – staggering! To put that into perspective, think of the dustcart that empties your bin. The rabbit's national diet would fill 225 refuse trucks each day, or over 82,000 truck loads per year. The good news (if you're not a farmer) is that much of this is recycled. The rabbit's droppings, like a horse's, are still full of nutrients and eventually biodegrade into the soil.

## RABBIT PRESSURE ON A SUGAR BEET CROP

Be careful not to confuse rabbit grazing with deer sign. Often, you'll find both signs in the same crop. The low nibbling of the coneys producing a stepped effect alongside the higher browsing of the deer. In brassica (such as cabbage) and tuber (such as sugar beet)

*Rabbit pressure on a sugar beet crop*

crops, the damage will be localised and low to the ground. Rabbits graze outward from the cover of the warren during spring and summer. On winter crops, they will venture far from safety during the long, dark nights, which is why lamping can be so productive. I'll discuss lamping in more depth later.

In hard weather, rabbits can cause considerable damage to saplings, which they'd usually ignore as a food source. Stripped bark up to 20 or 30 centimetres from the base will kill saplings and infuriate the forester. Deer also do this, but the damage will be at browsing height – too high for it to be rabbit – though the effect is the same.

*Rabbit buries are about 15 to 20 centimetres in diameter*

The rabbit has provided food for a host of predators which otherwise may have gone into decline. The buzzard, the fox, the badger, the stoat and the weasel all include it as a staple in their diet. As an air rifle hunter, you will never shoot larger species such as foxes. You haven't got a gun with sufficient power to kill cleanly. Yet the knowledge that you have foxes or badgers on your hunting land more or less guarantees you have coneys. Why? Because they are a staple diet for Britain's two largest burrowing mammals. Indeed, they will often share a warren with their prey. It's common for both to take up residence in warrens without the rabbits vacating – so look out for dens or setts. The ability to read the tracks, trails and sign of these 'higher' predators will help the hunter home in on prey activity from lower down the hierarchy. They will have found the rabbits' buries long before you; their survival depends on it.

Another good indicator of rabbits in the vicinity will be buzzards or other large raptors on your shooting land. Such a bulky predator will enjoy the hors d'oeuvre of mice or voles, but if they nest on your land, there's invariably a more hearty food source obtainable. So spotting raptor nest sites can be significant, too. Other clues that there are rabbits present (if their own sign isn't obvious) will be the presence of other lower predators, such the mustelids – stoats and weasels. Again, wild coney is a staple in their diet and watching either hunt is pure entertainment. Their methods range from snaking through buries, ferreting out their dinner, to dancing and writhing in front of their prey to mesmerise it... then striking like a snake with a viscious bite to the base of the skull.

## HABITAT AND HABIT

Rabbits exist pretty much everywhere on the British mainland. As with all wildlife reared in wild places, away from regular contact with man, they live in fear of us, and therefore generally shun us. That forms the whole basis of hunting – getting out there into the wild to first find our quarry, then working out how to get close enough to despatch it. For a wild creature rarely walks or flies in to greet you.

Direct evidence of rabbit presence can be seen in a number of ways. Let's look at these in more detail. Burrowing and delving along fencelines, under hedgerows and on hillsides is an obvious sign. Newly-thrown earth will hold footprints to indicate the occupant of a bury. Check the size of the entrance and the prints carefully. It may be the badger or fox we talked about earlier. Study the trails through grass or hedgerow leading away from a bury or den. A rabbit trail through grass will be about 15 centimetres wide. Follow it… and you should find those little nuggets of their faeces along the way.

Rabbits defecate or spray along their paths and use this as a scent marker to quickly find their way home. The pellets are easy to spot. Learn to tell how fresh they are. Are they dry and calcified, and therefore old? Are they dark and moist, and therefore fresh? Pick them up – don't be coy; they're only recycled grass! Are they warm? If they are, your rabbit could be very close.

Rabbits urinate often, too. In snow, you will see a regular splash of yellow. Obviously, this is indiscernible without snow, but the spray contains the pheromones that attract the fox, the badger… not to mention my lurcher. Rabbits have a tendency to follow a habitual trail and will hop over small obstacles (such as a tussock) at the same place, every time. Map these spots in your brain. Remember them well, for that will be where your target hesitates when you're lying in ambush with your rifle. Holes forced through hedgerows or shrubs will be about 15 or 20 centimetres in diameter. Mark these, too. The rabbit is a wary animal. It will exit through such a tunnel and stop to consider potential danger – a good time to shoot. Likewise, it will pause on its

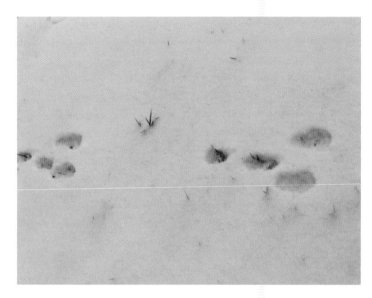

*Rabbit tracks in the snow – these show it moving left to right*

way back to scent the tunnel; there could be a stoat or weasel waiting within. It's another good shooting opportunity – though one that comes with a caveat: even in its death throes, the coney may 'kick' into the undergrowth. If this is thick briar, you may never recover it. It's better, if you want to recover it for the pot, to shoot it out in the open.

Rabbit buries are about 15 to 20 centimetres in diameter, normally with a 'fan' of dirt at the entrance, around 30cm or so long, sometimes more in sandy soil. If the entrance is a 30cm wide (or perhaps more), with a huge cascade of earth outside, it's more likely a fox's den (which is often a widened rabbit bury). If there's a series of wide holes with lots of debris pulled outside, it's probably a badger sett. Again, they will recycle a rabbit bury.

In sand, snow or wet mud, you get the chance to study the pawprints left by the rabbits on your permission. Use this information to find hidden warrens. Many folk read rabbit tracks back to front. The coney hops and sprints using it's forefeet (the smaller pads) to propel it forward, landing with it's large back legs wrapped around the front ones. Think of the kangaroo and how

it travels. The rabbit moves in the same way when in a hurry. If you want hunt rabbits, it's important to learn where they came from and where they went. Follow the tracks from start to finish and you'll know both where the bury is and where it feeds. Other than in deep snow, frost or a dewy morning, you rarely get the chance to establish this.

Thirty years ago, when I first began shooting rabbits, I held to a self-imposed 'close' season. No 'milky does' (in other words, females feeding kits) between May and August. That rule has long since evaporated. It's open season all year if I want to retain my shooting permission! The sensible airgun shooter, however, will 'farm' the coneys carefully. He will know when he's close to a complete pogrom on a warren and relax his attention to ensure future shooting accordingly. It's a fool who condones total eradication. If you enjoy (as I do) the glimpse of buzzard, badger or fox, would you want to eliminate its food source totally? I hope not. Let me put that another way – a hunter's way. Where you see the buzzard, badger or fox, there will be rabbits. Which means that you are needed, too. Take the rabbit out of that equation… and we're all gone; the predators will migrate and the shooter will be evicted, if not redundant.

Finally, the golden rule is that patient observation is the key to quarry detection. Just sit, watch, listen, learn and, in time, shoot.

## HUNTING METHODS

By far the biggest hauls of rabbits I achieve are through static hunting, ambushing warrens from behind natural cover or a shooting blind. Setting up late in the afternoon, I will pick a spot within range and downwind of the burrows, then simply sit and wait for the rabbits to emerge. Although rabbits will feed all night, they feed most voraciously just before dusk and will not only come out in numbers, but also remain closer to the warren. So the spot you choose needs to be close to

*Watch, listen, learn…*
*and shoot*

the food source, too. Patience always pays when ambushing rabbits – even after you've shot a few outside the buries. Give those that fled time to calm down. Let the warren settle and they will often emerge again within 20 minutes.

Stalking rabbits (walking about and trying to creep up on feeding coneys) can be effective, but success is more random. You're more likely to signal your presence through scent, footfall or noise. In many ways, this method is more challenging and enjoyable. Edging up to the gap in the hedgerow, or creeping up to the gateway to steal around with the rifle at the ready.

There are many factors to consider when stalking. The direction of the breeze; the terrain underfoot; the throw of your shadow; even the presence of other wildlife. The erupting pheasant or shrieking jay won't give a browsing rabbit much confidence in its safety and it will be highly alert.

## LAMPING RABBITS

Another method that brings heavy bags is lamping – shooting after dark with a gunlamp. Modern scope-mounted lamps are lightweight and extremely well designed, throwing a powerful LED beam out to 100 metres or more. This is really a winter method. Your rabbits have by now ventured much further from the warren and can be hijacked far out on low crops or grassland. Working into the breeze, the beam from the gunlamp is randomly switched on and off to pin-point grazing rabbits via their eye reflections. The light usually confuses the rabbit into freezing, inviting the shot. But be warned – working behind a lamp needs practice. The light will confuse you, too, and it's easy to think a rabbit is further away than it actually is – because instead of seeing a the full animal in profile, all you see is that reflected eye.

Lamping can be an exhilirating hunting method, but it can be disastrous, too. Make sure you know your land like the back of your hand as trips or falls can be a hazard. Always mark where you shot your rabbits, or you could lose them to the night (or a following fox!). Never shoot unless you recognise the quarry as rabbit, either. You could be pointing your muzzle at the farm cat. And always carry a mobile phone in case you get into trouble. Golden rule number one if you are setting out on a lamping expedition is to infrom both the landowner and the local police of your intention and where you'll be. That can save being interrupted by either. If they don't know better, they will have to assume poaching or other mischief.

## TIPS AND TRICKS

When ambushing rabbits (static hunting), don't shoot the first rabbits to emerge. Let the first scouts gorge for a while, which will give others the confidence to emerge. Watch the rabbit warrens for some time. Let the rabbits come and go and learn their runs. When you do shoot, always take out the furthest from your muzzle (but within your competent range). With a silenced air rifle, the rabbits left feeding are likely to turn to the sound of the expired rabbit in alarm rather than the source of the danger. This gives you the chance of further shots. Leave dead rabbits where they lie; don't gather them until you're finished. If you're working your way along a big warren and don't want to carry the shot ones, make sure you 'hock and hang' them on a fence or bush, safely out of the way of the fox.

Although stalking is generally done with the breeze in your favour – with it blowing into your face so the scent is carried away from your quarry – there are times when you can turn this around and use an upwind breeze to your advantage.

At dusk or dawn, if you suspect rabbits are already deep within a high crop (maize or brassicas), you can often flush a few by simply using your own scent. Walk down the crop's

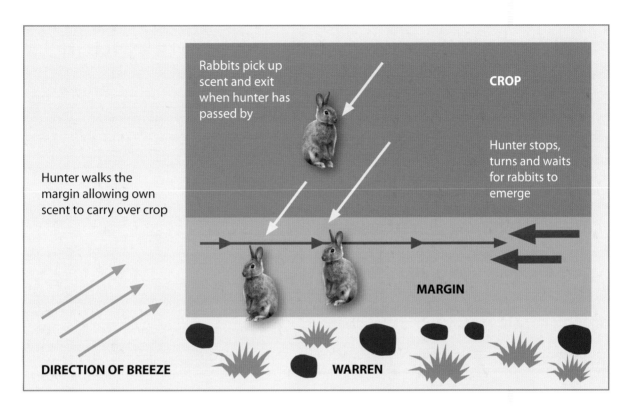

Rabbits pick up scent and exit when hunter has passed by

**CROP**

Hunter stops, turns and waits for rabbits to emerge

Hunter walks the margin allowing own scent to carry over crop

**MARGIN**

**DIRECTION OF BREEZE**

**WARREN**

margin into the breeze, then back up it slowly. Watch for rabbits, which may bolt at your scent, on the margin you have just walked.

Briars, stinging nettles, gorse and broom are worth checking for rabbit warrens. Any thick cover over vegetation, such as Old Man's Beard, will let daytime rabbits sit out in confidence. Look for signs beneath, and target these areas.

The rabbit will take its water from the dew on the morning meadow grass, or from the small puddles in the base of a broad-leafed plant such as dock or rhubarb. Remember this after overnight rain.

I carry a small LED torch in my bag at all times, night or day. A shot rabbit's nervous system often shuts down with a kick or twitch and this can send it instinctively down the nearest hole if you shoot close to a warren. In such a case, I always play a light down the bury to see if the dead rabbit is in sight and could be reached. Even if it isn't, there's an old warrener's trick that can sometimes recover your rabbit. Cut a long, thorny length of briar. Strip the thorns off the slender end with your knife, wrap the stripped part around your hand. Now play the thicker, barbed end into the burrow, twisting all the time – a little like rodding a sink drain at home. I've recovered dozens of otherwise lost coneys this way – the thorns wrapping around the fur so that the rabbit can be dragged out.

I can often mark the translucent ear tips of a wary rabbit among the tall nettles in a hedgerow. How? Because my eye has been trained by years of experience to search for aberrations in any scene. The huddled, dark form under a bush, looking for all the world like a rock or molehill wasn't there last time I passed by. Through the riflescope, the twinkle of an eye betrays the squatting coney... and the shot is taken.

*There are times when you can use an upwind breeze to your advantage*

Rabbit or hare? If you haven't recognised which by the ears (they're longer on the hare, with black tips), the mouth also gives a clue. The hare's top lip is split – hence the derivation of the condition harelip – as opposed to the rabbit's split bottom lip. When a hare runs from danger, it usually runs out into open land first. A rabbit will dart straight for cover.

## A TWILIGHT HUNT

Can there be any time more magical than that period between the setting of the sun behind tree-line or hedgerow, and its complete disappearance below the earth's horizon? The familiar name for this – twilight – conjures imagery of mystery and transition. This is truly a time for the hunter to sit peacefully on the margin, between wood and field, to watch the subtle change of players in Mother Nature's game.

On this sultry evening, I'm perched on some felled lumber, just inside the wood. At my rear, the subtle orange beams of fading sunlight between the tree trunks fall like spotlights on clouds of whirring insects. Midges, gnats, sawflies, chafers, darters, moths – the wood is teeming with lower forms of life. The drone and bustle of this winged ensemble draws in a peculiar audience. The magpies now find a final burst of vigour, lured by the opportunity of supper, and a cat-owl hawks amid the swarm. The scouts from the noctule bat colony have emerged and hunt blindly – but proficiently – above my cap.

Though observing all this from the corner of my eye, I'm certainly not idle. I've withdrawn a small pack from my gamebag which contains my lamping rig. And I do mean small, such is the progress made with modern gunlamps. I'm old enough to recall the days of heaving a weighty lead-acid motorcycle battery around in my pocket, trailing a long coil to an old motorbike headlight! Tonight I'm using a tiny Clulite lamp, purchased at a recent East Anglian Game Fair. LED technology, and not

## RABBIT DRESSING IN THE FIELD

There is nothing more annoying than stripping rabbits in the field and the meat getting tainted with dirt and grass. This is how I field-dress my shot rabbits without the meat touching the ground.

First squeeze out the rabbit's bladder. Lift the rabbit, unpaunched and using a sharp knife, cut off its hind and forelegs at the knee joints. Next, cut a long slit in the skin on one hind leg. Push in your thumb and peel the skin away all the way around to the other hind leg. With the legs free, hold the rabbit head-down and pull the whole skin down to the head with one sharp tug, revealing the stripped body. Peel the skin from the front legs. Hold the rabbit by one hind leg and cut a V-shaped vent into each side of the flesh, near the anus. Twist and pull the tail and anal duct away. Then find a branch, fence wire or gate and wrap the skin around it so that the coney hangs down, head upward. Cut through the stomach membrane from ribcage to groin, ensuring you don't cut into the entrails. Hook two fingers up into the ribcage, breaking the thin membrane that holds the lungs and heart. Pull everything (guts, lungs, heart, liver) down and out in one sweeping movement. All that will be left are the kidneys. Pluck them out if you don't eat them. Push one finger through the anal vent to clear it. Take a carrier bag, cut through the coneys neck and drop the clean, whole carcase into the bag – one clean, grass- and mud-free rabbit.

I've got this down to about two minutes per rabbit, but with much practise. Don't forget to remove the skin and head from its hanging point, where it could terrify passers by or annoy your landowner. The other advantage of this system is that you keep your kitchen clear of all that rabbit fur you have to clean up before the wife comes home – and you don't have to hide all the unwanted stuff from the bin-man. Well, at least only the bones!

the only LED masterwork in this pouch. I slip two lithium batteries into the body of the lamp, revived yesterday using the supplied charger. Though it has an optional on/off switching cap, I fit the coiled pressure switch to the lamp.

The Clulite comes with a clamp which fixes it above the riflescope. Ingeniously, the clamp has a ball socket which allows you tilt and turn the beam to where you want it. I select a post about 30 paces away and train my scope's centre on a knot in the wood. Then I operate the pressure switch and adjust the position of the lamp until the light beam and scope crosshair meet on the wooden knot. The beam is now zeroed to my scope. The final touch this evening is to add a light filter to the flip-up cover on the lens of the lamp. A clear filter is great in full darkness, throwing a narrow beam 60 metres. In the black of a November night, I say if you've got power, use it! In mist or fog, I use a blue filter as it diffuses the beam, but still gives a good light throw. If I've been lamping fields regularly, I use amber to tone down the brightness. The rabbits seem to be confused by the change and sit longer to watch my light.

As I'm going to be lamping at twilight, I choose the red filter. My Hawke 3-12x50 SR6 scope captures light well enough anyway, so adds an hour or more to my shooting without additional light. So here I sit waiting for my rabbits, as always, a wealth of contradiction. I have a scope, it's light-capture superb… but I've added a lamp! Furthermore, I've just stifled the beam with a red filter. Oh, and yes, I am lamping… but it's not fully dark yet!

Out across the meadow, the rays of the westering sun cast across the cirrus cloudbase and bathe my hunting stage in autumnal colour, like spotlights at a rock concert. Here, at the boundary of the wood, we're entering that time of day where colour dissolves into monochrome, then slowly into black. A time when the hungry adult rabbit shuffles out to

follow its kits. It comes cautiously, already (perhaps) pursued in its short lifetime by vixen, hawk, hound and human. It squats and grazes between tussocks of meadow grass and the nettle stands. Through the riflescope, I note an almost indiscernible tremor along the tops of the stingers… and then I know it's there. Between the plants, I can vaguely see its shape, but I'm unsure which way it's facing.

The gunlamp's pressure switch is Velcro-fixed to the front left-hand side of my rifle's stock. My left thumb strokes the switch, tempted. My right forefinger is also ready, close to the trigger. Tempted. My brain is playing umpire. If the coney hops out into the open, the right finger will lead. If it sits tight, the left thumb may have to take the play. I wait and wait. Two minutes pass and the rabbit is still in cover. I know from the movement of the plants that my rabbit *is* in there…

The umpire makes his decision. The left thumb sends a searing beam of red light into the nettle bed. My right eye, through the scope, sees a red, reflected iris mirrored between the leaves. The brain, which has interpreted this information many times before, calculates the distance and instinctively lowers the muzzle in milliseconds. The right forefinger synchronises with this fresh mental data and releases the pellet. A flip and a shudder amongst the nettles affirms success, and the red light is instinctively extinguished just after the pellet hits its mark. Which is why I use a pressure switch, and why it's on the forestock. My trigger finger is too busy with the follow-through to allow it to move in panic to push an on/off switch and turn out the lamp. Believe me, when lamping, you need that light out quickly once you've shot.

Leaving the shot coney where it lies, I wait patiently for the next one to appear. Again, it's that subtle commotion amongst the foliage which predicts a rabbit's stealthy progress. In the half-light, I can just make out the twitch of an advancing nose. Red light on, a solid

*A twilight foray with the tiny Clulite LED lamp*

identification of the eye position… and the rabbit somersaults out onto the grass and expires.

I sit still for a few minutes to slow my heartbeat and prepare for the next. The sudden screech of a disturbed jay warns me that Old Charlie may be close. The fox has probably scented blood on the breeze, so I leave my position and pick up the two rabbits, both precise head shots. I hock and hang them close to my tree-stump seat (where I can keep an eye on them) and, sure enough, the fox puts in an appearance. He bolts out into the meadow and noses around the nettles in confusion. He follows the blood scent towards my position, oblivious to my vigil. I stamp my boot and the fox freezes, stares curiously for a few seconds, then hastens off into the dark wood. I settle down and wait again, the daylight now seriously receding.

A female tawny owl's 'kee-wick' echoes around the wood behind me. My stomach rumbles to remind me that dinner beckons; I've come straight here from work, with no food since breakfast. The one last coney I desire slinks out onto the meadow, almost invisible in the gloom. The lamp flicks on, the beam picks up the red eye, the shot is released. I mark where the coney falls and relax my left thumb to switch the lamp off.

I hinted earlier that the Clulite isn't the only LED trickery in my kitbag. Clipped to the brim of my baseball cap are a tiny array of floodlights – an Orion cap-light from

Deben. I stretch the three coneys out on the grass, squeeze the bladders and set about paunching them. A quick touch of the switch on the Orion and I have enough light for the task. The lights are set to green, ample enough in twilight, though I could choose a full flood of white light, or a mixture. An excellent device which leaves both hands free for the messy job of paunching. Far better than using a torch between my teeth, which is how I used to tackle this job at night!

While I unclamp the gunlamp and stow away my kit, I leave the Orion cap-light on to assist me. Feeling watched, I glance into the wood and the eerie green beams pick up a pair of bright emerald moons about 20 metres into the thicket. Old Charlie is lingering nearby and will be drooling at the rancid scent of rabbit guts. So I leave him to his supper and leisurely wander down the track, toward the Jeep. Leaving the wood's edge, I'm surprised at how much natural light is still left on the open field. Yet in the gloom of cover, below the sun's last rays, the lamp has proved its worth. I'm suddenly conscious of the luxury of the new technology in my bag. Years ago, on pitch-black lamping nights, I'd have been broaching a hernia, struggling with a sack of coneys, a heavy spring-powered air rifle and half of a motorbike! I would never have dreamt of carrying that cumbersome gear in my bag for a simple evening sojourn. Tonight, I have just a gamebag, a light PCP air rifle, a hat-trick of fat coneys – and I'll have supper in my lap in time for the 10 o'clock news! ○

**Chapter**

**3**

# THE GREY SQUIRREL

An adept airgun hunter can be highly effective in controlling grey squirrels

## A GREY DAY

Shaking off the lethargy of the night's sleep, you slide from the drey and squat on a bough. It's an hour after sunrise and the chill winter air ruffles your fur. Your mate is already abroad; you scan the canopy searching for his movement. Nothing. Movement below catches your eye and you see him, digging in the loamy earth, a flurry of pine needles falling behind him. He drags out a rotting acorn and turns it triumphantly between his front paws. You scuttle down the trunk of the home tree, head first, food now firmly on your mind. Halfway down, he sees you and chases away with his prize.

On the floor, you put your nose down and search around. Eventually, you find one of your own caches and unearth the cob nut with a furious scrabble of your dexterous paws. Nut in mouth, you bob across the damp leaf mulch and hop up onto a fallen stump to take breakfast. As you nibble at the moist kernel, a chatter behind you alerts you to your mate's intention. Annoyed at having breakfast interrupted, you spit your anger. He advances, detecting the pheromones you are unknowingly emitting. Oestrus. Mating time. He sprints forward and you flee.

The chase is on... You dash upward, but he's closing fast. You leap across the flimsy branches to another tree. Your mate tries the same but misses his grip in his eagerness and falls, saving himself by catching a lower branch. You stop to rest on a thick bough and the hiss and spit of another squirrel nearby greets you. Another male. Younger. You flick your tail, flirting with him. He senses your readiness and you don't resist. He mounts you quickly. Then you head down again. Your old mate is coming up to meet you. You are trapped between two suitors. A leap of faith to the crown of a slender beech sapling leaves the two males in a face-off.

Time stops as the two threaten each other, hissing, with tails fluffed out. You join the spitting – but for a different reason. The two males have failed to see the two-legged creature standing on the forest floor about five trees away, watching them. Next to it is a huge four-legged beast, watching your suitors intently. The two-legged one raises a stick... and it spits its deathly venom to topple your mate's opponent from the branch. The four-legged animal runs in below to grab him as he hits the ground. You flee in terror, your mate following. The stick spits again and something smacks into the bark of the tree in front of you. The four-legged beast is below you, following your escape. You flip around the trunk of your home tree, out of sight, and scamper up into the drey where you lie, your lungs heaving. Moments later, your mate scrambles in beside you. You lie together, trembling, until the danger passes.

Later, in the darkness and warmth of the drey, your flirtation with both fresh genes and danger over, you allow your mate to cover you, too. You survived today. Inside you, whichever mate was successful, survival of your kind is already underway.

## A NATURAL HISTORY

Introduced to the UK in late Nineteenth century from its native North America, the grey squirrel (*Sciurus carolinensis*) wasted no time invading and colonising every corner of the landlocked UK, driving out our native red squirrel before it. There are now an estimated 2.5 million greys in the UK, compared to just 140,000 reds. The bigger grey doesn't attack the red, but with its twice-yearly breeding cycle, larger litters and therefore competition for the same food and ecosystem, it was inevitable that the grey squirrel would push the red squirrel close to extinction in this country. It also carries the squirrel parapox virus (SPPV), to which it is largely immune, but which is lethal to the more fragile red squirrel.

Its habits of bark-stripping during breeding seasons and nest-raiding in spring have put it firmly on the list of a 'shoot on sight' species. Foresters and conservationists have all recognised its danger to tree cultivation and to resident songbird species. In some areas, culls have been authorised (particularly to protect breeding sanctuaries for red squirrels) and, lately, calls for a national pogrom have been mooted – with even Prince Charles' backing! In urban areas, however, it is adored by the public. Good news, folks. The grey squirrel has officially lost its cute, bushy-tailed 'Tufty' image. Even some of the most fervent wildlife organisations and their supporters have had to concede that to allow such a dominant, non-native species to rule the British wood is madness. Despite this overwhelming evidence, the RSPB continue to imitate the ostrich and claim that songbird nest predation by *Sciurus carolinensis* is negligible. But we airgun hunters know different, don't we? All genuine country folk know. Moves to eradicate the grey and re-establish our native red squirrel are building in momentum throughout the UK and this is giving opportunity not just to trappers, but also air rifle hunters. For the humble air rifle is a very effective, safe and non-disruptive way of clearing grey squirrels. I know, because I cull hundreds every year.

A lively, inquisitive and entertaining creature, it will now always have a foot-hold and food source in our towns and cities. For this reason alone, a national cull is doomed to failure. In rural areas, however, the airgun hunter will always find work to do, and landowners asking for a reduction in numbers. Behind the fox, the rabbit, the rat and the woodpigeon, this is fifth most unpopular resident on a farmer's estate. On the forester's estate, it is third only to deer and rabbits in the pest stakes. An adept airgun hunter can be highly effective in controlling grey squirrels.

Becoming adept is all about knowing how, where and when to tackle this abundant and challenging quarry. The grey squirrel lives in a drey, a loose bundle of twigs and leaves made in the cleft of a tree or within a hole in the trunk. They breed twice a year, usually around February and July, the female producing three or four kits after a six-week gestation period. This is an important point for the hunter; more on that later. The young will be reach

independence within about 12 weeks.

Legend has it that the squirrel was present in the Garden of Eden. It was so shocked at seeing the mating antics of Adam and Eve that it fluffed up its tail and wrapped it around its eyes in embarrassment! God was so pleased at its piety, He made the fluffy tail a permanent feature. All I can say is thank you Lord, for giving me the perfect indicator of my hidden quarry! If the squirrel is a 'pious' mammal, then I'm the Angel Gabriel – for I know no creature more openly promiscuous in the British wood that than the grey squirrel. It has the fidelity and morality of a Premiership footballer!

## FOOD AND PREDATORS

The grey squirrel's natural diet is mainly vegetarian – acorns, beech mast, flower bulbs, hazel nuts, pine cones, maize cobs, sweet chestnuts and fruit. Never, however, underestimate their penchant for fresh songbirds' eggs and newly-hatched chicks. They are omnivorous and, as highly adept, intelligent and agile climbers and jumpers, will reach any food they set their sights on. The nickname 'tree-rat' hasn't been earned lightly. They have little fear when hunting up in the treetops and will even tackle the nests of birds as large as the jay. Hence those two are mortal enemies. Ground-nesting birds aren't safe either; they will strip a pheasant or partridge nest of eggs within 15 minutes. They're also a visible nuisance around bird tables, dexterously raiding feeders and seed left out for songbirds.

The grey squirrel only has one serious ground predator – the fox – though they are usually nimble enough to escape its clutches. Its biggest threat comes from the air, in the form of raptors. In Southern areas, this threat is low, though I have watched buzzards haranguing squirrels in the crowns of tall trees (with scant success). The grey squirrel's biggest threat, though, is man –

and he doesn't do anywhere near enough to control it!

## HABITAT AND HABIT

Like rabbits, squirrels can be found almost anywhere on mainland Britain where there is a stand of trees. They're not fussy, either. They will build their dreys in any tree – deciduous or conifer. Though if you shoot territory without trees, you won't see many squirrels. To find them feeding, simply look for food-bearing trees such as oak, hazel, beech or pine.

Greys traverse their terrain via a series of well-established highways (or low-ways). Their movement and direction of travel is often highly predictable, habitual – making hunting them easier for the shooter who takes time to simply sit and watch for a while. Signs of shallow digging on the woodland floor are a sure indication of a nearby drey – even if you can't see it. The one 'mark' you'll rarely see with squirrels are their faeces. They're as rare as the proverbial rocking-horse squit. Signs of feeding – like fir cones or maize cobs – can identify the culprit. Those little, dextrous paws can turn a cob easily and the cast-away remnant looks the same as when we eat a pear.

*"Don't bother looking for grey squirrels in mid-winter because they hibernate."* I heard this nonsense on a leading Norfolk radio station wildlife piece recently, when we were enduring heavy snowfall. I was just a tad confused, because in the back of the Jeep I had half-a-dozen grey squirrel corpses that had just succumbed to my gun. And trust me, they weren't asleep when I shot them! They were highly active, scratching under the snow for their hidden caches of beech nuts, or dancing through the conifers above me. Again – and there is no sentiment in vermin control – they are vulnerable in such conditions. I called the radio station to correct their mistake, trying to explain that true hibernation is a complete

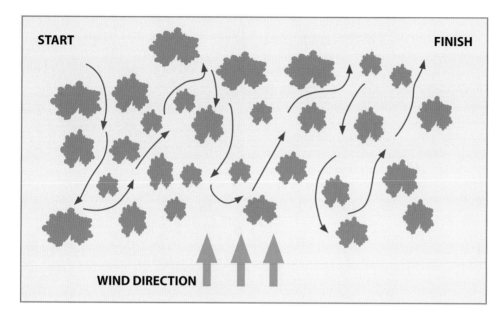

*Stalking through the wood in diagonal lines will force the greys into a corner*

shutdown of external senses and a deep sleep which closely resembles death. Squirrels may retire to the dreys in inclement weather for long periods, but they come out regularly to feed. I even offered that hedgehogs truly hibernate, as do dormice. As you would expect, my advice wasn't reported back to the public on the programme. So when little Jimmy from Norfolk takes his biology exam and is asked to name an animal that hibernates, he will probably say a squirrel – and the sad bit is that he will probably get a mark for being correct! A reflection of the media and academic ignorance of our own countryside and its inhabitants. On mention of hedgehogs, though, I *do* know that if it emerges from hibernation – but then returns to it – you can be sure that winter is far from over.

## HUNTING METHODS

Like rabbits, I find the best way to target grey squirrels is through ambushing them. Find those highways, pick the right times of day… and you will get good bags of greys. You don't particularly need heavy camoflauge or cover,

either – just patience, silence and stillness. The perfect time of day is an hour after dawn, or before dusk. Although you will see random activity all day, that will depend on the weather. In hot periods, they will take a siesta and retire to the cool of the drey during the hottest parts of the day.

On what I call rainbow days – sunshine peppered with showers – shooting squirrels can be at a premium. They hate rain and will lie up in the drey, but as soon as the warmth of the sun between showers hits the drey, they will scamper out to feed, regardless of the time.

Ambushing feeding 'tables' is another sure way of guaranteeing success, though you might have a long wait. Tables are those stumps and fallen boughs in the wood covered in shredded and splintered nut kernels. Any one squirrel could use several of these, however, so visits are random. The squirrel is a lone feeder, so never expect to see several at one time.

Using a dog to assist when squirrel shooting is useful. Not only can they track scent on trails and rides, but they can play 'second man' to drive squirrels around a trunk, back into your line of fire. A disturbed grey will often seek shelter on the opposite side of a tree trunk, hiding from you. A trained dog (I use my lurcher) can be sent to that 'hidden' side, thus forcing the grey – which will always react to the most immediate, moving threat it perceives – back to your side of the tree. Just make sure you are standing back far enough to engage the squirrel in your scope and execute the shot. I use a technique to stalk through the wood, working in diagonal lines to force the greys into a corner.

At this point, a plea for responsible shooting. Please don't get drawn into the 'drey shooting' technique I see used by many shotgunners. This form of squirrel control makes me shudder, even with a cartridge gun. It can't guarantee certain despatch within the drey, and what if the drey is inhabited by something other than a squirrel – like the long-eared owl, which favours old dreys as a nest? The airgunner's single pellet fired into a drey is unlikely to kill, only maim.

## TIPS AND TRICKS

The grey squirrel will mate roughly six weeks before February or July, so during December and May, watch out for squirrel mating activity – because this is often when they are most vulnerable, chasing up and down trunks or along the woodland floor in a state of urgency, yet utter concentration. They are so focused – the females on escape and the males on pursuit – that they are often oblivious to the watching hunter. I've even had squirrels run across my boots while standing in grey squirrel mating territory. A loud click of the tongue will bring them to a halt on the floor. They are most vulnerable, though, while pinned against a trunk catching their breath.

Winter is a great time to thin out greys, when the leaf canopy has receded and they are most exposed. On damp, misty mornings, when the dew drops cling to the branches above, squirrels give away their presence by

*You need to deliberately under-shoot (aim low) when taking elevated targets*

## SHOOTING ELEVATIONS

I've read all sorts of technical articles about shooting elevated targets with a legal limit air rifle. Almost all of them have baffled me, mainly because the ballistics of such a low-powered rifle and its ammunition are too variable to allow set rules. You just can't use pure mathematics to determine a one-fit recommendation to the beginner, so I won't even try. The basic principles are simple, however.

If your gun is zeroed at 30 yards on the horizontal, the pellet arcs up as it crosses your sightline, and drops into your target as velocity decreases and gravity pulls it downward. The higher you aim your pellet, the more gravity will pull on it as it travels towards your target. So, if your target now sits 45 degrees up in a tree, but still at 30 yards from your muzzle in a straight line, gravity will be pulling hard at the pellet. Thus the arc will be flattened. If you use your centre crosshair, that will result in missing the target, high. What gravity is doing to your pellet (in reducing this arc) is having the same effect as bringing your target closer to you. So you need to deliberately under-shoot (aim low); I'd use the 25-yard mil-dot instead of the 30-yard crosshair in this scenario.

But that, folks, is far too simple. The power of your gun and the weight of the pellet mean that you need to practise this meticulously with your own rig, and as often as possible. Shoot at apples, conkers – anything that sits high up and at any angle until you get a feel for the range adjustment. Perversely, this same effect applies when shooting downhill. Don't ask me why, as I'm no physicist. And we haven't even mentioned the breeze. That's a black art – and why I get more satisfaction from one, cleanly executed, elevated shot than a dozen horizontal ones.

showering down the moisture. Similarly, after heavy snow, their movement above sends small avalanches to the floor, exposing their position.

If a younger squirrel spots you, and therefore danger, it will often perch in a cleft of a bough, hissing and chattering. It's a very distinctive sound. Older greys tend not to do this; experience lends itself to flight rather than challenge. Yet you can sometimes crouch for ages trying to identify where the sound is coming from, for squirrels can 'throw' their voice as adeptly as the magpie. Be patient and don't move, because that little hissy-fit also involves a flickering of its bushy tail. If the animal can see you, you must be able to see it, too. You will eventually spot it – and that gives you a static target.

A squirrel running at you on the ground probably won't see you, even if you are in the middle of a woodland ride. Look at its eye position, either side of its head (like the hare). Simply squat slowly and click your tongue loudly. It will halt in its tracks, allowing you to shoot.

But never, ever assume a shot squirrel is dead. They have a skull like a walnut kernel, assuming you take the head shot (I don't, normally), which can be difficult to penetrate. Take a long twig to the shot squirrel and rub it over its eyeball. Look for a blink reflex. (You can do this with rabbits, too). If it blinks, place your muzzle between eye and ear – point blank – and finish the job. A numbed, shocked squirrel that comes alert as you pick it up could bite right through a finger. Just remember its natural diet of nuts; those jaws are mighty powerful!

I mentioned drey shooting earlier. There is a useful technique which draws on this without the risk of indiscriminate maiming of either grey squirrels or other innocent occupants of a drey. Using a multi-shot PCP air rifle, you can plug a couple of pellets into a branch close to a drey in quick succession. This will often force squirrels to exit the drey. A few loud clicks of the tongue as they flee can see them stop still long enough for a shot.

## BANDIT COUNTRY

One of my permissions is an estate which only raises gamebirds for shooting on Boxing Day, every second year. There is, as a result, a healthy resident population of wild pheasants. I noticed that they were taking a hammering one year from predators. Foxes taking the adults, corvids and grey squirrels taking the eggs. It was Sunday morning. The church bells tolled in a distant tower as I arrived to try help a population besieged by bandits. I felt like Clint Eastwood, riding into town to support the weak and defenceless. Cue the music…

The first thing that struck me as I walked into the wood was the comfortable cushion of damp mulch beneath my boots. After weeks of near-drought conditions, moving across the brittle leaf-litter had made stalking difficult, to say the least. The breeze was a mere zephyr, kissing my sun-parched face. As I edged between the trees today, I was so silent, so stealthy, I almost stepped on a doe lying tight beneath a thicket near the path. The deer rose and fled, barking as she went, her bobbing white rump marking her passage. I stopped to let my heart rate settle – a big beast getting up at such close quarters certainly makes the adrenalin course through your blood. I moved on and, just as my heartbeat had stabilised, a hen pheasant crashed from cover and exploded along the ride with that infuriating alarm call that tells every creature in the wood that danger is near. My pulse flat-lined again for a moment, and I considered the irony of her panic. She had just fled from the only guardian and protector of the eggs that I was sure she'd just abandoned. Tempted to search for the nest, I resisted. Much as I would have liked to gaze upon the clutch of olive eggs hidden nearby, I knew that my curiosity would disturb.

The first grey squirrel I saw was frolicking up the ride in the opposite direction to me. Though I had the favour of the breeze, the sun was at my back and the squirrel faltered, my large silhouette too obvious. It flashed away and scurried up a pine bole. I edged close to the tree and passed around it slowly, just glimpsing a flick of bushy tail working away from me. The grey squirrel's usual method to avoid threat is to hide. I stooped, picked up a large pine cone and threw it beyond the other side of the trunk. As it hit the ground, the grey scuttled around into view, gripping the trunk, but now three metres higher. I raised the barrel too conspicuously and the squirrel, a nimble youngster, marked the movement and escaped before I could shoot. The next one didn't, however. It was up on a branch above one of the dank, midge-infested ponds – immobile and easily picked up in my Hawke Sidewinder scope. A touch of hold-under to compensate for the elevation and the Air Arms Field pellet sent it tumbling. Tom Daley, the Olympic diver, would have been proud of the 'half-pike with somersault', but the entry into the pond lost it valuable points. Too big a splash!

On a different ride, I found clear evidence of infanticide. Lying on the grass were two

*Beware the man with only one gun!*

empty pheasant eggs. I examined them. The colouration was subtly different, so I reckoned they had come from different nests. The entry method through both the plundered shells was the same, though. As I turned the shells on my palm, I guessed the culprit was a magpie. Why? The eggs were out in the open (though just the two), and it would take a long, wide mouth to move them there. The crow, a bolder bird, generally feeds where it finds. The long indentations in the shells told me magpie, too – the membranes torn away by a long, slender beak.

Deeper into the forest, I disturbed another squirrel, yet another juvenile. It sat on branch watching me, not sure if I posed a threat. Had the shot missed, it would have known for future reference. Life (or death) is like that. Often, you only get one chance to make a crucial decision. The next grey was foraging on the forest floor. Older, hungry, confident and committed. I allowed it to get within 30 paces, then clicked my tongue loudly. Suddenly, it didn't seem so confident. Suddenly, it wasn't going to get any older. My Weihrauch HW100K-S rifle was absolutely singing today. Three down.

I'd worked my way around the first circle on a figure-of-eight path back to the Jeep. I often do this (park centrally and hunt a figure-of-eight path) as it allows me to cover a large area and work all aspects of the breeze and the terrain. With the tailgate open and the gun beside me, safety catch engaged, I stood and enjoyed a hot coffee from my flask and tucked into a sandwich. A flash of black and white from floor to tree, just 20 paces away, almost made me choke. Magpie! Then another danced around a nearby trunk and flew up to join its mate in the crown of a Scots pine. As I watched, one darted down and swooped out into the wood. The other descended onto a lower branch, cackling and looking agitated. The penny dropped quickly. It was their nest site.

I finished my lunch, in no haste, all the time watching the birds flying up and down the tree-line and darting into the treetop. They were obviously too preoccupied to be concerned by the Jeep, so I picked up the gun and decided to use the open tailgate door as a hide. But, as so often happens when hunting, the magpies threw me a curve-ball. One of them swooped down and started to forage on the track where the Jeep was parked – in front of it and on my blind side. I edged around the motor and it was still there, on the floor. Thirty? No, 35 paces. The shot was clean and it flopped, wings open, on the grass. I left it there so that I could concentrate on its mate, which I expected to go ballistic. It didn't. It had fled. I waited half-an-hour, but as it didn't return to the nest, I recovered the shot bird and moved on to cover the second half of my figure-of-eight foray.

Half way down the track to the lower wood, a squirrel hissed, balanced on top of a flint wall. I knelt slowly as it flicked its tail angrily. I drew breath, exhaled and settled the crosshairs. The rifle hissed back and number four was in the bag. I moved on and checked a blackcap's nest in a briar patch that I'd noted recently with five eggs in it. But now it was empty, half-trashed and no egg shells around. Stoat or squirrel, who knows? But I was simmering now. I had been trying my best to guard this nest, and those of several other species, but I couldn't be here

night and day. As I looked on in despair, a tiny wren fluttered, chastising me, from the same briar patch and just two feet away. I checked further and found its homely moss-lined nest tucked into a hole in the flint wall behind the briars, complete with six, tiny dotted eggs. I prayed that it was the squirrel I'd just shot that got the blackcap's eggs. But if it was a stoat, then these wren's eggs would also have little chance of incubating. Such is the fragility of songbird survival in a British wood.

The next grey squirrel that crossed my path bore the full wrath of my anger. I don't generally track squirrels. They're either there in my scope, or I wait for them to track toward me. This one popped up just 20 paces from the wrens' nest, again on the wall. Spotting me, it scampered up into a holly bush, looking for cover. I couldn't see it, and that bugged me. I launched a quick shot of .22 lead into the woodland floor just beyond the tree. The ruse worked. The grey ran out onto a branch, more worried at the threat behind it than in front of it, and paused just long enough for me to draw a bead. Number five – except it dropped behind the wall. I would recover it when I'd crossed through the gate at the wall's end. I felt a bit better now, some balance restored.

In the lower wood, I watched a pair of jackdaws busying at their nest; I was in no mood to shoot them. They may be on the General Licence – and cull them I will, where necessary – but they do little harm in this wood. I enjoy their aerial antics and seeing them slip flawlessly into a nest hole just a few centimetres in diameter is a delight. As I stood watching, they even started to dive at me! Concerned at my interest. The 'jake' is a plucky little crow. As I moved into the neatly mowed clearing in the wood below the Hall, I glanced at the tree stump in the middle. I had to double-take, not believing what I was seeing. Egg shells – lots! I stepped over to examine them. Only one creature would be arrogant enough to collect such a number of eggs and

*A pheasant egg, cleaned out by a squirrel*

pheasant poults that hadn't made it out of the shells due to bandit activity.

I waited close to the clearing, just watching and listening. Nothing ventured out into the open, but I saw a squirrel travelling overhead, following a highway along the branches from the Old Hall gardens back to the wood. It stopped only once – and that once was enough. On my trek back to the Jeep, another young grey squirrel stood on the wall. It dared to rattle its tail in indignation at my passing, and hiss its disapproval of my company. Now, I'm a reasonably tolerant man, but this apprentice nest-robber had picked the wrong day to mess with a seasoned gunslinger who had just witnessed the pillage of several of his charges. I had no crisis of conscience in silencing its protests with a pellet. It fell on the right side of the wall and eight squirrels for eight pheasants seemed a reasonable revenge. I called it a day, climbed the hill back to the Jeep while whistling an Ennio Morricone tune from the 1964 Spaghetti Western, *A Fistful Of Dollars*: An eye for an eye… ○

drag them out, one-by-one, into the open to feast at the same table: the grey squirrel. And this one had been very industrious. The egg shells were all pheasants', and of various hues (meaning different clutches). I picked them all up, matched the broken pieces and counted at least five, perhaps six. Added to the two I found earlier, that was perhaps eight

# THE BROWN RAT

## THE LAIR

She wriggled and freed her dry teats from the squirming, pink, blind offspring, hurrying toward the exit of her lair. She was exhausted, but the mewling of her young at their abandonment forced her forth. She needed to feed now; replenish her energy. At the gape of the lair, she paused, her whiskers testing the breeze. It was nearly dark in the grain shed and she sensed the scent, presence, and movement of her kind. Slipping beneath the pallet that covered her lair, she put her nose down to follow a well-worn trail. One that she hadn't tracked for days, during the parturition. She scuttled along the base of the shed wall, only stopping briefly to spray. Up over a few straw bales. On top, she met another female and stopped to touch whiskers. This exchange told her that she wasn't the only new mother abroad. As she ran towards the grain pile, many more of her kind joined her from all directions.

She clambered among the piled ears of barley, gorging. She glutted, urinating when her full stomach pressed on her bladder. Still she gorged, fighting for grain among a host of her kind, all scrapping and writhing in greed and possessiveness in the dark. Then suddenly they were bathed in warm red light. The movement stopped. She froze, with the others. A spit of air and a 'whump'… then the light went out. The female next to her rolled over and the scent of blood washed across the grain heap like nectar. Several of her kind fled. She paused, tempted. As the light went on again, two males and a female were already sniffing at her dead companion. Another 'whump' and one of them bowled down the heap into her. She ran for the wall, suddenly remembering her youngsters. She flashed back along the shed wall and met a male head-on, carrying a pink morsel in his jaws. The scent of lactation swamped her in panic. She rushed past him and dived under the pallet.

*A picture of innocence, yet the rat will devour even its own young*

*At the lair's entrance, she met a large male. He was exiting her nest-stop. She recognised his musk immediately – her mate, the father of this litter. In his jaws he held a pink nestling. She smelt the blood of her young and spat. His black eyes shone fiercely in threat and he scrambled over her, to escape her wrath. She edged down into the lair, her instincts already telling her it was in vain. Her nest was empty. Plundered by her own mate. Her own kind.*

## A NATURAL HISTORY

The brown rat (*Rattus norvegicus*) has been a British resident since it first clambered along the ropes of docked ships from the Far East and Russia in the Eighteenth century. If the rabbit is considered fecund, just step back a moment and consider the rat: capable of producing up to 15 young in a litter, five times a year! Little wonder, then that – unchecked – they populated these islands within years, driving our native black rat almost to extinction. Thankfully, modern rodenticides and their application by astute farmers means that only about five per cent of broods survive on our farms. Best we don't mention the towns and cities where rats thrive on the excess of our consumer society. For the rat is a foul creature that will eat almost anything, dead or alive – even its own young, or its own dead. It is this propensity for survival that makes the doom-mongers speculate that, should the ultimate cataclysm hit planet earth (be it natural or nuclear), just one creature will emerge from the wreckage. The brown rat. Having watched them all these years, I wouldn't argue with the theory.

Rats tend to be territorial and live in tunnels and runs under buildings or in hedgerows. They are largely nocturnal and move around using their nose, whiskers and fur to follow trails. With a body length of around 25 centimetres, and a tail of equal length, they are much larger than mice.

I mentioned rodenticides, but in many areas, rats have built up a resistence to Warfarin-based poisons and so often survive application of this control. Another testimony to the rat's quick-fix, evolutionary history. Though the rat is a dreadful pest, these poisons are anti-coagulants which inflict a slow death. They are an absolute necessity, don't get me wrong, yet the point I want to make here is that by comparison, death at the hands of an air rifle hunter is far quicker. So never feel any guilt; like the squirrel, the brown rat is a 'shoot on sight' species.

## FOOD AND PREDATORS

If I was to draw up a list of what makes up the brown rat's diet, it would take up the rest of this book! It's the ultimate omnivore. So let's concentrate on those elements of its diet which make us want to control it. And it's often not so much what they eat, but what they spoil that causes concern. The 'easy' diet for the rat is grain – wheat, barley, oats and suchlike – and if it's heaped in a silo, so much the better. It also has a penchant for eggs – from chickens, gamebirds or anything ground-nesting. And chicks. In urban areas, the rat will feast on the detritus of modern living, swarming over bins full of food waste, invading unhygienic kitchens and even thriving on the foul waste in our sewer systems. I once had to pull up my garden deck due to the activity of an elusive, solo rat which had stored a larder of rotting, putrid dead frogs beneath the framework. Half-eaten amphibians, stacked up for harder days – the stench was awful.

A bloody rat resident right under my nose! I was incensed. I cleared the frogs, poisoned the hole I found under the brickwork of the house, and when I was satisfied I had culled my visitor, relaid the deck. A few weeks later, the smell was back. I took up the deck again, cleared more frogs, pushed a hosepipe into the hole, sat my lurcher close by and once I'd turned on the tap, the rat flushed. It fled up a deck stanchion, tried to run along a rail and was snatched in mid-run and shaken to death. Proper job.

The rat has many enemies and no friends. It is predated by cats, weasels, stoats, foxes, owls, buzzards and badgers. What effect the eating of a rat has on these creatures, Lord only knows.

## HABITAT AND HABIT

During the warmer months from April to September, rural rat colonies tend to migrate lock, stock and barrel into the hedgerows and ditches surrounding cereal crops and streams. Here, they delve a labyrinth of tunnels. Rats love water and swim strongly. When colder weather sets in, rat colonies move back to the warmer havens in and around farm buildings, digging in deep behind and beneath the building fabric. Here, they cause huge nuisance for they will gnaw through pipes, cables and even brickwork to establish their runs and nests. They can cause flooding, electrical short-circuits and, even, fires. One of the divisions I manage in my day-job is a refuse collection business. We recently had to move a couple of trucks from their parking area at a waste transfer station because rats on the site had tried to nest within the body of a vehicle and had gnawed through the power take-off cabling, which operates the bin lifts on the truck. The truck was brand new and it cost us a fortune to replace the cabling as the damage was excluded from the warranty!

It's the brown rat's habits, though, which make it a very firm pest control target and a public enemy. The rat carries a number of diseases from which it is immune, but to which humans and their pets are highly susceptible. These are carried in their urine, their blood and on the fleas they invariable harbour. They carry trichinosis, salmonella and, worst of all, leptispirosis (Weil's disease). The latter is present in their urine and given that rats mark their runs with sprayed urine constantly, they contaminate everything that they contact. Weil's is an often fatal and debilitating disease

in humans and dogs, attacking the kidneys and causing jaundice. In cattle, it will induce stillborn calves or cause infertility. The rat can be responsible for a whole plethora of health issues in man and beast, without anyone actually knowing they've been in contact with leptospires. Merely because a rat passed (or pissed!) their way. That is why the rat is another shoot on sight species, and why you should never handle a rat, dead or alive, nor anything you know it has sprayed without extreme caution.

## HUNTING METHODS

Rat hunting with an air rifle can be very effective in the right conditions. The rat is a fast, nimble sprinter and an expert climber, so shooting them on the move is not the way to tackle them. Probably the most effective way is using a gunlamp and ambushing their feeding points after dark. They shun

*Brown rat on waste heap – infection on legs*

bright, white light – so the use of a colour filter on the beam is imperative. Red, green or blue. It's also worth changing the filter during a session as they will quickly associate the colour of the beam with danger. Best to confuse them a bit! Winter evenings in poultry houses or grain silos can be productive. Get there before dark and set up in a corner behind equipment. Check the runs first and establish, via their droppings, where they are entering or exiting – then just wait for the night to fall. Make sure all shed lights are off, even low-level emergency lighting. Wait until you hear squealing or scampering – then switch on the beam.

The beauty of the airgun is that you can comfortably work between 10 and 30 metres with little risk of damage within the building. Obviously check you have backstops for errant pellets, and make sure you don't damage troughs or other agricultural equipment. If working a poultry house, try to shoot away from the birds and try to avoid ricochets. Head and upper body shots are lethal on rats at such close range, but never handle corpses unless you are 100 per cent sure they're dead. It's better to waste another pellet than risk a bite. Make sure you clear up when you've finished, too. I use a mechanical litter-picker or disposable gloves to collect the corpses. Dispose of those corpses responsibly; you don't want the farmer's kids running into the farmhouse kitchen waving a dead rat at your host or his wife! Nor do you want livestock such as pigs feasting on them.

Other areas plagued by rats are piggeries and spoil pits. I often target these during twilight (dusk) as rats will nest below pig-pens or in pits. Targeting them at their nests can be easy as they will frequently be venturing in and out to feed young.

The other nirvanas for the rat shooter are

obviously waste transfer stations or landfill sites. With such a steady food source, if you can get permission, these are often alive with rats, even before dark.

## TIPS AND TRICKS

Rat shooting is fairly simplistic, but you often have to get the lively critters to stop still long enough for the shot. There are various ways to do this. Some shooters use sticky mixtures to make the rats pause long enough to dig in and eat, peanut butter or jam being typical. The use of a squirrel or rabbit corpse, belly slit open, around nests and pits will pull feeding parents from underground. On grain piles or on waste sites, you won't need anything but fast target acquisition.

I read of shooters down-zeroing their rifles when rat shooting – say from the usual 30-metre setting to 15 – but I find this unnecessary. The air rifle has two zero points anyway – usually between 10 to 12m secondary zero and 28 to 32m primary zero in .22 calibre. It takes little adjustment in the scope to nail rats between 10 and 30-odd metres – just knowledge and practice.

Put some thought into your rat shooting selection, too. When they're swarming over waste or grain, get to learn which are the matriarchs; these rule the rat roost. The males are subservient and often a bit smaller. Target large, heavy females where you can; they are probably pregnant (and there won't be many times that they aren't). Shoot these as a priority, as you're invariably taking out up to 16 rats with one, single pellet. If you're too sentimental to do that, you really shouldn't be in the barn…

Make sure you've got your wits about you in the dark – and be prepared for surprises. Rats may run over your boots (so tuck your socks over your trousers!), up your back and even over your cap! (So definitely wear one!)

If you are unlucky enough to get bitten, seek immediate medical treatment. Leptospirosis is a killer, but not if detected and treated quickly. For this reason, too, never leave a shot rat in a static water source such as a cattle trough. Get it out quickly, and then get rid. Warn your farmer if necessary, so that he can drain and cleanse the trough.

Finally, don't underestimate the culinary experience associated with rat shooting, details of which you'll find in Chapter 25.

## THE WASTE TRANSFER STATION

I arrived at the site late in the afternoon, as the dust was settling on another busy day in the transfer station. This remote tip does exactly what it says on the tin – teams dump both general waste and dry recyclables in the huge shed here, it gets segregated and, throughout the day, a couple of 400-ton bulkers ferry the waste either to landfill or a recycling facility. It's a tidy and well managed site, but I'm here this evening for a reason – curiosity. The workers tell me that wherever I might have shot rats before, I will never have seen rats like the rats that I'll meet here. Multi-coloured and as big as cats, apparently!

It's just after 4pm and the dustcarts are all finished. I'm invited into the office, where the staff are clearing up the day's paperwork, to have a brew before I set off into the sheds. I'm intrigued as I look around the mess room – there are identification posters of bird species everywhere. Outside the windows, there are bird tables and feeders. The office explains how diverse the bird population is out here and immediately I'm envious. This site is set in an enclave between the river and the sea, on wetland levels. It's surrounded by deep, rank dykes and marshes – hence the rat population. I suddenly realise that we're not talking skinny, urban bin-raiders here; we're talking wild dyke rats, capable of murdering moorhens on their nest. By now, as a serious ratophobe', I'm getting a bit twitchy…

The resident workers explain to me how, as soon as all vehicle movement has stopped,

*That's a shoe box – so a size 10 rat, without the tail!*

two resident creatures emerge and slip into the sheds. Feral cats thrive and breed around here, and the guys look on these with some affection because they feed on the other residents – the rats. Though many of the rats come in from their lairs in the dykes, most reside inside the concrete A-frames that shore up the fabric of the building. Poisons are effective but, rats being rats, they just keep coming.

The rats are big and bold, I'm warned, and unusually coloured – for which there's a simple and logical theory. This site, even before the transfer station was built, has been used to tip waste since Admiral Nelson was a boy. Live domestic rats have been dumped here and have survived, inter-breeding with *Rattus norvegicus*. The resulting population is almost the post-apocalyptic mutants you would have nightmares about after reading a James Herbert novel. I'm even told that one of the digger drivers had pushed a monstrous white rat from the garden waste pile with the digger this very afternoon!

So off I went, in to face the denizens from hell, armed simply with a camera and an air rifle (albeit a multishot). To be honest, I was wishing I'd brought a flame-thrower or a Thompson sub-machine gun! Entering the huge shed quietly, I was relieved to find that the lights were on. A couple of feral pigeons flashed off one of the waste piles, making me flinch. They headed up into the rafters, to perch and watch me. In the corner, in the gloom, I caught movement. Two huge creatures were rummaging under the heap of putrescence that was the landfill pile. One piebald, one chocolate-brown. Jeez – they *were* massive! As big as cats, no lie. I knelt and opened out the zoom lens on my camera, focusing into the shadows. My nightmare rats were… cats! Shabby, mange-infested feral moggies, rooting through the putrid food waste. I relaxed.

A rustling behind me on the recycling heap made me turn, just in time to see a leathery tail withdrawing into a gap under the wooden wall that covered the oil tank. The tail laid there, in full view, but I couldn't see the other end of its owner. Then it disappeared. I edged nearer with the camera and the rat flashed from the hole and ran into the waste paper pile, a mere blur in my lens. It stopped, and started to forage among the pile. I stood 10 paces or so away, clicking away with the camera. A very large, but ordinary, brown rat. Yet looks don't deceive when it comes to pest control. I edged the rifle sling from my shoulder, let the camera drop on its neck strap and sighted up. Ten metres – that secondary zero point – and, thus, a cinch of a shot. As the rat crashed into the cardboard and paper behind it, another three or four dived from beneath the pile and dashed to safety. Interesting!

I walked over to the landfill heap thinking, quite reasonably, that if the recyclable pile housed so many, then the rotten stuff must be heaving. I was wrong. There was no sign of movement among the mountain of split black sacks and rotten foodstuff. I lifted a bag at the bottom and heaved it to the top to disturb the pile. Still nothing. Above me, the feral pigeons fluttered in irritation at my presence, then settled back to their vigil. The two cats sloped out through the shed door, staring back at me. I'd obviously interrupted their sickly feast.

I paced quietly back to the recyclable waste and immediately saw another modestly-sized brown rat scavenging. It flopped into the heap at the shot and another pushed its head and whiskers up to investigate the noise. Three down now. I waited a while longer and another appeared at a gap in an A-frame, sensing the air with its whiskers twitching. Smaller than the others and with some white on its front, like a squirrel, I plugged it before it could retreat.

Beneath the paper and card I could hear panic and rustling. I was intrigued that the rats seemed to be more particular about their

*One pregnant female equals about 17 adults – so well worth one shot*

food than the cats. The recycling waste is always marginally contaminated, but only with higher grade, prepared food waste; the dregs of fast food or ready-meal cartons, yoghurt pots, cheese wrappers, crisp packets and the like. The pile itself is light and airy, easy to creep around from beneath. The cats, if they tried to negotiate the pile, would sink beneath the lightweight material. They wouldn't be able to gain purchase with their paws to sprint after prey. The landfill pile opposite is stuffed with putrescent, heavy sacks. Difficult to negotiate, except on the surface. A rat would have to dig for its food, tear open bags and would be vulnerable to those predatory cats. Rats aren't stupid, as this place proves.

Outside I could hear the staff getting ready to lock up, so I called it a day. Four rats in 20 minutes told me that an airgunner could have a festival here.

"Shoot any?" enquired one.

"Yep, four," I replied.

"Where are they, then?"

"In the paper pile. And I'm not climbing through that crap to get them!" I retorted, a little embarrassed.

"No worries," one of them intervened. "The cats will clear them by morning. Big beggars, though, aren't they?".

"Naaah, just normal rats," I answered.

"Best you come back at midnight, then." I was advised. "When the monsters come out to feed!"

"Sadly I'll be busy lamping rabbits," I lied, returning an equally wry grin.

I thanked the staff for their hospitality and drove away, promising myself I'd spend a winter evening here if I could swing it. That little rat with the white belly had me intrigued. You know what they say about no smoke without fire...

Something else had me smiling to myself on the long drive home. I realised I'd been so focused on purpose today that I had forgotten my phobia. Threatened with monster rats, the ones I'd shot had seemed like mice. Yet that first one, I swear, really was as fat as a two-litre drink bottle – and, head to tail, almost as long. ⬤

# THE WOODPIGEON

## SQUADRON LEADER

*He lifted his head from beneath his wing and shuffled out from beneath the damp ivy, along the branch. Shaking the moisture from his broad wings, he flapped them a few times then flew up to a high twig at the top of the tree to survey the landscape. A fine day; a good flying day. Bit of a breeze from the west, but that would add to the fun.*

*A quick squit, another flap or two of the old wings to loosen up and a salutory 'coo' to summon the rest of the chaps… and the squadron leader took off. Behind him, the ivy breaks came alive with the clatter of grey wings as the rest of the squadron burst forth. They soared high, in formation. He took them on a circle around the power pylons, just to test their technique. "Good show, chaps." He flew on, passing over a field of bare plough. He took them down low, circling to look for seed. Nothing. "Poor show, chaps. Onwards!" They flashed over the next blackthorn hedgerow, skating within inches of the barbs. No casualties. "Good flying, chaps!"*

*"Aaah, peas! In we go boys. No shirkers! Tally-ho!" For two hours, the squadron plundered the peas, unhindered. When his crop was bursting, he rallied the others and set off back to the roost. They were heavy and weary now, from all that rape and pillage, so he led them low back over the hedgerows, following the pylon cables. Over the first hedge, the squadron leader spotted snipers. A net, set out crudely behind a pile of straw bales. He wheeled quickly away, but in the salvo that followed, a few of the outlying fliers took flak. As they tumbled from the sky, the rest of the squadron put on the after-burners…*

*Back in the roost, the squadron leader took stock. "No problem, chaps. War is war. Safety in numbers and all that." After allowing a couple of hours to digest the food in their crops, he led them out on their second sortie of the day. He whisked them far around the anti-pigeon gun position they'd crossed*

*Woodpigeons settling on clover*

*earlier, keeping high and vigilant, then dropped them onto a rape field where they gorged all afternoon. Just before sunset, he took his glorious squadron back to the roost. He strutted up and down a branch, encouraging his squad.*

*The airgun hunter hidden in the ivy, some 30 metres away, wondered what the hell this crazy pigeon was doing. With a whisper of his rifle, he dropped the squadron leader to the woodland floor. There was a flutter and fluster among the trees. A few pigeon flew out, wheeled around and came back. The sniper took a few more before calling it a night. The flock were in disarray. Yet, next morning, a new squadron leader would emerge. This airgunner had won a battle – but not the war.*

## A NATURAL HISTORY

Ask me what my favourite bird is and I would probably say the sparrowhawk , a bird with whom I associate. A small, vigilant hunter

with the ability to strike when unexpected . Ask me my second favourite, and I'll say the humble woodpigeon (*Columba palumbas*). Without a doubt, the woodpigeon is an iconic sight in the British countryside. Study it for a time and you'll come to respect it, too – particularly as this bird will give you, the airgunner, some of your most consistent and enjoyable sport for a whole lifetime.

Woodpigeon numbers have increased two-fold in the UK since the 1950s; it is one species that's adapted and thrived under the regime of modern agricultural practice. The introduction of oilseed rape as a winter crop and our recent mild winters in Britain have combined to completely overturn the natural balance which traditionally thinned out their population. Thousands upon thousands used to either starve or freeze to death. The estimated three million population recorded by the Ministry of Agriculture in the 1960s is now estimated to be nearer a flock of 10 million. The woodpigeon is now officially Britain's most numerous wild bird; even in suburban gardens, the national average has increased 665 per cent in the past 30 years according to survey data. With an average weight of around 500 grammes and a crop – the storage pouch beneath its neck – that can hold up to 200 beans, it doesn't take a mathematical genius to work out the woodpigeon's capacity for agricutural damage. Yet it's not just that. It's the gregarious nature of the bird that causes damage; damage that's estimated in the region of £3 million per year.

Woodpigeon nests are familiar to most country folk; a flimsy platform of dead twigs on a bough, typically between three and seven metres from ground level. The birds usually breed two or three times a year, but even on this subject, the ornithologists are tearing up the text books. Recent mild winters have seen extended breeding. The female lays two, round white eggs (hence the term 'pigeon

*The woody's nest is a flimsy platform of dead twigs*

pair') which hatch in three weeks; within a month, the squabs will fly. Although most birds survive less than a year, they can live for up to 16 years.

## FOOD AND PREDATORS

Food – therein lies the problem. Although the woody will eat natural wild fodder such as beech mast, berries and buds, it has a penchant for growing crops. Especially young crops and seedlings. As mentioned, woodpigeon are gregarious, and they communicate well. They flock in huge numbers to descend on freshly-planted seedlings such as brassicas and peas. They flight down in their hundreds onto ripe beans, rape or kale. Wind-flattened corn or barley is another favourite, where they can easily reach the ears at ground level. These 'flash-mob' tactics often decimate acres of crop in one visit. Farmers' deterrents – like scarecrows, gas cannons – simply move the flocks about and are, therefore, largely ineffective. What makes this worse is the woodpigeon's amazing metabolism. It moves fast and often, so feeds often. They will usually settle to roost late morning, digest what's in their crop and then fly out to feed again. Double trouble for the farmer!

The woody has numerous predators other than man. Fast-flying raptors such as goshawk, peregrine falcon or sparrowhawk, will intercept them in flight, while feeding or at roost. These attacks are one of nature's most amazing spectacles. I once watched a sitting sparrowhawk, preening itself on the woodland floor, while observing woodies coming in to roost in an ivy-covered elm about 30 metres off. I was there because I was targeting them, too. But through my magnified riflescope, I couldn't see a single feather amongst the dense ivy. Suddenly, the spar started its chiming – a loud, piercing bell-like sound – and lifted off. The panic in the ivy was tangible and visible, but too late. The hawk hit the ivy like an exocet missile. There was an explosion of downy, white feathers and it emerged from the other side carrying a woodpigeon, then descended to the floor far away to feast.

A fair few woodies fall to the fox and domestic cat, through cunning stalking, and the stoat will climb and take brooding females from the nest, or the chicks if hatched. Ironically, the other creatures that decimate the eggs in woodpigeon nests are other vermin, such as magpies, crows and grey squirrels. They're obviously not doing a good enough job, so shoot them, too!

## HABITAT AND HABIT

Habitat is pretty irrelevant when hunting woodpigeon. They can be found everywhere, even on the coast. But beware. Under the rules governing the General Licences, woodpigeon should only be shot if there is no other means of controlling them (such as scaring them) and only in the interest of crop protection. You are not allowed to shoot only 'for the pot' – your primary purpose must be for pest control – which is a shame. Assuming the breast meat represents a quarter of a mature woodpigeon's half-kilo weight, that equates to around 800 tons of succulent meat that you're only meant to flap your arms at and scare away! Shooting them from a rocky outcrop or off your garden bird table is not likely to satisfy that criteria – though in the latter case, if you have a vegetable patch at the end of the garden, you'd probably have a case.

The woodpigeon's habits are the key to culling them successfully with an air rifle. They feed, at least twice a day. They roost in numbers, twice a day. That gives opportunity. They target crops, so you can hazard a good guess as to where they'll be. They follow regular flightlines between roost and crop. Learn these. They often pause in flight to rest on a branch or twig – hardly surprising if they've got 200 beans in their crop! Learn where. They drink often, too – so work out their watering holes.

The woodpigeon is the Wayne Rooney of the bird world. At first glance, you could underestimate it. Not the most handsome of birds and tending to look a bit overweight, it completely transforms when in motion. In flight it is magnificent, soaring, jinking, turning on a sixpence and evading its predators. This speed on the wing is its salvation, as when it's in the field, it knows that physical survival depends on fast, evasive tactics. It watches from afar, hovers around the action and sweeps in to make its mark when it spots that the defence is weak. Just like our Wayne…

## PIGEON FLIGHTLINES

Far better shooting men and writers than me have preached the 'flightline' dictum. John Darling, Archie Coats and John Humphreys all advocated that successful woodpigeon shooting – and particularly decoy placement – relies on careful observation. It comes back to my points made earlier about wild creatures and habit. Woodpigeon flight can appear random, but watch them carefully and you'll notice that they navigate via lines and waymarks. They may follow the line of telegraph poles or the path of a hedgerow.

Sometimes it's simply from tall tree to tall tree. It may be from National Grid pylon to pylon. These flights are most certainly not haphazard – they are linked to roosting and feeding patterns. From night-time roost to food, back to roost and digest, out again into the fields for more food, back to a roost and digest; so it goes on.

They will have several roost choices. You need to spot these and time the patterns of movement. Be careful to time it by the sun, not the clock. Pigeons don't wear watches and a change from GMT to BST won't change *their* timing one iota. As they fly, they are scouting, their keen eye looking for opportunity. That's where decoys come in. Placed beneath (or close to) a regular flightline, you are trying to get the birds to deviate from their path. So your decoy pattern needs to look convincing.

## HUNTING METHODS

I'm not going to pretend for a moment that the air rifle is the most effective way to control woodpigeon. The shotgunner can (and does) take huge bags of crop-raiders with a well-placed net, a good decoy layout and a sackful of cartridges. It's bloody expensive, though!

The defence of crops, the relentless battle against the grey hordes, is a war of attrition. In any war, there will be heavy artillery. That's the shotgun fraternity. In any battle, there will be room for a sniper – and in the case of the woodpigeon war, that's the hunter with the air rifle in his shoulder.

My favourite (and most productive method) is roost shooting. As there are a couple of times a day when the flocks return to the trees – first to digest food, then to retire for the night – if you've been watching them diligently, you'll already know where these roosts are. Sometimes, though, you'll stumble across roosts by accident while stalking your shooting permission. Even when the birds aren't there, you'll find evidence of large areas of pigeon guano (squit) below the trees.

The key to roost shooting is to be in place before the birds return – so mid-morning or an hour before dusk. They'll settle in the side of the wood sheltered from the breeze or wind. Evaluate that and pick a spot on that side, too. Make sure the breeze is at your back. If the sun is at your back, so much the better. I'll explain the reason for both later. Set yourself up in deep cover, but with a good all-round view of the wood's canopy. The woodpigeon is a highly vigilant bird and quickly spots movement, like a pink face or the glint of glass. Although I don't go to the extreme of a face net (simply because I feel claustrophobic in one), many shooters do. I wear a baseball cap, but I'm fairly dark-skinned anyway from hours spent outdoors. If you have a full-set beard, you probably won't need a face net. The use of a sunshade on your scope will cut

*Using secateurs to trim obstructions*

down light capture a tad during an evening shoot, but will also reduce the chance of a pigeon catching that glimmer of glass until it's too late. Dark, subtle clothing is the order, or camo if you prefer.

The silenced multishot PCP rifle lends itself immensely to roost shooting as there's no need for unnecessary movement when re-arming the gun. The sidelever cocking mechanism on my Weihrauch HW100K-S can be actioned in a split second, innocuously. I always keep a pair of secateurs in my gamebag to trim away any close twigs or foliage that will deflect a pellet, too

So… you're in place, armed and ready. After a patient wait, the birds start to flight in above and around you, and you get that rush of enthusiasm on seeing the first target. Take a deep breath… and *hold* your fire. Trust me, it's hard to, but it's worth it. Let the birds alight in numbers before taking out the first. Let them hustle for the best spots in the roost. Allow them some confidence. Woodpigeon flocks come to roost randomly, and minutes apart. They will circle the wood and check it out first, then land *into* the breeze. Remember that, always. That's why I earlier said have the breeze at your back – the birds will land facing you, presenting that huge pink breast and head. If the sun is at your back, it won't reflect off your scope, the biggest reason for pigeons flashing off hastily when you raise your muzzle. When the time is right and many birds have settled in, pick a target, ease the gun up very gently and keep it there. Don't loose a pellet on a restless bird, it will be gone before the pellet strikes – and so, too, will all its comrades. And remember, you are about to take an elevated shot, so compensate for this. (Refer to page 43 for advice on elevated shooting.)

Now, there is a lot of controversy about where best (on its anatomy) to shoot a pigeon with an air rifle and I'm only going to add to that. The purpose here is pest control, as

accurately and humanely as *possible*. Note
the emphasis of that word. So now is where
you'll be glad you spent all that time plugging
pellets into targets the size of a 10p piece in
practice, or shooting conkers from the horse
chestnut tree. I'll tell you later what I do, but
you'll have to make your own judgement call
on this. With the right shot, the bird will
drop like a stone from its roost. That will
cause more disruption than your silenced
shot. When it does, some of its comrades will
panic and fly, though usually not far. Some
will flush, circle and settle again. Many will
stay and that's why the multishot PCP is the
tool to use. Leave fallen birds where they lie
to collect later, but do make a mental note of
where they fell as it may be dark when you
go to pick up!

Decoying pigeons on growing crops or
harvested stubbles is mildly useful and a
tactic I often employ just because it satisfies
the hunting need. Luring and baiting any
quarry is a challenge, pitting your wits against
theirs. For the airgunner, with a single small
projectile, it's a testing activity. Just watch a
woodpigeon feeding on the ground and you'll
soon appreciate that. They are rarely still. The
shotgunner takes his decoyed birds during
that moment when they soar in to join the
false birds and flappers on the floor, before
they get a chance to realise that something isn't
right. The airgunner, though, has to wait for
the random landers and take the opportunity
quickly when it comes. While I certainly take
a few on the floor, I get far more woodies in
the sitty trees above the decoys – but to draw
either target (the lander or the percher), you
first need to set an effective decoy pattern as
outlined in the tips and tricks section further
on in this chapter.

You will often hear or read the term 'sitty
trees' in relation to shooting avian quarry. Many
birds have vantage points where they perch to
observe the terrain and watch for threat before
descending to feed. The airgun hunter needs

*Don't loose a pellet
on a restless bird – it
will be gone before
the pellet strikes*

*A sitty tree – the roost shooter's nirvana!*

to learn these, or at least anticipate them. Trees with high or wide boughs and scant in leaves – like dead trunks or lightning-struck trees – are a perfect example. Birds will gather singly or in numbers before feeding. I have many regular trees on my permissions where I know that if I set up for a while in cover, eventually a corvid or pigeon will chance by to take a rest and decide its next move. Fruitful places for the airgunner.

There are others where I know, because they overlook a growing crop, that if I set up a decoy or two, birds will be drawn down to use them to check out my decoys, rather than land straight on the floor. A bare, exposed branch is usually more conducive to a result than waiting for a grounded bird to stop still among farrow or, worse still, obstructive stubble which can deflect a pellet.

Never neglect water sources if you're after woodpigeons, either. Of all avian quarry species – and I suspect because of that heavy metabolic rate – they are the most copious drinkers. Watch for them at puddles, pools and water troughs. Opportunistic shooting, for sure – but, then, hunting with the air rifle often is.

Finally, a word of caution. Make sure that you know how to identify the woodpigeon and distinguish it from a stock dove or turtle dove. To accidentally shoot either of the latter is highly illegal and could see your gun confiscated and a potential prison sentence. If you can't see that disctinctive neck flash of the woodpigeon – unique to the bird – then don't shoot. If it has a green, irridescent neck flash, it's a stock dove; if it has a black-barred neck flash and wing plumage like a kestrel, it's a turtle dove. With confidence, you'll soon learn to recognise a woody – even a juvenile which, just to confuse matters, doesn't develop that white collar for four months.

## TIPS AND TRICKS

I shoot hundreds of woodies every year and I have a freezer full of ripe, plump pigeon breasts. If a woodie presents on a bough with just head and neck showing, I'll take the neck shot. This is a rare shot for me as I prefer the high percentage game in pest control, as my freezer testifies. A slender, but fragile target, and the .22 pellets I favour will snap the neck easily at ranges up to 30 metres… if you hit it. A slight deviation any side and the pigeon will fly free when you miss. So I prefer the heart-stopper – and pick a bird that ideally presents its breast full-on. The woodpigeon's heart is located behind the wing joints. Some airgun experts will tell you that a shot through the rich breast muscle of a woody won't penetrate the bone protecting the heart. They will advocate head shots only. But watch the weaving, bobbing head of a pigeon, even at rest, and I'm willing to bet that there isn't much pigeon meat in their freezer. A shot within the range I've stated will penetrate both the breast muscle and the bone. Placed either side of the blade of breastbone (sternum) itself, and below the crop (the sack which

holds its undigested food), it will strike the bird's heart, or near enough, for the ballistic trauma to stop it beating. To really understand this, I would strongly recommend you study any bird's anatomy.

Decoy patterns for the airgun pigeon shooter don't need to be as scientific as for the shotgunner, if you take my advice and draw them to a sitty tree rather than the ground. For a sitty tree, you only want the birds to be curious enough to perch. The decoy itself, though, is important. I use flocked (velvet coated) shells or FUDs (fold-up decoys). The latter, with their ultra-violet paints, mirror the woodies' own irridescent plumage and can be set to look as though they are either feeding or watching from the ground. In breezy weather, I have a handful of Sillosock decoys, too. They

*It's well worth targeting water points*

*That white neck flash is a woodpigeon trademark – and a useful target*

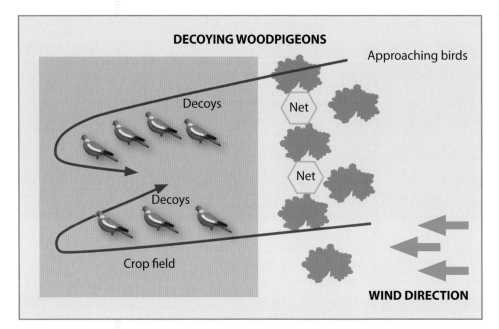

**DECOYING WOODPIGEONS**

Approaching birds

Decoys

Net

Net

Decoys

Crop field

**WIND DIRECTION**

*Decoy patterns for the airgun pigeon shooter don't need to be as scientific as for the shotgunner*

are silky, balloon like decoys that billow in the breeze and look like a moving bird. Make sure that you set the heads facing the breeze – a trait of the live woodpigeon when it feeds. If you want to shoot birds on the ground, set a pattern that allows a bird to land through the back, into the breeze, and escape easily through the front. Watch real flocks. Birds won't drop into crowded areas; they land at the perimeter and work their way inwards.

If you need to break cover to collect upturned birds – those shot carcases where the white underbelly will warn over-flying birds and negate the effect of your decoys – use the dead birds as additional decoys to expand the pattern. Keep a handful of wire supports in your bag. I use sections of coat hanger wire, trimmed to about 15 centimetres long, which take up no space at all. These are spiked under the dead bird's chin, then into the soil. Please remember that any amount of pigeon-like birds will bring curious woodies flying over low to check them out, but air shots are the shotgunner's arena. You need to make your

pattern convincing enough to make them land on the ground, or in a nearby tree. Don't expect huge bags – just enjoy the few you do get.

## THE SHORT STRAW

All around me, the harvest has been brought in. The vast dragons that gobble up the barley and wheat have stayed their smoking breath and the golden ash cloud has settled. The plundered prize of grain is winding its way to flour mill or brewery. Bread and beer for the masses. Farmers sit at their PCs satisfying bank managers that overdrafts have been honoured and everyone is happy. None more than me – for the aftermath, the month of stubbles, is mine for the taking. I have a short window of opportunity where both woodpigeon and corvid will be scouring the short straw and clearing up the surplus grain left behind by the combine. A surplus which declines each decade due to the efficiency of modern machinery. The large rolled bales of straw dot the landscape like the discarded cartridge

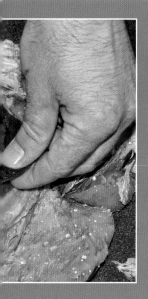

## BREASTING OUT

There are two types of quarry which, when shot, I never discard unless there are signs of disease because their meat is simply too tasty – the rabbit and the woodpigeon. I prefer to dress rabbits in the field, but the woodpigeons always come home first. The only meat worth salvaging on a pigeon (to my mind) are the two, lush breast medallions. To get to them, you have to pluck out the downy breast feathers. In the field, this leaves one hell of a sign that a predator has been at work – you! White feathers floating around on the breeze beneath a roost will soon see it abandoned, so take them home first.

Feathers floating around your house won't endear you to family, though – so, before plucking, hold the bird under a running tap and soak the breast thoroughly. Now pluck the feathers under the running water and the weight will keep them in the sink. When the breast is clear, run a sharp knife gently down the skin on either side of the breastbone so it can be peeled back towards the wing joints on either side, exposing the dark breast meat. Take a sharp fillet knife and trim the medallions out on either side, following the breast bone closely. Down from the top of the breast bone and out to the wing joints on either side. Wash these thoroughly in a cullender and they are then ready for eating. If you're going to freeze them, pat them dry with kitchen towel and drop them into a freezer bag. Freeze immediately.

Clearing up is now easy. Put the rest of the carcase into a doubled carrier bag, pull the sodden feathers from the sink and add them to the bag. Tie tightly and put in your waste bin.

---

shells left by a Goliath's shooting party. A magnificent sight, again short-lived. The arid summer has brought short stalks. This straw is almost as precious now as the ears of grain borne upon it. This is stock fodder which will be in low supply. I shall pity the equestrian this winter. As I look across fields holding 20 bales where once there were 50, I can guess that bedding and feed straw will cost dearly this year. Thus the teleporters and trailers are already busy gathering in these bales – they're far too valuable to expose to the rain and spoilage. I need to act quickly.

Today, the edge of the wood, next to the stubbles and below a flight-line, is perfect. For a quick session like this, I use a brilliant bit of kit, the telescopic Pigeon Shooter Blind, made by an American company called Hunters Specialities. Its Realtree fabric dictates placement within a tree-line or hedge, but it can be put up in minutes and moved quickly if necessary. Let's face it, we don't always pick the right spot, first time. There is nothing more frustrating than an elaborate net set-up in the wrong area when pigeon are on the move. This blind is attached to telescopic poles to adjust height, and its metal spikes can be driven in to even the hardest ground. If you need to move, you simply drop the poles to minimum height, roll it up and relocate. My small squadron of FUD woody and crow deeks pack into a waterproof stash-sack. Put the three pieces of kit together (blind, seat and flat-packed decoys) and you're talking modern, lightweight, quick-set pigeon decoying here.

With the net in place, I arrange the deeks in a simple random pattern that's typical of post-harvest grain scavengers, and sit back to wait. This isn't intended to be shotgun-type red letter day shooting, with bags of 200-plus birds. This is an airgunner's set-up – and my idea of 'red letter' is half-a-dozen birds. If you're a shotgunner, please don't scoff – we 'popgunners' place our single, small projectile into a target the size of a 10p piece. We might not get many birds, but when we do, they're all edible; no dental bills

*Filleting out a pigeon's breast medallions*

necessary and the farmer still appreciates the effort. If I'm honest, I get far more birds roost shooting in winter – but this decoying game is wonderfully relaxing sport on an autumn evening. Primarily 'pest control', of course.

As I settle, the heady aroma of wild watermint surrounds me. Behind, in the wood, the harmonics of a life much simpler than mine (yet no less stressful) catch my ear. I sit, mesmerised, considering what drama or natural sub-plots are occurring. The low, guttural chirrup of marauding magpies means trouble for some poor creature, though nests are now clear and fledglings long gone. What mischief can they be up to? More appealing to the ear is the robin's song and the distant

*Placing FUD decoys on stubble for a relaxing evening's sport*

chorus of a nightingale. Even the murmur of my quarry, that gentle cooing, is cleansing. Below this, the drone of insect life; buzzing, whirring and relaying the incessant quest for pollen. A gentle nip on my lower arm reminds me that this quest is often for blood. I twist the gnat between my fingers, wakened once more to my own purpose. Everything here, around me, is hunting – for food, for pollen, for blood. For survival.

Shooting through a net, as opposed to over it (which the shotgunner does) isn't as easy as it first looks. Your perspective on range is warped, vision confused by the shield between you and your quarry. The scope doesn't lie, your brain does – before you sight up. The

*The view through a net is confusing to the eye and brain, so employ range-markers*

pigeon that lands at 30 metres will look further away through the apertures in the net. I overcome this optical illusion by placing a couple of my decoys as range-markers, pacing 25 and 35 from the net. Any live birds that land are quickly judged by their proximity to these two decoys and, therefore, perspective is regained.

Without the aid of flappers and rotary deeks (pretty useless to an airgunner), I rely on the natural curiosity and greed of the woodpigeon to draw them to ground. Many will pass over; some will double around to inspect the decoys again but few will actually land. When they do, I need to draw a bead swiftly – they won't take long to realise that the flock they've joined is false. Now, this may be controversial in some quarters, but I don't hold by the nonsense that every shot taken with an airgun should be a head shot. Just watch a feeding pigeon. That tiny head, the size of a 50p coin, is bobbing and dabbing at grain and makes an almost impossible target at 25 or 30 metres. Watch the body, the centre of the fulcrum. It hardly moves. So I prefer to tuck my .22 pellet close to where the wing joins the breast. This is

where the heart lies, and if a .22 pellet with its residual power at that range can smash a rabbit's skull, it certainly stops a pigeon's heartbeat. I've got a freezer full of untainted pigeon breasts to prove the point. Add the stubble factor – the head more often out of sight than the body – and this shot is, excuse the pun, a no-brainer. The heart shot relies on exactly the same responsibility for accurate shooting and respect for quarry as the head shot. It just makes more sense in the reality of the circumstance. The only disadvantage of the heart shot is that it often turns the pigeon over on impact. If that happens, retrieval of the bird will interrupt shooting – but interrupt it you must, as an upturned bird will deter others from landing.

As the birds are passing regularly, but appear reluctant to land, I decide to add another decoy nearby. The bulky sentinel of a single crow can often kid the passing woodpigeon into a false sense of security. They seem to understand that this most wary of birds won't land unless it is totally confident of its own safety. The FUD crow deeks aren't too convincing close up, but they are very

*Defintely not a red letter day!*

effective from a distance.

The sortie brought just four birds to the bag in two hours. There was a bonus rabbit, too, which ventured along the wood's edge. I breasted out the birds behind the net, then skinned out the rabbit. All the offal went into a ditch for Charlie and Brock to fight over later. It was the sort of autumn evening when I wished I had a small stove and a skillet pan. A sizzling, pan-fried supper under a harvest sunset would have rounded off the session nicely – but, alas, practicality won over poeticism and I sent a text to my good lady to say I was on my way home! I harvested some of the water-mint leaves before leaving. I'd had an idea for a new pigeon recipe… ○

# THE COLLARED DOVE

*Food store spoilage is the collared dove's main crime*

## A NATURAL HISTORY

If I have a particular affinity to the collared dove (*Streptopelia decaocto*), it's for two reasons. One is that the first chick to hatch on the British mainland did so in 1956, the year of my birth. The other is that in 55 years, it has made as much of a nuisance of itself nationally as I have! Crossing the Channel from Europe after a century of spread from the East (Turkey and Greece), there's now an estimated quarter-of-a-million pairs breeding in Britain. The emphasis being on 'pairs', as the bird is iconic for its lifelong loyalty to one partner. As such, it represents a loyalty and fidelity not often noted in the bird world, except in large species with isolated territories such as eagles and buzzards.

Like the woodpigeon, it breeds several times a year on a skimpy platform of twigs holding a pair of white eggs. The woodpigeon's sleepy, five-syllable bass note murmur on a summer's day differs from the collared dove's higher pitched, three-syllable '*coo, coo, coo*'. Dressed in a silken, lightly-tanned plumage that's almost pink in the sun's rays, it has a marked, narrow black half-collar around its nape. Train your scope on such a bird and look into its soft, beautiful and doe-like eye, and you'll most likely gulp with guilt before releasing a shot. I certainly do. Yet watch it for a while and you will realise why it is now firmly on Britain's General Licence.

A common garden bird table visitor now, it will plunder and beat off rival feeders (songbirds) with same acrimony as the woodpigeon, to which it often surrenders simply because of the imbalance in size. If the woodpigeon is the heavyweight (the Mike Tyson) in the bird table arena, the collared dove is the middleweight (the Pretty Boy Floyd). The reason for its bad reputation and addition to the vermin list, however, is due to its proliferance around the farmyard and grain silos. Not just because of its grain theft, but like its cousin, also because of the spoilage

*A delicate bird but highly edible*

it causes on fodder and stored grain – and its ability to deplete food left out for gamebirds and poultry.

## FOOD AND PREDATORS

The collared dove's diet is very similar to the woodpigeon's, but without the overt crop-raiding or flocking – grain, seeds, buds and shoots. It's a bird that has adapted and spread due to living close to human habitation and available food sources, so it's rarely seen in remote areas.

Predators, too, are the same; I have found hundreds killed and plucked by sparrowhawks over my hunting lifetime. Cats and foxes take advantage of their grain-hoovering tendency, too, which is far too predictable for their own safety.

## HABITAT AND HABIT

Collared doves can be found anywhere there is a human supply of seed and grain. They will nest in hedgerows, low trees, inside barns or outhouses and in the gutters of houses. Where there are houses with bird tables or farms, they'll be close by.

These doves are fiercely territorial, and where forced to share resource will fight and squabble with rival pairs; it's in total conflict with their serene appearance. Fighting between rival males is common, I often witness this.

## HUNTING METHODS

There is nothing complicated about shooting collared doves and their preference for human habitation means they aren't as nervous or as wary as the woodpigeon. Quite simply, target their food sources and sitty trees. If the woodpigeon has a slender neck and small head, the collared dove's is smaller still – hence breast shots are quite adequate. The breast medallions, while smaller than a woody's, are just as tasty. They can be extracted in the same way (see page 67).

*If you're a romantic like me, try to shoot them both*

## TIPS AND TRICKS

Collared doves don't roost in flocks, but they have two tendencies which makes them quite vulnerable; I've hinted at these earlier. The first is their territorialism. Around the farmyard, there will be several pairs competing for spilled grain or poultry feed. While I have never been able to discern a 'hierarchy' as such, each pair will often wait in turn to visit a food source. They stack up like aeroplanes waiting to descend at Heathrow, albeit this holding pattern is in the trees. I often target those in the sitty trees as well as the ground-feeding birds.

I make no bones for dwelling on the collared dove's fidelity. Like the magpie, if you shoot one, its mate will often exhibit an almost human level of anger and distress. Flying in to inspect its dead mate, chastising and flapping around, overlooking the scene for ages. For this reason, I often get the pair – and am much more comfortable if I do, for obvious reasons. A colleague of mine is convinced that if you shoot one collared dove, it's mate will die of a broken heart. A romantic view – and obviously untrue. I mentioned earlier, too, the fighting between males. I'm sure that many of the battles I witness are the result of mismatches caused by my own 'divorce' of mated pairs! I have to say, too, that the females seem to enjoy the attention and rivalry – another almost-human trait, perhaps? ○

# THE FERAL PIGEON

## A NATURAL HISTORY

The feral pigeon, as we now know, is a descendant of the rock dove – so both share the same Latin name, *Columba livia*. I know, it's all rather confusing, isn't it? Rock doves, stock doves, ring doves… That's why it's important for the airgun hunter to learn a bit about quarry!

The rock dove 'proper' lives almost exclusively on the rugged coastal cliffs of Western England, Wales and Scotland. Let's ignore this bird, other than to say that many of its urban, feral cousins still carry the distinctive light grey upper, green nape and two strong black wing bars. The rest of the ferals are a mish-mash of colouring and plumage, following hundreds of years of inter-breeding with foreign birds introduced to fill the dovecotes that helped feed the Lord of the Manor and his serfs in medieval Britain. Many of these evolved into the racing-pigeon, too, by the way – more on that later.

Feral pigeons are smaller than woodpigeons, and about the same size as a collared dove. Their nest is a scrappy affair: just a few twigs and feathers – enough to stop their two, white eggs from rolling away – on a ledge or rafter. They breed all year round, raising up to three broods a year.

## FOOD AND PREDATORS

Feral pigeons consume up to a fifth of their body weight in food per day, which equates to a quite voracious appetite when you consider them in flocks. Food is mainly grain and berries, though in an urban environment, they will eat virtually anything – they're a bit like an avian rat.

Predators are the usual suspects – sparrowhawks, goshawks and farmyard cats.

## HABITAT AND HABIT

The modern feral pigeon plagues our towns and cities, often openly fed by a public ignorant to its capacity to harbour disease. Yet it's a severe pest in rural areas, too. In the absence of the rocky cliff ledges of its ancestor, it nests on ledges or beams, both inside and outside buildings. As a very sociable bird, the colonies that gather cause immeasurable damage to buildings. Its acidic guano decimates brickwork, cladding and historic statues. On the ground, it forms a film as treacherous as black ice.

Once a colony is established, it's difficult to eradicate, though many public authorities have tried to. Not just because it breeds so readily, but because as soon as anyone wages war on it, there is invariably a public outcry from serial 'pigeon feeders'. By wiping the smile off Nelson's face with their guano, even the iconic flocks in London's Trafalgar Square have incurred the wrath of the authorities, though, and consequently suffered culls. Over here in Norfolk – coincidentally Nelson's county! – I do my best to exact revenge when I can. Pigeon nets which prevent them flying and landing on ledges, live falcons, decoy owls and all manner of deterrents all fail to eradicate the pest. I often visit Norwich railway station and chuckle to myself when I see the trio of plastic hawks perched around the beams staring wild-eyed, but impotent, at the horde of ferals picking and pecking around the commuters' ankles!

Around the farmyard, feral pigeons are just as destructive, but far more easily tackled than in the city. Their main sins will be plundering grain stores and spoiling animal fodder with their guano. Like the other doves, they can carry a host of unmentionable diseases, as outlined on page 166. In a rural environment, they almost exclusively nest inside man-made structures, like barns and sheds, or under bridge parapets.

## HUNTING METHODS

You will have noted my cynicism regarding the futile deterrents used by authorities with a pigeon problem. I firmly believe that the

most cost-effective, clinical and humane way of dealing with feral pigeons is the air rifle. Many professional pest controllers use them when able to carry out the work discreetly and away from critical eyes. On rooftop sorties in factories and city centres, some even use the rifle to destroy eggs on nests without causing structural damage or disturbing the public.

Hunting is hardly the right word for culling feral pigeons. They are totally dependent on man for food, so are far less suspicious or cautious as other doves. Simply ambushing feeding points (obviously not the market square!), or nesting sites in barns and warehouses, is all that's needed.

## TIPS AND TRICKS

As most feral pigeons culls will be carried out in or around human habitation, sticking to a sub-12 ft/lb air rifle is essential. In fact, many who control the feral pigeon population will advocate a mid-powered rifle with as little as 8 or 9ft/lb. Regardless, always check that you have a safe backstop before firing, and be conscious of what damage a ricochet from a miss may cause. This especially applies around livestock – as does clearing away shot birds.

One of the best ways to set up in a barn or warehouse is somewhere in shadow, with any available light or sun at your back. The birds entering the building – and there will be constant traffic – won't be able to see you. Let them settle on the beam. They will be fidgety at first, but once they've settled, they will be still enough for a head shot. If – and this often happens – you kill the bird where it sits, try to dislodge it with another pellet or two so that you can dispose of it. Leave all shot birds where they are until you've finished, though.

*There's that Barnett bloke again. You divert him and I'll go squit on his Jeep!*

Ferals aren't as flighty as woodies and will often ignore a cull going on around them.

I mentioned racing-pigeons earlier. These are simply pedigree 'ferals', carefully bred for their speed and homing instinct. They are someone's property and, technically, it would be illegal to shoot them – although if you inadvertently despatched one while routinely going about avian pest control under the standard terms of the General Licence, you have not broken any law. Remember that ferals are gregarious and flock. If you come across a lone feral, please don't shoot it until you're sure it's not a racing 'straggler'. If in doubt, let the bird pass. Racing birds that lose the pack often settle with feral colonies, too. I have myself inadvertantly shot racers among feral flocks, not finding out until collecting the corpse and finding its leg 'ringed' or wing-feathers number-coded. In all cases, I've taken the care to recover the ring and send it (anonymously, I confess) to the secretary of a local (or the identified) racing-pigeon club. All birds are registered, so the ring is a bit like a dog's micro-chip. At least, then, the owner would know that the bird wasn't coming home and it's a practice that the Royal Pigeon Racing Association strongly advocates.

Finally, I don't eat feral pigeons. Some people do – but that 'avian rat' affinity to scavenging puts me right off even trying. They are prolific carriers of campylobacter and salmonella due to their scavenging which is, of course, why we are allowed to shoot them. ○

# THE CARRION CROW

## THE VIEW FROM THE CROW'S NEST

*You've spent half your day in flight, the other half scavenging for food. As birds come, you're sturdy... but still at risk from higher predators. Your continued survival depends on your ability to fly from danger, swiftly; this may come from below or above. Through the wonder of evolution, you have developed a sharp eye, a vice-like beak, powerful wings and talons that would make even the buzzard envious. In the air, you are superlative. On the floor, you are vulnerable.*

*Watching from the bough of a tree, you are midway between the crucial parameters of safety and danger. You gauge every pending threat or opportunity using your hearing and your sight, driven by two instincts that fuel your very existence – eating and breeding. The need for food is a dynamic driver. The call of a mate is another. The beseeching squeal of your hungry fledgling will pull on your psyche and implore that you assume almost desperate duty during rearing – a duty that will drive you to self-neglect, exhaustion and near suicide in the quest for food.*

*When you, yourself, departed the egg which cosseted you as an embryo, you already knew your enemies. For this knowledge was pre-programmed into your DNA. One of the most dangerous of those threats you can now see, bumbling toward you on two legs, through the tree-line. A tall, awkward animal, incapable of flight. It moves with little grace, yet it has the capacity to kill you from a distance. You can sense its malevolence as you gaze, but you have an inherent ability to judge distance. When it stops about 100 crow-lengths away, you glide away to a further corner of the wood and return to your vigil. Danger, for now, averted...*

## A NATURAL HISTORY

I doubt that I would be seriously challenged by any experienced airgunner if I were to say that the carrion crow is one of the hardest quarry species to target. And I *will* say it. *Corvus corone* and its Northern hooded crow cousin, *Corvus cornix*, are legendary for their intelligence and their acute vigilance. At first glance, they appear to be the most drab of the corvid species, but closer examination reveals a subtle mixture of blacks and greens among their plumage. They are distinguishable from rooks by their stout black beak (the rook's is pointed) and the lack of a white face. The hooded crow – or hoodie as it's known – has a mantle of grey plumage. I never have the privilege of seeing hoodies in my neck of the woods, so I can only relate my experience with the carrion crow.

There is an old saying: "If you see crows, they be rooks. If you see a rook, it's a crow." Crows tend to be furtive, isolated birds, generally seen alone or in pairs. Rooks are highly gregarious and flock in numbers, though, so the saying bears much truth. And it is that isolation and acute wariness that makes the crow so difficult to target with the short-range ballistics of an air rifle.

Crows pair for life and nest in remote trees, often where they have a commanding view of the countryside. The nest is a solid platform of dead twigs, lower in profile than the rook's, and is often used for years. I have passed under the same nest along the Acle Straight (where trees are rare, set amid the coastal marshes) in my Jeep for six years on my way to work, and every spring a pair of crows has bred in it. Probably the same pair.

Though they generally raise a single brood if left undisturbed, the crow has a deeply rooted survival instinct. On estates where keepers destroy nests (perfectly legal under the General Licence), crows will rebuild elsewhere and breed again.

Around four to six eggs are laid between March and July, depending on weather conditions. Unlike magpies, who marshal their nursery brood around all summer, crow parents are intolerant of their own young and soon harry them away to find their own territory. The crow is much like me; three's a crowd... and to be avoided!

*Carrion crows are very solitary birds, and always on vigil*

## FOOD AND PREDATORS

The clue is in its name really, isn't it? Yet though the carrion crow is adept at finding dead meat and detritus, it has the omnivorous, varied diet associated with all corvids. It will eat anything it needs to, just to survive. That, unfortunately – for I highly respect this Einstein of the bird world – means it will plunder nests and take both eggs and chicks.

Compare the crow to its mammalian equivalent, the stoat. Sitting atop a high bough in the centre of its territory, it misses nothing. It watches the hen pheasant scraping her meagre nest. It watches the chaffinch bringing moss into the hedgerow. It watches the blackbird fetch grass fronds to weave its nest. It also knows where every nest is. The crow enjoys an egg of any size for breakfast… or lunch, or supper. If the nest is impenetrable to its vice-like beak, it will wait and watch patiently over ensuing weeks for the feeble fledgling to emerge from the security of its nursery – and then strike. For the crow – and the airgun hunter needs to note this – has a formidable memory. Like the stoat, once the crow has focused on a prey, the prey stands little chance of survival. The big difference is that the crow will prey on the vulnerable; the stoat doesn't even know the word vulnerable!

The crow's leaning toward feasting on carrion is legendary, to the point where poems have featured it; even films have, too. It will devour the flesh of anything presented, including the afterbirths of cattle or sheep and roadkill mammals. Its uncanny ability to sense weakness (vulnerability) and death has given the crow its reputation as a harbinger of death itself.

The carrion crow has few natural predators, other than higher mammals (fox, man) and raptors. I can count on two hands the amount of sparrowhawk kills I've found on crows in my lifetime. They have always been fledlings, with the whitish feathers streaks that display immaturity. Foxes account for a few adult kills

– but, as with the dead woodpigeon remnants I find, I can't explain how they make the kills. Perhaps they simply stumble upon sick or injured prey?

## HABITAT AND HABIT

Crow territory is anywhere and everywhere with respect to what I've said above. Though their preference is open space in which to nest, they will venture wherever food is available. Acutely tuned to threat, they will act fearlessly in the urban garden, but are elsusive in their natural rural environment. The crow hunter needs to be a patient individual, and I stress the word individual. This bird will study a potential food source for an hour before venturing in to feed. Any sign of human activity and it will abort its mission.

Sit in the cover of a wood and watch carrion crows (or rooks) feeding over a freshly-sown crop. They will sit out from the tree-line, perhaps 50 to 80 metres as they are distinctly uncomfortable with a reduced horizon. That's pretty understandable when you watch them fly. For a medium sized bird, they don't take off or land well; they are quite clumsy. Compare them to the similar-sized woodpigeon, which can turn on a sixpence and flash away like the sparrowhawk that may be on its tail.

Crows leave themselves a wide take-off or landing area. We need to remember that when hunting. If you are hiding up, watching crows (or rooks), you will learn much about them. Particularly their voice, which reveals much about their intentions and state of mind. If the rook is a tenor, the carrion crow is a bass tenor. Study them long enough and, from the call, you will learn to distinguish which species is calling '*gun, guun, guuun!*' to warn its neighbours. For that really is how it sounds. The carrion crow has a much deeper, more gutteral call than the rook. If you hear that call, you are not being paranoid – it's actually seen you! If you hear a more relaxed, again gutteral '*caaw*' – evenly spaced and a

few seconds apart – the bird is calling in its mate. The crow is secure, safe. Sit tight, for it will soon come in to feed.

As for visiting sign, it is there, but seldom seen by most shooters. I can't personally distinguish between the footprint of a crow or a rook, but I can usually distinguish the trail. Both have the typical print of a perching bird: three forward toes, one backward, but with distinctive, separated lobes which you won't see on a woodpigeon track. The size is similar, but the crow usually walks, whereas a rook hops. Is that important? Only if, like me, you like to take a qualified view on which species predated a songbird or gamebird nest – and rooks, in true corvid style, will do so. The other sure sign of rook or crow presence are the disgorged pellets left at the base of fenceposts. The rook's tend to be brown and earthy, from the soil digested with grubs and seeds. The crow's pellet will divulge many more sins. Often, if you pull them open, you will find small fragments of bone, feather and egg shell – proof of their plunder and murder.

## HUNTING METHODS

Although you may occasionally shoot a crow on a walkabout session, definitely don't bank on it! They usually see you well before you see them. One of the hardest tasks you'll be set as a vermin controller on your permission (because they are predating gamebird nests), will be to target a particular pair of crows or their nest. Yet it can be done. As an air rifle shooter, you don't have the luxury of two barrels full of scattergun shot, like the shotgunner. The most reliable way to target crows is to bait them in to where you want them – or, to be more precise, close to where you pretend to want them! Remember what I said above. The crow is a very vigilant bird. Their intelligence and memory means that once seen abroad with a gun, the human carrying it will be marked as a threat.

My editor, Nigel Allen, once recounted to

me a tale that proved to him crows have the ability to identify which gun you're carrying, and whether it poses a threat. Many years ago, he'd visited a Welsh smallholder to photograph a magazine article. While shooting with his camera, a wily old crow danced around, about 60 yards away, unconcerned by the Theoben break-barrel airgun that Nigel's subject was holding. The man told Nigel that the crow knew he had an air rifle, which is why it appeared so unconcerned. Nigel (understandably!) didn't believe him. The chap went inside and brought out his .22 BRNO rimfire. The old crow screamed in alarm and flew off to watch from about 200 yards away! When the man put the rimfire away and brought the Theoben back out, the crow returned to its closer watch point.

At the time, Nigel was gobsmacked, and admits it's a personal experience he recounts to few for fear of being laughed at. But having watched crows for over 40 years now myself, it's a tale I actually have no trouble believing. When intentionally hunting crows, I will approach my intended cover, or hide, on the blind side – even if it means a long hike – and carry the gun in a slip over my shoulder. I don't do this for any other vermin species.

## TIPS AND TRICKS

Remember that old saying I mentioned earlier? "If you see crows, they be rooks. If you see a rook, it's a crow." Well, despite their usual solitude, crows are quick to join a rook and jackdaw throng (and tolerate other crows) in two events. Mobbing over a threat, or plundering a food source. Use that as a random method for crow culling – though, again, don't stake your life on it.

Let's assume you have your eye on a particular pair of crows, for it will usually be 'the pair'. You have two options – and both

*Corvids often mob together – a crow and jackdaw bagged from the same spot*

work. You either go to them… or they come to come to you. I know which I prefer – when *they* come to *me*.

Baiting or decoying crows can be very effective methods for the air rifle hunter. It needs a bit of preparation and forward thinking, though, such as keeping back an intact rabbit or grey squirrel to use within a few days. I find that a three- or four-day-old coney makes excellent bait when slit open and its paunch pulled out. There is some debate as to whether birds have acute olfactory senses, indeed that they can smell at all. Believe me, though, I'm convinced corvids can. The riper the carrion, the quicker they home-in on it!

I like to place bait out in regular spots, too; this conditions corvids to actually look for food. For instance, as I don't cook squirrels, I often deposit their shot carcases in regular places on my permissions. A quick incision through the belly ensures that the fox, crow or badger cleans them up by next day. So if I'm targeting a corvid nest, I make sure I leave them close to the nest tree, but near enough to cover to come back with the gun a few days later. That 'near enough' statement is important. Remember what I said about the crow's reluctance to land close to the tree-line? Drop your offering about 30 paces out into the open. That way, you're conditioning the birds to come in at least that far – and then you can bait at that distance when the time comes.

Remember, too, that crows prefer to feed on the ground. Bait left on top of a straw bale or a gate post will attract suspicion. You'll get away with that when using eggs, but rarely carrion. The crow isn't that stupid; in fact, recent studies show it to be one of the cleverest of the bird species. It easily spots fake plastic decoys, too. I consider flocked decoys to be more effective than 'plastic' when it comes to duping crows. Yet another baiting method I use *doesn't* involve carrion. The crow will scavenge on almost anything, so I save all my

vegetable peelings – potato, carrot, swede, peppers and such like – and scatter them on the ride outside a wood or a shed.

There is much written about needing to be under solid cover, and being in there early to target the crow. This is absolutely right – and there's the rub. To bait out 30 metres from the tree-line, you need to disturb the scene, even if you crept up via the back door. Therefore, 'early' means just before dawn, because the crow is one of nature's earliest risers. Place out a gutted coney, spread the paunch and retire to the trees.

I generally don't use a hide for crows – just solid, natural cover. I will have to remain motionless for ages, though. The crow spends much time studying its environment, so a misplaced net or the parched, dying leaves of a prebuilt 'natural' hide are soon spotted. The best way is to just become a shadow under natural cover. Use a sunshade on your scope to reduce chances of a glint from the glass. Dress drably, or in camoflauge. Prime your rifle ready for a shot… and sit tight. If a crow comes down to the bait, it will land many metres away and take a good look around before hopping in to feed. Be patient. Until it actually dips its beak into the paunch, it is on high alert. Once it has those succulent entrails in its bill, it's yours for the taking, though. But even if you're successful, don't move another muscle, except to re-arm the rifle. If the crow's mate is around, it will either flee immediately or come in to harry its fallen partner in confusion. As with collared doves, whose fidelity is legendary, the kindest thing you can now do is shoot the mate, too.

I mentioned earlier the crow's tendency to evict its young when they're fledged. Take advantage of that if you've been nest-watching and cull the young in those first few days, when their confusion keeps them within the nesting territory.

There is another old adage which say that crows can't count. An old countryman's ploy

*Setting out a flocked (velvet) decoy crow*

is for two or more people to approach a hide or a building. All but one depart and the crow will be fooled into thinking it's now safe. This ruse certainly works with magpies – I've often used it around the farm buildings. But I'm still not sure that the crow is that easily fooled!

To me, testing my fieldcraft against such seasoned quarry is the definitive challenge. Hunting the crow, rook, magpie, jay or even the woodpigeon is much more challenging than the unsophisticated (though necessary) culling of small mammals, like squirrels and coneys. There is far more to consider when hunting bird species. Should I bait them in with a food source or set decoys? Should I simply hide in cover and ambush them? Are they best shot on the floor, or on the bough? With an air rifle, I definitely won't shoot birds in flight. I consider any vermin bird species to be at its most vulnerable when it's on the

bough. Most birds (and particularly corvids) will only settle on the ground if they are far from cover, which for the airgunner usually means out of range. There are exceptions, of course, the main one being baiting-in with carrion; bolder birds will flight in to feed (though not before watching for an age).

Knowing when and why to tackle avian pests is essential. The time when the winter crops are pulled in and the ground is prepared for the spring-sowing of deep-rooted crops, such as potato, is ideal. The deep furrows drawn across acres of soil turn up the grubs and worms which have lain dormant all winter. This is a terrific time to be secured in the cover of the wood as legions of carrion crows, rooks and jackdaws gather in the trees waiting for the huge ploughs to withdraw. On such days, I thank Mother Nature for the abundant, evergreen ivy which provides

*A red letter day on
the black bandits*

cover beneath the beech. On such days I'm reminded of how crucial all those practised elevation shots – at crab apples, fir cones and horse chestnuts – were. High shots demand hasty evaluation of angle and range, making them all the sweeter in their accomplishment. I shoot too few of the black hordes in winter due to lack of foliage as cover (even when using their corpses as decoys), so they often flock in again to ransack the pea seedlings that follow the beet crop. Certainly too few to make any serious impact for my farmers' liking.

A thaw after snow offers a better prospect, shooting from a pop-up hide. The swamped meadows and water-splashes are enticing to carrion crows and magpies. The shallow pools not only make ideal bathing pools for the magpies, but also draw up the worms, which attract the crows. Hide shooting offers the chance to watch other wildlife, too. ○

# THE MAGPIE

## THE FORTRESS

*You're perched on the crown of the tree, exhausted. For over two weeks, you have flown from the woodland floor to the top of this ancient Scots pine. Probably two hundred times a day. Each and every time with a stick or a twig, to weave in to the gradually-growing nest. Your mate has done the same. Four hundred journeys a day between you. The last few days have definitely taken their toll. You have had to cover the nest, your fortress, with a domed roof to thwart the attentions of your corvid kindred; you're well aware that a carrion crow pair are building a nest just a few hundred yards away. That domed roof was hard work, needing softer pliant twigs cropped from living wood.*

*Yet still your mate wasn't satisfied, her urgency greater than yours. You had covered her two weeks ago and she would produce the fruit of that union within days now. She was abroad in the meadows, courting with danger, lifting horsehair from the barbed-wire fence and rabbit fur from outside the warrens. As she put the final touches to the nest, you were now on vigil – and that vigil had already borne results. As your nest was nearing completion, you were watching all the other birds starting their own construction. From this lofty viewpoint, you could see where the yellowhammers were weaving a tidy nest in the grassy bank below a rowan tree. The robins were dragging moss and horsehair under the old farm trailer. Aside the crumbling flint wall that bordered the track, you had seen the chaffinch pulling moss into the thick ivy that had pulled the wall down. Along the ditch, near the telegraph pole, you had watched a cock pheasant cover his hens. The eggs would be thereabouts, somewhere, when they lay. Vigilance would find them; all these observations were etched in your predatory memory…*

*Movement below disturbs you and you cackle in alarm. Two animals are beneath the fortress: two legs, four legs. You fly away, a safe distance, chiding them as you flee. When you're sure they're gone, you return to the nest, flying in low through the shrubbery, cautious and vigilant. Arriving at the tree, you cackle in alarm. Close by, brazen and*

*threatening, is a wide-eyed bird – a raptor! You screech your disapproval and your mate comes to support. Together, you circle the low trees and shrubs, shrieking, trying to flush the threat – but it doesn't move. You come in closer, both mobbing the passive owl. But still it doesn't budge.*

*As you both stand, screaming at the unblinking, orange eyes of this stationary attacker, a subtle whisper from nearby breaks the impasse… and your mate tumbles untidily from her perch. As she hits the floor, you go beserk, flashing around the branches above her. You drop to the floor, next to her, to nudge her inert form with your beak. The fortress had been breached before it had even held its intended occupants.*

## A NATURAL HISTORY

Over the past 40 years, the British population of the magpie (*Pica pica*) has multiplied ten-fold and is now estimated to be close on two million birds. I'm afraid I totally refute claims by national bird protection organisations that this explosion bears no relationship to songbird decline. I've seen them in action around smaller birds' nests all too often. Like the grey squirrel, magpies enjoy the sanctuary of urban parks and gardens, where they can feed and breed unchallenged. Consequently, as fast as the vermin controller can eradicate breeding pairs, the voids are filled by this urban overspill.

Magpies raise just one brood a year, but it's a large one – the female laying from five to eight eggs. Watching a pair nest-building is an education and perhaps the only time I feel any empathy for these birds. Their industry is phenomenal, flying from ground to tree thousands of times over many days to weave a huge dome and line it with mud. For some reason, the pair will often half-build a nest then abandon it and start again in another tree. It's a trait shared by the wren, but in his case, the polygamous male sometimes builds a few nests and chooses females to occupy them. With magpies, they both build… so who makes the decision to move is open to

question. To form the arch over the nest, they will bend and break supple live twigs from surrounding trees using their bill as a tool. Once the eggs are laid, the birds appear to alternate the brooding, the male sitting while the female feeds. Don't try to identify which is which, though; it's almost impossible to sex magpies on the wing.

During brooding, magpies are fiercely territorial and the hunter can take advantage of this. More on this later. Once the chicks fledge, they stick closely as a family for many weeks, the parents chaperoning the curious youngsters everywhere. It's totally different behaviour to the carrion crow.

Putting an age on magpies is usually fairly easy. First-year birds will be shorter in tail, lighter in weight and will have straight, pointed bills. The older the bird gets, the plumper it gets; the tail extends and the bill thickens. Ancient birds – though there aren't many left on my own permissions! – can be identified by crooked bills and thick claws. Left undisturbed, magpies can live for many years and become extremely canny. I've had some very interesting challenges hunting birds that have been long-established on new permission. Miss them just once with the rifle and you will chase them for months, for the magpie is a bird with an acute memory. Yet that memory can be put to your advantage, albeit eventually. The parents are good

*A magpie's nest – a a huge dome, lined with mud*

teachers, too and will lead the young to feed in the way they, themselves, have traditionally feasted. In my first book, I recount a tale, fully photographed, of an unusual pest control mission where the youngsters inherited a very macabre trait from the mother.

## FOOD AND PREDATORS

Magpies are omnivorous – they'll eat meat or vegetable – yet their preference is meat, carrion or a juicy egg. Like most corvids, it has a morbid reputation for delving into the result of some other poor creature's demise. Most folk will only see the magpie feeding as they hurtle along a highway and see it flutter away at the last minute from the mangled, bloodied corpse of a road-kill rabbit. For rabbit, read also badger, fox, deer and squirrel. Basically, if it's pink, red, fresh and dead, then it's perfect magpie fodder. This is no bad thing, when you think about it. They act as Britain's little vulture, picking clean the bones of human guilt – for who hasn't felt guilt as their wheels bump across a living creature caught in the headlights? The problem with the magpie, however, is when there's no road-kill, it will resort to murder and infanticide.

Magpies breed early, and that's for a reason: an evolutionary necessity. Usually, by the time their fledglings are abroad, it will be May or June. The songbirds, many of which will have travelled thousands of miles to breed here, will just be hatching chicks. Like its cousin, the carrion crow, the magpie will have been training its dark, beady eye across its nesting domain and will have marked every movement. It has seen the greenfinch dragging moss into the blackthorn hedge; the blackbird weaving its comfortable bowl in the poor cover of the azalea. It has watched the partridge prepare her shallow scrape; the hen pheasant creeping into her grassy bank time and time again. The prospect of new life – better still, the prospect of life just emerged – will excite the magpie and its now

*Britain's little vulture, feasting on road-kill*

maturing family. They are 'chavs'. The avian 'muggers', watching and waiting outside a natural supermarket to rob the small, the weak, the vulnerable. They are cowards, too. You will never see a magpie push a pheasant from her nest. Nor even a feeble chaffinch. They will wait for the parents to leave, then sneak in and burgle, or encourage its young to do so. I've even watched them then steal the proceeds from their own young. Yes, the Fagin of British birds.

These birds vie with the carrion crow to be first on the hunt once the sun is creeping up. They will scour the lanes and roads for last night's casualties, and they will check out the farmyard. During lambing or calving season, you'll mark them in the tree-line, waiting for a juicy placenta to peck at.

The main predator to worry the magpie is the shooter. I will always preach 'respect' for quarry. Yet, by that, I mean a clean despatch. If I'm driving a country lane, I will swerve to avoid a startled rabbit unless it shows signs of myxomatosis. When I see a magpie feeding on a road-kill rabbit, I hit the accelerator! (Never got one yet, though; sometimes I wish I drove a Lotus Elan rather than a Jeep Cherokee!) Mind you, it's illegal, so probably just as well.

Sparrowhawks take a fair few magpies in flight, and I occasionally come across fox kills. That's a stalk I'd love to see, for the maggie is such a wary bird.

## HABITAT AND HABIT

The magpie's habitat is extensive and they are found just about everywhere – town, park, garden, woodland and farmland. Nor are they fussy where they nest, be it a remote stand of tall trees or a high, tangled hedgerow. The nest will usually be almost impenetrable, though, and hard to spot until autumn's leaf fall. I've never known a magpie use the same nest twice, but they often build close to an old nest. Recently, I watched a pair carefully dismantle an old nest and move most of it, twig by twig, to build a new one about 200 yards away. That indicated a level of intelligence that I'd never previously associated with the magpie. Bear that in mind…

Keep an eye on puddles and pools after rain, particularly in summer as magpies love a good splash to clean the mites and ticks from their feathers – and they're very vulnerable when wet. You can often tell if a magpie has been using a puddle by checking for prints in the mud around the edge. Its track is distinctive, often marked by the trail of that long tail between its footprints.

*La Gazza Ladra*, Rossini's famous opera – which translates to 'the thieving magpie' – has given the bird a reputation as a thief of any trinket which sparkles or glitters. I've been watching, shooting and photographing magpies all of my life. In an age when such practice wasn't frowned upon (when I was between 10 and 13 years old), I raided many a magpie nest after their eggs, but I never found any evidence to support this. In these latter years, where I have sat for hours watching magpies build nests, rear young and raid nests… also nothing. In fact, the mere glint from my binocular or riflescope lens sends them away in a flash, rather than bring them in.

I've heard it said that the glint of a dead rabbit's eye is what attracts them down. All I can say is that it had better be very freshly shot, because that glint soon disappears once a rabbit has expired. Conversely, mirrors *do* attract magpies, and I've seen them attacking the side mirrors on parked tractors. Actually, it's only because they can see what they believe to be a rival magpie on their territory, rather than a the mirror's sparkle. This is the same principle as employed by the Larsen trap; an interloper (the live Judas bird inside the trap) will provoke this highly territorial bird to try to chase it away. I should point out, though, that the use of a mirror to deliberately attract birds down to shoot them is against British law.

The Wildlife & Countryside Act, 1981 states that it is illegal to use any form of artificial lighting, mirror or other dazzling device with which to hunt avian species (although there can be exceptions). Mind you, if you happen to be close to a tractor…

Throughout the breeding season, the magpie pair are dedicated to family and territory, rarely tolerating other magpie intruders. In winter, though, the families often merge and flocks of 10, 20 or 30 birds are common. We can assume that this is when the younger birds pair off and eventually set up their own territories. It's also these congregations that gave rise to old the children's rhyme 'one for sorrow, two for joy…'

## HUNTING METHODS

Stalking magpies is generally a frustrating and fruitless exercise. They can spot movement with uncanny ability. The only time I actively stalk them is when they're nest building and are preoccupied (and exhausted). The best way to hunt maggies, is to ambush them in familiar haunts, or to get them to come to you.

Magpie shooting around the farmyard is usually easy, laying up in the shadows and waiting for them to come in to plunder cattle fodder or grain. In the wood and field, it's more difficult and a good pop-up hide or nets are useful. Baiting-down is effective – a gutted rabbit or a couple of broken hens' eggs laid out in a makeshift nest are irrestible to these corvids.

While crows detest the tree-line and its hidden threats, magpies rely on the cover and security of it. Bait close to the trees, very close, and the chances are that you will actually take your bird from a bough overlooking your bait, rather than at the bait itself.

## TIPS AND TRICKS

Most people are familiar with the rattle or cackle of the excited magpie, but how many of us recognise the low, throaty chuckles and gurgles of a relaxed magpie browsing through a wood or hedgerow? I can't demonstrate these in a book, but you will learn them when hunting from a hide for any duration. The bird will move in stutters along a fairly regular highway. If you hear a sound, probably best described as like a contented baby gurgling in a cot, you have a magpie close by – and it's also relaxed and unalert. If you've laid bait, such as a gutted rabbit, and the bird spots it, you will know. That rattle will start. The bird will helter-skelter up a tree to get a better view, cackling and calling for assistance, for the magpie is a murderous, yet cowardly, opportunist. Be patient. Even if other magpies arrive, nothing will happen until they've made lots of noise then gone silent for some time.

It's a poker game – and if you move or make a sound, you've lost. Only when the bird is happy that there is no spoof, no threat, no man or fox or cat near, will it descend to feed. Then it will do so with a flourish, usually soaring straight to the bait. Always mark the 'trails' which they follow through the wood or along the hedgerow. Watch them approach and anticipate where they will perch next. Be ready with the rifle. Notice that as a magpie approaches the base of a tall tree, it will spiral up – a reverse helter-skelter, round the trunk, up through the boughs – and emerge at the top. Train your gun up there before it reaches the crown.

The magpie's memory can be its downfall, if you're cunning. Simply drop rabbit paunch or squirrel carcases in a regular spot and the birds will get used to the food source. They will add this cursory checkpoint to their daily patrol. One day, you'll be in cover waiting for them to call by…

The air rifle hunter should note that most nests have two holes – an entrance and an exit. An important point, as the birds will pause at an entrance, but flash out of an exit. Target them as they enter. If you really want to plague a pair at their nest, take along a little owl decoy. Wait until both birds are away from the nest and set it close to the nest tree. When they return they will go beserk if they spot it. They won't attack it. Instead, they'll dance around nearby, trying to drive it away – a good shooting opportunity. A flocked magpie decoy can be effective, too, for the same reason as the Larsen trap. The nesting pair will want chase off the intruder.

The parents' chaperoning trait is a good chance to shoot those older, more elusive birds. Their loyalty to the young is remarkable for a usually cowardly bird. The young are easily shot in the first couple of weeks out of the nest. They are green, curious and incautious. If you can down one or two, the parents will be frantic. They will harry-in close to their fallen young and show themselves in a way you would never see otherwise. I once fought a running battle with an old hen magpie for six years, and it was this method that finally brought her to book. The biggest haul I've had in a single session at a family was five – four young and an adult. The other adult saw sense and flushed the other two youngsters away to survive.

## BAITING MAGPIES

I mentioned about baiting magpies. If you need to target a bird, but haven't had a chance to shoot some bait, drive around the lanes and find a nice, mashed-up road-kill. If using your own shot rabbit or squirrel, slash the

*Staking out a magpie's nest in early spring*

*An effective magpie teaser!*

belly, from groin to ribcage, and pull out the intestines. Lay the animal out, white belly fur on show and the guts spread out, in a prominent position – a hummock or mound is good. If using hens' eggs, make sure you crack one open and leave the yolk on view. Make it easy and tempting for your quarry.

Retire into cover and wait; wait for however long it takes. Take your knitting with you, or a pack of playing cards to play solitaire because you could have a very long wait! Yet you can make it easier. Carry a Faulhaber rattle. If you hear magpies anywhere near, give it a shake or two. Not too much, just enough to draw in an inquisitive bird. Once you have a taker, just sit tight and quiet. If you can draw a bead on a bird overlooking your bait from the tree – it will be cackling like a fishwife – then do so. If you need it to land and feed, allow it to feed.

When a magpie first lands on the deck, it will do so right next to the bait – but it will be on high alert. Let it move in and take a peck or two. Once the bloodlust kicks in, its concentration will be on feast, not threat – so then shoot at your leisure. A magpie at eggs is more tricky. It may try to lift and steal the broken egg, so squeeze the trigger as soon as it has its bill on the shell. Alternatively, taunt the birds at the nest site with an owl decoy, which will craze them as they perceive the threat to their brood. ◯

# THE ROOK

## THE ROOK ROOST

I had lived in Norfolk for 13 years, but had never taken the time to visit the legendary Buckenham rook roost. I'd read articles about it on websites. So, on the last working day of the year for me (and an early escape from work), I called in on the way home. I was eager to see this spectacle (from a hunter's perspective).

I trundled the Jeep down the narrow lanes, praying that the threatened afternoon rain would hold off. I drove through to Beighton, swimming upstream against the empty sugar beet trucks returning from the Cantley sugar processing factory. I followed a sign to Buckenham, then finally hit the sign for the station. Station? Well, trains do apparently stop at the tiny platform now and again!

I donned my boots and wrapped well against the chill easterly wind cutting across the marshes. Buckenham Fen harbours an RSPB reserve, set in the levels surrounding the River Yare as it snakes its way from Norwich to Great Yarmouth and the sea. Even on this cold afternoon, the car park was busy; this was definitely twitcher country. In fact, I felt a little inferior without a spotting scope and tripod! Not part of that particular club, I grabbed my camera and headed over the railway crossing, toward the reserve. It was early yet, but I wanted to get my bearings.

The marshes are dotted with alder carrs – fens overgrown with trees – to right and left. In fact, there were already rooks coasting into the carrs, fussing and fretting. Some were landing to feed in the soft loamy soil of the water meadows. Standing close to the station, with an hour to go to sunset, I was a little confused. The birds were drifting in from all points of the compass. Where was the main roost? Was I in the right place?

I stopped a passing scope-wielder and asked him. He looked me up and down as if I was gone-out (the local expression for mad). "Rooks? They're everywhere!" he replied. Not very helpful – he'd obviously crossed 'rook' off his twitcher's-list years ago and wasn't prepared to revisit it. Then I watched a party of four serious birders approach. Dressed in green from top to toe, they were carrying so much spotting equipment and camera gear I wondered if Simon King was in their midst.

"Rooks?" That same daft look answered me. Then his colleague said: "Apparently there's a sizeable corvid roost here?"

"Yes!" I offered, excitedly. "Like twenty-thousand-plus birds!"

They sniggered to each other. "Sorry, we're not local." And off they marched. I figured they'd probably been watching humped-back cranes or ruffle-bottomed ducks, or some other exotic waterfowl.

"What's wrong with rooks?" I thought. These are the folk who spend so much time looking for the unusual that they fail to see the ordinary. The sort of people who say that magpies don't predate songbirds, more than likely.

I hijacked another dejected looking birder, heading back to his car. He'd obviously missed the baggy-arsed bittern. "Don't suppose you have a light, do you?" he asked, before answering the dreaded rook question. I drew out my Zippo lighter like Clint Eastwood on bandit duty and flipped open the lid. "Rooks?" I reminded him, withholding his salvation. "There's a sign in the car-park," he offered. A half-answer. I thought about closing the lid on the cigarette drawn expectantly between his lips, to snap it in half. He drew from the flame, exhaled in relief, then said: "They'll be in soon. Sometimes this wood, sometimes that one." He pointed east and west. Great!

I walked back to the car park to read the sign. Best viewing point was the car park or station platform. I was suspicious, checking for a pay and display sign. There wasn't one. It was still early, though more and more rooks were drifting into the carrs to the west. The light was dying, and there were fewer rooks than I had hoped for. I headed back to the station car park and took up a vigil from there.

More and more rooks floated in, dropping into nearby trees, on to telephone wires and landing in the winter barley crops. They came in twenties and thirties. Behind me, in the car park, I was conscious of more cars arriving. Perhaps a train was due? No – soon the car park filled with rook-spotters. Suddenly, I felt vindicated. I wasn't the only rook fan here!

The rooks now descended in their hundreds, but it was hardly spectacular. People shuffled around, looking disappointed. Out to the north, we could see throngs of rooks wheeling and descending, a mile away. A lady came up to me to ask if she was in the right place? I explained that I was a 'rookie' here, too.

The rooks gradually stopped calling and squabbling. The air went quiet. Everyone in the car park, bar me and one other old chap, got into their cars and drove off. It was anti-climactic. Like watching a firework display without a finale. I pulled my trainers from the Jeep and sat on a low fence, changing out of my boots. The old chap came and sat next to me. "First time?" he asked. "Yep, first time."

"Listen!" he almost commanded. I stopped lacing my trainers to listen. "I can't hear anything?" I said.

"Exactly!" he replied. "Just wait."

And then it happened. First in the distance, then all around me, I heard a rising crescendo of rook shout. A growing buzz, an electric chatter.

*Rooks thronging to an evening roost site*

*Like white noise. It rose in volume as the old chap pointed to the deep blue sky over the eastern carrs. The horizon above the wood filled with clouds of black whirling spectres, wheeling and circling and crying as they floated high, then descended into the trees. Thousand upon thousand upon thousand lifted from the fields around us and span in a vortex around the wood's stark canopy, each and every one sucked down into the roost, and oblivion. The noise was awesome, epic, captivating – like a thousand fireworks crackling and buzzing for at least 10 minutes. Ten-, maybe even twenty-thousand rooks.*

*Then, as suddenly as it had started, it was over. I was still sitting, jaws agape, when the old chap enquired with a smile: "Worth the wait?"*

*Driving home, I reflected on what I had just been privileged to witness, and have witnessed many times since then. Folk travel the world, thrill-seeking. Pyramids, Grand Canyons, swimming with dolphins, once-in-a-lifetime opportunities often artificially manufactured. Me? I had just seen many of Norfolk's rooks go to roost. It didn't cost me a penny, and I'll never forget that 'first time' as long as I live.*

*Now, with my gun on my lap, waiting for rabbits at sunset, when the rook throng heads over, I at least know where they're going…*

## A NATURAL HISTORY

Can there be a more quintessentially British bird than the rook (*Corvus frugilegus*)? Any rural scene is inevitably sprinkled and freckled with the black forms of this industrious crow going about its daily business. With the British population now estimated at around three million, that's probably not surprising.

Distinguishing rook from carrion crow is easy. Compared to the sombre, stout-beaked crow, the rook looks almost clownish. It has a long, sharp beak and – except in immature birds – a white face. Its appearance is one of having dipped that beak into a saucer of milk.

The crow has thin, bare legs, whereas the

rook has a pair of baggy trousers made of feather. The call is different, too. The crow 'caws' where the rook 'craas'. As explained in the chapter pertaining to the carrion crow, while crows are generally seen solitarily or in pairs, rooks will be numerous.

In spring and summer, these highly sociable birds gather in the colonies which we call rookeries. They are the rooks' township, their ghetto, their 'hood. Dozens of shabbily-built nests in a stand of high trees which they use for generations. There is a longstanding belief on many country estates that the abandonment of a rookery portends bad luck, even death, for the estate owners. As in any colony, there's constant conflict, jealousy, squabble and noise.

The rookery is an interesting place to watch, if only to understand the intelligence and opportunism of this bird. During nest reconstruction in February and March, you will see some steal twigs from a neighbour rather than venture out to find their own. You will witness 'proximity battles', when one nest is expanding too close to another. You will also see, however, how co-operative the rook can be. Once the three to six eggs are laid in March or April, each nest is sacrosanct; rooks don't steal eggs from a neighbour even though these corvids are, like any crow, partial to other birds' eggs. When the chicks have hatched, and feeding them is of prime importance, watch how organised the rookery becomes. There is a constant relay between the nearest food sources and the rookery. There is a contingent of guards to watch the young and protect the nests. Approach a rookery during this time, and the attention you get will make you will think you are in a Hitchcock film! The boys from the 'hood will rally together to try to drive off any intruder.

By early May, the fledglings will be stretching their wings on boughs alongside the nest, hence the young birds are commonly known as 'branchers' by the shooting fraternity. Rooks

*The rookery is a busy ghetto, bustling with both conflict and co-operation*

will stay in the rookery until late summer or autumn, then leave it to congregate in nearby roosts, where hundreds of rookeries will combine forces to face the winter.

Winter rook watching is fascinating, too. At dawn, when the congregations leave their roosts driven by the need to feed, they fill the sky with noise and the slow beat of wings. Similarly, as the sun sets, they labour back with equal clamour and (often) an amazing display of unity and common purpose. Many people won't have a clue where they came from at sunrise, nor where they're heading at dusk. Yet, find a winter rook roost and you will have found black gold. For there is no more spectacular show in natural Britain than the last few minutes before the rooks take to bed. Rooks are masterful in flight, especially when riding the thermals or fleeing an approaching storm.

There is a commonly-reported trait among rooks that they occasionally hold a parliament, wherein a large gathering of birds will congregate on the ground to judge and pass sentence on one or two individuals who have breached the rules of the rookery. I've never seen this, though I can understand how this could be misperceived. The gathering for roost as described above results in much squabbling and fighting for ground space.

Some of the myths surrounding rooks bear commentary. It's said that if they build the rookery nests high, it will be a fine summer, and vice-versa. I fail to see this, for the rookery is a fixed site and the rooks reoccupy old nests. The new generation will build wherever there is space, be it high or low. They say that if a rookery is abandoned on an estate, bad fortune will follow. This is perhaps partly true, but the events are the wrong way around. If an estate falls into disrepair and no arable farming prevails, it makes natural sense for the colony to move to a more abundant feeding ground. An old saying associating imminent bad weather with rooks flocking to roost early in the day is absolutely true, though – and one which I always heed when out hunting. When they flee the ploughland for the trees, it's time to wrap up well and plan your exit. It takes the threat of severe weather to stop rooks feeding.

## FOOD AND PREDATORS

Rooks are as omnivorous as all other crow species. Some of the birding fraternity will claim that the rook is the farmer's friend due to its penchant for soil-inhabiting grubs, like leatherjackets (cranefly larvae). There is some truth in this, but the reason the rook is on the General Licence is due to that gregarious nature. A rook horde descending on a newly-sown field is as persistent and destructive as a woodpigeon flock. It's the British locust, if you like. Rooks occasionally feed on carrion when pressed and I have had rooks come down to bait, though I've often thought they came down for the bluebottle flies, rather than the meat on offer. Many of us will have witnessed their antics and intuition around urban waste such as the leftovers at motorway service stations. Their ability to 'reason' is beyond doubt, as you watch them unwrap a discarded chip bag or unlatch a castaway burger carton.

Rooks love craneflies (Daddy longlegs) and in September will flock into meadows where these are hatching from beneath the grass. Again, a useful trait for the air rifle huntsman to know. Unfortunately, this iconic bird follows that other crow family tendency, too. It will take the eggs and chicks of ground-nesting birds when the chance arises, which puts it on the wanted list for the gamekeeper and pest controller.

The rook has few predators other than man. In some areas of Britain, however, the rook is a staple food for peregrine falcons and goshawks. I personally can't ever recall having found an adult rook killed by a sparrowhawk – which seems a little strange as the rook's breast meat used to be a staple human food

and therefore ought to appeal to a raptor. The children's old rhyme, *Sing a Song of Sixpence*, makes reference to the gentry's love of rook breasts baked in pastry, viz: four and twenty black birds baked in a pie. Not a delicacy that's ever taken my fancy, but some country cooks swear that it's worth trying.

## HABITAT AND HABIT

The deforestation of Britain has been credited as the reason for the rook's population increase over the past few centuries. The rook has thrived in areas of open agriculture and villages. The abundance of grubs and worms in tilled soil coupled with newly-sown seed mean that the rook and the tractor – a good name for a pub, that! – go side by side through the seasons. Rookeries will generally be found close to remote human habitation, probably not without good reason. Not only does the rook like the feeding opportunities we supply but, like the carrion crow, the rook likes a high watch-tower. Think about it – many churches, castles, stately homes and farms were built on high ground for exactly the same reason.

Habit is the same weakness in this black centurion's armour, as with all crows. It goes to the same fields repeatedly, in numbers, so it's easy to find rooks on the ground. It returns to the same nest or roost, depending on season. It follows the tractor. And the seed spreader. Such predictability make it vulnerable as it's a bird with a nature that's easy to second-guess. The rook has other habits, however, that protect it immensely. The rook flock always has a scouting contingent and a rear guard. They move like a military platoon. The scouts will advance and soar around a potential feeding area. They will shout 'safe' and drop to feed, or scream 'danger' and lead the platoon away. If safe and the flock lands, the rear guard will patrol the skies in shifts, taking turns to drop and feed. Its habit of nesting close to human habitation is protective, for unless it's the month of May, few landowners will allow you to target the birds at the nest or close to their own home.

Its other means of survival is the same as the crow. It rarely ventures close to the tree-line to feed. Except for one reason – the plough.

## HUNTING METHODS

I'd best cover the May method first, though I'm reluctant to call it 'hunting'. There is a tradition on many British estates to shoot the fledgling 'branchers' from their perch, before they learn to fly, on or around the twelfth of May each year – some airgunners even refer to it as their 'glorious twelfth'. Though not a practice I find particularly sporting – the branchers are too young, too vulnerable – it

does give the chance for young guns to learn how to shoot elevations. But nor would I want it stopped, for it is as traditional as the Boxing Day pheasant shoot, or as the Christmas fox hunt used to be. Removal of these traditions erodes the freedom of choice for the rural community and, therefore, the shooter. This particular method is simply not for me.

Baiting rooks can be random, unless with a shot rook from the same flock. Bring one down and the whole flock will mob around their dead comrade. They will sometimes come in to an egg bait, but only with extreme caution. Ambushing rooks from a hide is an option, but it still takes a lot of cunning to achieve this. Like all corvids, catching them in a sitty tree is one way of getting some in the bag.

*Rooks descending on freshly-sown seed can decimate a crop before it starts to grow*

## TIPS AND TRICKS

I mentioned earlier that rooks usually avoid the proximity of a tree-line. To ambush rooks, you need them within 30 or 40 metres of that line, depending on where you set your hide or cover. Several years ago, I sat in cover waiting for a pair of magpies to visit their nest. I was at the edge of a wood, behind an ivy-covered, fallen beech. In the field next to me, a tractor and plough was making the quarter-mile trawl up and down, followed by a throng of rooks. The birds, dozens of them, continually leap-frogged each other. Obviously to dive at the freshly exposed grubs and earthworms. As I waited for the absent magpies, the tractor's turns brought it ever closer to the wood – and the rooks came with it. Mentally I gauged that

each sweep of the plough threw over a strip of about eight yards or so. The margin was about 10 yards wide… so the final three sweeps of the plough would bring the rooks within 34, 26 and 18 yards as it came nearer to the tree-line.

As soon as the machine turned at my end of the wood for the 36-yard strip, I huddled down and readied the Weihrauch. I can remember thinking: a hundred birds and just 14 shots in the magazine! (I had another mag, fully laden, close by.) As the tractor pulled away from me, in they came. The rooks fussed and fought over the leatherjackets and worms, behind the noisy tractor. My silent shots were lost in the mayhem. First sweep – three birds down and not a complaint from the flock, who were still all squabbling behind the steel blades. Second sweep – the driver paused for a minute or two, looking at the dead birds in his last furrows. Behind him, I had just shot another four! On the final sweep, he stopped just 15 yards from my position and switched off the engine, lifting his cap and scratching his head in the cab. He'd seen the

*The sitty tree is often the place to target rooks – especially the 'scouting party'*

four corpses. Then the penny dropped and he scoured the tree-line. I waved my camo cap lightly and he saw me. He gave the thumbs-up and gunned up the noisy diesel engine again to move on. Behind him, the penny had dropped for the rooks, too. The clamour behind the plough was much more restrained – and I only shot one more bird after that.

But it's a ploy I've used several times since, and I have to say that the deep furrow of the potato plough is more productive than the lighter screws used for a crop like barley. (The deeper furrow throws up more grubs and worms, and thus attracts more birds.)

Shoot a scout and you're on to a winner. This is where baiting can be of benefit. Try to get one of the scouting party to land close by, usually in a sitty tree, and nail it. Others will be watching, so when one bird goes down, corvid mayhem will ensue. Not just the rooks, either. A murdered crow, of any species, draws a corvid CSI team. The Crime Scene Investigators. They mob, shout and complain. Some will make the same mistake as the deceased, landing on a bough to get a better look. That's your next chance, with rooks in particular. ◯

# THE JACKDAW

*The jackdaw often flies with the rook, but is a more adept aviator*

## A NATURAL HISTORY

Where the rook flies, the jackdaw accompanies it. While some would say they have a symbiotic relationship in that they complement and help each other, most would say that the 'jake' rides with the rook for far more selfish reasons. The jackdaw (*Corvus monedula*) is a bold and sassy crow. Bold enough and fast enough to steal in and take the food that its larger cousins covet. Its aerial acrobatics put the woodpigeon to shame, and the woody's are admirable. I can sit and watch the jinking and wheeling of the jake for hours when they're doing no harm.

Though gregarious like the rook, to the point where it may share the winter rook roost, the jackdaw doesn't nest with it. Jakes prefer a hole, a cleft in a tree or – often to its downfall – a chimney. It is that last tendency which generally gains the attention of the airgun shooter or pest controller. Jackdaws like their nest to be hidden, but accessible. To that end, a pair – if they're determined to nest there – will fill a chimney from the ground up until the platform is just a foot or so from the top. In reality, in this modern era, few people use a chimney, so they aren't causing a problem except to old houses relying on open-hearth fires. The nest is lined with a luxurious mixture of horse hair, wool and fur gleaned from the pastures nearby – and, often, comically plucked straight from the back of some hapless beast! Most of the nests I attend to are in hollow trees on game-rearing estates; they're hard to find unless you watch the birds for ages. They're always well concealed and always accessed or exited with stealth by the attendant parents. The jake can be a very vocal bird, a mimic and a social talker to its own kind – but never near the nest.

Jackdaws are only two-thirds the size of the carrion crow or rook. Brighter of eye and with an almost smokey grey mantle, they can easily be recognised on the bough or ground. Like most crows, they raise only one brood, which is usually of about four to six young.

## FOOD AND PREDATORS

This handsome small crow lives predominately on worms, caterpillars, slugs, berries and seeds. For most of the year, it's harmless – but when it has young of its own to feed, it can become a ruthless little predator. Its size and its inclination to explore holes and crevices make it an avian match for the weasel. I once watched a jackdaw methodically take five pink fledglings from a greater spotted woodpecker's nest. On its first exit, I was confused, thinking the woodpecker was moving its chicks for some reason. The dark bird had flashed quickly from the hole and I hadn't figured it was a jake. I had the sun in my eyes and was watching the whole scene in silhouette. By the time the third chick was removed, I'd moved position and still hadn't figured out that this was theft… until I saw and heard the distressed parents flashing around nearby trees. As it plundered the fourth, I noticed that the jackdaw paused momentarily, with its head out of the hole, before flashing away. Five minutes later, it was back for the fifth… and my scope was trained on the hole. As the jake's head appeared, I shot and its momentum reeled the raider out of the hole to plummet to the ground, the chick still in its beak. The woodpeckers were going mad. I moved in removed the jackdaw and the chick, which was already dead, crushed by that firm beak. Leaving quickly, I hoped that there were one or two more fledglings left for the parents to raise. Alas, when I returned to the hole a couple of weeks later, there was no sign of activity; the nest was abandoned.

Jackdaws have few natural predators. They are usually too fast and too agile in the air for the sparrowhawk. Grey squirrels will often attempt a raid on their eggs, but usually fail. Like rooks, jackdaws organise well around the nursery trees. Some will guard, while some fetch food.

## HABITAT AND HABIT

Despite its tendency to socialise with rooks, the jackdaw is a mainly a woodland, quarry or clifftop bird. It differs from the magpie and jay in its preference for the high boughs and canopy. You will more often hear jakes than see them when in the wood. As they are noisy birds, the 'jackery' – forgive me for making up such a word to describe a jackdaw rookery, the clump of trees where they nest – is easy to find. It's the nests themselves that are the challenge. You can walk around the trunks, staring up and failing to spot any sign, unless you are lucky enough to spot some nesting material. They don't clean the nest, and never defecate at the hole or cleft. They are masters at disguising the presence of a brood. When the chicks hatch, though, you'll often hear their pleading from deep within a bole – a harsh, plaintive chorus from within a seemingly talking tree!

Jackdaws are rarely still. Even among a large flock of feeding rooks, you'll soon spot the jakes by their smaller profile and their tendency to rocket away in small parties, then wheel about and return.

## HUNTING METHODS

That last-stated jackdaw trait – restlessness – makes it a difficult bird to hunt, should you need to. Having said that, if you get a 'chimney clearance' mission, you'll find that the birds, like feral pigeons, are very tolerant of approaching humans where thay have been nesting among them. Like feral pigeon control, it's not really sporting, but it is necessary. The birds can be sitting ducks. Out in their natural environment, though, your best chance is ambushing from cover or a hide.

Baiting brings random results. They are canny birds and will dart in with a flourish

*A jackdaw's nest, deep within the cleft of a tree*

to steal a morsel from a crow. They will rarely venture in before the larger bird has started feeding. I'm not sure about you, but when I have a jackdaw and a carrion crow in my scope, it will always be the latter that takes the pellet. Roost shooting jakes from beneath the 'jackery', hiding under ivy cover, is more difficult than with woodpigeons, but I've shot more jackdaws using this method than any other. I've also shot jackdaws at water feeders and puddles in summer. They love to bathe, probably to remove ticks and fleas.

## TIPS AND TRICKS

Jackdaws mount a high watch over their nest trees and travel over the top of the canopy. A careful stalker can get underneath these trees if there is adequate cover. Find a clear path, through the greenery, up toward the birds and, if you have mastered the 90-degree elevated shot, you will cull jackdaws. Practise these shots on pine cones or conkers whenever you get a chance. Unless you know your gun and your scope intimately, this is the second most difficult shot you'll ever execute (the first being the five-yard blur-in-your-scope shot). You're into Isaac Newton territory here. Gravity versus trajectory. I get such different results with different guns that I'm not going to offer any advice other than to practise, practise, practise – and with just the one rifle!

Another tip I'm going to give you is when looking for jackdaw nest trees, keep your nostrils open. The nests give off a very fox-like musky scent. On heavy, dull days with little breeze, this odour, though subtle, will be hanging in the air. My theory on this is that it's because jakes nest for generations in the same holes. I've already said that they never defecate immediately outside the nest – but they do within it. The odour is not unlike that of a seabird colony, for the same reason: guano. ○

## A NATURAL HISTORY

A shooting newcomer could be forgiven for thinking that the jay bears no relation to the crow family. Until they study it for a few years. The anatomy, the beak, the claws – most importantly its often hugely-understated predatory nature. Some ornithological reference books will argue that the jay is 'vegetarian'. I'm very sorry, but my experience tells me that the jay is as omnivorous as the magpie. I will concede that it is less prone to feasting on carrion (yet it does, when pressed), but show an egg to a jay… and then tell me it's vegetarian!

Having said that, the Eurasian jay (*Garrulus glandarius*) is famous for its association with oak trees. Specifically the acorn, the tree's seed. It loves acorns as a food source. It buries them prior to winter's hardships, much like the squirrel. The jay, though, seems to have an inferior memory compared to the squirrel and hence has been long credited as an 'oak planter' – the forester's friend.

I wouldn't argue that at all, but I would pose a simple question to conservation groups. Why can't they accept that the beak that cracks an acorn can crack an eggshell or break the tiny bones of a songbird chick? They do, for I've seen it. The jay hasn't been pursued by gamekeepers for 200 years without justification or, for that matter, added to the General Licences without reason.

The jay's fame and name has contributed to its reputation in popular social history. It's azure wing feathers were much sought by milliners in a less eco-sensitive age. They were also prized then – and still are now – by the fly-fishing fraternity. The name 'jay' was also applied to dressy women and ladies of ill repute in times past, which I consider a bit unfair. When did ladies of ill repute ever steal songbirds' chicks?

Jays tend to nest much lower than other crow cousins, building a scruffy, leaf-lined cup of twigs in the fork of a tree or bush. They raise just one brood from a clutch of four to seven eggs, breeding between April and June. They are protective, territorial birds and mate for life.

I once reported a very strange experience with a jay, having shot its mate a week earlier. I had been targeting the pair at their nest, tucked deep into a low elder tree covered in ivy. The pair, on a game estate, had evaded me for nigh-on three years and had an annoying habit of screaming my presence to every other

creature. Having spotted them nest-building, I set a pop-up hide along the fence-line and left it for a few days. The ploy paid off, and just a couple of hours' wait gave the opportunity to cull one of the pair. The other fled. I removed the hide.

A week later, walking the same hedgerow, the shriek of a jay revealed the surviving bird sitting on a prominent bough of the nest tree. I walked up to within 25 paces and the bird just sat watching me. If that wasn't confusing enough, the bird gave a low croak and turned on the bough to present its breast. I raised the rifle, expecting it to fly off. It didn't. It croaked again and tucked its head down. I lowered the muzzle – it just wasn't a sporting shot – and made to walk past. The jay immediately scolded me, opened its wings to present its breast and settled again on the branch facing me. Now, call me soft, but I could only deduce that the bird was begging for an end to the misery of losing its mate. So, with a heavy

*The jay hasn't been pursued by gamekeepers for 200 years without justification*

heart, I obliged.

I couldn't face shooting another jay for several months after the incident.

## FOOD AND PREDATORS

As mentioned earlier, the jay's dominant food source is the acorn. Like the woodpigeon, it has a crop on its neck in which it gathers food. It will glean young, succulent acorns from the oak trees and bury them in shallow caches on the woodland floor or in surrounding meadows.

Acorns, however, are seasonal. Once the caches have been depleted during winter, the jay turns its attention to springs offerings – which include songbird or gamebird eggs and chicks. It will also supplement its diet with other nuts, grubs, insects and flies.

The jay's predators include sparrowhawks, but as a fast, furtive bird, few other species – man included – can get near it. The almost psychopathic hatred between the jay and the grey squirrel is vested in three, obvious reasons. They compete for the same territory; the same food sources (acorns and nuts); and the grey squirrel will readily steal the jay's eggs from its open nest. I regularly hear the treetop Mexican stand-offs between squirrel and jay – one screaming, the other hissing and spitting!

## HABITAT AND HABIT

If you have oak trees on your permission, you're bound to have jays, for the acorn is a staple in their diet. The footprint is similar to the magpie, but smaller – yet I challenge you to find one! The jay spends the least time on the floor of all the corvid family, except when recovering cached acorns, though it can be baited-down to eggs.

The shooting of jays is a subject of much debate. Is it friend or foe? That, I suspect, depends on whether you are a forester or a gamekeeper. Buried acorns in the forest floor are often neglected and develop into the next generation of oak plantation. Yet the jay, the most striking bird in the family *corvidae*, can't resist a pheasant, partridge or pigeon egg. Often, this is the only evidence you will find. Shooting jays will largely be dictated by the habitat on which you shoot and the desire of your landowner. Its raucous scream, conveying caution to every living creature within half a mile, is the jay's most infuriating trait. If it spots you stalking rabbits and does this, I'll guarantee you'll want to shoot it if you get the chance! Watch a rabbit warren and watch their reaction to the sound of a shouting jay. Wild creatures know the signs of distress that surround them. The hunter needs to learn these, too.

The jay's flight is very distinctive – a horizontal, but bobbing flightpath. But beware! One other bird, of a comparable size, has a similar flight – the green woodpecker. In silhouette, they look similar while flying, unless you can note the woodpecker's longer beak. It's the landing that is generally different. The jay will alight on a branch still horizontal, head down, tail back. The woodpecker will land vertical, head up, tail down. For Lord's sake, don't take a shot unless you are absolutely sure, though. The green woodpecker is protected under law, even though it (and its greater spotted cousin) take as many songbird chicks as jays, such is the curiosity we call 'law'.

## HUNTING METHODS

Some of my methods have been hinted at already. To be honest, I'm very selective when it comes to hunting jays. On some land, I'm content to let them pass unharmed. Where they are disturbing my other hunting activity due to their warning calls – particularly rabbit warrens, where stealth is essential – I will try to remove them. In songbird copses, they are definitely fair game due to their predatory habits. In game coverts, they are shoot-on-sight quarry. Actually, they are more than that.

*A jay's flight flaps, then soars*

They are a quarry to be ambushed, stalked, baited and removed. Pheasant and partridge eggs on the ground are highly vulnerable to jays.

## TIPS AND TRICKS

Baiting jays with eggs, I've already mentioned. My set of rubber imitation hens' eggs – one carved and painted to look like a broken egg with yolk – have accounted for dozens of jays over the past five years, confirming the jay's fondness for going to work on a egg.

Placing the pretend clutch on a fencepost in full view can often prove irrestistable to jays. Like the magpie, the jay doesn't take the cautious approach of the crow. It's too impatient; it just flashes straight in silently, a kaleidoscope of blue, white and brown. Be ready for a quick acquisition in the scope and a quick shot. Miss at your peril, though – because you won't fool the same bird twice.

Oak ambushing is productive so long as you've been watching the trees in autumn.

After a good squall, when mature acorns have been shaken to the ground, you can often see jays gathering the windfall to bury it. Use the opportunity. Jays are very vulnerable when it comes to caching (burying) acorns, too. For a creature with just a beak as a tool, this is arduous activity. Their concentration is so focused on the task, it gives the shooter a distinct advantage. Some would say this is unsporting, but the hunter needs to reflect that for 90 per cent of the time, it's their quarry that holds the advantage. Hunting is all about recognising the weak spots and opportunities to achieve the despatch. If you cannot exploit these, you will never succeed as a hunter. If you respect these – as in my suicidal jay story earlier – you become an even better hunter.

## PLAYING THE BLUES

I set off on a reluctant mission one particular weekend, and I was in little mood for the challenge. Only because I was under the weather. The man-flu that had laid me low for a week was no excuse to refuse a request to reduce the inordinate number of jays in some of the coverts. I could take some relief in the fact that least my choking cough had receded, beaten into surrender by my regular medicines (cigar smoke and more than a spoonful of whiskey). In an effort to stem the flow from my nose, my good wife prescribed a splash of Olbas oil on a hankie, which I refused, point blank – it was an aroma acrid enough to empty a wood of all wildlife within minutes! No, I'd just have to sniffle my way through the weekend's work...

I dubbed it a 'reluctant mission' because I'm usually tolerant of jays unless they are disturbing a hunt. Their rise in numbers over recent years has been noticeable, though. For the same reason as the increase in the magpie population – far too much sanctuary in public parks and urban gardens. Even on shooting estates, the perceived political incorrectness of the gamekeeper's gibbet has encouraged the jay's rise in numbers. Just 20 or 30 years back, the gamekeeper would have been rewarded for the number of vermin displayed on his gibbet, and the jay would have been much prized. Every shooting man knows how difficult it is to get close to a jay and most are shot 'off-hand', purely by chance. There are a few ways to target jays, but they take cunning, patience and a clear brain. I was in short supply of the latter two on this weekend.

Two hours' observation in the coverts, mainly spent wiping snot from my upper lip, determined my tactics. There were at least four distinct jay territories, with pairs patrolling each. One pair had a family of fledglings in tow, which were following the parents everywhere. The pheasant fledglings weren't under threat as they were too big for a jay to wrestle, but next year's egg clutches would be if the young jays were allowed to pair off and breed nearby. Other bird species were still at risk, though. A damaged, empty moorhen egg close to the nest site showed all the signs of corvid predation. The other adults were raucously harassing grey squirrels in the crowns of nearby oak trees and that observation decided my tactic – an old ruse, often used with success.

There is a fierce rivalry between the jay and the squirrel. They both compete for the acorn crop and both store it for winter feeding. The jay is threatened by the grey squirrel's inclination toward egg predation – not just the raiding of songbird nests sought by the jay, but also the jay's own eggs. The blue crow's pathological hatred of the squirrel can often be employed to good effect. So first of all, I hunted down a grey squirrel and shot it. That was the easy part over!

I always carry a clutch of rubber hens' eggs in my gamebag. One is doctored to look as though the shell is broken and showing its false golden yolk. I ripped up handfuls of ryegrass and paced out into the meadow, about 30 paces from the tree-line at the edge of the covert, close to where I'd seen the family group. Weaving the grass into a rough garland, I set it around the rubber eggs to like a ground nest. Then I positioned the dead squirrel to look as though it was raiding the nest. Next, I trekked back to my Jeep and returned with a shooting blind, which I set up in deep cover at the wood's edge. The blind itself faced back into the wood, while an elder bush gave me the cover to look out into the field. There was very good reason for this. With the squirrel looking as though it was in the act of thieving, I doubted that the jay family would actually attempt to raid the fake nest until it had left – and I was right. Jays and squirrels are like rival football fans. There is always lots of 'come and 'ave a go if you think yer 'ard enough' banter, but rarely any real physical conflict.

The blue clan hadn't yet noticed my lure, though they had been screaming from cover, watching my strange antics. The disturbance caused by setting up the blind had chased them further into cover, so now I needed to draw them back. Around my neck, on a lanyard, I had one of the most effective predator calls I've ever owned. It's called a Foxcaller, the brand name. Picked up at a gamefair for under a tenner, I have used this to not only call in foxes to photograph them (you don't shoot foxes with airguns), but also to squeak in owls and corvids. A quick blow through this device will stop a squirrel dead in its tracks, or draw a rabbit to its haunches above long grass. With a bit of ingenuity and practise, you can imitate a jay call, too. You just need to ease off the plastic screws at either end to loosen the metal reed within. That's exactly what I did – just a couple of harsh rasps – and I sat and waited. No reaction. I gave a couple more bursts, then heard reply from within the wood. Another jay joined in the chorus, closer to me. That was enough to start the whole family off. One more quick rasp from me – to bring them to the tree-line – and I was in business. Game on...

If you want to shoot jays, you need to be able to identify their flight and their profile quickly. The flight bit is easy – short, sharp wingbeats and a bobbing flightline. Often, in profile, the raised crest on the jay's head will define it in silhouette. I had jays alright, but they were still too distant. When they noticed the squirrel at the fake nest, all hell broke loose. There were raucous screams as the birds flew up and down just inside the wood, scolding the (dead) squirrel. I watched quietly from behind the blind, trying desperately to stifle my sniffing and resisting the urge to sneeze. I knew the birds wouldn't attack the squirrel, so it was branch shooting that I was planning.

The first chance soon came, when one of the younger jays ventured too close to my hide and paid the penalty. If this had been one of the adults, the normal circumstance with jays, then the action would have been over. The bond between adults and offspring is particularly strong in the family

*corvidae*, and so the parent birds went wild. They flapped around their fallen youngster anxiously, screaming blue murder – but all they succeeded in doing was drawing the other siblings into sight with them. I had a clear tactic now: shoot the young and the adults will stay near. I took down two more of the fledglings before the parents realised the danger and beat a retreat, the rest of the brood following them.

I knew they wouldn't be back again, so I collected the dead birds and snipped off the indigo primary wing feathers for my angling friends to recycle. These are much prized by fly-fishermen. I took the corpses (including the squirrel) away from the area and left them in a ditch near a badger sett, where they could be hoovered up by the cubs overnight.

Despite this success, I had unfinished business. Next morning, I returned to the

*The jay's primary wing feathers are prized by fly-fishermen*

same spot, setting the shooting blind under a different tree. Instead of three eggs, I baited out with two, set in the open without the dead squirrel in attendance. Again, with a false nest woven around them. This time, though, I had a long wait. A few passing rooks scouts wheeled in to study the eggs, but moved on quickly, immediately suspicious. A lone magpie announced its curiosity from deep within a nearby blackthorn bush, but also declined the free feast. Its call, though, was most beneficial. Corvids draw corvids.

Soon the jays homed in on the maggie's chattering, shrieking as they came. I sat ready with the air rifle barrel poked between some hazel rods. After what seemed like an eternity, that bobbing flight down towards my dummy eggs had me easing off the safety catch. An adult jay flashed to the ground, about 10 metres away from the prize. It looked about warily and hopped in, a few steps at a time, pausing to look around for threat. I waited until it was just 30cm from the eggs, until it looked focused, then released the pellet to hit at the tuck of the wing. Whether it was because they'd heard the quiet discharge of the air rifle, or simply the witnessing of the adult's assassination, I'll never know – but the remaining few jays departed in a clamour.

Four jays in two days was sufficient for me. I can go six months between shooting these small, gaudy crows, whose ugly call contradicts their handsome appearance. Yet in nature, that's often a trend. The green woodpecker, the magpie and the goldfinch are perfect examples. Nice suit, shame about the song. The jay is just the same: lovely looking bird – shame about its habits! ◯

# THE MINK

## THE BLACK ASSASSIN

*As dark as night, as elusive as a Jinn, she slunk from her den, delved beneath the tangle of roots of an ancient willow. A tree which, when it first sent its tentative tendrils through the earth to claim its place on the riverbank, did so in a time when she and her kind were never a feature of the British wetlands. At the exit, her whiskers bristled and her nose scented the cool evening breeze. Her face revealed a devil's white-fanged grin as she sensed the sweet aroma of feather, fur and fin. She slipped into the cold chalk-stream, paddling with her head above the water. The glint of silver scales caught her eye and she slipped below the surface, her ripple unseen. She stroked low, her purpose and senses keen.*

*Above, near the surface, she saw her prey. The mouth that seized the rainbow trout showed no grace. The tussle amid the reeds; the flick and the splash; the haul to the bank; the fish thrashing until she sank her teeth into it. The evisceration uncompromising – then the moonlight feast...*

*Yet still she wasn't sated. Her blood lust roused, she went on, to the hen-house. Up inside the hutch, the panic of the birds sent her into a frenzy. She slashed and lashed and spat and slaughtered. The flood of light which signified her departure left her unable to drag a single bird out with her. It didn't matter; they were surplus to requirement anyway.*

*The chicken farmer stood scratching his head, his bantams murdered, many decapitated. No sign of fox incursion. No breach in the fencing. Nothing. The work of the devil?*

*The devil slid back along the riverbank, back to her den beneath the crack-willow, her white grin glittering in the moonlight. White teeth, stained with the crimson of blood-letting.... and a soul as black as sin.*

*The mink resembles a dark brown ferret*

## A NATURAL HISTORY

The mink (*Mustela vison*), a mustelid resident in Britain, is not a natural European species. Since its escape (or deliberate release) from fur farms in the 1950s, it has gained a foothold in the UK's countryside and can probably never be totally eradicated as that other escapee, the coypu, eventually was. The mink is far too elusive.

Significantly larger than our native mustelid, the stoat, the mink resembles a dark brown ferret and, when wet, can look jet-black. Mink breed in late winter and produce a litter of up to seven, two months later in April or May. Young mink leave the mother by late summer and can venture up to 30 miles to define new territory of their own, which explains their rapid spread. Mink are rarely seen, but the results of their hunting, their droppings and their tracks, often are. Although fair game for the air rifle hunter, most would go a lifetime – like me – without ever having the chance to shoot at a mink. I live and hunt close to the Norfolk Broads, where mink are numerous. I can count on one hand the number of times I've glimpsed mink about their mischief. At no time did I have a rifle in my hand and, to be honest, if I had, I'd have never acquired the target fast enough to despatch one.

## FOOD AND PREDATORS

If the stoat is a voracious predator, it pales into insignificance alonside the American mink. Its reputation for wanton slaughter is what first attached it to the General Licences. It will take fish of its own size, amphibians, ground-nesting birds, small mammals, rabbits, gamebirds and poultry. Like the stoat and the fox, it will slaughter for fun, not need. Stories abound of single mink massacring nearly 200 pheasant poults in a pen and cleaning out trout hatcheries in a night.

They have no known natural predators.

The only dead ones I've found have been roadkills; their biggest natural predator (by far) is man – and for good reason.

## HABITAT AND HABIT

Mink thrive around around streams, rivers, ponds, lakes and fisheries as they are superb swimmers. Mainly nocturnal, they do sometimes hunt by day and are confident climbers. They generally nest in rabbit burrows, gaps in walls and low holes in trees.

Although solitary animals, they have one trait which the trappers here on the Broads tell me is their downfall. They follow each other's trails, either to mate or to defend territories.

## HUNTING METHODS

By far and away, trapping is the most effective way to deal with mink. Broadland trappers use floating rafts (mink rafts) with baited cage traps to good effect. Having caught one, because of that 'following' trait mentioned above, they invariably catch more

*The high-percentage solution to mink on the Broads – the raft trap*

*I often find signs of mink, but have never seen one with my feet on dry land*

soon after. The good news is that it's illegal to release a trapped mink back into the wild – they have to be humanely culled, which means shot.

Although I've seen fleeting glimpses of mink from a canoe on the river, I've never chanced on one on dry land. If you know a trapper, you can get to shoot a mink, but it won't be hunting. I have turned down this opportunity myself; the call came when I'd enquired about a chance to hunt mink and a conservation officer with a full trap and a conscience asked if I would help. I was 40 miles away at the time, so couldn't help him. For me, though, the challenge is to shoot one in the wild – and I've a sneaky feeling I may never get to do that in my hunting lifetime.

## TIPS AND TRICKS

I'm going to have to pass on this one! But I promise that when – or if – I finally get to shoot a wild mink, I'll put into print how I did it… ○

# THE STOAT
# AND WEASEL

*A mooching stoat – too fast even for my camera to shoot it*

## A NATURAL HISTORY

There is absolutely no doubt in my mind that the most efficient and exemplary indigenous hunters in the UK are the stoat and the weasel. Both are nimble and lithe, often first noticed standing on their haunches sniffing the air like a meerkat, yet they are rarely watched for long.

The stoat (*Mustela erminea*) is the larger and more curious of the two. It is a dreadnought hunter and will tackle prey many times its own size. For this reason, particularly as it can clear the poults from a pheasant or partridge nest in minutes, with the same sort of wanton slaughter as a fox, it is firmly on the control list of shooting estates. It breeds just once a year, mating in early summer, and the female doesn't produce young until the following spring – though the brood will be large, up to 13 kits.

The weasel (*Mustela nivalis*) is also on the control list for similar reasons. Once you've seen just one of each species, you'll know how to distinguish them; the stoat is twice the size of a weasel and has a discernible black tip to its tail. The diminutive weasel is Britain's smallest carnivore and is just as concentrated on its hunting as its larger cousin. Its head is the largest part of its body, but designed for stalking into the tiniest of holes. Indeed, rumour has it that the weasel can slip through a wedding ring! Weasels breed twice a year, giving birth (usually during March and June) to around six kits.

## FOOD AND PREDATORS

One of the stoat's primary food sources is the rabbit. Like a miniature heat-seeking missile, once it sets its sights on a coney, the beast is invariably doomed. The stoat will track it to its death. Often, that will be a chase below ground, ferreted into a stop, then slaughtered. Above ground, the stoat will launch itself at the rabbit's neck and pin it. I have only witnessed this once in my life and I swear the rabbit froze solid as the stoat sunk its teeth into the back of the coney's neck. Within a minute it was dead – and I'm certain it died of sheer fright. On another occasion, I missed the kill but watched a stoat rolling a rabbit at least six times its own size into the mouth of a rabbit hole, and then drag it below ground.

Stoat family outings are a delight to watch and I've seen these several times. The mother leading a clutch of sinewy youngsters out to romp and mock-hunt. They wrestle and squirm, like a ball of snakes – it's no wonder that myth and legend has them down as pack-hunters and baby killers. Nonsense, of course. As mentioned, it's a pest when it takes up residence near poultry or game, where it will indiscriminately take eggs, chicks or adults. But the stoat isn't all bad. Another of its staples is the brown rat, which it also pursues relentlessly amongst its own nests and tunnels. Any creature that will tackle a full grown rat, itself a fearsome fighter, is one to be reckoned with.

The weasel, due to its size, sets its sights somewhat lower and feeds mainly on mice, voles and young rabbits. It is, though, a notorious thief of ground-nesting birds' eggs, and so attracts the same attention to control its numbers.

Both stoats and weasels are occasionally predated by foxes, owls, raptors and cats. Their biggest killer, though, is man – either intentionally with tunnel traps, or accidentally with the car.

## HABITAT AND HABIT

Stoats and weasels can be seen exploring holes or tunnels and slipping along the the top of low walls. They can be glimpsed snaking along the edge of rabbit warrens or among the cover crops where game birds are nesting. Habitat is varied, and they can be found almost anywhere that prey is sufficient. It is their proclivity for nosing in and out of tunnels that makes their control by gamekeepers most effective using tunnel traps.

Stoats are magnificent climbers – a fact overlooked and unknown to many. I have found stoat-killed squirrel kits below the drey with those trademark punctures in the back of the neck. Only recently, I tracked the back-lit silhouette of what I thought was a young squirrel scratching slowly, head-first, down a conifer trunk. As it hit the base of the tree I raised the scope to shoot, only to see a stoat, standing on its back legs glaring back at me. My shock and the stoat's quick sideway jink meant it survived: I missed by millimetres.

## HUNTING METHODS

Any creature that puts the brown rat high on its diet is okay by me, so I am very selective about shooting stoats and confess to having shot very few over the years. In my first book, *The Airgun Hunter's Year*, I related how I baited and shot a particularly troublesome stoat on a pheasant shoot, using decoy eggs. If there are poultry or game around, I feel it

*The stoat's food source includes the rabbit*

*A pair of weasels chasing in play. (Far too quick for the airgun shooter)*

my duty to cull them. If they are just sharing a warren or rat-run with me, I prefer their company and entertainment. I have never shot a weasel (other than with a camera, and only then poorly) as they are simply too fast for even the most adept airgunner.

## TIPS AND TRICKS

Both stoats and weasels can be squeaked into view when you've seen them darting around a hedgerow or warren. Like the fox, they just can't resist the sound of a rabbit in distress and curiosity will get the better of them. That's the easy bit! Where they will appear from is always a lottery, and shooting them when they appear is a Herculean task for the air rifle huntsman. They jink and fidget, skip and squirm – which is why baiting them with a hen's egg can be useful. They then have to stop to try to either feast on it, or roll it. Unlike a round pheasant egg, rolling an oval-shaped hen's egg is difficult for such a small animal.

*The weasel is simply too fast for the airgunner!*

## WEASEL CORNER

Though we shooters often crave thousands of acres of permission, what we actually find is that on most of it, all the action happens in a very small area. It's what's often referred to as the Pareto Principle – the 80:20 rule. In vermin control terms, this means that 80 per cent of your success comes from 20 per cent of the territory. Little more than a year back, I was lucky to secure a 300-acre permission on farmland where there are also gamebirds laid down for seasonal shooting. Tucked away at the end of a game covert, sandwiched between a crop field and a cattle pasture, I found an ivy strangled corner from which I have enjoyed hours and hours of productive pest control. It is one of those natural geographic points where all manner of wildlife converge.

I saw her long before she saw me. I was tucked under an ivy break on a bank looking along the rain-filled dyke. The woodies would be in soon for their late morning break, crops full of plundered peas. The rifle was lying leisurely across my lap, armed but with the safety engaged. Next to me lay my gunbag and poised on top was a DSLR camera 'just in case'. Atuned for any unusual movement, my hunting eyes first noticed her when she hopped up on top of a mossy fallen branch, her rufus back and snow white front in total contrast to the emerald moss. She was 40 metres away, slipping and snaking under twigs and over bough-fall, coming ever nearer. She paused, 30 paces away, between the netting of the empty poult pen and the embankment. Her whiskers twitched frantically, and her black little beads of eyes scoured hither and thither. My mind dithered between rifle and camera. As she slipped under a rotting branch, I laid the gun aside and went gently for the camera. Too late – for in that wink of an eye, she'd emerged on a stump just 10 metres away and saw my fingers wrap around the camera. Her tawny form slithered out of sight in a flash. I drew my Foxcaller from my pocket and tried to tempt her back with a few distressed rabbit calls – but she was gone.

It wasn't the first time we'd met, my little weasel and I. I've watched her several times since I found this small vermin crossroad at the edge of the coverts. That's why I've named it Weasel Corner. In her honour. How do I know the weasel's sex? In truth, I don't, but she is so camera shy that I have likened her to a svelt, little supermodel avoiding the paparazzi (me)!

I went back to my vigil. The pigeon were proving elusive, too.

I poured a coffee from my flask and listened to the birdsong. Suddenly, the song turned to panic. The angry chit of the wren, the tick of the robin and the pip of the blackbird. I supped at the coffee, amused that a single little weasel could cause such a commotion. Then, as I stared at the scolding robin, a grey stone plummeted from the ivy above and swept him from his perch, carrying him fluttering through the shrubbery and out of sight. The blackbird reacted first, sweeping from the bushes and almost hitting my face as it flashed out into the meadow beyond, screaming blue murder as it passed. Somewhere in the cover beyond, I could hear the sparrowhawk plucking out its kill. The ripping and tearing didn't take long, for a robin is a meagre morsel…

Somewhere near, I heard the weasel scolding again. She had probably smelt my coffee and took deference to it. From the corner of my eye, I noted the flick of a bottle brush tail. I laid down the plastic coffee cup and it tipped over, the last of my rich brew spilling across the floor. I raised the rifle to my shoulder and trained the scope in the direction of the tail. It was flickering angrily, the squirrel hissing, yet its body unseen. I took my eye from the scope to look below the branch where it sat. There on the leaf mulch was the weasel, with a vole in its jaws. It skipped forward and the squirrel followed, above, but now in full view. The pellet that toppled the squirrel chased off

*Stoats can be squeaked into view*

the weasel once again.

Overhead, a clatter and crash signified 'incoming'. I pulled up my snood, covering my chin and nose. Another came in. Then another. One woodpigeon landed with its back to me and just 20 paces off on a low bough. The pellet struck true, between the shoulder blades, and the others swept away as the bird hit the ground.

The sudden deep trundling of a diesel engine bumbled down the edge of the covert. I peered through the ivy to see a large cherry-picker appear, making the ground vibrate. I caught a flash of white scut as a rabbit I hadn't even noticed disappeared below ground nearby. I stayed in cover to watch what was happening. It soon became obvious. The trees were encroaching on the power lines nearby and the team started up their chain-saws. I packed up and slid away toward the Jeep, unseen, as the racket started. Was that a flash of rufus fur I saw again as I passed the pens? I started to wonder who was following who…

But she should be safe from my gun – forever. For what would Weasel Corner be… without a weasel? ○

Chapter

15

# WEATHER CRAFT

## FORECASTING QUARRY BEHAVIOUR

Climate changes and weather fronts obviously affect the behaviour of quarry. The beauty of airgun hunting is that it has no 'season' – so if you learn how to anticipate, and how to adapt to, different weather conditions, there will be few days (if any) where you cannot get in some shooting. I tend to watch internet weather forecasts closely and plan for days ahead, including contingency plans. I also use a digital weather station at home, which is far more reliable for local trends than the general internet sites. It gives a fairly accurate trend forecast for the day ahead, allowing me to prepare what clothing and kit I need to take hunting with me.

## COLD WEATHER

In extreme cold, rabbits hold down in their buries and squirrels change their feeding patterns to adapt to the chill. Woodpigeons will be more particular about their choice of roost and choose deep cover to avoid the bitter winter winds. Corvids hold to form, but they flock more tightly as the weather hardens. It's not unusual to see magpies or crows gather in groups of up to 30 birds, not both species together, but flocks of the same species. Rooks? Well, probably the most resilient of all British vermin species, they carry on about their feeding in large flocks. Higher predators will be very active, culling the weak and vulnerable. You will see many fox, weasel and stoat prints in the snow around your land as they harry the hard-pressed ground mammals, like rabbit, vole and mouse.

This is the attitude the hunter needs to adopt. There would be some who would advocate relaxing attention to vermin control in such harsh conditions – but I don't hold with that opinion. Vermin is vermin, in sunshine or snow. Just think of all the advantages most pest species have over you,

the hunter, in spring or summer. The lush leaf canopy, the tall crop cover, the thick hedgerow. Winter exposure and lethargy now give you some advantage and I see it as Mother Nature's way of restoring balance. You can take advantage of this but, to have any impact, you must be prepared to endure the same, hard conditions. When you think about it, though, the hunter is able to prepare himself much better than a crow or squirrel for a day in sub-zero temperatures.

I make sure I have an array of specialist kit and clothing and have rarely missed a day out in the field (even in temperatures touching minus 15 degrees Celcius) in the past few years. I've run myself very close to hypothermia on a couple of occasions, but that was because I simply wouldn't call it a day. (As many will know, there's always that last opportunity you just don't want to let pass by... or the deep, red winter sunset that you can't resist watching!)

## KEEPING WARM

The key to longevity in the cold is to employ lots of sub-layers to ensure a build-up of warm air beneath your outer layer. I favour a long sleeved T-shirt under a micro-fleece top under a micro-fleece or quilted outer coat. There are some superb shooting mitts on the market now, with flaps that tuck back to allow your fingers the freedom to find the rifle's cocking bolt and trigger. Cold fingers won't enable good trigger technique and for that reason, I use either disposable chemical hand-warmers or my Zippo rechargeable warmer to regularly warm my fingers between targets.

One of the most under-estimated areas of attention by shooters are the feet. On hoar-frosted ground, it will be your feet that 'radiate' cold into your body, slowly and subtly. Once your toes are frozen, your discomfort will be a hunt-stopper – so I wear a good pair of thermal socks outside a pair of lighter under-socks, tucked into waterproof leather boots lined with lamb's wool insoles. If you have a head like a snooker ball with stubble (like me), then a snug, fleece bob-cap is essential. Add a neck warmer or snood to pull up across a wind-chilled face and you're almost ready for a full day out. The preparation doesn't stop there, however. Make sure you load a few magazines of pellets in the warmth of your home, to prevent fumbling with cold fingers in the field. This is why the PCP multi-shot rifle is king for me; reloading single pellets into a springer in an arctic wind is a recipe for frostbite. Keep your magazines unloaded and separate from your rifle while travelling to your shoot, or you'll be breaking the law by having a 'loaded' gun in public. Finally, a flask of hot soup, tea or coffee will be guaranteed to add an hour to the cold hunting day.

## RAIN

If you hunt for the pot, hunting only in fine weather will seriously lessen your supply of meat for the family table. If you control vermin for the farmer, they won't be very impressed if you don't show up just because its raining. (*They'll* still be working!)

Personally, I take a perverse satisfaction in walking back down to my Jeep, drenched and muddy, with a bag full of rabbits, pigeons or squirrels. My farmers are out in all conditions and they know that vermin is, too. To see me out in the same conditions lends some credibility to the permission they have granted for me to shoot on their land.

Rain, strange though it may seem, is one of the most benevolent weather trends that Mother Nature offers to the switched-on airgun hunter. Hell's teeth! Don't fret about getting your precious rifle wet – the most common excuse I hear for shooters not venturing out on rainy days – you can towel it down and oil it to stave off rust when you get home.

This is where it pays to keep an eye on that digital weather station I mentioned earlier. You need to play your aces when you know that rain is imminent. If you're expecting a period of sustained, torrential rain, head for the rabbit warrens before it arrives. Coneys have an in-built sense of prevailing weather fronts. As the pressure drops, they'll slink out to feed, driven by a natural urge to stock up on food as they will be underground for some time. An ambush along the warren will pay dividends, because the nearer the weather front gets, the more the rabbits are prone to venture out – even when you've shot a few. They are preprogrammed, mentally, to feed urgently. Take advantage of it. Similarly, after a prolonged period of rain, the rabbits will need to emerge to feed. If it's been pouring down relentlessly for a day or two, get into position again to meet them coming out.

*The key to longevity in the cold is to employ lots of sub-layers*

## GUNS AND MOISTURE

If you choose not to shoot when it's wet then, in Britain, you'll get precious few hunting days in a year! So never worry about taking your rifle out and about in wet weather – but take a few extra precautions to ensure that your rifle (which is simply a tool) doesn't suffer from too much exposure to water. I use a sunshade on my scope, in the rain, to keep raindrops off the lens and reduce fogging. If I have to sling the rifle over my shoulder while moving around, I either cover the shade with a flip-up cover or a cloth (both kept in my bag). A wet rifle is easy to tend when you get home: detach the action from the stock (it won't disturb your zero) and dry everything off with a towel, including inside the stock itself. Don't store the gun in its slip, still wet. Raindrops can turn into rust spots and could cause long-term damage. Allow everything to air-dry for an hour or so, then wipe action and stock down with a light coating of gun oil and reassemble the gun. The key is to do all this immediately you get home. Make a ritual of it – it only takes 10 minutes.

*A magpie, hunting winged insects in a meadow*

Some of the best days for hunting are what I refer to as 'rainbow days' – where heavy showers are punctuated by spells of hot sunshine. These are excellent days to target grey squirrels and woodpigeon. The squirrel detests getting wet and will head for its drey at the merest sniff of rain. Just like the rabbit, it will sense approaching showers and will scamper about searching for food. During the squall, you won't see squirrels at all, but when the warm rays of the sun breaking through cloud heat the drey, out they'll come again to feed before the next downpour. Usually, greys are most active just after dawn and just before dusk. On these rainbow days, they will be darting in and out of the food caches like a ballboy at Wimbledon.

Woodpigeons behave differently on rainbow days, too. They fly lower across the hedgerow and stick close to the copse or wood. On clear days – cold or warm – they fly much higher. As the squirrels disappear into the drey, the pigeons arrive, looking for cover from the rain – and that gives the hunter the opportunity to target them at roost. They seem to enjoy warm rain and sit cooing under cover, giving away their positions... but it takes a very cautious stalker to find them. Once a stalked pigeon stops its murmur, the game is up. It's sensed your movement and one more step will see it clatter back out into even the wildest storm.

Corvids are staunch wet-weather birds and will be seen flying in all but the most torrential rain. Rooks and crows will feast on wet earth in ploughland or meadow for grubs and worms driven to the surface by the vibration of falling raindrops. A tight, sheltered spot under the canopy at the wood's edge can pay dividends near freshly turned soil. Magpies are more reluctant in rain. They will flutter far beneath the foliage and you will hear those curious chuckles and churrs as they approach through the wood. In heavy foliage, they can be hard to spot – but after sustained rain, like any bird, they often give their position away by sending a shower of raindrops from the canopy. After a heavy deluge has passed, watch for magpies and jays rain-dancing in the wet meadow grass. They haven't gone crazy; they're snatching up the bugs and flies that have been waiting beneath the soil as larvae for the trigger of rain to hatch. In spring, it will be the May-bugs. In autumn, it will be crane flies (sometimes misnamed Daddy longlegs). On that point, the only saving grace of the magpie is its fondness for hawking mosquitoes and midges as they hatch.

Don't ignore the puddles and pools left after heavy rain, either. They will bear the prints and trails of visiting wildlife – which is always useful intelligence – and they also create watering points for many vermin species. Crows and magpies love to bathe in these pools and are often so distracted they won't sense a hunter's cautious approach to within range. Rats, of course, delight in swollen watercourses and ponds.

## SUNSHINE AND HEAT

There is no doubt that a fine day will see the woods, fields and farmyard busy with wildlife. Those days when the mercury threatens to burst through the top of the thermometer can be less fruitful, though. There are three very distinctive times when the potential for hunting and the behaviour of quarry changes significantly during a hot, summer's day.

At daybreak, Mother Nature often adapts to weather extremes in a way which the hunter would do well to mark and remember. The rabbit warren will be alert to the increasing warmth in the soil as the dawn summer sun creeps above the horizon to burn off the morning mist. Coneys will emerge to shake off their fleas and lope indolently far from their burrows to lap the dew from broad leaved brassicas and weeds, or to nibble at the wet crops. A heavy mist will blanket both your scent and the sound of your air rifle. The rabbit stalker who is prepared to leave bed early will not only enjoy the moist, silent ground on which to walk. Even if you shoot nothing, this is a magnificent time of day to be out: the chorus of birdsong; the fox retiring from its night's mischief; the startled deer you encounter in the mist.

Such a dawn is also the time for other vermin to be prowling. Crows and magpies, the earliest of avian risers, will be on the wing. For them, the fresh roadkill will have already attracted the buzz of bluebottles and alerted them to a fair feast. The hedgerow rat will still be foraging before retreating from the rising sun. The weasel and the stoat will be snaking toward the same rabbits that you covet. Only when the sun has breached the horizon will the grey squirrel leave its drey to feed for an hour or two. For as much it hates darkness and water, it won't abide high temperatures, either. Watch the margins between the maize crop and the wood to ambush the squirrels as they venture out to steal the ripening yellow cobs.

Noon is a barren time for the hunter on a hot summer's day. Once the sun reaches its zenith, shooting opportunities will be few.

*Still enough light for another coney or two*

When I'm out and about, I will be bathed in inspect repellent and I will be sitting in heavy shade or behind a leaf-net, just watching the world go by. I normally have a sunshade on my scope, come rain or shine, but on a bright, sunny day, it's crucial. I will probably have a few flocked decoys set out, as the only creature likely to be busy in the open field is the woodpigeon. They will be fast and wary, the merest glint from your lens will spook them into flight. Setting up close to a water source – a drinker or a pool – can pay dividends as magpies love to bathe. Be warned, though, you'll likely pay a penance, too; where there is water, there will be the midge and the mosquito! (Hence my insect repellent.) The odd rabbit will emerge to browse and cast off the plague of fleas which inhabit the warren. It won't be far from its bury, though, so your shot had better be accurate and terminal, lest it flip back into the hole beyond your reach. Most sensible creatures will be deep in shade, waiting for the sun to drop and the air to cool.

Dusk comes as a relief to the hunter at the end of such a glorious day – but few will have the stamina to last that long. Nor is it sensible. The wise hunter, during a hot spell, will pick either dawn-to-noon forays, or hunt noon-to-dusk. Don't ever miss an opportunity to do the latter; if ever Mother Nature blessed us with the spectacular, it is sunset on a summer's evening. The lowering sunlight highlights a rich harvest both in the air and on the floor. Thousands of winged insects, driven to hatch in the heat, whirligig above the field and margin attracting the magpie, the carrion crow and the jay. They will dance and pogo between the dandelions and the daisies, pecking at the bugs. Their colourful, gaudy plumage and lack of rhythm are reminiscent of my youthful animation at a Clash concert. If you're lucky, you'll also see that superb little raptor, the little owl, hawking.

The coneys will now emerge in numbers, the kits scuttling about first, the adults following later. Sit very quietly. Let them chase and frolic. Give them confidence and let the adults join the party before starting the cull. Watch the grey woodpigeon flocks wheel and dive against a crimson canvas as they head toward the roosts. Mark them well, for those roosts are your winter and rainy-day target areas. The grey squirrels come back out to take some supper before night descends. Me? I'll sit quietly and pick off those juicy, fat, adult rabbits. Then I'll rest and watch the white form of the barn owl ghost across the meadow. When the creeping fox looks like a dark wraith and the blackbird ceases it's evensong, I'll head for home.

## HUNTING IN THE SUN

Ironically, hot weather hunting can be more discomforting than cold, for many reasons. During a freeze, you can add layers, don hats, slip on gloves and adjust to the temperature. When the heat's turned up beyond comfort point, while you can lighten clothing, you can't keep removing the layers! Even reducing cover to camo trousers and a T-shirt can bring added threat through sunburn and insect bites. If I'm out in the heat, I wear a Tee, cover my head with a baseball cap and spray my skin with insect repellent. I haven't yet found one that is totally effective, so a few bites are always par for the course.

Stalking in sunshine can be challenging. Bear in mind that if you move with the sun in your face, you risk detection from the glare of your scope lens or specs. If you move with the sun at your back, you throw shadow – so always try to hunt across the sun's rays. Mirage effect can make range-finding difficult if ambushing a warren across warm ground with a shimmer above it. Take a test shot or two at a clump of nettles, prior to hunting, to check your distance.

Dealing with shot quarry needs extra care in hot weather. Recover rabbits as soon as possible so that they don't get fly-blown. Hang them in shade and paunch out just before you leave the field. If you've had shot pigeons pegged out as decoys for hours in high temperatures, ditch them when finished rather than take them home to eat. They will be crawling with bacteria.

## PORTENTS AND SIGNALS

Though I choose to shoot in all weathers, adjusting my tactics to cope with the changes is important. Weathercraft is also about anticipating those changes and guessing when you are going to need to take action. Most weather changes are fairly obvious in a temperate county with big skies, such as Norfolk, where I hunt. There will be many hunters out there who have to deal with potentially lethal climactic changes – snowfall, avalanche, flood, hill fog and suchlike. In the main, my weather eye is always on rain, thunderstorms, mist and wind. Long-term planning relies on the Met Office and the digital weather station.

Often, the flora and fauna around you will give clues to longer-term weather patterns. Heavy autumn harvests of berries on blackthorn (sloes), rowan, elder, holly and similar shrubs will be gorged on by birds and indicate a hard winter. In recent years, I've still found this to be true – but the duration of hard weather is shorter now.

Medium-term signs are quite reliable. For example, seeing a full moon hanging in the east at the same time as the sun sets in the west will usually bring a frost by dawn. The old rhyme about 'red sky at night, shepherds' delight. Red sky at morning, shepherds' warning' is vested in truth. In the same way, the colour of the moon will portend conditions due to the cloud formations causing the colouring. A red moon means windy conditions; a pale moon signifies rain; and a white moon, clear conditions. Despite some of the advice you read about lamping being fruitless under a full moon, a pale full moon is definitely a lamping moon for me. With rain coming soon, the rabbits will be abroad, feeding before the rain hits. Most weather fronts pass across a region within six hours – remember this; it's plenty of time to get a planned hunting session in.

There are serious signals to watch for, too.

My coastal and marshland friends tell me that if the dyke-rats come out into the open fields in numbers to feed on tuber crops like sugar beet, or into the woods to feed on fallen acorns or beechmast, severe floods will soon follow. This makes perfect sense as the rising water table is probably threatening their tunnels and driving the rats into the open.

Short-term planning, out in the field, often relies on Mother Nature's own forecasters. These can be living creatures or they can be plants. Mistle thrushes (nicknamed 'stormcocks') and blackbirds will sit high and sing their hearts out at approaching storms or heavy rain. The robin does the opposite, singing low in the shrubbery, instead of on a post or high on a hedge. Swifts and swallows hawking insects low down indicate a storm front approaching. The insects are driven low by the humid air preceding the storm. If, like me, you hunt close to wetlands and dykes, the sudden stench of ditchwater is another sure sign of the storm front. For the same reason as the low insects – it's the odour of fungal spores released by humidity, held low by moisture and driven before the breeze carrying the weather front. Many creatures prepare their fur or feather for the onslaught.

*A useful tool for the hunter – a digital weather station*

Crows and pheasants peck and preen. Pheasants are definitely worth noting. Their life is spent mainly on the ground so they 'listen' with their feet. As a Eurasian import, they have genes which take them back to the earthquake zones on distant continents, where a tiny tremor on the earth signals that it's time to fly up to roost, to relative safety. Pheasants will sense an approaching thunderstorm miles away and clatter to roost in large numbers, crowing in alarm. You'll wonder what the heck is going on but, trust me, an hour or two later the storm will be overhead.

The hare and the farmyard cat will sit washing their faces and whiskers with their paws as heavy rain approaches. My lurcher will start eating grass, whining and getting agitated an hour before a thunderstorm hits. Rooks will circle high and tumble among the thermals, hours ahead of the storm. If you see them beating home, wings low to the field, well before dusk, get closer to your car or home; there's a hell-raiser coming your way.

Certain flowers detect humidity and close their petals, too – like scarlet pimpernels, ox-eye daisies, chickweed and dandelions. Rain portents, for sure. ◯

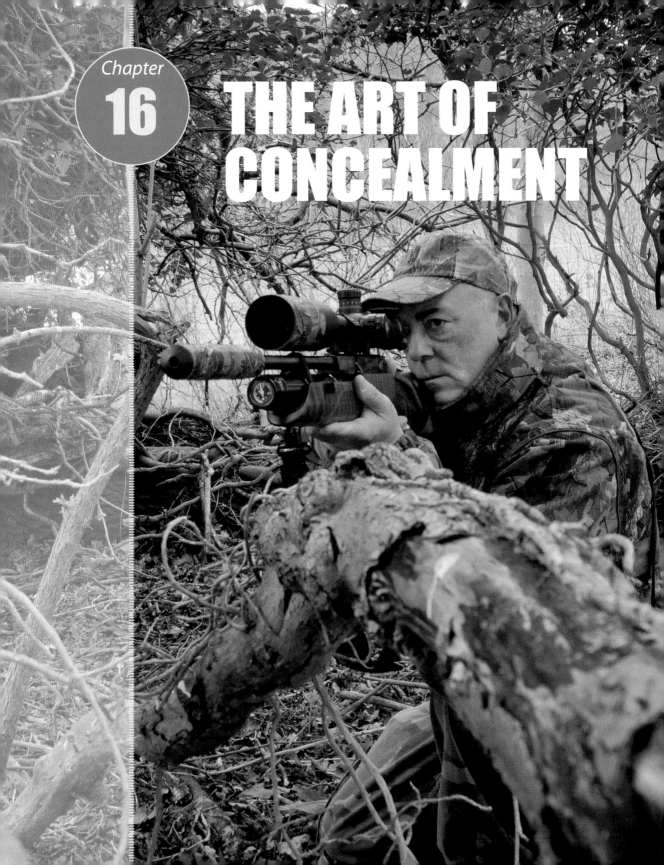

# THE ART OF CONCEALMENT

## THE BLACK ART

Concealment is an all-embracing term and a vital part of fieldcraft. There is much more to the art of concealment than sitting in hides or squatting behind leaf-nets. It's about movement, stealth, shadow, melting into the landscape, be that the wood, field or farm.

One of the first lines of defence that an airgunner's quarry uses is its vision. Avian quarry has pin-sharp eyesight. Other species rely on the olfactory sense and can scent you before they see you. Most have great auditory sense and can hear you coming. Rabbits, in particular, will feel you approaching, the vibration of your footfall. Animal and bird senses are finely tuned to detect the slightest change in the natural order. The passing shadow; the glint of light; the crack of a twig; the warning of another creature; the creak of a gate; the clunk of a car door; the breaking of a barrel; the muffled cough… and a myriad other signals.

So you can see that concealment is not just about the visual element of not being seen. It's also about not being heard, felt or smelt. Hiding all these things from your quarry is the real art – the black art. Learning it takes a lifetime, while mastering it will never truly be achieved. Yet every mistake that you make will etch itself in your memory and you will gradually eliminate the most basic errors. You will teach yourself, through those mistakes, to move slowly and deliberately. To think carefully about the consequence of every action (and possible reaction) during a hunt. To see the shadow or shade as a friend. To check the breeze constantly. To scan the path in front of you before every few steps. To watch for the scouts and sentinels that your quarry post in the tree-line. To pause every few steps and take stock of everything, constantly and habitually.

Your ear will become tuned to the arena in which you're operating. You will learn the subtle differences in bird sound – how to differentiate between peaceful song and chatter, and the sound of concern. The scold of the wren or the pipe of the blackbird should alert you that your movement is too fast, too threatening. Slow down. The thumping of the rabbit's paw will tell you it has felt your footfall and is drumming its warning to the warren. Tread more lightly. The flapping of the woodpigeon's wings, making ready to fly. It has sensed your progress. Check the throw of your shadow before moving on. If your movement is unsettling the wood, stop for a spell. Let the curious come to you, and let the others regain their calm.

Concealment most certainly isn't just about wearing camoflauge clothing. In fact, I didn't start wearing camo until about eight years ago, when modern patterns became more natural and subtle than the old DPM gear. I used to hunt quite successfully in simple drab, olive greens and browns. The advances in hunting clothing technology over recent years have certainly been phenomenal, to the point where the industry has finally cracked the code that was most important to me when selecting gear. Silence. The two-dimensional, monochromatic vision of most quarry has been recognised, and modern camo patterns definitely help you blend into the hedgerow or tree trunk.

More importantly, the new micro-fleece fabrics are superbly silent. Much thought is being put into making clothing supple, so that you can bend, squat and kneel without sounding like a breaking branch. Metal zips have been replaced with rubber – no more morris dancing around the wood! Utility pockets have been added. Mind you, I find that some jackets have so many pockets, I forget where I put the knife or the jay call or the spare pellet magazine! The only thing that the big manufacturers have failed to get right so far are the trousers. Too long or too narrow, I usually find. They aren't too important, though. Rabbits never see my

*The thumping of a rabbit's paw will tell you it has felt your footfall*

legs – they don't live long enough – and avian species usually only see me squatting. Hopefully, by then, it's too late. What is important, and why I like baggier trousers, is flexibility. To climb a gate or slip through a fence without castrating myself.

Consideration of kit though, with regard to concealment, is not to be disregarded. I use multi-compartment angling bags – which I find are designed better than many so-called shooting bags – but I have to snip off their metal zips and replace with toggles cut from bootlaces to keep them completely silent when I'm on the move.

Footwear is a controversial topic. Two of the most influential air rifle hunting writers I've ever enjoyed reading advocate wearing soft trainers to promote silence and allow for a 'feel' of the ground underfoot. This has never worked for me. I spend hours and hours every week in the field, in all weathers and always wear a pair of stout, waterproof, leather boots with a Vibram sole for grip. My feet stay warm and dry and I've learned how not to 'feel' the ground by avoiding obstacles. I can walk, like an Indian in moccasins, in the most littered woodland. It's fieldcraft; it's concealment – and it simply takes concentration and practice. Generally, my lurcher makes more noise than me in a wood or on a field margin and, if you know your dogs, you'll know that few pass by more silently than a lurcher.

As for visual concealment, that is a sub-art. The clothing mentioned earlier keeps your colour profile minimal, for though most creatures won't see 'in colour' they *will* notice high contrast. So in your movement around wood, margin or field, you need to aim to keep that contrast as subtle as possible. In the wood, avoid open areas such as clearings. Slip from trunk to trunk in shade, if you can. Use the cover of the canopy to hide your progress. Constantly, consciously, think 'cover'. Wear a baseball cap to shade your face; therefore your sparkling eyes and your intention, for I swear that wildlife can read malice aforethought in your eyes!

The recent tendency towards ghillie suits amuses me immensely. If I couldn't get within 20 or 30 yards of a rabbit or corvid with my current level of fieldcraft, I'd give up shooting rather than wear one of these ridiculous outfits. We're talking about putting a coney in the pot or knocking over a crow, not life-threatening survival here! Your quarry can't shoot back, so why go to military extremes? I often find it awkward enough to pop into the local shop after an early morning rabbit sortie wearing my camo fleece. All I want is a paper and bottle of milk, but the staff behind the counter are hovering over the personal alarm button. Lord knows what would happen if I walked into the shop looking like an unpruned hedge! I'm sorry, but while they may have a use for a specific and difficult target (mink comes to mind), I just think they are the lazy hunter's solution to avoiding real, up-close stalking and fieldcraft technique.

When walking crop margins, hug the areas

## REVERSE BEHAVIOUR

One of the most important pieces of advice I can give is that you must always take the opposite action to your quarry. If your quarry is moving, perhaps a foraging rat or squirrel, then stand stock still. If your quarry freezes because you are moving (such as a rabbit caught in the open), then keep moving away, avoiding eye contact. You have just triggered a natural defence mechanism for many creatures. If you pass on, they will relax. If you stop and stare, they will panic and bolt. If your quarry goes upward, like a squirrel climbing a trunk, get as low as you can and freeze. Blend in to the floor. This confuses the creature and it will usually stop long enough for a shot. If a bird or squirrel comes down to the floor, do the opposite – slowly stand as high and as straight as you can. Blend into a tree, become a tree. Your ankles and shins won't intimidate them at all – but your face and eyes will if you squat and meet their gaze close to their viewing level.

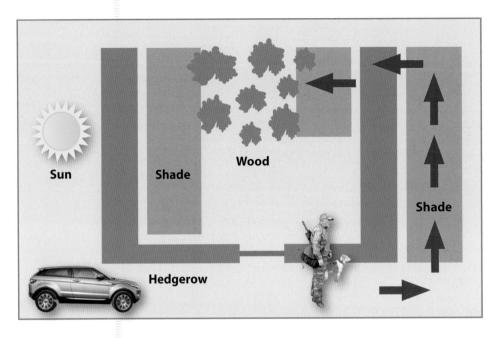

*Approach a wood using shadow and cover*

of maximum shadow and high vegetation. Usually that will be a hedgerow or the wood's edge. On some tall crops, like maize, it may be the crop itself. Never cross open fields if it can be avoided. Take the long way round and keep to the blind side of hedgerows or trees. Woodpigeons or crows watching a hunter approaching over open land will be long gone when you get to them. Most will be gone even taking the longer route, but fieldcraft is about raising the odds in your favour. You just did, if you took my advice – because the quarry on the blind side of your approach will still be there.

Furthermore, don't advertise that you are carrying a gun. Wear it slung over your shoulder on open land or margins until you reach the area that you intend to shoot. The crow's favourite alarm call is 'Gunnn! Guuunnn!' as I've already mentioned.

## THE AMBUSH

When it comes to ambushing quarry, artificial hides help, of course, but they have to be first set up. The hunter who blunders into a wood

with half-a-ton of kit and stomps straight to the intended set-up point will empty the wood of wildlife in minutes.

The self-constructed, natural hide – one that's built on the fly using off-cuts of local soft wood and vegetation to look in tune with its surroundings – is one I personally never bother with now, though many hunters still do. Life is far too short and hunting time is too precious for me to even consider these. To build a hide this way, large enough to accommodate a hunter and their kit, takes (me) hours. While it's being built, your quarry is watching, listening, scenting and feeling your activity. When it's finished, you can't then use it (or will need extreme patience), because nothing will come near or fly over your hide for ages. You have just distressed the natural environment too much. Please forget advice about leaving your new hide to 'weather' for a few days to allow quarry get used to its presence, too. When you go back a few days later, your hide will look like a bonfire heap! The cut foliage will be tinder dry, the leaves will have died and turned over

and you will now have a dry hide against a lush backdrop that looks so unnatural that vermin will give it a wide berth.

The traditional camo net and poles, used by pigeon shotgunners for years, is a useful hide. I prefer a spiked pole set, with kick plates to drive the spikes into even the hardest ground with my boot. I use a variety of camo leaf-nets, depending on the season and natural background. This gear is great for a quick set-up on any species; the poles and nets can be wrapped around a tree trunk, set against a fence-line with a dark backdrop or put up close to a woodland clearing. Weight isn't too much of an issue when transporting them as they aren't heavy, but length certainly is, even with telescopic poles. I tend to use mine on a planned ambushing mission. I also carry a set of carbon rods with mine – the type used to make small tents rigid – to prop the tops of the nets. This stops them sagging and adds weight to stop them flapping in a breeze. Nets can be set and dressed with local vegetation very quickly (hunting journalist and friend, Mat Manning, is a master at this) to

target difficult vermin such as crows. They can be set up in minutes, with little disturbance. Job done. When you're finished, you can dismantle the hide in minutes, too – though disentangling nets and removing vegetation can be tricky. If you're pigeon shooting, the nets can be packed and moved swiftly to follow changing flightlines. A distinct asset in any hunter's kit.

One of my favourite tools for semi-instant concealment is my fold-up camo blind. If I want to move about quickly and target ground-based vermin, such as rabbits or foraging squirrels, this is a God-send. Mine is the Backpacker Pigeon Blind, an ingenious American fold-down, but integral, version of the net and pole concept. It packs into a 70cm-long quiver bag, weighs just grammes and can be moved around my permissions swiftly. It has lightweight carbon poles and metal spikes, a slick and extendable pole clamping system and a Realtree camo fabric. The net is riveted to the poles, so you just roll it out – no tangled leaf nets to battle with. Excellent for spot-ambushing on a whim.

It can be set near a fence-line to break up my profile or wrapped around a tree trunk in a wood. I've shot hundreds of otherwise unapproachable rabbits from behind this hide by setting it close to open or fence-line warrens. I can set up, wait, knock out a few emerging rabbits, then move along into the breeze and reset.

One must-have for me is a pop-up hide – a camoflauged tent for hunters. I've owned several of these since they appeared (they're an American invention). Due to their size, roofed structure and being totally waterproof, they make a perfect haven on a cold, winter's day or a wet, squally one. The one I've used for the past few years is the Hideout, bought from the Deben Group. Lengthwise, it's a bit of a burden to carry, so a planned campaign item. I often use mine as a base for hedgerow or woodland shooting. I get claustrophobic, but this hide is spacious enough to spend hours in, and I haven't only shot many vermin species from within it, but also captured some of my best wildlife photographs. That, alone, is testimony to its discrete presence – when positioned correctly, of course.

*A pop-up hide can be set in minutes – and moved at a whim*

Farm machinery
makes excellent
cover and quarry are
used to seeing
it there

The hunter should never underestimate the efficiency of the static hide for concealment – the farm building; the shed; the outhouse; the barn; the redundant tractor; the pig pen; the myriad of old structures dotted around farms. Wild creatures are familiar with them. They pass them every day. They feed, breed, nest, sleep, shelter and even defecate in them. They anticipate them being in their planned path or flight, so they don't fear them. They also offer the hunter refuge and opportunity during the icy November gale or the fierce July lightning storm. Where you seek shelter, you quarry often will, too. I frequently sit in the gloomy corner of a barn on a squalid day to shoot feral pigeons and woodpigeons flying onto the rafters. I target scavenging rats, magpies seeking scraps and jackdaws plundering the grain stores. No need for nets or other devices – your concealment is generally the tactic of surprise; these visitors just don't expect to meet an airgunner lurking in the shadows.

So, to my ultimate hide – the natural one. Most definitely my favourite form of concealment, for I value the fresh air, the scent of the wood, the sight of the sky and a light load. The fallen tree trunk, the ivy overhang, the low conifer, the nettle cluster, the elder bush – all these, and many more, can hide the air rifle hunter in just moments. Vermin are familiar with the scene in which you've hidden yourself. There is no construction needed, nor any disruption to the surrounding environment. Nor is there anything to pack away when you've finished your task.

One of the first things I do after a serious gale is to scour the woods to check for fresh tree falls. These make superb hides, best taken advantage of while the leaves on them are still alive. The problem, of course, is that this sort of incidental natural hide is only usually available in summer and autumn, when the foliage is lush. Yet the evergreen overhang (ivy, mistletoe, holly) can be found all year round. One of the staple tools kept in any bag that I carry is a pair of secateurs, which I use to trim out portholes for my scope and barrel when in the thick cover of evergreen shrubs. These spy-holes can be used over and over again, particularly when roost-shooting woodpigeons. They are a place in which to shrink when you sense that the wood and its occupants have become alert to your presence and are excessively disturbed. ○

# TRACKING AND TRAILING

## SIGN LANGUAGE

When it comes to sensory advantage, we hunters simply can't match our quarry. They have the benefit of acute olfactory and aural perception – they can smell and hear significantly better than humans. The one thing we have in common is sight. But we have superior powers of reasoning and, arguably, memory. Recognising the tracks, trails and signs of wild creatures is a prerequisite of successful shooting and hunting. So, too, is remembering everything you see and learn to use as a reference point for the future.

I often take more pleasure from sign-reading – the nature detective role – than I do from the actual execution of a shot at a wild creature. This is part of the real hunt; the pitting of wits against your quarry's, which so often precedes the stalking or ambushing or baiting. The challenge is immense, but doesn't take a lifetime to learn. Pondering over the footprint of an animal or bird; noting the twist of fur caught on the barbed-wire fence; studying the run eroded in the grass or muddy bank; picking up and turning the broken egg-shell; dissecting the scat of a creature with a twig. These small things add to the interest, the intellectual challenge, of a hunt.

I like to investigate crime scenes: what slaughtered the pheasant hen? Who left the scatter of pigeon feathers? What raided the grain store? The hunter needs to learn these things, if only to justify the hunt itself. Unlike common law, though, you – the walking, stalking judge and jury – just need to establish a balance of probability to pass sentence on moral grounds. You do not need proof beyond reasonable doubt; understanding that will help you sleep better at night.

There are a number of signals that help the hunter establish presence, activity, location, health and habit of quarry. These include prints, runs, feeding sign, residual sign and defecation.

There are important pointers to help you transfer the signs you read into the identification of quarry. Footprints are relative to the overall size of a creature. Study your quarry intensely. How does a bird hold on a perch? Gauge the size of its feet in relation to its body. Watch it walk, or hop, on the ground. Imagine what its print will look like. Do the same with small mammals. Which are the bigger paws – front or back? How are they carried when they lope – a canter or a sprint? All important signs. Examine the claws and paws of quarry you've shot. Watch a squirrel turn a nut or egg before eating it. Pick up the remnants when it's gone (or you've shot it) and study them. Remember the marks and indentations. Sit and study the travel of creatures, like rabbits, rats and squirrels. What makes them pause, stoop, hop, squat, climb? These behaviours will seem unimportant… until you come to track them. To cover all these for every quarry species would need a book of its own, but I feel I must relate those of the most common airgun quarry.

## TRAILING BIRDS

Let's start with the hard part – footprints. Corvids and doves (including woodpigeons) have what are known as perching prints. Three forward toes and one rear toe, which grip a bough to hold them steady. When splayed out on the floor, these prints look very similar for all our quarry species. The subtle difference is size and gait. Crow, rook and woodpigeon prints are similar in size. Telling crow from woodpigeon is easy. The crow's print will show two of the forward toes closer together than the third. The back toe will look longer than the forward three; the print of the woodpigeon will be much more even – all three forward toes equally spread, and the rear toe the same length as the middle front toe. That's the print sorted – but the bigger clues are in the gait, the walk or hop of the bird you are trying to identify.

If you watch how your quarry travels on the

*Carrion crow on left, magpie on right*

ground, you'll see that the crow generally hops toward bait or a puddle. So the prints of both feet are side by side. The woodpigeon walks – struts – forward, and its trail is distinctive for a peculiar reason. I can remember my old gym teacher cuffing kids around the head for running with their toes turned inward – pigeon toed, as he called it. This is why – the woodpigeon walks with its feet turned slightly inward, and the trail confirms this.

The smaller corvids and the collared dove or feral pigeon display similar trails to the above. Their prints will be much shallower, due to their lighter weight. In very soft ground or snow, the magpie will often leave an intermittent straight line behind its footprints – its long tail carving a trail of its own. If you're lucky, your bird will leave a take-off print on the ground, where the first sweeps of the wings leave a trail. These immediately show the actual size of the bird. It's rather like an X-ray.

Feeding sign is more difficult with bird species. Again, though, think size. The indentations on a raided egg shell will give clues. Long, narrow 'V' shapes snipped out are usually magpie; broader ones will be carrion crow or jay. It doesn't matter – all you need to know is that a corvid has stolen the eggs, so

you have work to do as a pest controller!

Pellets are the regurgitated detritus that a bird disgorges because its internal digestive system can't cope with it – fur, insect wings, egg shell, bones, mud and tiny beaks. Many bird species produce these, not just owls as is commonly assumed. I've never been a massive fan of the BBC's *Springwatch* television programme, but if I have anything in common with one of its presenters, Chris Packham, it's my enduring love of punk rock and a proclivity for picking through the pellets and faeces of wild creatures to understand what they've been eating and what their state of health is. Which is why I know that even

*Magpie take-off prints in the snow. Note the wing-beats*

the humble rook will raid songbird nests and feast on a dead (hopefully!) mole. The mole claws were a one-off, but I've regularly found chaffinch and blackbird hatchling beaks in rook or carrion crow pellets. I've never found a magpie pellet, and I'm not sure if they produce them. If Chris reads this, maybe he'll have some in his collection he can show me...

Bird faeces – aka guano – are worth studying. Not just for the aforementioned reasons, but because they will also show the airgun hunter what the bird has been eating and, perhaps more importantly, where it fed. If you stumble across significant amounts of guano on the floor of a copse or wood, then you've probably just found a roost – either corvid or pigeon.

A hunter's treasure trove, unless it turns out to be a starling roost (they're currently on the protected list).

## TRAILING MAMMALS

If you can't spot rabbit sign, then I'm afraid you probably shouldn't be holding an air rifle – and you should certainly book an appointment at Specsavers! You also shouldn't even be thinking about hunting live quarry unless you can pass the test of fairly simple quarry recognition, which includes its sign. Although I've hunted the rabbit for three-quarters of a lifetime, these seemingly benign, yet highly destructive, mammals are the easiest on which to test your tracking and trailing skills.

*Checking rabbit runs through grass*

The signs along an established rabbit warren are easy to see. Lots of rabbit droppings; scratched earth, probably open buries with fresh earth cast outside; the yellow splash of urine on the leaf or dirt; nearby crop damage; a flick of grey or brown fur here and there, usually the result of an over amorous buck exerting his dominance over a reluctant doe. In short – litter, urine, excrement, discarded clothing, signs of overt sexual activity and vandalism. (Sounds a bit like many city centres on a Sunday morning...)

Spotting remote or woodland warrens can be a bit more challenging. You need to get an eye for the run in the grass, or the clump of fur on the barbed wire. One thing is a certainty: all runs lead back to the buries, even if only one or two holes. Snowy or dewy mornings will display the rabbits' overnight movements like the map on your sat-nav. Use the GPS in your head to lead you to the buries and then remember where they are. You now know, from the trail, that these are live ones.

Do you know how to read rabbit tracks? I once set a Christmas quiz for work colleagues, where I asked them to identify the makers of various prints and trails in the snow. I knew that they would probably recognise rabbit tracks, so I made the test harder – which way was the rabbit travelling? They all got it wrong! Watch rabbits lope along – the two, small forepaws stretch forward then they drag their large rear paws up and around the forepaws into a hop. Therefore, the large prints are the *leading* edge of the trail, not the trailing one.

Study grass runs carefully, because the rabbit is a habitual traveller. It will pause and hop over the same hummock, or stop before passing under the same fence-line or tree trunk every time it meets the obstacle. Learn and remember these points, for that pause of theirs is your invitation to shoot. You should be anticipating it, if watching the beast.

Rabbit feeding sign among crops is low-

*Some little tell-tale signs as to the culprits here!*

level gnawing of tubers like sugar beet, and the severing of fine-bladed crops like barley. In spring woodland, they will dig out bulbs – so where you see snowdrop or bluebell stalks scattered about, you have found a rabbit restaurant worthy of ambushing from cover. These are short-lived harvests for the coney, so they'll be back very soon if you're patient.

Rat-runs are a different matter for the shooter. Around the farmyard, they're reasonably obvious and always littered with the rats' oblong droppings. Out in the country, though – in the ditch or pit – you can easily miss them. The rat loves water and filth. At the flight pond,where the ducklings are vulnerable, or along the dyke, you may find their distinctive prints. In wet conditions or snow, you will see the single, central line that follows the footprints. Unlike the squirrel, the rat can't hold its tail aloft, so it drags it behind wherever it skulks. This includes through its own scat and spray, which is why you especially must never pick up a shot rat by its tail.

A rat's lair isn't simple to spot, unless you are tracking its prints. Nor is it easy to shoot a rat at the entrance. They are naturally cautious at the nest and sprint in and out, particularly if they have young below. However, like many mammals, they often need to defecate on exit from the lair (it's that habit thing again!), so

*Study paws to learn their tracks*

look out for the latrines close to the nest – piles of rat droppings. This is where they will pause on exit… and this is where to shoot them at their most vulnerable.

Grey squirrel footprints are distinctive due to those long claws that allow them to climb so deftly, yet don't retract when the animal is on the ground. The rear feet are double the size of the front ones and their trail is similar to that of the rabbit, but it travels the other way – the squirrel doesn't hop, it canters, so the front paws mark first. In snow, for instance, the direction of a squirrel's trail can be seen heading in the direction of the smaller prints, opposite from the rabbit's print.

Trailing greys after fresh snowfall is easy using this sign and one other; if the critters are in the canopy, they form little avalanches of snow as they move along the branches. Don't bother looking for squirrel droppings, though – they're are as rare as rocking-horse manure. They obviously defecate, but where and when is a mystery to me. Feeding sign is common, however – gnawed and split cob nuts or acorns; stripped fir cones; nibbled maize kernels; and occasionally a topped egg shell. Grey squirrels use regular feeding spots and these are worth hiding near, in ambush. Low tree stumps are a favourite, which they use as a table.

## NATURE DETECTIVE

While tracking and trailing is about identifying potential culprits and understanding what vermin species are abroad on your land, the true nature detective won't want to stop there. He'll want to analyse any unusual activity in more detail and try to fathom out what actually happened, why it happened, and when it happened. What was the motive? Will – remembering that habit is the biggest weakness in your quarry's armour – it happen again? Fieldcraft is more than just anticipating what lies in front of you as a hunter on a shooting permission. It's also about understanding what went on while you weren't there – the target area's history. But how do you go about examining a crime scene? Let's work through some of my recent experiences and how I arrived at the conclusions that I did… rightly or wrongly!

I stepped from a narrow, overgrown woodland track on a shooting estate into a dewy, yet sunlit, grassy clearing. It was about 7am, a late spring morning. The turf was almost manicured, nibbled tight – an oasis in a thick plantation beneath the nearest habitation (the Hall), just 400 metres away. In the centre of the clearing was the low-cut stump of an ancient elm, barely clearing the grass. What attracted me was that it was covered in egg shells. On examination, large, olive-coloured shells – pheasant eggs. I didn't touch a thing. I walked around them first, and looked carefully at the grass; rabbit-grazed grass… and rabbits don't eat eggs. I was looking for a trail – and I found two. One barely discernible track, a mere skim through the wet grass, coming from the rhododendron bank below the Hall. The other, a slender track coming from a hollow on the opposite side. I'd already decided the egg-thief's identity. Then I looked at the egg shells and doubt crept in. Two different shades of olive, meaning two, different nests. Some were topped off and drained – typical squirrel work. Others were fragmented, with the distinctive jagged indents of a corvid beak. Both egg types had the same signs. I looked more closely around the stump. Some swirled bird droppings, containing tiny shell fragments.

Conclusions? No corvid normally brings eggs out into the open. They can't carry eggs this large without difficulty. The trails told me that a grey squirrel had carried them there from two, separate nests, and at different times. I'd love to have seen this. The trails told me it was carrying them blindly, its teeth through the shells, head half-buried inside. The tracks would be wider if it rolled them here. Squirrels use tables – whereas corvids eat as close to a plundered nest as possible. What corvid had collaborated here, though? A carrion crow wouldn't venture this close to the Hall. No, magpies. Magpies came in to clean up after the squirrel had feasted – hence the beak marks.

So, how did I use this intelligence? I ignored the squirrel – I could get that any time. I broke a couple of hens' eggs on the stump a few days later and sat waiting in that covered track. I was right. The pair of magpies couldn't resist the open offering. Well, an ex-pair; I widowed one of them (the other got away). I hit the squirrels hard around the Hall that weekend, and have never seen that table used since.

Another interesting crime scene: I broke carefully through the bushes on an embankment overlooking a grassy ride full of wet, muddy ruts churned up by tractor wheels. It was just after dawn on a damp spring morning. I was hoping to catch a rabbit or two sitting out along the extensive warren here. Looking along the ride, into the breeze, I saw two rabbits alright. About 40 yards off, but lying flat on the grass between the ruts. Strange – they were obviously dead. My first thought was poachers... and that they were still here. I retreated back into the cover to watch, but after 10 minutes, no-one appeared to retrieve the coneys, so I walked

*Only one bird has a beak long and slender enough to do this – magpie!*

slowly down to them, watching around me for movement. Nothing. I stooped to feel one of the rabbits – it was still luke warm; dead less than half-an-hour. I turned it over. It was clean – no sign of a dogs or foxes jaws having held it, though its eyes were bulging. The other was the same, leaving me perplexed.

I looked around at the dewy grass. No sign of boot marks. There was some sign of disturbance in the wet grass, between the buries and the corpses. I scouted around while trying to decide what had killed this pair. Reason told me it could be a fellow airgunner, someone who had shot from nearby, but not recovered the rabbits – so I examined each, between eye and ear, then the heart area. Nothing. I looked along the muddy tractor ruts... and then found the clues I was looking for.

Fresh, and deep along one of the ruts, was the thick imprint of a bike tyre – a mountain bike. In among this, were fresh stoat tracks. I checked the other rut, the nearest to the embankment. More stoat prints in the wet mud, coming inward from the wood. I picked up one of the rabbits, turned back the fur on the back of its neck and squeezed. Two blobs of blood showed where the stoat had buried its fangs and inflicted the killing bite. Same with the second rabbit. The clever little assassin had hit two, dragged them out, then been disturbed by an early morning fitness

*I shot the pigeon, but note the running fox trail behind it*

freak. A few days later, I stepped out of the hedge at dawn and nearly gave the trespassing mountain biker a heart attack. I've never seen him since – nor the stoat for that matter.

The main point about nature detection is to study scenery carefully for clues, particularly where a kill has occurred. Know what the predator was, where it came from and, if possible, where it went. Learn to tell the difference between how creatures attack or dissect quarry. The sparrowhawk, for instance, will pluck feathers from the woody's breast and cast them about it leaving a circle. The fox will tear the woody apart from the wings, inwards. The badger will turn a rabbit inside-out, leaving just an empty pelt, whereas the fox will devour everything, perhaps just leaving the paws. The squirrel will top the gamebird's eggs as we do a boiled egg, but the corvid will drill a hole and suck out the contents. Magpies will drag a songbird's nest from position to raid its contents, but the jay will dip in furtively, leaving the nest intact. Rats will drive a hen pheasant from her eggs and eat them in the scrape, whereas squirrels will remove them to dine at leisure. Learn these things; they will help you understand the environment you share with your quarry and help you to ultimately become a better hunter. ○

# RECOGNITION

## QUARRY RECOGNITION

If shooting quarry accurately and cleanly is important, making sure you don't shoot another species in error is equally important. Not just because it's unethical, but also because shooting any bird not on the General Licence could see you in deep trouble with the Law. Quarry recognition requires a bit of homework on your part and, also, a wealth of experience in the field. Here are a few hints and tips on how to avoid some basic mistakes with the most common species.

By far the most common errors made by over-exuberant airgun hunters happen around doves and pigeons. The woodpigeon (with its broad white nape spots) and the collared dove (with its narrow black necklace) should both be instantly recognisable. The problem species is the rarer and protected stock dove. It has the same, iridescent green nape as the woodpigeon, but without the white spots. It has the same grey feathering and pinkish breast. Slightly smaller, it is easily mistaken for a woody – so the golden rule is look for the white neck flashes before taking a shot.

It would be easy to mistake a stock dove for a feral pigeon and shoot it, but ferals tend to congregate while stock doves are lonesome doves. The fragile, and increasingly rare, turtle dove isn't a bit like any of the legal doves. It has several flashes of black on its neck and the wings are the russet colour more familiar with the kestrel. Never shoot a dove or pigeon unless you are certain it's a legitimate pest species.

If you are lucky enough to live in an area where the red squirrel is breeding, you will need to know how to quickly define the distinct differences between grey and red squirrels. Shoot a few greys and you

*The hare – but airgunners have more pressing vermin to deal with*

will soon realise that at certain times of the season – and at certain ages – they carry a lot of red fur, too. The true British squirrel, the red, is smaller than the grey and has larger, prominent pointed ears. Think 'Tufty'!

When it comes to recognising rabbit from hare, look at the ears in proportion to the head. The rabbit's, like its head, are shorter and more rounded. The hare's ears are long and narrow, with dark tips. Its head is more elongated. If you are staring at a 'bunny' through your scope, but are unsure which of the Lagomorpha genus it falls within, the eyes have it! The charcoal blink of a rabbit is passive and anxious; the wild stare of the hare's brown eye is distinct and the stuff of legends – the witch's eye!

Though some airgunners shoot hares with a sub-12ft/lb rifle, they do so with little respect for its heavier skull. I don't generally

touch them, even with my higher-powered, FAC-rated air rifles. They are innocuous in pest terms, living out their lives in relative solitude, nibbling at crops when they need to, yet without the rabbit's voracious destructiveness. I read Brian Plummer's wonderful tribute to the hare, *Lepus*, when I was in my twenties – and, as a young man who hunted them with lurchers, it completely changed my view of the animal. Written by a true hunter and scripted through the eye of the beast, it is a book I would recommend to anyone who thinks the hare fair game, and wants to understand it more. Now there's another thing – the hare is formally classified under law as game in the UK, so it has seasons in which you are permitted to hunt it... and I wonder how many air rifle hunters know it's still illegal to hunt a hare on Sunday? Personally, I think we have more pressing vermin to deal with than the brown hare.

I've studied wildlife long enough to have a mental encyclopaedia of song, silhouette, gait or flight. It would be impossible for me to get that knowledge onto the written page. I can, though, give a few examples to steer you toward the patterns to look for when you find yourself deep in-country and trying to learn how to distinguish between the shootable and untouchable. Some of this has already been mentioned in the quarry chapters at the beginning of this book, but it's important enough to reiterate here.

The bobbing flight of the jay is most characteristic – a couple of wing beats, then it drops down, flaps again to lift to the flight-line, drops again – and, you'd think is easy to spot. But watch a green woodpecker; it has exactly the same motion in the air, it is of a similar size and in silhouette could be mistaken for a jay. When the jay lands, it usually lands horizontally – beak in line with tail – then sits up. The green woodpecker lands vertically, coming to a sharp stop on the bough, when it hits the brakes, head up. If your jay lands head-up, don't shoot – it's probably a green woodpecker.

A woodpigeon coming in to the wood to perch or roost will circle and clatter in, face to the wind. It will alight on a high bough, or perhaps on an exposed branch some six metres or so up from the floor. The stock dove will flutter in gracefully and low; the wind won't be a factor and it will land either on the ground or within a metre of it. Few woodpigeon would arrive in that manner – so hold your fire.

Song and sound often gives an early indication of quarry presence, approach or state of alert. The air rifle hunter needs to learn these. We all know many of the common ones – the magpie's machine-gun rattle; the jay's shriek; the crow's '*guunn!*' But what of the more uncommon sounds?

The chuckle and gurgle of a happy baby in a buggy? Magpie – incoming and totally relaxed, unaware of your presence. Use the opportunity.

The dull, rhythmic thump amongst the nettle bed? Rabbit – drumming its rear foot, warning the warren of danger. Is it you or a fox it's sensed? Check the breeze.

A shrill scolding in the hedgerow or grass? A weasel or stoat has sensed you. You won't see it now, unless you can squeak it out into the open using a distressed rabbit sound.

The blackbird, rocketing low-level through the wood with a long, jarring alarm call? Human – and probably you! But if the alarm call is distant, you may have human company elsewhere in the wood, so take care with your shooting. Note, though, that the blackbird reserves its '*pip, pip, pip*' call for ground-level threats, like a rat or stoat, and follows the threat, scolding it. Another useful signal for the hunter.

The chatter and hiss of the grey squirrel needs to be learned. The beast will be squatting somewhere nearby, fluffing its tail

in anger. They have an uncanny ability to throw their voice like a ventriloquist. Scour the trees carefully and you may spot the tail flicking, and therefore find your target.

Listen to the murmur of woodpigeons at roost. Tempted though you may be to stalk them, thinking that the sound indicates security and contentment, you couldn't be more wrong. Think about it – can you sing in your sleep? They are inviting company, so will be highly alert. Wait for the sound to stop. That's when the head tucks down and the eyelids droop. Now venture inward, keeping to cover and shadow.

## CROPS, TREES AND SHRUBS

You can't aspire to a PHD in hunting unless you're prepared to get the knowledge. You are a human being endeavouring to compete with quarry in their natural landscape. Unless you get to know that landscape as intimately as them, you will have only mediocre results. Strutting around fields and woods, lofting a rifle randomly at speculative targets, isn't hunting. It's shooting. Therein lies the difference between a shooter and a hunter. A hunter studies the habitat and landscape carefully, observing patterns, change, rhyme and reason for quarry behaviour. A hunter knows how to anticipate opportunity and plan for it, rather than simply chancing on vermin. If this sounds very Zen, then I make no apology. Anyone can call themselves a shooter. You just pick up a rifle and shoot it. But only a qualified few can truly call themselves a hunter. The word itself is a definition of a skill – a person who seeks out and kills or captures game.

Growing crops are often why the landowner gives you, the airgunner, a mandate to shoot vermin species on their estate. Spend some time studying crops. Know how to identify them during the various stages of growth. Understand when the seed is likely to be drilled, which creatures will attack them as

*Looks like carrots this time, gang!*

they ripen and when they will be gathered (for harvest time is a bumper time for vermin control). As the crop develops, its raiders will have burrows, lairs, roosts, dreys and nests close by. Seek them out. You don't have to learn each variety of crop, just their types. Grass crops like wheat, barley, rye or oats, will be plundered both at seed stage and when the ears are ripe by woodpigeons and rooks. Broadleaved crops, such as oilseed rape, pea, cabbage, bean, sugar beet and potato, will come under attack from above and below. Pigeons will raid rape, pea and bean fruits as they ripen. Rabbits will be gnawing at the tubers of beet, carrot, swede and potato. Give a warren of rabbits a crop of cabbage or lettuce nearby and they will be in Nirvana.

Note, though, that unlike rats – who will up sticks and rehome to the hedgerows or pits to follow the grain crops – rabbits never move the warren, despite what you may have read in *Watership Down*. They take pot luck. I can imagine old Bugsy sitting outside his hole, watching the tractor drilling and thinking 'I wonder what's for dinner this spring?'

What shrubs make up the hedgerow? The hedgerows we see now are generally the remnants of the man-made boundaries laid during the land enclosures of the 18th Century. Hawthorn and blackthorn were a choice due to their ability to spread, and their barbed thorns which prevented passage. Both are favourite haunts of magpies and jays, for exactly the same reason. Their density protects both nest and bird. Elderberry, holly and mistletoe, which have seeded and established among the thorny shrubs and trees, will attract woodpigeon – particularly when their fruits are ripe. Mistletoe is especially fascinating as it has no root in the earth. It's a parasitic shrub, its seed often dropped into the split bark of a tree in the faeces of a passing bird, so it often springs up

relatively high in a host tree. Boring? Consider this, then: it can only germinate when both a male and female gamete have been deposited – in order to be fused – together. Look around the wood next time you see mistletoe and marvel at how Mother Nature put those two necessary seeds together. Probably in the pre-packed fertiliser package of a lump of bird squit, which slid conveniently into the open crevice of bark cover on the tree it now covers. The birds that gave it birth now nest in it, roost in it and feed on its fruit. So they will spread the seed again, elsewhere. A cycle that confirms the symbiosis that surrounds Mother Nature.

Learn how to recognise these bushes and their berries. The hedgerow also harbours songbird nests – like those of the blackbird, chaffinch, linnet, dunnock, greenfinch – while its base will hide ground-nesting species such as pheasant, partridge and yellowhammer. See a magpie acting suspiciously around these and you can be judge, jury… and executioner.

Is a tree merely that to you? Just a tree? To the wild creature, the tree can be a complete ecosystem. It may hide it, home it, water it and feed it. The oak tree is a perfect example of this. The grey squirrel will build its drey in the oak's cleft. It will scamper easily up its deep bark when pursued and disappear into a hollow. In summer it will cavort in its lush canopy, and in autumn it will harvest the crop of ripening acorns, eating some and burying others at the oak's base.

The mature beech is a hunter's true friend and worth knowing intimately. Its raised roots hold rainwater like small troughs, which will be visited by squirrels and jays seeking to slake their thirst. In high summer, its broad-leafed canopy gives both shade from a searing sun and shelter, like a huge green umbrella, from the rainstorm. Hazel and beech both produce nuts – squirrel fodder. Jays love lime trees, not for the fruit

*To the wild creature, trees are a complete ecosystem*

so much as the aphids, which gather on the sticky fruit. Magpies and woodpigeon can't resist the fruits of cherry, whitebeam, alder or rowan. Know the tree, know the fruit… know the opportunity.

On a final note, though I love most trees, there's one particular woodland type I absolutely detest – the 'alien' conifer plantation. The regimented rows of commercially-planted conifer trees we so often see are a dark, dense and impenetrable canopy that allows the magpie and jay to nest or the grey squirrel to build a drey with no fear of retribution. I'm convinced that many counties destroyed the native red squirrel population through such commercial planting. Few things but that tick-bearing horror called bracken can grow beneath the permanent shade in loamy soil polluted by a perpetual carpet of rotting, acidic pine needles. I have such 'mirkwoods' near me and you can walk them for an hour or more without hearing a single bird sing. Devilish places – give me the splendour and vibrancy of a deciduous British wood any day. ○

# Chapter 19

# GAINING PERMISSION

## OPENING GATES

One subject that gets would-be airgun hunters emotive – even jealous – is the gaining of land on which to actually hunt. You have spent months on the shooting range, at home or at a club, with your new gun, fine-tuned your visual range-finding, had safety drummed into you by your mentors, can shoot groups the size of a 10p piece. And now you want to test yourself against live quarry… but can't get the opportunity because you can't find a shooting permission. It's a frustrating chicken and egg scenario: how can you prove yourself and build up a reputation if you can't get started in the first place?

Let's get one thing clear from the start. This book is based on the simple principle that no-one 'gets knowledge' unless they are willing to put in the hours to learn. If that applies to hunting quarry, it definitely applies to hunting for land on which to shoot, too. The magic keys that open the door to permission are knowledge, observation and opportunity.

Get these right and you will get permission, eventually.

I get a fair amount of correspondence about the subject from new shooters. People email me and beg for a share of my permissions. I have to remind them that it's not my land to give away. They ask if they can accompany me, to get experience. Trust me, I've tried that and regretted it on my permitted shooting land – so I now have a golden rule: I'll help anyone near enough to where I live on *their* permission, when they get it. Honestly, this process is part of being a hunter. If you can't hunt down the land, you can't hunt down its quarry – but here are a few tips to help you on the way.

If (like me) you live on a sururban estate, imagine a couple of kids from down the road knocking your door and asking if they can use your treasured back-garden as their football pitch. No chance! So put yourself in a farmer's boots when a complete stranger knocks the door and tells you he's got a gun and wants to

*When it comes to permission, the best opportunities come through observation and intelligence*

shoot things on your land, your back-garden. Deploy this approach and you may just get lucky, but if the farmer says no, you won't be getting a second chance.

So I'd always advocate a more sensible, and subtle, approach. Farmers and landowners are busy folk. Around me in Norfolk, where agriculture is a prime industry, my farmers are masters of many arts. If you think a farmer is someone who sits behind the wheel of a tractor all day, you need to do some serious homework before knocking that door of his. My farmer friends (for that's what they've become) make some of the managers and directors I work with in my day-job look like amateurs. They are cute businessmen and women. They are entrepeneurs, employers, strategic analysts, investors, even speculators – and they work 24/7. When they've shaken off their muddy boots and spent a couple of hours on a PC looking at the latest trading prices before placing a harvest at market; when they've just run the payroll for their farmhands; when they've just seen an up-to-date drought forecast; when they've just been told by the vet that their sheep flock has blue-tongue, the last thing they need is someone knocking the door asking if he can cull a few rabbits! Respect that. Get to know what farming (or game rearing) is about before attempting to get permission. Get knowledge, because when you do strike lucky, you're likely to be tested. Which is why, in this book, you must not pass over the previous chapter on crops, trees, flowers and shrubs; these are all part of the apprenticeship.

The late, great John Darling advised the subtle approach in his book *Air Rifle Hunting*. He, as I have, recognised that often the best opportunities come through observation and intelligence. Seeing or hearing that a landowner has a 'problem' makes it easy to offer help rather than a blind, speculative approach. Drive the lanes and watch the crops and fields. Spot the rabbit pressure on a new

crop or the woodpigeons flocking onto new seed. Stop and talk to farmhands and offer a business card. Don't ask for permission to shoot – ask if you can be of help! And to raise their eyebrows, tell them it will cost nothing.

Having said all the above, priming the local area with a simple business card (through the letter box) is a good tactic, but I would only advocate doing that once you have your first permission and some experience under your belt.

So, you've leaned over a fence and talked to a farmhand about that scourged patch of sugar beet. He's passed your name to his boss… who then calls you up and invites you to go and meet him. You've made it through to the interview stage – but how, exactly, do you prepare? Ask if he wants to see your gun on the day; don't take it otherwise and dress smartly. First impressions count. ○

## MEETING A LANDOWNER

Don't dress in that dreary 'I'm an airgunner and proud of it' DPM camouflage. Don't wear any camouflage. The landowner will categorise you. If you've taken my advice and know the farming community, you'll just wear simple, casual clothing. The footie top won't impress – and don't politicise, either. Leave your old 'Ban The Hunting Act' T-shirts back at home – they're about as relevant now as my old Sex Pistols T-shirts! Be conservative, with a small 'c'.

Show your insurance document. Gently insist on a safety tour of the land to establish boundaries, public footpaths and such like – it will set you up as a responsible shooter. Ask for a look around the farmyard, if that's included in the permission. What days are worked there? Does your farmer have children, cats, dogs? What vermin species are allowed – a very important question as many farmers like jackdaws, rooks and hares and would rather they weren't controlled at random. Find out permitted times of access. Contact numbers. Parking arrangements. Does the farmer want a rabbit, pigeon or two? All these aren't just simple etiquette, they're important to your landowner, for safety and for your retention of the permission.

If you've been told to bring your gun, it's probably for a reason – so be prepared for a target test to prove your accuracy. If that worries you, you're not ready to ask for permission yet.

*A professional-looking business card can open gates to permission*

# Chapter 20

# SHOOTING CRAFT

## AROUND THE FARMYARD

Military and security forces aside, there are very few individuals in the British Isles who are allowed to wander around an area, inhabited by humans, carrying an armed rifle. Sporting shooters often enjoy that privilege, though – so they need to know how to exercise that freedom with nothing less than exemplary behaviour. The difference between you and your government colleagues is that you will hope to shoot your gun, and often. The airgun hunter, with even his comparatively feeble rifle, has the same duty of care to ensure he is in total control of his actions. When I refer to the farmyard, I also mean around any human habitation – the factory where you may be culling feral pigeons; the stately home where you've been asked to clear the jackdaws from the chimneys; the urban garden when you've been asked to remove the rats around the poultry pen; the golf greens plagued with rabbit incursion; the riding school where coneys are digging fetlock-snapping holes. All of these places demand extra vigilance and care when using an air rifle.

None of this makes shooting a chore, though – nor should it worry an accurate and competent shooter. In places like this, the airgun hunter can really make a mark simply because they can complete their task discreetly, with no disruption to daily activities if they're experienced enough.

Working in these environments simply means weighing up the potential danger posed by a shot, rather than simply executing the shot. This soon becomes second nature; I would describe this as mental risk assessment on the move. You will learn to listen for signals that could indicate the shooting either needs to be done cautiously, or stopped altogether. The sound of an approaching motor; the tractor firing up; children laughing. Horses neighing can mean they're being approached by a human. Cattle are clock-watch feeders, just like dogs, so when you hear them bellowing

in the sheds, it's because their body clock is demanding food. That may mean a farmhand will appear any time soon.

Think of your own personal safety, too. Farmyards can be hazardous places. Don't get in amongst heavy stock like bullocks unless you know what you're doing – and certainly don't fire a gun from in their midst. Even a silent air rifle can panic stock and cause a stampede – as can a dead feral clattering down from the rafters. One of my favourite sniping points for ferals is sitting up among the warm hay bales. Make sure the stack is solid and balanced. If you topple off, you're not only likely to harm yourself – but it won't do your rifle a lot of good either! Watch where you're walking; there will be sharp machinery tines, barbed wire, cattle slurry, engine oil and a myriad other 'slip, trip or fall' hazards.

In and around any buildings, always be conscious of when it's time to make your presence known and stash your rifle. If you're interrupted, disarm your gun and lay it aside. Go and meet the interloper – try not to surprise them – and explain who you are, what you're doing and who gave you permission to be there. If it's apparent that they need to be around for some time, politely leave – you'll have plenty of other opportunities to shoot. I often have to do this – when equestrians decide to muck-out the stables; when the stockhand needs to feed the herd or, perhaps, when the service engineer turns up to fix a broken tractor.

Farms and buildings are hardy places and, technically, there isn't much that can be damaged by a soft, lead airgun pellet designed to flatten when it meets maximum resistance. Nevertheless, your host doesn't expect damage to property or harm to stock. Glass is an obvious weak point, which could embarrass you if you're not careful. So are plastic corrugated roofs and plasterboard partitions. Beware of ricochets and their consequences, both to you and to farm animals. I'll hold my

*Note the rat-bait box behind me – not a place for an inquisitive dog*

hand up to the former – I once tried to shoot between the bars of a steel cattle gate just two yards away to hit a magpie feeding on spilled grain and the pellet hit the gate and whizzed straight back, glancing off my cheekbone, a centimetre below my left eye. Thankfully it had lost most of its momentum. Always try to ease your rifle muzzle past any obstacle before taking the shot. If you can't, leave the shot. With regard to damage, if you do make a mistake, report it and offer to pay for it. Better that than a phone call from your landowner telling you that you're not welcome anymore.

Personally, I never take my lurcher into the farmyard, nor any other inhabited shooting area. His mere presence will unsettle stock, as well trained as he is. There's also the risk of an encounter with the farm dogs or cats. There is another, more prudent reason, too. Most of my farmers use rat poison in abundance to protect their fodder and grain – and it just isn't worth the risk of my dog getting a little too curious.

## RANGE-FINDING

Mastering shooting accuracy is soon achievable on a range or using static targets. Air rifles are generally reliable tools once you've learned a bit about power curves (in the case of a PCP) and trajectory. The situation radically changes, however, when you take your gun out into the fields or woods to shoot live quarry. All of a sudden, the comfort factor of knowing the distance-to-target you enjoyed at the club range or your back-garden has evaporated. You will find yourself having to make snap judgements of range, under the added pressure of having limited time to do so, else your quarry will be long gone.

Here are a few techniques I use to either fine-tune this black art, or at least make the process easier. The first is a simple, passive technique which you can do without a gun in your hands – therefore anywhere, anytime. I owe this one to Dylan, my lurcher. In the depths of winter, when I can't get out in the fields after work, he still needs to be exercised – but a walk around the block with a leashed dog is terminally boring for me, so I've invented a game which adds some spice for him… and improves my shooting to boot. It's the lamp-post game – though for lamp-post, read any inanimate object. As the dog does that regular dog thing and cocks his leg, I look forward and pick out a small landmark or object, make a snap judgement as to how many paces away it is… and then stride toward it to check my accuracy. Over the years, I've got this judgement down to within a pace at 40 paces. Light conditions affect vision and judgement, so I practise this in all weathers – mist, strong sunlight, night-time. It's simple brain-training for the shooter, without firing a shot.

Out in the fields and woods, I use several tricks to keep spatial awareness – distance consciousness – refined. Stalking through woodland can be the most difficult. Rows of tree trunks can cause a sense of optical illusion and make distance judgement difficult as your brain tries to adjust its sensory focus. This is the time to use the mental ruler technique. By way of regime, I practise this every few months by placing a couple of objects on the deck

and pacing out 10 yards (my pace is about a yard) between them. They could be a couple of fir cones or broken twigs. After pacing, I then just squat, look back to the first and map the distance in my mind. Then I pick out a further, random subject (like a tree stump or a nettle stand) and then, in my mind, I roll out the 10-pace ruler, mentally 'turning it over' to meet the subject. One full turn would be 20 paces; an additional half turn would make 25 paces… and so on. Having mentally mapped it, I then pace to the target to see how close to the actual range I'd guessed. The floor of the wood or meadow is pretty horizontal and so easier for the brain to measure than the vertical confusion of a stand of trees. Try it – this mental ruler technique really does work.

For ambushing a rabbit warren along a field's edge, there's another, fairly simple technique to employ without pacing out the distance – which, of course, would disturb the rabbits below ground. Use the fence-line itself. Farmers rarely deploy their fence posts randomly – they will be regimented, pushed into the ground at measured intervals of, say, three or five yards. These are an obvious visual

*The mental ruler – a useful range-finding technique that really works*

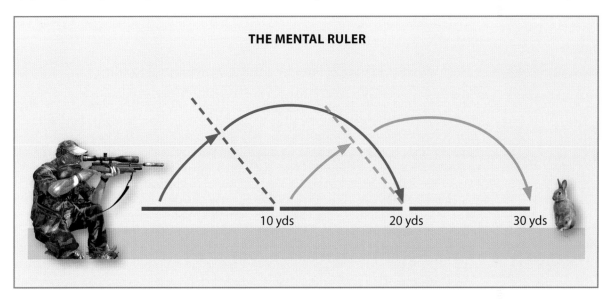

**THE MENTAL RULER**

10 yds    20 yds    30 yds

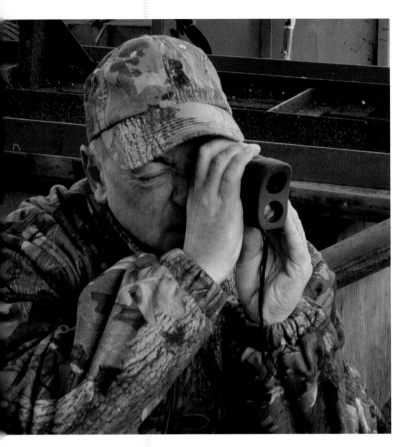

*A digital rangefinder is a useful piece of kit – but it's not for snap decisions*

the device to measure – superbly accurately, I must say – the distance to a shrub, a tussock or a stand of ragwort outside the buries. That's all I need. The device goes away, and when the rabbits emerge, I have natural distance markers mapped in my head. That one by the ragwort? Eighteen yards. The buck browsing by the tussock? That's a 27-yarder.

I will reiterate, though, that for the walk-about air rifle hunter, nothing beats the ability to lock onto the distance to your quarry using your own, practised eye.

## CALLS AND LURES

Almost any creature can be stopped in its tracks or turned in its flight with the right sound. I carry a selection of calls and lures in my shooting bag and there's one permanently attached to my car keys, which are always in my pocket.

The Faulhaber rattle is a small, sealed drum filled with balls which, when shaken, does a pretty good job of imitating the magpie's vocal 'rattle' – though skilled fieldsmen can create the same effect with a matchbox and a few pellets. The rattle is a useful lure when you can hear maggies close by, but can't see them. They're very territorial, so on hearing a strange rival on their patch, magpies will usually want to investigate. Four or five shakes, every fifteen seconds or so, is enough. Don't overdo it – or you'll be sussed and scare the birds away.

My jay call is a small, alloy sealed trumpet with a diaphragm inside. When blown, it makes a rasping noise like an irate jay. Again a useful lure, but it's a shame that it isn't made in a darker colour. That silver cone sparkles too much and is easily spotted.

My Acme crow call is a slender black trumpet with a reed inside its split stem. Practise with this (including cupping your hands over the end) and you can learn to imitate most of the black corvids – jackdaw, carrion crow and rook. This call is most

aid to quarry distance. You note the posts are every five yards, and the rabbit is five sets of posts away from the one you're sat against. So… a 25-yard shot. Easy.

This idea can be applied to a lot of agricultural scenarios, actually. Maize stalks are often equidistant due to modern machinery. The plough furrows are set apart equally. Anywhere there is a pattern on the farm or in the plantation, there's the capacity to quickly judge range with assured accuracy.

I now often use a digital rangefinder. I used to scoff at these hi-tech devices until I tried one. As a hunter, there is no way I'm going to drag a monocular device from my pocket to check distance to my target before every shot – but it can be used as a preliminary shooting aid. To ambush a warren, for instance. I will use effective when you croak like mad, loudly, to pull-in distant crows or passing flocks.

By far the best artificial call I carry is the Foxcaller on my key ring. So good, I have two others – one in my bag and another in my camera bag. Probably the best £10 the airgun hunter could ever spend – but why? Airgunners don't shoot foxes, right?

The Foxcaller is a slim, plastic call based on that old grass-blade-between-your-thumbs principle we all tried as kids. Twin plastic plates sandwich a metal reed, with plastic screws at both ends. When these are tightened, the high pitched squeal produced when you blow through it sounds like a mouse or a distressed rabbit. This will call in stoats or weasels, as well as foxes. This sound will also pull in opportunistic predators, such as carrion crows and magpies. If you loosen the end screws a tad, you can produce harsher sounds – such as the jay's shriek or an owl's screech. I can call buzzards on the wing down close to me, perfectly imitating their mewing. On a recent family holiday in Devon, we sat by the glowing embers of a barbecue one evening and (imitating the kee-wick of a female tawny owl), we all sat listening to four or five male tawnies drawn close to us in the woods. We responded to every call with their hoots – and it was music to my ears.

Perhaps the most effective call you'll ever own costs nothing, and is always at hand when you need it – your own mouth. You just need to spend time practising how to imitate animals and birds. Out in the wood or field, you don't have to worry about how foolish you feel trying this (and you will!). Get it right, though, and it will pay huge dividends. I've never found a squirrel call more effective than my own chatter and hiss – and I can gurgle and chuckle with the best of magpies. But the one art I've never mastered, despite my father-in-law being an expert, is the distressed rabbit squeal made by sucking on the back of your hand.

*Left to right: magpie rattle, jay call, Foxcaller and crow call*

## HYGIENE CONSIDERATIONS

Those who have followed the hundreds of magazine articles I've had published will know that I'm a stickler for hygiene when handling dead quarry. Photographs of me gutting rabbits in surgical gloves have brought their fair share of derisory comments, most particularly on web forums which are generally populated by hardcore hunters (or so they'd have you believe!) and 'flamers' who just like to criticise anyone and everyone. I avoid such sites now as although there are some genuine hunters on these forums, the majority are armchair experts – and people who spend all their spare time at the keyboard of a PC can't be spending much time out in the field!

Back to the gloves. Consider the reasons for many species being on the General Licences, or enjoying exemptions under the Wildlife Acts. Let's work through a few obvious ones first, then tackle some less obvious reasons for my caution. No-one in their right mind would handle rats without taking precautions against Weil's Disease (*Leptospirosis*). This debilitating disease, caught from the bacteria swimming in nearly all rats' blood and urine, can be a killer. Even hardcore rat hunters pay respect to this and handle dead rats

*Picking up – but not just a pigeon; this bird could be carrying psittacosis or campylobacter*

survive in water sources – are all bacteria the airgun hunter could potentially be handling every time they pick up a dead bird. Does that worry you? It should – unless, like me, you instil some simple hygiene discipline into your hunting.

And what about passive mammals, like the rabbit or the grey squirrel? It's in gutting-out coneys with gloves on where I have been subjected to ridicule – yet what if I told you I've had a nasty bout of septicaemia (blood poisoning) through handling rabbits? Not a dead one, admittedly, but I thought it was dead when I dragged it from hole into which it had jinked after the shot. As I dragged it out, the two rear paws went off like a chainsaw and left me with a deep laceration in my knuckle. I despatched the rabbit manually and went about my day. A few days later, I was almost a hospital case.

What if I told you that a young man in the next county to me tragically died around the same time after handling a dead rabbit? He contracted septicaemia, too, from the bacteria *Pasteurella multocida* (a bacterium in rabbit flu). I didn't find either incident amusing. Indeed, I count myself very lucky that I was put on antibiotics immediately I felt unwell.

What if I told you that rabbits are a primary host for the tapeworm in its extraordinary life cycle? The tapeworm grows in a predominantly carnivorous host, such as a fox... or us. The fox will defecate and shed the worm's eggs onto vegetation or pasture. The eggs are eaten by browsing vegetarian mammals, such as rabbit or sheep. The eggs lie dormant until the nursery host (our rabbit) is eaten by a carnivore (fox... or man!). Then the egg hatches and the tapeworm grows inside the secondary host's gut. The hunter can avoid being part of this cycle by making sure he doesn't come into contact with those eggs which, if unnoticed, are destroyed in the cooking process. To expand on this a little, a strange story:

with gloves, shovels or litter-pickers. No argument. (No loss of kudos.)

One of the conditions of the General Licences when it comes to shooting birds is that they are shot 'to preserve public health or safety'. There's good reason for that statement. Putting aside bird flu – possibly a pandemic waiting to happen in Britain – wild birds by the very nature of their activity carry all manner of disease. Woodpigeons, collared doves and feral pigeons can carry a variety of health-threatening or lethal bacteria in their faeces. These can be left on grain and crops intended for human consumption. Some of these bacteria can be simply inhaled from dried faeces by farm workers or factory food-processing staff. *Psittacosis, E. coli, Salmonella, Campylobacter* – the latter two can even

I once had a shot rabbit laid close to me while I was ambushing more along a warren. After 10 minutes, the rabbit's gut was wriggling. I'm used to that with pregnant does – but this was a buck! I tried the blink test – running a twig over the rabbit's eyeball – but there was no flinch. Dead. As it was already getting cool and stiff, which confused me, I gutted the rabbit and it looked as though its intestines were outside the paunch. They were pumping, alive. Curiosity got the better of me and I used my knife to unravel the mystery – a 45cm tapeworm coiled between fur and paunch; it must have been wrapped around the rabbit three times! Extracting it with a couple of twigs, I laid it out on the grass, watching it writhe. A pale, blind and repulsive parasite, I took a poor photograph with my then-cheap camera as I was puzzled. The worm had skipped a cycle... unless the shot rabbit was a carnivore. It taught me, there and then, to have a lot more respect for the tapeworm threat. I wouldn't fancy one of them inside me, for sure.

Anyone want to buy some gloves yet? If that hasn't convinced you, be aware that a strain of cestode (tapeworm) predominantly carried by foxes or dogs, called *Echinococcus multilocularis*, is spreading fast in Northern Europe and is threatening to cross the Channel to the British Isles. If it does, you will certainly want to check your rabbits carefully. Small mammals are the intermediary host... and the disease it carries has a 90 per cent mortality rate in humans!

I've fallen foul of squirrels, too. I rely on glasses or contact lenses for 20/20 vision these days (I prefer contacts to hunt in as specs tend to mist up in the cold or have to be continually wiped during rain). As an infrequent lens wearer, my eyes tend to become dry and itchy when out hunting for a while, so I rub them. One winter, though, a few years back, I kept getting bouts of conjunctivitis after visiting the Old Hall wearing contact lenses. My purpose for being there is purely to control squirrels and, upon visiting my doctor – who knows I hunt – about the eye problem, he joked that I'd probably got myxomatosis! The penny dropped. As I don't eat greys, I don't gut them... so I don't wear gloves handling them. I was rubbing my dry eyes constantly. Squirrel pox? Who knows? But as soon as I started to use a small bottle of dry anti-bacterial gel to cleanse my hands every time I'd handled a squirrel, the eye problem disappeared. Coincidence? Maybe? Or maybe not...

Another hygiene consideration as a hunter of small vermin, is responsible disposal of dead quarry. Your farmer or landowner will be highly grateful at your despatch of rats, feral pigeons and other species, but that gratitude will turn to anger and loss of your shooting permission if you leave these infested carcases sitting on top of the grain pile or amongst the animal feed. For example, Leptospirosis is a common cause of infertility and premature birth in cattle. Make sure you clear up after

*Using gloves to check for tapeworm egg cysts beneath a rabbit's fur*

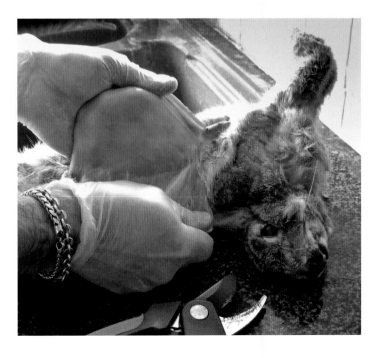

*The tiny sheep or deer tick – some can infect you with Lyme disease*

your shooting. In open country or woodland (if your dead quarry isn't edible), hide the corpses discreetly. Not only can they upset other passers-by, but they can be dragged home by the farm mouser or the cattle dog. Left hidden in a ditch, nature's overnight cleansing team – aka the fox and badger – will soon nose them out and clear away the evidence.

Finally, ticks. Commonly known as the sheep tick (*ixodes ricinus*), this is a misnomer as they will lodge in the fur of or feather of any warm-blooded creature. In summer and autumn, the sheep pastures and deer coverts are alive with these tiny, spider-like chiggers. They're carried on a host, brushed off on foliage… where they cling on and wait for their next host – the passing bird, beast or human. As soon as they find a host, they will instinctively crawl for a nice, warm and moist spot (armpits and groins are perfect on humans) where they will bore into the skin to find their favourite food, blood. As an airgun hunter, you will regularly invite their attention as you crawl over grass and squat in the cover of shrubbery. Trust me, they'll find you eventually – and I've certainly had my fair share.

But now the frightening bit: some (not all) ticks carry deadly *spirochete* bacteria (specifically *borrelia burgdorferi*) in their saliva which, when transferred to your blood stream, can cause Lyme disease. This slowly developing and debilitating condition is often referred to as the 'mimicking disease' as its symptoms mirror many other conditions (arthiritis, meningitis, palsies, glandular fever). As such, many doctors fail to recognise the cause as Lyme disease and misdiagnose. Another sinister factor is that if you've failed to recognise that you've been drilled by a tick, the borrelia bacteria can lie dormant for months or years before these symptoms kick in. By which time treatment becomes very complex – so if you know you have been bitten by a tick, seek medical help immediately. Preventative antibiotics could save a lot of grief later. Prevention is better than cure, too. After hunting, you should shower and take some time to check yourself thoroughly. It soon becomes a natural part of the post-hunt ritual.

None of the above should scare or deter the air rifle hunter, though, if you understand the importance of in-the-field hygiene (and accept it's necessary, rather than taking the Michael). The biggest health threat you face when out in the field is yourself – in the safe handling of your gun. ◯

# THE NEXT GENERATION

## PASSING IT ON

There is no better way to illustrate my thoughts on introducing youth to shooting than to repeat a story previously published in *Airgun Shooter* magazine. When I was a youth, I was so desperate to own an air rifle that I resorted to all sorts of illicit and secretive means to deceive my parents. Some worked, some failed miserably – with the inevitable consequences. You can't push a youngster to follow your path in any sport or pastime; they need to *want* to follow you. It's even worse for a youngster if you're held up as 'expert' in your field. The following story, I hope, reflects that. Often, motivation is better served with subtle psychology and encouragement – but definitely not criticism, nor misplaced expectation.

I can't praise enough the work done by the BASC, ATEO (Airgun Training and Education Organisation), the organisation Pass It On, and the plethora of club members up and down the country who devote time to training our country's young airgunners. They must have the patience of Job. What they can rarely teach on a practical (hands-on) basis, though, is fieldcraft. That's firmly down to hunters to pass on, with our offspring at our sides. That's no easy task unless those youngsters want to learn. The following account of a trip out with my own lad, Sam, probably just demonstrates my own frustration – but I include it in this book as it may amuse those of you who have tried to teach fieldcraft. (Forgive me, Sam!)

## THE SORCERER'S APPRENTICE

When it finally appeared, it stumbled down the stairs, still wiping sleep from its eyes. It wore grey trainer socks, camo trousers and a dazzling white long-sleeved T-shirt. The

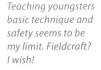

*Teaching youngsters basic technique and safety seems to be my limit. Fieldcraft? I wish!*

Sorcerer had been pacing around since 6am and had considered throwing a bucket of cold water over it, or leaving without it – but a promise is a promise, and the Sorcerer had waited for it to emerge in its own time.

"Hell, Sam! Since when did we go hunting in skateboard gear? Get that b****y T-shirt off and find some proper socks! Quickly – I've been waiting half the day already!"

Sam, my (then) 14-year-old, reappeared in a black T-shirt and, contrary to the story so far, he'd actually been begging me to take him shooting. As he helped load up the Jeep, he enquired where we were going, and what we'd be after. At least it was the right question – I'd have winced if he'd asked how long we were going to be!

At the farm, I set up the .177 calibre Webley-Venom Sidewinder for Sam. Its 25-yard zero was spot-on and after a quick lecture to remind him of the golden safety rules, he was plinking away at the metal targets I'd set at 20, 25 and 30 yards with this sub-12ft/lb precharged pneumatic. Soon, the Sidewinder was out of air, so getting out the FX pump, I challenged the vigour of youth to fill its own gun.

After a few downward strokes, the fill valve started to hiss, leaking air. "Pump faster!" I instructed Sam – the O-rings needed to swell and seal.

"It's lifting me up, Dad!" exclaimed Sam, his chest trying to hold down the pump.

Laughing at him, I took over – but after a few strokes, I could feel the pump pushing back at me. I took a deep breath and wellied it – and 15 long, deep strokes later, the valve finally broke open and we were in business. I kept going, finally collapsing in a heap on the turf, wondering how long it would take the paramedics to bring me oxygen, but smug in the knowledge my lad would be impressed by the feat. How wrong was I?

"Dad, let's bring the air bottle next time. It'll be easier for you!"

Then it was time to do something that I *am* good at – hunting. We packed up the targets and I set another safety rule for Sam: "Don't you dare let that damn gun run out of air!" I asked Sam if he had preference.

"Pigeons," he declared. "Can we set up some decoys?"

We drove out to a wood's edge, under a regular woodpigeon flightline, and Sam helped to put up the shooting blind and lay out the decoys. I showed him how to set a horseshoe pattern with an area for birds to land or fly through. He also set up a flocked crow deek to add some 'security' to the scene – pigeons often feel safe if they see a wily crow feeding near them.

We settled down behind the net to wait. After 10 minutes of silent fidgeting, Sam asked: "Why haven't any pigeons landed?" I encouraged him to be patient; the flocks must still be feeding somewhere else.

"Dad, I'm hungry," came a plea shortly thereafter – so out came the ham rolls and a drink. The rifles were laid aside, disarmed, and while we ate, a squadron of grey flashed from the wood behind us, circled once and dropped among the decoys.

"Woodies, Dad. Let's shoot them!"

"Go on, then," I gesticulated.

Sam rushed to load a magazine, push the muzzle through the netting and cock the Webley.

"Where are they?" he enquired, searching through the scope.

"They took off before your eye even reached the scope," I explained. "You need to be set up, ready, in order to bag landing pigeons."

Sam couldn't understand how they could see us through the net and I told him they couldn't. "The second you pushed that muzzle through the net and made it flutter, they sensed danger."

Fifteen, uneventful minutes later and Sam declared he was bored with pigeon shooting, so I suggested we stalk along the edge of a nearby warren. Putting Sam two paces behind me – safety on, muzzle down – off we went, me walking like a prowling cat and Sam shuffling his size tens like a cross-country skier...

Up the line, among the nettles, I saw a pair of flickering ear tips and held up my hand to halt Sam. He kept shuffling until he was alongside me. He saw the flash of tawny fur part the nettles and disappear under the fence.

"What was that?" he enquired.

"That, dear boy, *was* a rabbit." There was emphasis on the 'was', and despair in my voice.

"You stalk forward," I suggested, which roughly translated meant now find your own flipping rabbit! Sam set off and I stayed way behind him. I wasn't watching a stalk – I was watching an American GI on 'point patrol' in Vietnam. I half expected him to lean the barrel over his shoulder, pull a smoke from his pocket and light up. He turned to me.

"Naaah, nothing here, Dad." I watched two young coneys creep under the barbed wire

behind him, but I didn't let on, though. It would have been cruel to tell him.

Next we drove over to a copse with a good squirrel population. Sam enjoyed this 'jungle patrol' much more as we silently slipped from tree to tree, communicating only with hand-signals. I was impressed when Sam tracked a grey through the treetops and 'stayed' his shot when the squirrel failed to stop long enough. It showed an increasing level of respect and maturity, and he was duly praised.

But I had so desperately wanted Sam to bag something; this was *his* day. So I deliberately missed two low-level squirrels which he'd offered to me.

"Not like you to miss a couple of sitters, Dad." I, of course agreed and suggested we both needed more practice by saying: "How about going out again next week, then?"

"Yeah, Dad, that'll be cool. I enjoyed today."

The Sorcerer smiled to himself. Sometimes the black arts need to attempted and desperately sought – not demonstrated – to be appreciated. ○

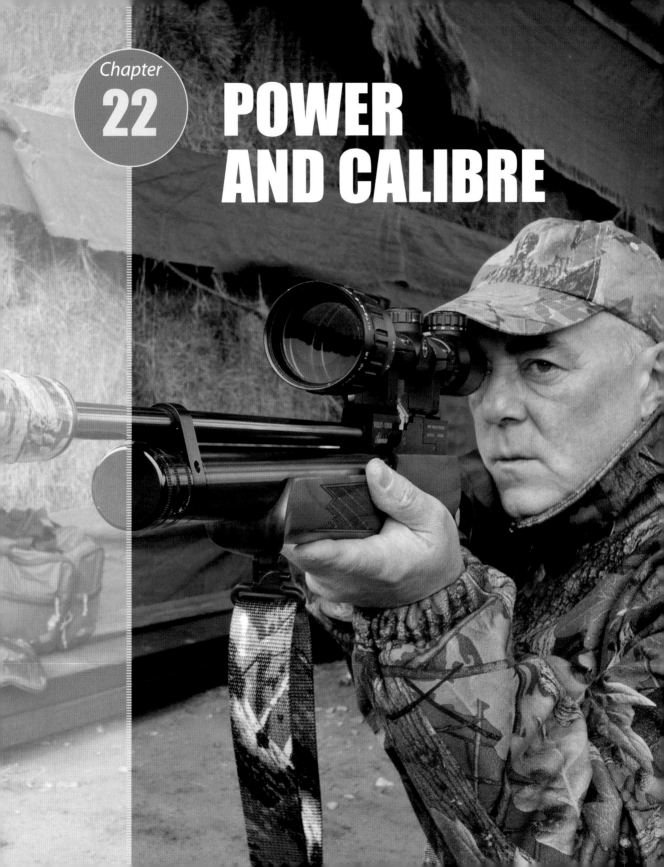

# POWER
# AND CALIBRE

## UPPING THE POWER

At the outset, I said this book was written for the workaday, sub-12 ft/lb airgunner. And it certainly is. Yet the newcomer to airgun hunting will be tempted, as we all are, to seek to bridge the gap between the legal limit air rifle and the rimfire rifle. The solution, they will think, is the FAC-rated air rifle (FAC meaning firearms certificate). Under current British law, to own an air rifle with a power rating exceeding 12 ft/lb requires a licence from your local police authority authorising its use. To gain one (as with the shotgun), you need to satisfy the police that you are a fit and proper person to possess a firearm. You need permission on land considered (sometimes inspected as) suitable for firearms' use. You need references (from persons of good repute) as to your good reputation and your sound health and mind. As part of the application process (and at anytime thereafter, randomly), you will be visited by an FEO (firearms enquiry officer) to establish that you meet the licence conditions, the main ones being purpose of ownership (pest control), possession of a gunsafe to secure the gun(s) and certifiable land/permission. All of this is a healthy and useful process in my opinion. Even if you don't have any intention of owning an FAC rifle, I will repeat something written earlier in this book: I would always advocate a gunsafe in your house, even for sub-12 ft/lb airguns. Children are eternally curious and masters of deception. I was, you probably were… and it's highly likely your children will be. Lock your guns away and eliminate the risk.

The FEO will want to know what gun you are considering. It will have to be nominated on your licence. Model doesn't matter. Sound moderators (silencers) need to be added, too, or you can't add one to your rifle without breaching the licence. Each gun is registered retrospectively, and individually, on an FAC by the RFD (Registered Firearm Dealer) and by you (sending details to the licensing constabulary). If you have a good FEO and a reliable RFD, you won't encounter many problems.

So, given I make it sound so easy to own an FAC-rated air rifle, why do I rarely use one? If you've read the greater part of this book and haven't simply jumped to this chapter, you'll realise by now that it's the hunt – not the execution – that floats my boat. There are some creatures that demand distant approach (due to their furtiveness) or high-power ballistics (due to their size). Deer and fox illustrate that need. Potting rabbits at 150 yards with a .22 rimfire rifle is pest control, not hunting. Nothing wrong with that. Knocking down a crow at 100 yards with a .17HMR is the same. Me? I like to 'hunt', which means getting up close and personal. Some people do the quick crossword in their newspaper; I always tackle the cryptic one. Some folk eat ready meals; I cook from scratch. Some hunters drive right up to the wood; I walk up (where I can). Some hunters want a gun to cut the distance; I want the challenge of cutting that distance so I can look my quarry in the eye.

Then… why do I *own* an FAC air rifle? Because, sometimes, I need to use the quick and easy option to satisfy my landowner. High-powered, FAC-rated air rifles certainly have their place in any hunter's gun cabinet – but they will never give a true hunter the enjoyment or the versatility of the legal limit rifle. The additional safety considerations make it a totally different animal. It's almost unusable around the farmyard or in buildings. Backstops need very careful consideration as the pellet will carry further. They're air-gobblers, too, at least in PCP format. That's alright if you carry a diver's scuba tank or manual pump around, but if you intend to spend all day in the field (as I often do), that means frequent trips back to the motor if you're having a busy day.

My current FAC rifle is exceptional. Custom-engineered from a little-used .177

calibre Webley-Venom Sidewinder precharged pneumatic that I'd bought for my son to use. Its relative redundancy and Sam's growth means that he can share my Weihrauchs with ease nowadays, so I had it converted to a shorter, carbine model and swapped its barrel for a .22. The gun was then specced at just 20 ft/lb so that noise was minimsed (and the shots-per-charge count kept reasonable). With the superb Weihrauch silencer added, it is the quietest FAC gun I have ever owned. The sacrifice paid for chopping the barrel was reduced air economy and it will fire about 40 shots on a full 200BAR charge. In reality, to hit the sweet spot on the power curve, that's really 25 usable shots. Using 16-grain Air Arms Field Diabolo pellets, it's incredibly accurate out to 50 or 60 metres. Almost the perfect air rifle if you ignore the air economy.

So, again, why do I use it so rarely? The answer is simple – over-penetration. Unlike the shotgunner, we air rifle hunters rely on placing a single pellet with high accuracy into a point on our quarry's anatomy that will bring about a clean despatch. It doesn't matter whether that's the brain or the heart and lung area. If that pellet transfers its ballistic shock to the right area, it will kill clinically. It will shut down the nervous system or stop the creature's heart. The FAC rifle allows you to do that at longer distances and performs excellently at 40 or 50 metres.

Most of my shots, however, are taken within 15 to 30 metres of my quarry. At these close ranges, I've found the pellet often passes right through a creature, even head shots, with an inevitable result. The failure to transfer shocking power – but to obviously severely maim a creature – means death only after prolonged pain. That is totally unacceptable to my hunting ethics and the anti-thesis of the hunting creed. Which means that although I do, occasionally, employ the FAC rifle, it's only where I've tried and failed to get within range with a sub-12 ft/lb air rifle. Generally, that

*High power is useful for long distance sniping*

will be hunting crows near pheasant release pens, or rabbits in open warrens, where both species are making a nuisance of themselves far from my nearest available cover. In other words, my FAC rifle is a cop-out, used only when my skills as a hunter are totally foiled and my landowner insists on a result.

## THE CALIBRE QUESTION

Oh hell! Dare I go here? What is the best calibre to use for quarry hunting? This debate rages around the airgun fraternity ad infinitum. Have you ever sat an exam or test and you are warned at the beginning that there's no right or wrong answer? Well, it's the same when it comes to the question of pellet calibre.

I, personally, always shoot quarry with the .22 calibre. Yes, I've tried other calibres – but I will always continue to shoot quarry with this calibre. So if you're wondering why – and I'm not open to dialogue on this, from anyone, because it bores me – these are my reasons for not wanting to partake in the .22 versus .177 calibre debate… and for flying the .22 flag.

There is less chance of 'right-through-your-

*Loading pellets into a magazine on a freezing winter's day – .22... every time!*

quarry' penetration. Known as overkill, it's a situation which often leaves quarry injured, not cleanly despatched. Especially at close ranges.

Larger surface area means less penetration, means more ballistic shock to the kill zone. Ballistic shock excels over absolute accuracy, and no true walkabout hunter can guarantee the latter. Unless they are a liar, that is, or prepared to walk past quarry that the farmer expects them to remove.

I know my trajectories intimately enough not to need the flatter trajectory boasted by the .177, the usual benefit put forward for exponents the smaller calibre. Learn how to shoot your one gun/pellet/scope combo... and trajectory is never a problem. If you're an air rifle user, with the objective of trying to make the shot as simple as possible, then you're not really an air rifle hunter. Go buy a .17 HMR rimfire, a firearm, then report back how much permission you get? The shooting will be easy – but don't expect much permission to shoot over.

The .22 pellet is easier to load in extreme conditions. I shoot all year round, and at night. Fumbling around, reloading a magazine with even tinier pellets, in freezing conditions or while lamping, isn't efficient or fun for me.

Air economy is better with .22 pellets. More shots per air charge in a PCP air rifle means longer in the field. Logic may tell you it's the other way round, but it isn't – the .177 is less efficient. Guns are designed to release more air behind the smaller, lighter pellet to ensure it reaches its target. If you shoot a springer, it'll be more effort to cock, and the heavier spring will give you more recoil to control than a .22 of equivalent power.

Ergo .22. I rest my case. ◯

# Chapter 23

# THE AIRGUN HUNTER'S DOG

## THE HOUND

I use the masculine gender throughout this chapter with no intent to offend. Please interpret 'man' as 'human', for many of the best dog trainers and hunters are, indeed, women. But I write it thus, as will become apparent, because it relates directly to my relationship with my own dog.

For thousands of years, man – the hunter – has employed the use of dogs to help him to gather food for the pot. Sometimes directly, using the hound as his weapon. Often indirectly, using the dog to scent-out prospective quarry, mark its presence or retrieve shot game. Like so many hunting disciplines, the airgun hunter's dog needs specific traits and a particular kind of training to make it a useful companion.

The airgun's biggest advantage is its short range and deadly silence. It stands to reason, then, that if an airgun hunter wants a dog alongside, it has to possess the quietest of tongues. A yappy, unruly dog will have all your quarry running or flying for cover in seconds. You will work over all terrains, including among stock and around the farmyard, so a hardy, steadfast and superbly-trained dog is needed. A dog that nips at the fleeing ewe or looks at the poultry as fair quarry will soon lose you your coveted permission. You will work through the game coverts and over the open field, so your dog needs to be taught to resist the temptation of the sitting pheasant or the sprinting hare. It needs to be trained to drop at the flick of a finger if you spot quarry; to resist running in front of your rifle; to retrieve when you need it to; to lie back and stay while you explore the open gateway or the ditch. In short, its behaviour in the field with you must be nothing short of impeccable. The dog must have a good nose, to mark the inhabited warren or lair. It must have enough intelligence to learn to anticipate your next

*The airgun hunter's dog is a very personal choice. My lurcher, Dylan*

## FROM THE DOG'S PERSPECTIVE

As the airgun hunter's dog, you will demand much from your master. A warm bed, nourishing food and exercise – even if shooting isn't on the agenda. You need clear instruction and training, so that you know what pleases your master and what annoys him. You have a short event memory, so you want to be told immediately – and clearly – if you have done something wrong. A simple 'No!' or 'Bad!' will suffice, not a beating or a kick.

You want, always, to be confident enough to return to your master's side – even if you got it wrong. You need to be allowed to free-run often, in safe places, to burn off your energy. You want to enjoy a share of the hunting spoils now and again, so that you understand why you're employed this way. You need a pat on the head or a stroke often, acknowledging your loyalty, when he comes down from his bed in the morning and you're wagging your tail in greeting. In the field, when you have excelled, you would like the same. It tells you that what you just did was right and pleased your master. You need your master to understand your state of health as he would his own, and respect it. You need protection from disease and, due to your activity on his behalf, you may need medical help.

*A well-trained dog
is a wonderful
shooting partner*

movements (and react accordingly) when it hears the magpie's chuckle or the squirrel's hiss. It must be tolerant enough to lie next to you, patiently, while you ambush a warren and be stealthy enough to stay close to you during a stalk. It needs to be fit enough to spend dawn through dusk with you in the wood, and athletic enough to find its own path under, over, or around the hedge or gate. As an airgun hunter, you will demand much from your dog.

The airgun hunter's choice of dog is his own – and, indeed, many breeds of dog would fit the criteria specified above. Some breeds clearly wouldn't, though – too much voice, intractable in training, too high a chase-and-kill instinct, too much sight, too little nose.

My choice – the breed I've favoured since my youth, but have not always been able to have by my side due to personal circumstance – is the lurcher. The lurcher isn't a mongrel, but a deliberately cross-bred pot-pourri of terrier nose, pluck and intelligence, coupled with sighthound speed, silence and stealth.

Readers of my magazine articles down the years will know my Bedlington/sighthound cross, Dylan. Thanks to intensive, early training, he is almost the perfect airgunning companion. I say 'almost' because there are situations in which it would be unfair to take any lurcher. For instance, he doesn't accompany me when hide-shooting or when roost-shooting pigeons. Unlike the rabbit warren, there's no interest in this for him, so it's unfair to lie him in boredom or cold, where he would – quite justifiably – start the trademark lurcher whining when he's impatient.

This isn't a book about dog training, so all I'm going to say is this: when you have a dog that lies flat on its belly as soon as it hears a magpie chatter, or a woodpigeon clatter into a tree, then looks to you in expectation of the shot; when you have a hound that squats, rotates its ears like radar dishes and lifts its right paw to claw the air in the direction of an incoming squirrel still 150 yard away; when you have a dog that will lie flat at the flick of a finger and wait patiently while you creep to a gap ahead in the hedgerow; when you have that... then you have a wonderful partnership. Dylan is nearly nine years old as I write this book, approaching his retirement. He's going to be hard act to follow. ○

# THE ACT OF SHOOTING

## SECOND NATURE

Many shooting books would have put a chapter on 'the act of shooting' right at the beginning; I've deliberately left it until near the end. I'll admit I'd probably be the worst shooting coach in the world, so I'm not going to attempt a 'how to shoot' lecture here – but I will impart some of the principles that have helped me evolve into a competent shooter. The rest is down to you (if you don't already consider yourself a competent shot).

Once you've got the various components – the sequence – right, then the simple act of executing a shot is as natural as changing gears while driving a car. It becomes second nature, a flow of mental and physical actions that bear little analysis unless things are going badly wrong. I'm often asked to advise people on how to achieve this process, but that's very difficult to do on the written page. Nor would I profess to be a role model. Asking me to describe how to pull off the perfect quarry shot is like asking Top Gear's Jeremy Clarkson to teach you to drive, or U2's Bono to teach you to sing. Hardly perfect examples of their art, but both extraordinarily successful at it!

There's a subliminal sequence of events that occur between me sighting my quarry and actually achieving the kill. The first two happen in milliseconds. Mental confirmation that this is a quarry species and that the shot is achievable. By now the gun is at my shoulder and my brain is getting signals from my eyes and other sensors. Range, profile, angle, safe backdrop, breeze… Again, all in milliseconds. If any of these register as negative, an alert kicks in and the process pauses. If all are positive, my breathing steadies. My arm muscles tense slightly to support the weight of the rifle steadily. My thumb instinctively flicks off the safety catch. My index finger moves into the trigger guard, flat to the trigger blade. My breath gently releases and pauses, and I tickle the trigger.

As the shot is released, my eye stays on the quarry until it drops. My hand comes from the trigger area to recock the rifle's sidelever and my thumb returns the safety catch to on. All of this happens within three seconds; five seconds maximum (if all the sensor signals are positive). If they're negative, the shot may never happen. I'm quite happy with my shooting technique and have found, over time, that over-analysis can be far from constructive. Confidence breeds success, they say – and it certainly does in the simple act of shooting.

There have been times, though, when I've been guilty of failing in one important part of this sequence. A failing that, more often than not, is the cause of random or poor shooting, a low quarry-count and injury to quarry. 'Watching' the pellet right through to your target – the follow-through – is a massively important factor in successful and accurate shooting. When you think about it logically, it's easy to reason why failing to follow through causes poor results. If you've released the pellet and your over-eagerness makes you snatch back from the shot to watch your quarry from over the top of the scope, you often do so before the pellet has exited the barrel. So you've moved the point of impact, unwittingly. Disciplining yourself to keep watching through the scope will overcome this. I even recock with my eye still on the scope.

Buck fever is another common failing of the hunter. This is a bit like a golfer's 'yips' – when they miss a simple putt because they're over-eager. With the shooter, this manifests itself in the trigger snatch, instead of a simple tickle to release the pellet. As a writer, I constantly use the phrase 'pull the trigger'. I shouldn't, because you must never *pull* a trigger! Squeeze or press it. Tickle it. The pull, or snatch, also jerks the barrel's alignment slightly and, like the failure to follow through, subtly changes the pellet's ultimate point of impact. Just a tiny movement at the rifle end can translate, at the quarry end, a deviation which equates to a miss or an injury. The correct technique is to use the soft pad of your index finger, horizontal with the trigger blade, to gently tickle it back towards your face. (Good Lord, I'm teaching!)

Some of the other factors which will greatly influence the above sequence are fairly obvious. Comfort is important, not just in terms of warmth and the cut of your clothing, but also your shooting stance. For that reason, I practise shooting in every conceivable position. Although I always favour the kneeling or squatting stance, where I can use my upper thigh as a support, I can shoot very effectively from a standing position when I have to.

Freehand shots like this are often essential on a walkabout session. A new shooter will find they have to take time to get used to the weight of a rifle. Stance alters with balance and management of the rifle's weight, which is another good reason why I advocate one-gun hunting. It's not just about intimately knowing your combo's trajectory, it's also about your body being trained to handle that gun in any situation, any stance. If you constantly switch guns, you'll find yourself struggling with stance and balance. As a one-gun man, I don't have that problem. Incidently, if someone tells you they've been shooting rifles (any rifles) for years and you want to check the credibility of that statement, ask to measure their forearms. My right forearm is a good couple of centimetres thicker than my left through carrying and bearing the majority of the weight of my rifle on countless hunting trips!

I'm right-handed, but I practise Southpaw shooting. Indeed, I've shot rabbits and squirrels this way where getting into a position to shoot with my natural stance would compromise my hidden position. There is a hugely important reason for this practice, though. I have a recurring dream

*Though I practise and use standing shots in the field... I will always prefer the kneeling shot*

(nightmare?) where my only chance of shooting a mink – the only airgun quarry I've never shot – occurs when I'm forced to take a left-handed shot...

Eyesight is important. I recently spent the best part of a shooting year with spectacles. I'd been wearing contact lenses for many years, but a succession of eye infections made me give them up for a while and switch to specs. That happened mid-summer, and I enjoyed the new 20/20 vision afforded by my new glasses. Initially apprehensive that this change would affect the size of my bag, I needn't have worried. Yet, over the winter, as the climatic conditions became less favourable, I became constantly frustrated at wiping rain off my glasses, or demisting them when I stepped from my warm Jeep into a cold field.

Now, I've hit a compromise. I wear specs all the time at home or at work. Having found

an optician who will supply non-contract contact lenses, I've changed my habit. I just buy what I need every three months, wear them for shooting sessions only, instead of 24/7, and I haven't had an eye infection since. Nor have I missed a chance at a rabbit because I was staring through a fog 5mm in front of my nose!

Finally, one of the most important factors of successful shooting: self-control. It's the ability to weigh up an opportunity instantly, switch into shooting mode, calm your breathing, lift the rifle in a singular motion and allow your brain to take over. Once you've shot a few vermin species successfully, that brain – an amazing organ with its programmable memory – will take over. We call it instinct. Trust your instincts – you will become a more confident shooter and, with it, a better hunter. ○

# RECYLING, RE-USE & RECIPES

## SHARING THE BOUNTY

As a waste manager, preaching the recycling creed is part of the day job for me. It's also ingrained into my hunting life. I always think that part of the 'respect for quarry' ethos is attempting to make the best of a creature's demise at my hand. There's a kind of karma attached to this philosophy, and if you are a shooter who sometimes feels at odds with the act of killing, then you'll have conscience enough to think about the ecological value of the creature you have just despatched. Everything has value in death as well as in life. Earlier in this book, I've described how I sometimes cast a corpse into a ditch for the fox or badger. If I do so, it is a calculated act; on paths I know the scavengers will tread. Why would I do that? The answer is because that handful of squirrels (or corvids) – which I choose not to eat – may satisfy the hunger of old Charlie or Brock that night, and they won't pursue the rabbits so vigorously. Ergo more rabbits for me – which I *do* eat.

If you have ferreting and falconry friends, or know folk who rescue raptors, you should save your unwanted bag and send it their way; fresh meat will always be appreciated.

Swapping meat is a useful trade for for the hunter, too. The stalker's dogs will appreciate some rabbit now and again and can earn you some fresh venison. Farmers may want some rabbit or woodpigeon in exchange for beef, lamb or pork.

I regularly pass on spare rabbit joints and pigeon breasts to my grandmother-in-law, who is of an age to appreciate them and know how to cook them. (She was gamekeeper's wife.)

However, I never sell rabbits or woodpigeons to the butcher. In the past, I've found them too fussy – and far too tight regarding fair recompense!

## BAIT AND DECOYS

If you have a chest freezer, it's worth keeping back a few samples of shot quarry to use as decoys or bait on future shooting sessions. Real birds always look far better than fakes, so to have a magpie, crow and a few woodies in the deepfreeze is, actually, worthwhile. If you've shot a scrawny rabbit or a squirrel, keep one of each back for baiting out. With all the above, make sure you double-wrap each, separately, in plastic carrier bags. Defrost them the day before a planned session, too, because you can't manipulate or gut them when they're still frozen stiff. Use them only once, then dispose of them. You'll soon get into the habit of keeping one of each quarry species – not rats, though! – back after a successful outing.

One, further tip: make sure you tell your partner what's in the freezer. I won't be the first – nor the last – shooter to upset their other half when they've opened a bag from the freezer to see what's inside and were greeted by the rigor mortis-induced scowl of a terminated Tufty!

## THE COOKPOT

If we are what we eat – and we eat what we hunt – then we are truly wild, truly at our quarry's level. Since man first picked up a spear or bow, hunters have celebrated their catch

*At least three meals here… and some bait for the corvids*

# IL PICCIONE NELL'ORZO (Pigeons in stubble)

## Ingredients

(Serves four)

- 8 pigeon breasts (i.e. 4 birds), 120g sausage meat
- Wild mint (about a dozen leaves), washed and finely chopped
- 1tbsp mixed herbs
- 12 button mushrooms
- 500g fusilli pasta
- A jar of tomato flavour pasta-bake sauce
- Grated cheese
- 2 tbsp olive oil
- 1 bottle red wine – must be Italian!
- 1 garlic ciabatta loaf
- **Side salad:** Iceburg lettuce, radish, tomato, cucumber, spring onion

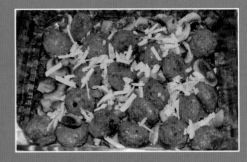

*Add herbs, sliced mushrooms and grated cheese to the minced and seared balls of pigeon breasts and sausage meat*

## Preparation

You need to get into the spirit of Italian cuisine for this one so, first, pour yourself a large glass of wine. Then finely mince the pigeon breasts and sausage meat and mix both together. Don't use too much of the sausage meat; it's there only to bind the pigeon meat, not drown its flavour. Add in the chopped mint and the mixed herbs.

To help along that Italian feeling, simmer the fusilli pasta in a pan of boiling water for about 12 minutes to soften it. While the pasta is cooking, form about 20 small, smooth balls of the meat/herb mix. Slice the button mushrooms. Heat the olive oil in a wok and then add in the meatballs, searing to brown and seal them. Add in the mushrooms and lightly fry.

You'll be able to smell that mint by now, and another glass of the red wine may beckon! Drain the excess oil from the wok and tip the meatballs and mushrooms into a deep lasagne dish. Sprinkle over a handful of grated cheese while hot (to melt) and then drain the pasta before tipping it into the lasagne dish.

Pour the pasta-bake sauce over everything and mix the whole lot thoroughly, so that the sauce covers the meat, mushrooms and pasta . Use your spoon to push all the meatballs below the top level of the mix. Next cover the top of the mix with a liberal sprinkling of grated cheese and place in the oven, pre-heated to 180° C for 20 minutes. Put in the ciabatta loaf for the last 10 minutes to warm it.

*Cover with cooked fusilli pasta, over which is poured some pasta-bake sauce with a final grating of cheese to top off*

*Ready to serve, having cooked for 20 minutes in a pre-heated oven (180o C). Scrumptious!*

## Serving

Dish out the pasta bake, letting the meatballs show through and dress one edge with salad. This represents the pigeons (meatballs) in the stubble (pasta) and the edge of the wood where you placed your nets (salad) to shoot them. Add ciabatta slices to represent the straw bales.

and offered thanks to their respective gods for its provision. I'm not saying that my family dance around the table or sacrifice virgins in gratitude for me potting a rabbit, but they do enjoy a well-prepared meal brought from the field to the plate. I have numerous recipies for the airgunner's quarry and there are many books dedicated to the subject of the cooking of game in which vermin like rabbits and woodpigeon are included. While this book isn't intended as a catalogue of recipes, I must share with you one of my favourite ways to eat woodpigeon.

Woodpigeon breasts are a very dark and rich meat. Delicious pan-fried with onions or added to casseroles, on their own they can be quite 'gamey', with a liver-like texture. They are, however, a delightfully cheap and easily acquired meat with which to experiment. On one pigeon shooting sortie, with my nets surrounded by water-mint, I had an idea:

it was seeing the birds settling in the harvest stubbles that inspired the name for the recipe you see opposite...

## RAT PIZZA

*(Serves one)*

Only kidding! After an evening's rat shooting in the chicken sheds, go home, take a long hot shower, pick up the phone and order a 12-inch pizza for home delivery. Pour a large glass of red wine, congratulate yourself on having exorcised the world of a few of the most horrific creatures that exist in it – then sit back and scoff your pizza in a glow of self-admiration.

But if you don't finish the pizza and turn to the bin with the wasted remnants, think again about where these will go... and what will probably feed on them. With that thought in mind, order a 9-inch pizza next time. Love food, hate waste... and don't feed the rats! ○

*While sitting behind a net, surrounded by the smell of wild mint, a culinary idea was conceived...*

# Chapter
# 26

# THE LAW

The air rifle is a hugely maligned tool where the press and general public are concerned, and quite wrongly so. It's estimated there are around seven million airguns in circulation in the UK; the government has never put an exact figure on it as, in the past, it was a relatively unregulated gun. A handful of incidents each year – by the ne'er-do-goods, irresponsible morons or (tragically) youngsters who have stumbled on an unsecured rifle and misused it – have given rise to calls in many quarters to either ban or licence this superb and efficient pest control tool.

I firmly believe that this needs to be put into perspective. Personally, I would rather my 16-year-old son asked for an air rifle than a moped – his chances of surviving to the age of 21 would multiply a thousand-fold. Analyse the illegal or tragic incidents surrounding air rifles and you'll find two common factors. The transgressors are usually urban, not rural, individuals and they are usually not youths, but idiotic adults. The recent shift in law to raise the legal age of ownership from 17 to 18 years of age – typically knee-jerk politics – ignored that latter fact. Licensing would be unpoliceable in Britain (England, Scotland and Wales), although airguns have been licenced in Northern Ireland, a throwback to the politically-troubled times. And, of course, the Scotland Act, 2012, is set to bring some form of airgun-specific legislation north of the Border. As this first edition of the book goes to press, the exact details of what laws Holyrood may impose are unknown. Be that as it may, the tragic events in the UK over recent years have proved that licensing is worthless in the face of individual, psychological behaviour.

That is true of not just guns, but also motor vehicles. Yet, strangely, I've never heard a call for a ban on cars because some idiot decided to get drunk and kill someone while driving.

Nonetheless, some of the recent legislation in Britain I find completely sensible. The need for an airgun retailer to register an address. The need to sell 'face to face' via a registered firearm dealer rather than through mail order. It all helps to prevent future nonsense and misuse. Some of the current laws (which apply to all forms of shooting) are derived from common sense. Such as not being allowed to shoot across the boundary of your permission, or having to carry your gun in a slip, with no ammunition in it, while passing through a public place. Simple, safety-based rules. The more recent addition of gun security rules (Crime & Security Act, 2010) shouldn't have affected most responsible airgun users. I've always locked mine away securely so that no 'unauthorised' hands can get to them.

At risk of over-simplifying the law, I'm not going to write a list of current legal requirements for ownership of an airgun – laws change and I don't intend to release updated editions of this, a hunting book, just to keep up-to-date with any changes in legislation. So I am simply going to refer you back to the safety advice I gave earlier in this book – check for legal compliance with the BASC (in Britain), or your state laws anywhere else in the world.

However, if you do happen to be reading this book in a decade's time, I just hope that all the lobbying and hard work that organisations like the BASC do on airgunners' behalves has paid off... and you can, under the right conditions, still walk into a gun shop to buy an air rifle for controlling vermin. ○

# ACKNOWLEDGEMENTS

Few people know that I used to be a keen road runner and marathoner. I only once broke three hours for the marathon – but it was a milestone in my life. The relevance? Writing this book has been like running that marathon. Years of training brought down to a gruelling race to beat a personal deadline. Instead of energy and oxygen, it has been fuelled by knowledge and experience. Getting to the finish line has meant digging inside my head for every bit of hunting nouse I could redeem. So a special thanks to my wife and family, who have endured my selfish single-mindedness while running this particular race (and for their constant toleration of my isolation, both when hunting and writing).

Thanks to all the team at Blaze Publishing for producing such outstanding presentation of my work, month after month in *Airgun Shooter* and, frequently, in *Sporting Rifle*. To my editor, Nigel Allen, for persuading me to keep writing when I could so happily have retreated back into the countryside where my only deadline is the setting sun! Thanks, too, to Tracey Allen and her team at The *Countryman's Weekly*. And to the readers of my scribblings who, whether through praise or criticism, inspire me to capture the moment and transmit it to the page.

The reader who has endured thus far will know that I'm not precious about my rifles; they are just tools. Yet the guns I pick leave no excuse for poor marksmanship. For designing perfect tools for the job, I thank Weihrauch (and importers, Hull Cartridge), BSA, Webley and Simon Atkins, The Airgun Doctor.

Finally, and most importantly, to the people without whom I would have no access to hunt. They rarely see me, often have no idea what the results have been – yet they never deny or question my presence. A hunter without land to shoot over is a like a jockey without a horse. Lady Anne Prince-Smith and her staff, Ed and Victoria Jones, Oliver and Hannah Arnold, Trevor Moy, Jimmy Hall – your land, its vermin, its game and its wildlife are my inspiration. I thank you immensely. ○

*Ladies, gentlemen, dear readers: I need to leave you.*

*The rooks are beating out from the roost; rabbits are abroad; rats skulk in the grain shed; magpies are raiding the blackcaps' nest. The fields are swollen with crops; the wood is verdant; the pheasants are crowing for help.*

*It's been a pleasure. But the lurcher is whining incessantly – and the gun is calling my name…*

# INDEX

# ABOUT THE AUTHOR

Ian Barnett discovered his hunting genes as a boy, while kicking around the woods and fields of Hertfordshire. Home-made bows-and-arrows evolved into catapults and, as the years advanced, into hunting with lurchers and air rifles. As a youth (much to his shame now), he learned much of his quarry lore, fieldcraft and stealth collecting birds' eggs, snaring rabbits and poaching hares or pheasants on nearby estates. Maturity brought responsibility though, and Ian legitimised his hunting.

The air rifle became his 'speciality' tool, though he had to park his hunting activities for a while to concentrate on career development. In 1999, Ian moved to a new job and new life in Norfolk. He soon established the trust of several landowners and, as well as hunting at every opportunity, began recording his experiences with a daily journal and photographs. Following a very strange request to shoot a magpie from a cow's back – a feat only safely achievable with an air rifle – Ian sent the story and pictures to a leading shooting magazine. Though it was submitted more out of curiosity, it kick-started a secondary career in airgun hunting photo-journalism.

Since then, Ian has written for *Airgunner*, *Home Farmer*, *Shooting Times*, *Sporting Shooter* and *Sporting Rifle*. He now regularly writes for *The Countryman's Weekly* and is a permanent fixture on the team of the award-winning magazine, *Airgun Shooter*. Ian's first book, *The Airgun Hunter's Year*, was published by Merlin Unwin in early 2011 (ISBN 978-1-906122-28-7). An anecdotal, often poetic, journey through the 12 months of a hunting year, it imparts many secrets to successful air rifle hunting.

Ian's other great passion is wildlife photography and his growing portfolios can be seen, online, at www.wildanglia.co.uk. Web-goers can also touch base with Ian at www.facebook.com/wildanglia.

# Walks For All Seasons
# Lincolnshire

# WALKS *FOR* *ALL* *SEASONS*

# LINCOLNSHIRE

## HUGH MARROWS

BRADWELL
**BOOKS**

Published by Bradwell Books
9 Orgreave Close Sheffield S13 9NP
Email: books@bradwellbooks.co.uk

British Library Cataloguing in Publication Data: a catalogue record for this book is available from the British Library.

1st Edition

ISBN: 9781909914278

Print: Gomer Press, Llandysul, Ceredigion SA44 4JL

Design by: Erik Siewko Creative, Derbyshire
eriksiewko@gmail.com

Photograph Credits: © Hugh Marrows


Maps: Contain Ordnance Survey data
© Crown copyright and database right 2014

Ordnance Survey licence number 100039353

The information in this book has been produced in good faith and is intended as a general guide. Bradwell Books and its authors have made all reasonable efforts to ensure that the details are correct at the time of publication. Bradwell Books and the author cannot accept any responsibility for any changes that have taken place subsequent to the book being published. It is the responsibility of individuals undertaking any of the walks listed in this publication to exercise due care and consideration for the health and wellbeing of each other in the party. Particular care should be taken if you are inexperienced. The walks in this book are not especially strenuous but individuals taking part should ensure they are fit and able to complete the walk before setting off.

# WALKS FOR ALL SEASONS

# INTRODUCTION

WELCOME TO 'WALKS FOR ALL SEASONS' IN LINCOLNSHIRE!
FOR MY SECOND VOLUME WITH THEM BRADWELL BOOKS
HAVE INVITED ME TO CHOOSE WALKS THAT ARE IN SOME
WAY PARTICULARLY ATTRACTIVE AT CERTAIN TIMES OF THE
YEAR — OR SUITABLE FOR YEAR-ROUND OUTINGS; HENCE
OUR TITLE! THESE TWENTY WALKS THEREFORE HAVE BEEN
CAREFULLY CHOSEN WITH THAT BRIEF IN MIND.

They do indeed show their best side at certain seasons of the year, so see the 'Basics' panel for individual route guidance. I must, however, stress that all are interesting throughout the year and will, I hope, encourage exploration of Lincolnshire's countryside in all seasons. We are this time being a little more adventurous by including a few slightly longer routes compared with those in our previous 'Walks For All Ages' volume. The majority, however, remain suitable for family groups or the 'occasional' rambler with distances ranging from a mere 1½ miles to the longest of 8¾ miles. And some of the longer routes also offer shorter options!

My choice again attempts to introduce readers to as wide a variety of scenery and places of interest as possible by encompassing a broad range of locations; from north to south, from the fenland coast to the hills of the Wolds and the vales to the west.

The 'Basics' panel accompanying each route will help you choose walks within your (or your family's) abilities and you can work up to the longer outings as experience develops. Note too that where possible the 'Start Point' information gives a postcode for satellite navigation users – though in a few cases, where this is in open countryside, these may be only approximate.

Readers should bear in mind too that the countryside is a changing environment. The route guides and maps are as accurate as we can make them but footpaths do occasionally get re-routed and other changes may occur where new stiles or kissing/bridle gates are set up. Strong, waterproof footwear is advisable as inevitably some routes encounter uneven ground and/or short distances over arable land, not to mention some seasonal mud. Also an unfortunate sign of the times is that some country pubs are closing – although encouragingly a few sometimes re-open again! Nevertheless it's wise to check if you are relying on them for refreshments. Our route guides and maps should get you round all these walks without difficulty but I always recommend having an Ordnance Survey map to hand – if possible the relevant Explorer sheet. These larger scale maps contain greater detail and may assist in locating the start points more easily. We have used grid references in the 'Basics' panel too and this helpful – even essential – map-reading skill is easily learnt since all OS maps give an explanatory example. Remember it's always sensible to know just where you are – for example to plan an alternative route in an emergency!

The times given – perhaps we should say estimated – to complete each walk are just that: estimates! Readers know their own abilities best and will need to allow additional time for rests, picnics, pub meals, photography etc. Those who have pets or children accompanying them should be mindful too of the hazards that roads (even quiet country lanes) and water features can present. I must again express my thanks the landlords of inns, each of whom I have personally contacted, who have kindly consented to readers using their car parks as a starting point. Do show your appreciation by giving them some custom before or after your walk.

And last but not least . . .

Please remember, and follow, the Countryside Code! Amongst other things this gives guidance on dogs in the countryside. Some of my walks are on, or cross, nature reserves where dogs may, for obvious reasons, be unwelcome. Some of the other routes have sections where well-behaved dogs could be let off the lead at the discretion of their owners. Be especially careful when near livestock – particularly if they have young.

Remember too that the countryside is someone else's home or workplace and provides their livelihood; don't be the one to spoil it for those following in your footsteps!

Happy Rambling!

# ALVINGHAM

THIS EASY, SCENIC RAMBLE FROM THE VILLAGE OF ALVINGHAM NEAR LOUTH VISITS AN UNUSUAL CHURCHYARD AND INCLUDES A STROLL BESIDE THE LOUTH NAVIGATION.

We begin at the small car park close to Alvingham's picturesque and famous watermill. There was a mill recorded here as early as AD 1155 and since no other site has been discovered it seems reasonable to conclude that the present one stands at the same location; the mill you see today, however, dates from the 16th century and was enlarged in 1782. Children and other extroverts can try out the nearby village stocks.

We first see the Louth Navigation at Alvingham Lock. The technical sounding term navigation is correctly applied here since it was created for the most part by converting an existing watercourse, the River Lud, instead of digging a completely new channel – which would have been a 'canal'. Almost everyone still calls it a canal though! It opened in May 1770 and brought prosperity to Louth; indeed for a short while the town had a bigger fish market than Grimsby! It was not only the shipping trade that benefited the town's economy for subsidiary businesses became established too, one example being a boatbuilding yard near Louth's Riverhead.

In addition to the sea lock at Tetney seven more were needed to get the navigation the twelve miles, and raise it by forty-six feet, from Tetney and all these were within five miles of Louth; we see the remains of Alvingham Lock on our walk. Some locks, including Alvingham, were of a unique design with concave bays to their brick walls, an engineering solution to absorb the pressure from the embankment behind. The weight of the soil was intended to compress the bricks together instead of forcing the walls outwards, as was the tendency with conventional 'straight' walls. The success of this idea is evident from the good condition of the locks after nearly 250 years. Furthermore, the intention of the Navigation promoters was to trade with the Humber ports and as far afield as Yorkshire so the waterway and locks were built wider and deeper than normal, thus allowing seagoing vessels to work into Louth and avoid the hassle of offloading their cargoes onto 'canal' barges.

Eventually it was the famous Louth Flood of 29 May 1920, and the devastation it wrought at the Riverhead, that brought about closure. Trade had been declining since the coming of the railways to Louth in the 1850s, when the Great Northern Railway Company had also bought the Navigation Company. The financial difficulties that ensued meant that there was simply no money for the necessary repairs so, at a stroke, the navigation was virtually abandoned.

Nevertheless official closure order took another four years.

On our return to Alvingham there is the surprise of discovering not one but two churches cheek by jowl in the same churchyard, and walkers may now realise that they saw no church

in North Cockerington. This is a rare (though not unique) occurrence, but yet another oddity is that St Mary's, the North Cockerington church, is the nearer of the two to Alvingham! St Mary's has some 12th-century stonework and is cared for by the Churches Conservation Trust – and is usually open! Nearby St Adelwold's (Alvingham's church) is perhaps a century newer! Here, although the walk is almost done, you can take a breather on the modern 'Millennium' seat in the churchyard.

The surrounding fields were formerly the site of Alvingham Priory, founded around AD 1154 by St Gilbert from Sempringham, near Bourne. The priory survived until the Dissolution of the Monasteries in 1536 and today the most obvious remaining earthworks are in the fields between the village and the navigation. You'll see an information board as you leave the churchyard.

NOTE. There is a special parking area at the start point.

# THE BASICS

Distance: 4¼ miles / 7.5km
Gradient: Almost level throughout
Severity: Easy
Approx time to walk: 2 hrs
Stiles: None
Maps: OS Landranger 113 (Grimsby), Explorer 283 (Louth & Mablethorpe)
Path description: Country lanes and tracks; field-edge paths
Start point: The 'Two Churches Car park' Alvingham (GR: TF 366914)
Parking: As above (LN11 0QD)
Dog friendly: Yes; on lead on public roads
Public toilets: None
Refreshments: None on route but numerous choices three miles away in Louth

# ALVINGHAM WALK

1. From the mill walk back through Alvingham village, keeping ahead where two lanes branch off to the right (the stocks are at the second junction) and then take the first left down to Alvingham Lock. Cross the bridge and turn left beside the Navigation almost as far as a footbridge leading back into Alvingham churchyard.

2. Turn right on the signed footpath heading up towards North Cockerington. At a lane cross over into the grassy path of Church Walk. Follow this through to the next lane and there go left, then at a T-junction, turn right.

3. As you come to a double bend take the footpath on the left and at the next road turn left again. In just over half a mile, at a sharp left-hand bend, keep forward on a track to reach yet another lane.

4. Now bear left and in 350 yards you will come back to the Navigation at a bridge (High Bridge). Don't cross it but turn left through the kissing gate and follow the embankment back to the footbridge seen earlier that accesses Alvingham churchyard. Walk through this and the adjoining farmyard to return to the watermill and your car.

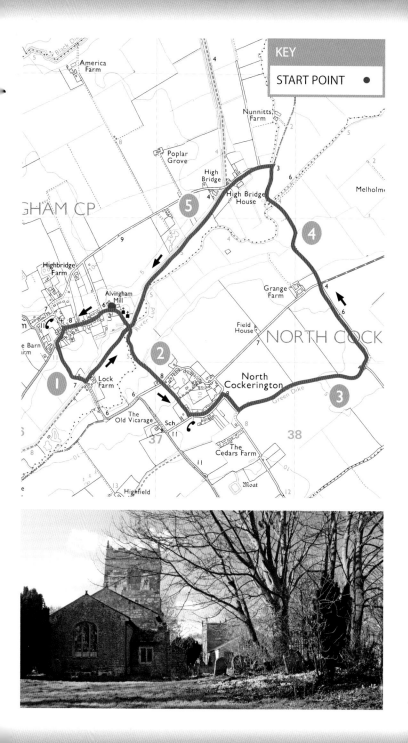

KEY

START POINT ●

# BARTON & BARROW-ON-HUMBER

THIS WALK FROM BARTON TO BARROW-ON-HUMBER ALLOWS US TO DISCOVER SOME REMARKABLE MARITIME HISTORY. WE RETURN ALONG THE BANKS OF THE MIGHTY RIVER HUMBER.

Barton-on-Humber has for centuries depended for its trade and wealth upon the Humber and its affluent past has bequeathed a particularly attractive architectural legacy. This is partly due to the local riverbank clays that have been exploited for brick and tile making. Many worked-out claypits are now flooded and some have become nature reserves such as the Water's Edge where this walk begins. Nearby is the amazing 450-yard-long Ropewalk (another important former Barton industry) built in 1767 and now home to art and craft galleries. And a café!

A few miles away Barrow-on-Humber is famous as being the home village, though not the birthplace, of a carpenter named John Harrison. He was actually born on 24 March 1693 in south Yorkshire, where his father was employed as a carpenter at Nostell Priory near Wakefield. Barrow, however, became his home from infancy and Lincolnshire has proudly adopted him as one of its 'sons' – for reasons explained below.

At first glance Barrow might seem an improbable location for nurturing great scientific advances, but we must remember the importance of shipping here, since Barrow Haven was also a small port. At that time there was the enormous problem of accurate time keeping at sea, essential to enable ships to calculate their longitudinal position. Harrison abandoned carpentry in 1714 to devote his energies to solving this problem when the Admiralty offered a prize equating to £1 million in today's money for a verifiable solution. His efforts resulted in his famous seagoing clocks, numbered H1 to H4, now displayed at Greenwich. Some of his early clocks were made of wood and one of these, commissioned by Lord Yarborough for Brocklesby Park in 1722, is still in working order! Harrison's eventual success in solving the longitude problem was followed by a prolonged battle, lasting until 1773, to overcome the Admiralty's political manoeuvrings and obtain his reward. The author Dava Sobel tells Harrison's fascinating story in her book Longitude.

Inside Barrow's Holy Trinity church is a small 'Harrison' exhibition together with a copy of an original portrait owned by the Science Museum. The church guide also contains a brief account of his life and work. He died on his 83rd birthday – 24 March 1776.

Wending our way back to the Humber we pass Barrow 'Castles', the impressive remains of a medieval motte and bailey, probably built around AD 1071 and with its moat originally filled from a nearby tidal creek that ran this far inland. It was occupied for some 300 years and today the earthworks still stand about nine feet high. (They are on private land but visible from the road.)

The railway crossed near Barton and at Barrow Haven links Barton with New Holland. It was built following the takeover by the Manchester, Sheffield & Lincolnshire Railway of the ferry service to Hull in 1848. This 3½-mile branch line to Barton opened the following year.

## THE BASICS

Distance: 8 miles / 13km
Gradient: Level throughout
Severity: Moderate
Approx time to walk: 4 hrs
Stiles: None
Maps: OS Landranger 112 (Scunthorpe), Explorer 281 (Ancholme Valley)
Path description: Nature Reserve paths, field paths, country lanes & river embankment
Start point: Water's Edge visitor centre, Barton (GR: TA 030234)
Parking: Water's Edge visitor centre (DN18 5JR)
Dog friendly: Yes – with care on roads. On lead in Water's Edge reserve
Public toilets: Water's Edge centre
Refreshments: Barton – café at Water's Edge centre: The Ropewalk café, Barrow – inns in the village (off route) and the Haven Inn near Barrow Haven

1. Take the path opposite the visitor centre onto a boardwalk over the lake. Follow the reserve paths, going left at the first junction and right at the second. At the third go left again, then right once more to reach the reserve exit at a bridge into Pasture Road (North).

2. Turn right to cross the railway and then veer right to reach the junction with Butts Road; now cross over into Pasture Road (South). At Falkland Way continue along the track opposite, which soon becomes a footpath. On reaching a footpath sign go through some trees and keep forward in the next field to another road (West Marsh Lane).

3. Still continue ahead, bearing right at the

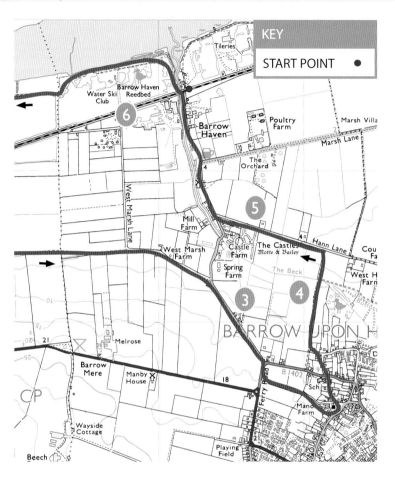

KEY

START POINT •

first junction. At the next junction join the pavement and bear right for 100 yards to a footpath on the left. After two fields a waymark directs you right into Barrow along Thorngarth Lane. Continue until you can go right into the churchyard. (Take time now to explore Barrow and visit the church.)

4. Return to where you entered the churchyard and cross into North Street. At the corner go left into Cherry Lane,

which becomes a track, and at the end of that join a field path by turning right. Follow this over a footbridge to reach another road (Hann Lane).

5. Turn left here, soon passing 'The Castles' earthworks on your left, and at a T-junction bear right. In 400 yards (near an inn) continue down the lane ahead until you come to the railway at Barrow Haven.

6. Go left over the railway bridge and then immediately right beside the Haven to reach the Humber bank path. An easy two miles returns you to the Water's Edge visitor centre, all the while enjoying magnificent views of the Humber and the bridge. Back at Barton explore the Water's Edge reserve and visitor centre.

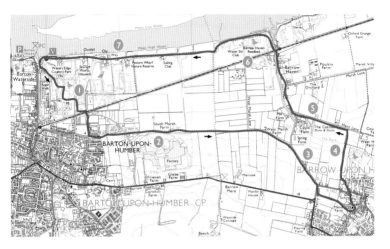

# BINBROOK & GREAT TOWS

This walk has wonderful views almost the entire way from the easily reached Wolds hilltops that surround Binbrook.

Binbrook's name derives from 'Bynna's brook', which flows in the valley below the church, and the town was a substantial settlement when the Domesday Book was compiled in 1086. From around the 1630s it even had a market but the rights to this were sold to Caistor around 1840.

The large and relatively modern church (1869) is in the Early English architectural style and was designed by the Louth architect James Fowler. It is dedicated to both St Mary and St Gabriel since Binbrook was once split into two parishes. By the 1840s both churches were in disrepair so the new church replaced both; hence the joint dedication. St Gabriel's churchyard, just off Grimsby Road, was abandoned but still survives with one large

section of a pillar at its centre and old gravestones propped up around the walls; it can still be visited and our walk passes the site.

Near to it is the village pump, raised above the road and with hitching rings so that horse-drawn water carts could be filled there; this was an important facility at harvest time when farmers brewed their own beer for their workers. It was renovated in 1996.

Opposite the pump is the Old Police House, built in 1852 when Binbrook had a lawless reputation and it became necessary to appoint a paid constable. The building originally contained a magistrate's room and cells. An inn has occupied the site of the Plough since at least the 1850s and at the other end of the Market Place was also the former Marquis of Granby inn, dated 1685 but now a private house.One of the few really significant events in Lincolnshire's history was the 'Rising' of 1536. This started in Louth where there is a commemorative plaque outside St James's church. During the Sunday evensong service on 1 October the vicar revealed the imminent visit of the Henry VIII's commissioners in connection with the dissolution of the nearby Louth Priory. The following day there were riots and a letter of protest was composed and dispatched to the king demanding the dissolution be abandoned. A march to Lincoln was then organised. Word soon spread and the men from Louth met more rebels from Horncastle, Caistor, Market Rasen and Grimsby at Great Tows on the Wolds (GR TF 226904) just south of Binbrook – their numbers possibly reaching 12,000. By Friday they were all in Lincoln.

Great Tows is still there – a large farm surrounded by trees – and can be glimpsed from our walk. The rebels' precise route is unknown of course but our walk brings to mind the spirit of those eventful days in 1536 as we explore the very countryside that the rebels must have crossed as they assembled.

The king of course refused their demands, the rebellion quickly crumbled and within twelve days it was all over. The leaders, including some clergymen, were executed and the episode gave rise to Henry's famous comment about Lincolnshire being 'the most brute and beastly shire in the realm'.

# THE BASICS

Distance: 6½ miles / 10.5km
Gradient: Gradual, mostly on level high ground
Severity: Moderate
Approx time to walk: 3 hrs
Stiles: None
Maps: OS Landranger 113 (Grimsby), Explorer 282 (Lincolnshire Wolds North)
Path description: Country lanes, farm tracks and green lanes; two arable fields
Start point: Plough Inn, Binbrook (GR: TF 210939)
Parking: Plough Inn, Binbrook (LN8 6DE)
Dog friendly: Yes. On lead in Binbrook and on roads.
Public toilets: None on route
Nearest refreshments: Plough Inn

1. Exit the rear of the inn car park and turn left along High Street then after 100 yards or so take the signed footpath on the right up a gravel drive between houses. The path passes through a small plantation of trees and then follows grass field headlands for just over half a mile to meet a farm track at a four-way footpath sign.

2. Turn left here and follow this track for a good mile to a road.

3. Turn right here and after a left-hand bend walk for approximately a mile to a right-hand bend; now turn left along a grassy bridleway. Follow this for another mile – there's a right-then-left zigzag about halfway – to the next lane. Keep ahead for 200 yards until this lane bends right and look that way towards the distant Great Tows.

4. Don't walk towards Great Tows, however, but turn left through the hedge gap at a footpath sign. Walk across the field to come alongside some woods keeping forward to reach a farm track. Now zigzag left then right to continue, beside more woods, but with the trees now to your right.

5. Follow a track high above a valley and past an information board and seat. Shortly pass through a small wood and, then keeping ahead downhill, reach a road at the edge of Binbrook.

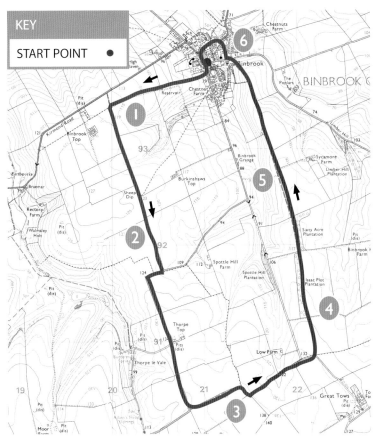

KEY

START POINT ●

6. Cross over, turn left and, just before the church, take the signed footpath on the right – be sure to pass to the right of the fence not up the gravel drive! At the next road go left. Beyond the water pump and the Old Police Station you can visit St Gabriel's churchyard. This is near the top of the hill and up the grass ramp across the road on your right. Finally at the Market Place turn left back to the inn.

# CAISTOR

This short walk explores the historic market town of Caistor along with the Water Hills – a local beauty spot.

The Caistor area has been inhabited since prehistoric times and was later a Roman castra or camp, from whence it derives its name, and a section of the Roman wall survives. The town sits on the west-facing slopes of the Wolds and has several springs that never fail even in the severest droughts.

Amongst Lincolnshire's market towns Caistor is unusual since, apart from the church and the Roman wall, virtually none of it precedes the year 1681. This is because, only fifteen years after the Great Fire of London, Caistor suffered its own devastating conflagration when almost all the town was lost.

We begin in the Market Place by the ornate pump of 1897 commemorating sixty years of Queen Victoria's reign before setting off down the picturesque Plough Hill to the Horsemarket. At the far end are the bright red doors of the former fire engine 'garage' dated 1869. Beside it is one of Caistor's springs – the Pigeon Spring. The former Methodist chapel, now a community Arts and Heritage Centre, contains a café.

In Fountain Street, which incidentally follows the line of the Roman town's south wall, is another roadside spring, the Sypher Spring. Then at the bottom of the churchyard we see the surviving section of Roman wall and an information board.

Above stands St Peter and St Paul's on the site of an earlier church possibly founded by St Paulinus in the early 7th century. The tower is the oldest part, being partially Norman, and there's a 13th-century door. Inside is a curious relic of a local custom – the Gad Whip. Until 1846 this was cracked, first in the porch and then over the head of the vicar, during Palm Sunday services. At the far side of the churchyard is the town's famous Grammar School, founded in 1631 and with the oldest part bearing its commemorative plaque easily visible.

We then head downhill to the perhaps surprisingly named Navigation Lane. This once led towards the ill-fated Caistor Canal that branched from the New River Ancholme near Brandy Wharf. The canal was four miles long with five locks but never reached Caistor, terminating

at Moortown 3½ miles to the west. Economically it was a failure since tolls were never sufficient to pay the interest on the loans raised to build it.

We return via Canada and the Water Hills, a steep-sided valley to the north of the town that contains yet more springs. The paths here provide spectacular views across the town and beyond to Nettleton Top, also westwards over the Trent Valley. It's well worth the climb! And on no other walk so short as this one can you say you have been to Canada – and back!

I am indebted to 'Sustainable Caistor' and the town's Civic Society whose nature and town trails inspired this walk. Their leaflets are available from the Arts and Heritage Centre. The Town Trail in particular makes a fine addition to this walk.

NOTES. There is also a car park off North Street with WCs. To find the Market Place from there leave by the corner near the toilets to cross High Street; then turn left and first right.

# THE BASICS

Distance: 3½ miles / 5.5km

Gradient: One steep descent and ascent, and some steps

Severity: Moderate

Approx time to walk: 2 hrs

Stiles: None

Maps: OS Landranger 113 (Grimsby), Explorer 284 (Grimsby, Cleethorpes & Immingham)

Path description: Town streets, tracks, grass and field paths

Start point: Market Place, Caistor (GR: TA 118013)

Parking: Caistor Market Place or off North Street (LN7 6TU)

Dog friendly: They will need to be on leads for most of this walk

Public toilets: At North Street car park or heritage centre

Nearest refreshments: Cafés, inns and chip shop in Caistor

# CAISTOR WALK

1. Start in the Market Place. Face the NatWest Bank, bear left down Plough Hill and keep left along Horsemarket to the old fire station; then return along the other side and by the Arts Centre go left into Fountain Street.

2. At the bottom climb the steps into the lower churchyard and walk past the Roman wall. (Visit the church now or later.) At the far end join a lane and bear left down the steep road of Cromwell View, keeping ahead at a junction and straight on into Navigation Lane.

3. After 350 yards bear right on the signed footpath immediately after the Grammar School sports ground. This crosses a footbridge before joining a road. Cross to the pavement opposite and bear left, and at a double bend (where the road bears left) keep ahead up Sandbraes Lane. After 200 yards veer right at a waymark onto a grassy path leading to a metal handgate. Go down steps, over a footbridge and up more steps to a fenced path and turn right. Follow this path to a kissing gate at a road.

4. Cross to the pavement opposite and turn right for 100 yards then bear left into Canada Lane. This climbs steeply at first to a junction with the Viking Way (helmet waymarks). There are good views from here over Caistor to Nettleton Top beyond.

5. The walk continues uphill for another quarter of a mile almost to the houses of Canada. Here a footpath branches off on the right across the head of the Water Hills valley – a fabulous viewpoint on a clear day – to another road.

6. Turn right downhill. Just after the traffic lights cross left into South Street and continue until you reach Buttermarket and the war memorial (with a relative of the author listed thereon). Now turn right back to the main Market Place.

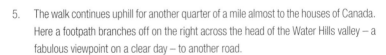

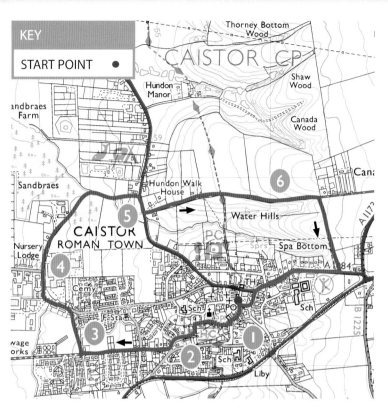

KEY

START POINT ●

# CASTLE BYTHAM

THIS (VERY) SHORT WALK AT CASTLE BYTHAM ALLOWS CLOSE-UP VIEWS OF PERHAPS THE MOST IMPRESSIVE CASTLE EARTHWORKS ANYWHERE IN LINCOLNSHIRE.

Furthermore, Castle Bytham village itself is one of south Lincolnshire's picturesque gems and well worth exploring in its own right. (In the author's opinion it is a strong contender to be considered one of the prettiest villages in the entire county.) It is crammed with visual delights including old stone cottages clustered along its narrow, sometimes steep, lanes, with a village pond, an ancient water pump, its church and inns.

Dominating all of this is the massive castle mound whose history goes back to Saxon times

when the locality was the domain of Earl Morcar, Earl of Northumberland. His name lingers on at the nearby 'Morkery' Woods. By AD 1086 the Domesday Book recorded the village as an industrial centre – hard to envisage now – with three iron works, presumably situated here on account of the plentiful wood supply, although since there is no local ironstone this must have been imported.

Following the Norman Conquest the manor was held by Drogo de Beuvriere, a relative of William the Conqueror, and a substantial stone castle was built, presumably replacing Morcar's wooden stockade. This is turn was destroyed after a battle here in 1221 but soon rebuilt again. This third castle lasted until the Wars of the Roses between 1455 and 1487. Some ruins stood until 1542, but in all likelihood you are now probably looking at bits of the castle as you admire today's pretty cottages. Near the castle, in St Martins, are clearly visible remains of the medieval fishponds.

The church, St James's, stands on a site that has probably held a church since Norman times. Inside is a strange curiosity, an ancient, wooden belfry ladder made from an old maypole and marked 'This ware the maypoul – 1660'.

At the top of the hill near the Castle Inn look out for 'The Priory' (on your right) with its church-like windows and guarded by a ship's cannon. It is the oldest house in the village, dating from around 1435 but with an early 16th-century frontage added.

At the village pond (where our walk begins) there is a ramp for sheep dipping and just round the corner in Water Lane stands the imposing village pump dating from Victorian times. The high point (literally) of our short walk comes as we return from the hilltop above the castle where the footpath gives stupendous views of its ramparts.

# THE BASICS

Distance: 1½ miles / 2.5km
Gradient: Gentle to moderate
Severity: Moderate
Approx time to walk: ¾ hr
Stiles: Seven
Maps: OS Landranger 130 (Grantham), Explorer 247 (Grantham)
Path description: Village streets, grass fields and tracks
Start point: Castle Bytham pond. (GR: SK 989186)
Parking: At the bottom of Castlegate/Glen Road at or near pond (NG33 4RJ)
Dog friendly: On lead – stock in fields
Public toilets: None
Nearest refreshments: Castle Inn and Fox & Hounds (both in Castle Bytham)

# CASTLE BYTHAM WALK

1. Face the castle and turn right back into the village. Climb the steps up the small triangular green to the bus stop and telephone kiosk at the front of the Castle Inn. (Those wishing to visit the church should go up Church Lane alongside the inn and return – then turn right.) Otherwise go left and then keep right from the nearby road junction for 250 yards before crossing over to a signed footpath on your left. This is by the former New Inn – now a private house!

2. Pass the garden to a stile and continue downhill to a footbridge with a handgate near the site of some medieval fishponds; cross the bridge and turn right to another stile. Keep forward to reach a derelict cricket pavilion.

3. Now turn left. Climb a third stile and begin a gradual uphill climb – with a fourth stile on the way – to reach yet another stile on your left above the castle. The castle site itself is on private land so stay on the public footpath, marked by a series of white posts, down to a stile in a fence. Beyond that look for a final stile and footbridge to your right; cross it and you are back near the pond where you began.

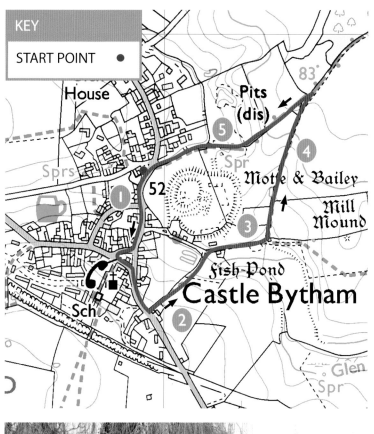

KEY

START POINT ●

House

Pits (dis)

83

Sprs

Spr

52

Motte & Bailey

Mill Mound

Sch

Fish-Pond

Castle Bytham

Glen Spr

# DONINGTON

INITIALLY THE LANDSCAPE AROUND DONINGTON MIGHT SEEM UNREMARKABLE WALKING COUNTRY BUT, AS IN MOST PLACES, INTEREST AND LOCAL HISTORY CAN BE SOUGHT OUT.

Donington is the birthplace of Matthew Flinders, one of Lincolnshire's largely unsung sons and heroes; indeed he is far more revered in Australia than in his home county. He was born on 16 March 1774 and he is commemorated by a plaque on the house presently occupying the site of his birthplace, close to the Black Bull, and by a statue in the Market Place with his faithful cat 'Trim' by his feet. (Trim's devotion throughout many voyages inspired Flinders to write a book in his praise!)

After education at the Cowley School, Donington and at Horbling young Matthew joined the navy aged sixteen and in 1791–93 sailed with the infamous Captain Bligh to Tahiti, later fighting beside Admiral Howe at the 'Glorious 1st of June' in 1794. Then between 1795 and 1800 came his first voyage to Australia, then called New South Wales; it was Flinders who was eventually to apply the name Australia. It was on this trip that he first met George Bass (from Aswarby near Sleaford) and together they circumnavigated Van Diemen's Land, now Tasmania. Their voyage proved it to be an island, thereby shortening the journey to Sydney given that ships had previously sailed round the south of the island. The intervening passage is now named the Bass Strait.

Back in England he married Anne Chappelle at the church in Partney, Lincolnshire on 17 April 1801 (where there is another memorial) before setting out for Australia again in July that same year. Whilst there he circumnavigated the entire Australian continent, being the first person to do so, but was shipwrecked as he set out for home. With a replacement ship he arrived at Mauritius – a French colony – but because his explorer's documentation related to the 'wrong' vessel he was arrested as a suspected spy (England and France being at war!). He was eventually allowed home in June 1810 after seven years in captivity.

His remaining years were spent writing accounts of his voyages and compiling his charts until he was taken ill early in 1814, seeing his finished, printed book only a few days before he died on 19 July 1814.

Donington itself is a former market town and was once an important centre for the hemp and flax trade with renowned twice-yearly horse fairs. St Mary and the Holy Rood Church is mainly in the 13th and 14th-century Decorated and Perpendicular styles and unusual in that the 143-feet (44m) high spire is offset to form the south porch.

Beyond the village as we approach the Eaudykes a short detour visits a memorial to six aircrew who perished here when their Avro Lancaster crashed in April 1944. The gently undulating Eaudykes area represents the remains of the medieval coastline for here was once 'Bicker Haven', a tidal creek stretching inland from The Wash. We also pass close to Wykes Manor, dating from around AD 1280 and probably then moated. Heading back towards Donington we see Baxter's Mill, possibly 18th century but certainly here in 1819. The sails were removed in 1913 and the tower became derelict.

## THE BASICS

Distance: 7 miles / 11.5km
Gradient: Level throughout
Severity: Easy
Approx time to walk: 3 hrs
Stiles: None
Maps: OS Landranger 131 (Boston & Spalding), Explorer 249 (Spalding & Holbeach)
Path description: Country lanes, field paths and grass tracks
Start point: Flinders statue, Market Place, Donington. (GR: TF 208357)
Parking: Market Place, Donington (or nearby PE11 4ST)
Dog friendly: Yes but leads needed when on roads
Public toilets: Park Lane, Donington
Nearest refreshments: Donington: Black Bull; chip shops and Chinese takeaways

# DONINGTON WALK

1. Cross the road and turn left into Park Lane (by the butchers) and then take the first right – still Park Lane – keeping ahead until this bends left. Now go right along a signed footpath and through the churchyard to the road. Turn left to cross the A52 by-pass and turn right.

2. Follow the A52 (there is a pavement!) for three-quarters of a mile and about 300 yards beyond the second junction (Day's Lane) cross to a signposted track. Almost at once this bears left and eventually right to join another lane. Now bear left towards Donington Eaudykes. (To visit the Avro Lancaster crash site first go right for 150 yards and return.)

3. Keep ahead at a T-junction and ignore the bridleway going left at a right-hand bend. At the second T-junction turn left for a few yards to a signed footpath on the right just before Wikes Manor.

4. Follow clear grass tracks and a headland path to join a lane (Pinder Lane) and reach another road (A152).

5. Turn left along the pavement for 200 yards then cross into Haw's Lane following this for a good half a mile to a sharp left-hand bend and then keep ahead along an unsigned track known as South Ing Drove.

6. Just before the railway take the footpath branching right, cross a footbridge and pass between a recreation ground and school to a road. The path continues thirty yards to your left between a wall and some new houses and enters Flinders Park. Go right to walk through the woodland area and at the far end reach the High Street. The Market Place is to your left.

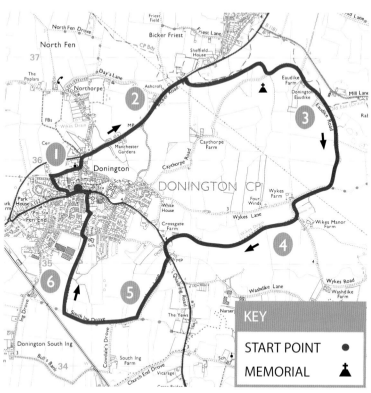

KEY

START POINT ●

MEMORIAL ▲

# FISKERTON & RIVER WITHAM

Country lanes and a riverside walk comprise this delightful walk from Fiskerton, partly along the Viking Way.

Fiskerton Church is dedicated to St Clement author of the Epistle to the Corinthians and has unusual 'clasping' buttresses to its tower supporting the 500 year old stonework. But its real curiosity is concealed, for the external masonry encloses the remains of a circular tower that may date from Saxon times.

To the north of the village, beside the Viking Way, is the site of the former RAF Fiskerton, a World War II airfield opened in 1943. A curious feature here was the installation of an experimental system known as FIDO – Fog Investigation Dispersal Operation – installed at only fifteen airfields. FIDO was an arrangement of pipes alongside the runways through which up to 1,500 gallons of petrol could be pumped each minute and burnt off so that the heat evaporated fog (it all sounds rather dodgy!). One of the final bombing operations from Fiskerton took place on 25 April 1945 when 576 Squadron attacked Berchtesgaden, Hitler's 'Eagle's Nest' hideaway in the Alps. The airfield was closed immediately the war ended in September 1945.

On the old airfield, beside the Viking Way and visible from the path, is the strange sight of 'nodding donkeys' operating a small oilfield. Oil was discovered here in November 1997 and production began in August 1998. The oil is piped to the Welton gathering ground a few miles to the north.

The River Witham's far bank once carried the Great Northern Railway's main line from London to the north built in 1848. Here too, when river traffic was the chief means of travel, was a bargee's inn called Five Mile House (from Lincoln that is!), which became part of the railway station. The station closed in July 1940 and the line closed after the final goods trains ran in 1981. Five Mile Bridge itself was installed in 1957. It replaced a vehicle ferry, which accounts for today's two 'No Through Roads' facing each other from opposite banks. It's worth climbing the bridge for the views.

For many thousands of years the Witham Valley to the east of Lincoln was mostly marshy reed beds and only in 1812 was the meandering river straightened downstream as far as Bardney. However, the area proved rich in archaeological finds and during the 1812 works finds included weapons and dug-out boats. (Apocryphal tales say that these were

so common they were used as logs on the village inn fire.) And discoveries continue to be made! Between Fiskerton and the river our walk passes the oldest site so far found although there's nothing to see above ground now. In 2001 some 195 buried wooden posts, dated to around 450 BC, were found in the field beside the footpath. Their purpose remains obscure but they were perhaps some sort of causeway or jetty.

More finds of weapons, jewellery, tools, bone and pottery, including Roman artefacts were, archaeologists believe, religious offerings to the 'Gods'. A reconstruction of the 'causeway' and some of the objects can be seen at 'The Collection' museum at Lincoln.

NOTES. Readers may park at the Carpenter's Arms by kind permission of the landlord; park at the rear leaving room for non-walking patrons. Unless eating at the inn please park considerately elsewhere in the village on Sundays when the inn is extra busy.

# THE BASICS

Distance: 4½ miles / 7.5km
Gradient: Virtually level throughout
Severity: Easy
Approx time to walk: 2¼ hrs
Stiles: None
Maps: OS Landranger 121 (Lincoln), Explorer 272 (Lincoln)
Path description: Village roads, bridleways and field paths
Start point: Carpenter's Arms, Fiskerton (GR: TF 050720)
Parking: At Carpenter's Arms (LN3 4HF)
Dog friendly: On leads
Public toilets: None
Nearest refreshments: Carpenter's Arms, Fiskerton

# FISKERTON & RIVER WITHAM WALK

1. From the inn car park turn right through Fiskerton for about half a mile and at the end of the village bear left into Hall Lane.

2. When this bends right keep ahead along the Viking Way, initially a short track but soon becoming a hedged bridleway that passes the old airfield and then bears right. At a first three-way footpath sign (where a path branches right) keep ahead; also ignore two more signposts where paths branch left.

3. About 100 yards after the second of these the path swings right to a fourth three-way sign. Now turn right with a hedge on your right soon passing some woods to reach a farm access track. Go right again onto a concrete road.

4. At a T-junction you are back in Hall Lane. Turn right for a quarter of a mile to a footpath sign near some woods and turn left alongside them. When the trees end walk ahead over an arable field towards another small wood where a path through the trees leads to a road. Turn right – there is soon a pavement – and continue until level with the 'Old Tannery' (B & B).

5. Now cross into the lane opposite and follow it down towards the River Witham. Immediately before the river footbridge, take the footpath on your right (the Viking Way again) along the river embankment.

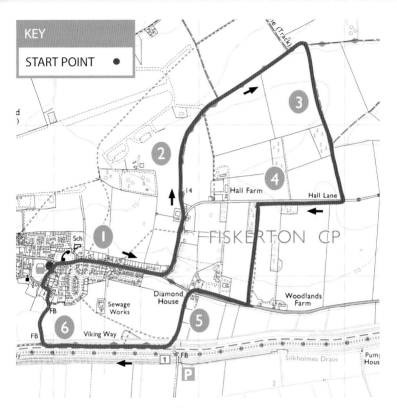

6. After half a mile cross the North Delph by the footbridge below you on your right. Follow a grass path by a fence to a junction and go left over another footbridge to join a lane and turn left. At the main road walk forward to visit church and return – or simply turn right back to the inn.

# FOSDYKE & RIVER WELLAND

THIS WALK PROVIDES A BRACING STROLL OVERLOOKING THE WASH, A VAST, WATERY WILDERNESS ALONG LINCOLNSHIRE'S EAST COAST. THE WALK RETURNS ALONGSIDE THE RIVER WELLAND.

Today's Fosdyke Bridge dates from 1980 and is the latest of several. The first plans for a bridge across the Welland here were made in the late 1700s but the earliest actually built was designed by Sir John Rennie and erected in 1815. Prior to that either a guide or ferry (or a combination of both!) was needed to safely cross the marshes. By 1836 Rennie's bridge needed major repairs but once completed the bridge lasted until 1911 when a cast iron replacement was built.

We distantly glimpse Fosdyke village; the name comes from the Saxon for 'Fotr's Dyke', but even so the leaden broach spire of All Saints Church, built in 1871, is prominent early in the walk. Nearer to the old sea bank can be seen the Middlecott Hospital, actually ten almshouses dating from 1625, paid for by Sir Thomas Middlecott.

The River Welland has been an important shipping route for centuries; indeed it may have been a Bronze Age immigration route. There was certainly access to the river from Stamford via a canal built to encourage trade with the Baltic ports as early as the 1670s. Fosdyke had, however, already been involved with shipbuilding and importing timber since medieval times, but silting was a recurrent problem and sometimes boats were carried overland to Surfleet on the River Glen tributary.

This meant that the Welland estuary saw the development of a variety of laws governing riverbank maintenance during the 15th century, many of which survived until the 1930s. The system of drainage dykes in the area was also largely in place by the early 1800s. Here too bank strengthening was pioneered in the 1830s by one James Walker, who used thorn branches and consolidated clay to minimise erosion. More improvements, including widening and straightening, have taken place since World War II.

Dating of the more ancient sea banks around The Wash is difficult and prone to uncertainty but they were probably begun in the early 13th century. There is no evidence for any being Roman in origin, even though the name of some stretches imply otherwise. The inner bank, which we walk first, just might be Saxon but is more likely to be early 14th century.

A curious situation arises just after Kirton Marsh pumping station for the sea bank, as it curves back south and inland, contrives to cross the Greenwich Meridian twice within the space of 300 yards or so!

Also the banks around this side of The Wash form part of the 290-mile-long Macmillan Way between Boston and the Dorset coast.

Finally – the marsh here is known for its bird life so bring your binoculars.

NOTES. Picnic on the outer sea banks with views over the Welland and The Wash.

## THE BASICS

Distance: 6½ miles / 10.5km
Gradient: Easy and level throughout but for accessing sea banks
Severity: Moderate
Approx time to walk: 3 hrs
Stiles: Five
Maps: OS Landranger 131 (Boston & Spalding), Explorer 249 (Spalding & Holbeach)
Path description: Old sea banks, riverside grass track and some country lanes
Start point: Ship Inn, Fosdyke Bridge. (GR: TF 318323)
Parking: Ship Inn (PE12 6LH)
Dog friendly: Yes – except for stiles
Public toilets: None
Nearest refreshments: Ship Inn, Fosdyke Bridge

1. From the inn turn right and cross the bridge and the river to a footpath sign near the boatyard. Follow the path along an embankment between houses and the boatyard onto a gravel track keeping forward a few yards to a waymarked gate on the right by a wall. Go up onto the riverbank and on reaching a concrete ramp and footpath sign veer left, away from the river along an old sea bank.

2. Initially tree-lined this has fine views towards Fosdyke Church and the Middlecott Hospital. At a lane cross a farm track and continue along the sea bank as it becomes more open. It soon swings sharp left and near a farm descends to a lane end in open countryside. Keep ahead on a much lower bank (though the route is clear), which shortly bears right to rejoin a full height section again. At steps leading to an 'Unclassified County Road' stay on the bank until it joins another road at a footpath sign.

3. Turn right along the road with the sea bank on your left for about half a mile and at a junction turn right onto the access track for Hundred Acre Farm.

4. In 20 yards leave the track, veering left from a waymark along a grassy sea bank and continue over two stiles. The path then becomes more distinct in a long field. Beyond a third stile, near a house and garden, join a track. Bear right at a footpath sign to a stile by a gate and keep forward, with a drain on your left until you arrive at Kirton Marsh pumping station.

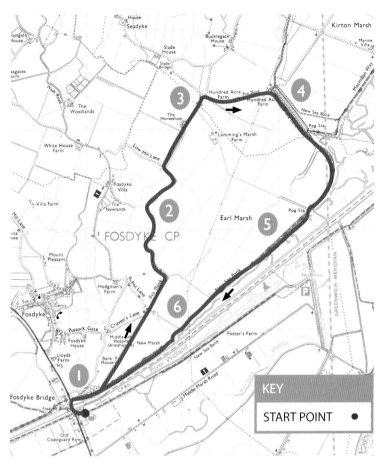

5. Climb another stile before veering right to a bridle gate giving access to the newest bank. Follow it, soon gradually swinging right; it is here that you twice cross the Greenwich Meridian! You will soon now come alongside the River Welland and after two miles arrive back near the Fosdyke marina.

6. Rejoin the outward route for the few final yards back to the A17 and the inn.

# FREISTON SHORE

THIS WALK EXPLORES THE RSPB RESERVE AT FREISTON
SHORE OVERLOOKING THE WASH. WHILST ENJOYING SOME
BRACING SEA AIR WE DISCOVER SOME LOCAL HISTORY AND
WILDLIFE.

The earliest sea banks here were traditionally considered to be Roman but are more likely to be medieval although the Saxons were probably the earliest settlers hereabouts in the mid 5th century. The coastline then was possibly a mile or so inland from today's RSPB car park. However, by the mid 18th century Freiston Shore was a popular seaside resort often referred to as the 'Brighton of Lincolnshire'. It boasted two hotels, between them offering around a hundred bedrooms and served by regular coaches from Boston.

The Plummer's Hotel (originally the Coach and Horses and later the Anchor Inn) took its present name from the family that ran it. The other was the adjacent Marine Hotel – still there too, but in ruins!

A bridge led from the Plummer's upper storey onto the sea bank, and modern ones still allow residents of neighbouring cottages to reach their gardens! In the 1840s the beach lay immediately beyond the bank and horse racing regularly took place; although presumably only when the tide was out, for it lapped the bank within yards of the hotel as late as 1908. Freiston's popularity declined, however, as the salt marsh grew and the railways reached Skegness in 1873. Following the disastrous 'Great Flood' of 1810 there were several failed reclamation schemes, particularly during the 1850s and 1870s, but most reclamation has taken place from the 1930s onwards.

During World War II much of Lincolnshire's coastline saw many defence fortifications built and those that remain at Freiston are perhaps the best preserved. Just beyond the Plummer's are substantial six-inch gun emplacements, ammunition stores, accommodation/sleeping quarters and lookout pillboxes.

The RSPB established their reserve here in 2000 and two years later, as part of the Wash Banks Scheme, the outer sea bank to the northeast was breached, partly to extend the reserve by creating additional salt marsh but also as a flood defence mechanism. More recently the reserve has been extended southwards by almost 200 acres of new wetland.

With another lagoon and small hide the whole reserve (lagoons, wetland and salt marsh) currently extends to nearly 2,000 acres.

The longer walk also visits the Lincolnshire Bird Club hide at Cut End, a remote spot and

wonderful birdwatching location. There are extensive views of the Witham and Welland river outfalls and across The Wash itself, which is one of England's premier salt marsh habitats. The two-storey hide opened in 1987 and was refurbished in 2009.

Passed on the outer sea bank as we head towards Cut End is a memorial to the inmates of North Sea Camp prison who began the bank's construction in 1936. The camp had opened in 1935 so this was perhaps the prisoners' first task but it achieved the reclamation of some 500 acres of land. One must doubt, however, whether many of them would have understood the somewhat pretentious Latin dedication plaque!

NOTES. The reserve is signposted from the A52 via Freiston.

# THE BASICS

Distance: 3½ / 5.5km or 5½ miles / 9km
Gradient: Ascents/descents onto and off sea banks – otherwise level
Severity: Easy to moderate throughout
Approx time to walk: 2 or 3 hrs (plus birdwatching time!)
Stiles: None
Maps: OS Landranger 131 (Boston & Spalding), Explorer 261 (Boston) (the last few yards to Cut End are shown on OS Explorer 249 (Spalding & Holbeach)
Path description: Grassy sea banks, surfaced road and reserve paths
Start point: RSPB car park, Freiston Shore (GR: TF 397424)
Parking: At RSPB reserve (near PE22 0LY)
Dog friendly: Dogs allowed only on a lead
Public toilets: None
Nearest refreshments: In Freiston village (2½ miles) the Bull & Dog and the King's Head; also picnic tables/seats at reserve car park

# FREISTON SHORE WALK

1. From the car park return towards the entrance ramp. (An RSPB Wetland Trail keeps ahead on the concrete road below the inner sea bank. The main route joins this in approximately three-quarters of a mile so you can follow this instead if you wish.)

2. Our route, which is grassy underfoot, turns left on the public footpath at the top of the ramp passing through a series of gates and gardens behind the Plummer's Hotel and going directly past the World War II gun emplacements etc. Stay on the bank top until the road and bank part company; the bank veering right and the road below going left. Descend left to a kissing gate at this point to join the road. Continue along it until you reach the boundary gates of North Sea Camp.

3. The walk now follows the grass track on the left that leads to steps climbing the outer sea bank. Once on the bank top the short route turns left back towards the RSPB lagoons (see 5).

4. Clearly visible to your right (on the longer route) some 300 yards away is the memorial. Walk just that far or continue the full distance to the Cut End bird hide. (It's about a mile each way!) Return the way you came.

5. Stay on the bank top until a path is seen descending leftwards by the southern edge of the main reserve lagoon; this leads back to the car park via the RSPB hide.

6. Alternatively a few steps further on another path bears left to skirt the northern shore of the lagoon. When this reaches some steps on the left turn off to follow the inner bank past the Marine Hotel ruins to reach the car park.

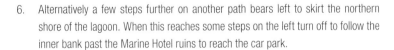

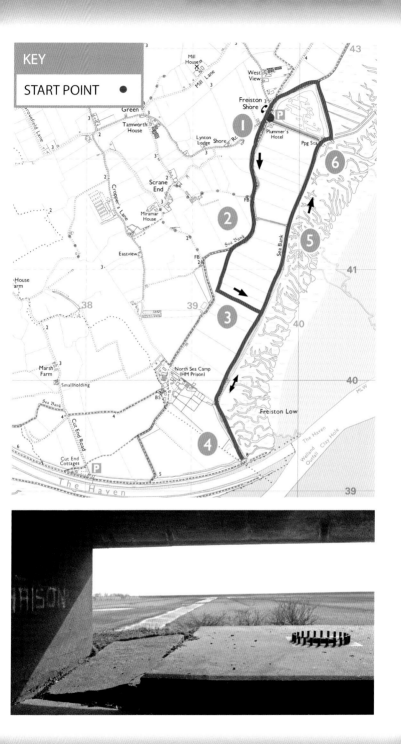

# FULLETBY (HOE HILL)

THIS WALK IS DIFFERENT IN THAT IT EXPLORES PERMISSIVE
PATHS CREATED BY THE LANDOWNER IN CONJUNCTION
WITH DEFRA AT HOE HILL, FULLETBY.

Special maps are provided at access
points and the route mainly consists
of clear, wide grass paths though
waymarks are few. Although OS map
details are given the paths used (except
near the start) do not appear on them.

Fulletby is one of Lincolnshire's highest
villages, located around the 135-metres
(about 440 feet) contour, and its name
with the Old Danish ending of 'by'
indicates a village, or farmstead, here
since the second half of the 9th century.
We know that the area was occupied
much earlier than that, however, for on
Nab Hill (to our left as we set off) there
have been archaeological finds from the
Early Neolithic age some 4,000 years
ago.

Hoe Hill, with its flat top, is deceptive
in resembling a prehistoric hill fort, but
the explanation lies instead in its geology as it is formed from a hard, erosion resistant
limestone known as carstone. Although it might have been occupied in prehistoric times
archaeological evidence is inconclusive. Fulletby is also unique amongst Lincolnshire
villages having an entry in the Guinness Book of Records.

The story begins in January 1816 when Henry Winn was born there; a remarkable man
destined to live in the village throughout his 98 years! At age ten his father died and he
left school to support his mother and the younger family members, but nevertheless
continued to educate himself at home. After marrying he opened a general store and
worked as a decorator, an auctioneer's clerk and later on as the village constable, Sunday
school teacher and local tax collector. Henry also set up a village sick club and by 1850
had founded a village library stocked with his own books.

However, in 1830, when he was fourteen, he became parish clerk and for this he achieved an entry in the record books. Initially he took on the role because the elected clerk was illiterate, but he subsequently held the job full time continuously from 1845 until 1910, a grand total of 80 years, which qualified him as England's longest acting public servant.

Although Fulletby had an earlier church the present St Andrew's dates from 1705 but was much restored in 1857. Henry Winn's grave may be found in the churchyard, directly opposite his former shop, now a private home but still with its old shop window.

NOTES. Verge parking is available at the start just east of Fulletby village at the T-junction (grid reference TF 302734). The access permits expire on 28 February 2019.

# THE BASICS

Distance: 2¾ miles / 4.5km or 3½ miles / 5.5km

Gradient: Some fairly steep ascents and descents

Severity: Moderate to hard

Approx time to walk: 2½ hrs: add half an hour for extension

Stiles: Four

Maps: OS Landranger 122 (Skegness & Horncastle), Explorer 273 (Lincolnshire Wolds South)

Path description: Rough grass fields, farm tracks and country lanes

Start point: Fulletby; at T-junction east of village (GR: TF 302734)

Parking: On verge (LN9 6JZ)

Dog friendly: Best kept on leads

Public toilets: None

Nearest refreshments: None on route. Nearby inns in Belchford, Tetford or Horncastle

# FULLETBY (HOE HILL) WALK

1. The footpath begins at a stile beside the entrance to Gorse Farm – by the water tower. Walk downhill aiming for the left-hand corner of Salmonby Carr Woods in the valley below and crossing two intervening stiles on the way. Do not cross the next stile by the corner of woods but turn right following the field edge round to another stile and climb that.

2. Turn left and drop steeply down to a footbridge in a hollow, climb the far side and continue over grass, keeping parallel to the woods and with some electricity poles to your left. Continue to a second footbridge in trees (it's about 50 yards right of the field corner), cross it and keep forward to reach a hedge. Then turn right on a grass field-edge towards Hoe Hill.

3. As the slope steepens cross a track and continue climbing ahead. The path curves over the shoulder of Hoe Hill. (The summit is open access – via a stile – but if you visit return to the path at the point you left it!) Descend the far side of the hill where a winding grass path descends by a hedge. At the bottom swing right through a thicket to arrive at two footbridges; cross the second one with an 'Access map' near it.

4. Now proceed uphill with a ditch to your left, and near the top curve right. You will soon see a track going left past the ruins of Hook's Barn; follow this to the road and turn right back to the start.

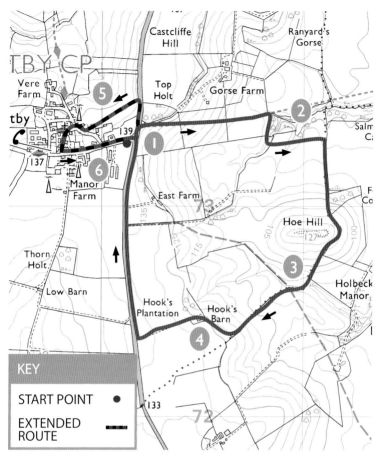

5. Continue past the starting point of the main walk along the Belchford road and just beyond the water tower go through the wide hedge gap on your left where there's another access map. (There are fabulous views here!) Walk down the left-hand edge of the field and in the bottom left-hand corner locate a short, fenced path and grass track leading to a road.

6. Cross into Church Street opposite and after visiting St Andrew's Church and Henry Winn's grave, go up Winn Lane, which is opposite the church gate. At the T-junction go left heading out of the village back to the start.

# MARSTON & HOUGHAM

THIS ROUTE ENJOYS CONSIDERABLE VARIETY WITH FINE VIEWS, TWO INTERESTING CHURCHES, SOME RAILWAY HISTORY AND EVEN AN ORNITHOLOGICAL BREAK.

Marston lies about six miles to the north of Grantham and our walk begins near the village school. This was built in 1861 to a rather unusual design that has a diagonally offset tower projecting from the main building and supported by a single column. Opposite the school a walled passage leads to St Mary's Church with its wonderful broach spire and Early English and Decorated period stonework. Inside a 'Thorold Chapel' contains monuments to the family who have lived at the nearby Hall since the mid 1300s; parts of the present hall date from the late 16th century.

Soon after leaving Marston we pass a nature reserve where a public hide overlooks lagoons installed in 1990 by the Anglian Water Board. These attract many species of birds so it's worthwhile stopping even though it's near the beginning of the walk! (Alternatively you could return later; there is a small roadside car park.)

Beyond the AWA waterworks is the East Coast main line railway between London, the North of England and Scotland built by the Great Northern Railway and opened in 1852. It became known as the 'Towns Line', since its route passed through Stamford, Grantham and Doncaster and by so doing replaced the original circuitous route via Boston and Lincoln.

Next comes a pleasant stroll beside the River Witham. Here, strangely, the river having mainly flowed northwards from its source is now somewhat obstinately heading west, away from the sea, to circumvent the high ground of the Lincoln Heath before it can then begin to head eastwards again towards The Wash. We see the river again at Hougham, by then heading north-west. Leaving the river we climb to the highest section of the walk along Frinkley Lane. The lane's present alignment probably dates from the Enclosure Acts of the late 18th century; note the difference in width either side of the Barkston/Hougham parish boundary at grid reference SK 917436.

As we turn down Manor Lane in Hougham a seat beside the Victorian village water pump welcomes us. Then on reaching the Witham again it's worth turning off the few yards to visit All Saints' Church. In the churchyard look out for the amazing collection of Hickson family memorials; eleven in one row alone with others scattered nearby and close to the porch. All Saints has some remarkable gargoyles too and, should it be locked, the clear windows allow a good interior view.

Finally Hougham Manor requires a mention. The present house is externally all early Georgian but this facade hides part of an 'interior' house dating from around 1620. Some masonry may even date from the early 1400s or possibly a Norman house whose moat has now mostly been filled in.

NOTES. Park considerately in School Lane, Marston and cross the railway line with care. In suitable weather picnic by the riverbank near Hougham Church.

## THE BASICS

Distance: 6½ miles / 10.5 km
Gradient: One steepish climb otherwise gentle ascents / descents
Severity: Moderate
Approx time to walk: 3½ hrs
Stiles: None
Maps: OS Landranger 130 (Grantham), Explorer 247 (Grantham)
Path description: Village streets, grass paths and tracks
Start point: School Lane, Marston (GR: SK 892436)
Parking: School Lane, Marston (NG32 2HH)
Dog friendly: On leads for most of walk
Public toilets: None
Nearest refreshments: Thorold Arms, Marston

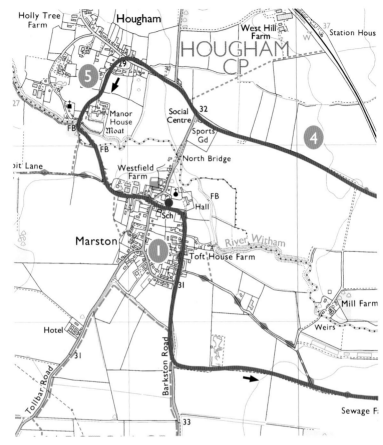

1. Set off along School Lane heading away from the main road and bear right into Barkstone Road. Continue until you are about a quarter of a mile outside the village and can turn left onto a track at a footpath sign. Some 200 yards along this a path goes off to the left to the nature reserve and bird hide. Return to the track and turn left keeping ahead until you reach a surfaced lane.

2. Go left here and at the waterworks keep to the right of the entrance following a track through a zigzag before passing under the East Coast main line. A clear path now meanders through

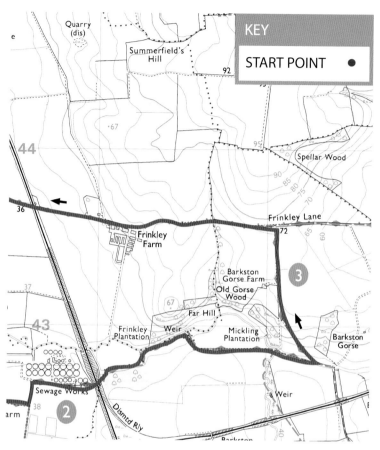

fields and alongside the River Witham. Eventually, at a footpath sign, it turns right uphill and then goes left to rejoin the river again near a bailey bridge. Cross this and keep forward for 200 yards to another footpath sign.

3.   Double back sharply left here, going uphill on a stony track to meet Frinkley Lane – a grass track – at a 'Restricted Byway' sign. Now turn left keeping ahead with some wonderful views that soon include Hougham Church spire approximately two miles away. Walk through a farmyard,

and beyond it keep ahead and cross the railway. Now head down a lane to a road junction just outside Hougham.

4. Bear right along the pavement and take the first left turn into the village. Turn left again on reaching Manor Lane and (passing the village pump) walk down to the manor entrance and a footpath sign and kissing gate just inside it. Now walk round so as to pass to the right of the house to a second kissing gate close to a footbridge over the River Witham.

5. Cross the bridge from which a clear path heads towards a kissing gate and another footbridge in a hedge. The walk now crosses a final field to join a lane on the edge of Marston village. Turn left and walk back to the inn at the crossroads by the school.

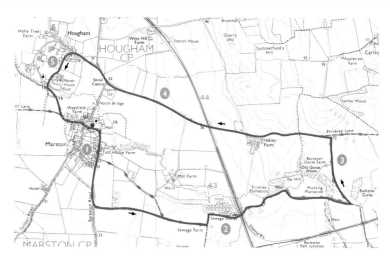

# MINTING & CHAMBERS FARM WOOD

HIDDEN IN REMOTE COUNTRYSIDE MINTING, GAUTBY AND THE LIMEWOODS NATURE RESERVE OF CHAMBER'S FARM WOOD OFFER A FASCINATING RAMBLE.

Firstly the Sebastopol Inn! The inn's unusual name is said to have originated after the Crimean War when a local soldier, safely returned from Sebastopol, over-celebrated, fell into a dyke and drowned. The building partly dates from the 16th century but only became a beer house brewing its own ale from around the mid 1830s when a landlord is mentioned in the 1836 census.

Minting is an ancient settlement and appears in the Domesday Book of 1086. Its church, St Andrew's, externally at least, dates only from 1864 although the interior has some 13th-century Early English stonework. Nearby are earthworks of the Benedictine Minting Priory founded about 1129, but by 1421 a 'Grange', that is a working ecclesiastical farm, belonging to Mount Grace Priory in Yorkshire.

Ramblers cannot fail to notice the striking contrast between Minting Church and the little Georgian All Saints at Gautby, built in 1756 by the Vyner family of Gautby Hall. As prosperous City bankers and goldsmiths, they had made the coronation regalia for Charles II. Their Gautby house lay to the south-west of the church in an area still named on OS maps as the 'Great Park'. However, it was demolished in 1872 when they inherited a far grander home at Newby Hall in Yorkshire. Thankfully their delightful church survives with some Vyner family monuments within.

Chambers Farm Wood is one of the largest woodlands in the area, which collectively comprise 'The Lincolnshire Limewoods'. These ancient woodlands, that are known to be more than 600 years old, are rare survivals and are particularly special as they contain many small-leaved lime trees (Tilia cordata) that are uncommon elsewhere. Consequently the Limewoods are a National Nature Reserve, protected not only for their trees but also for the many species of plants and animals that they support. Chambers Farm Wood has several conservation projects under way to increase populations of

such species as bats, tree sparrows and the Brown Hairstreak butterfly. In 2002 another important project was begun to re-introduce dormice when 16 micro-chipped pairs were successfully released. Its success has seen an increasing expansion throughout the neighbourhood. Information panels at the visitor centre explain more about these initiatives.

NOTES. Details of other waymarked walks within Chambers Farm Wood are obtainable from the visitor centre.

# THE BASICS

Distances: 7½ miles / 12km or 8¾ miles / 14km

Gradient: Level throughout

Severity: Moderate – but only on account of the distance; the going is easy

Approx time to walk: 3 or 4hrs

Stiles: None

Maps: OS Landrangers 121 (Lincoln) & 122 (Skegness), Explorer 273 (Lincolnshire Wolds South)

Path description: Country lanes, grassy and surfaced woodland tracks. One meadow if visiting Minting Priory site.

Start point: Sebastopol Inn, Minting (GR: TF 187735)

Parking: At inn – but please advise landlord before setting off (LN9 5RS)

Dog friendly: on leads on roads; leads mandatory in Chambers Farm Wood reserve

Public toilets: None

Nearest refreshments: Sebastopol Inn, Minting

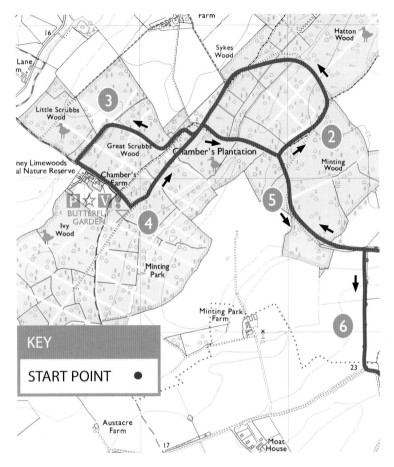

1.  Exit the inn car park and turn right through Minting village (along Grundy's Lane) to a junction near the village hall and there keep ahead on the unsigned track opposite. After a mile when the main track bends left continue ahead along a tree-lined track and past a vehicle barrier to enter Chambers Farm Wood. Continue until you reach a triangular clearing where there is a waymark for the 'Red Route' trail.

2.  Bear right along this following a woodland track. This soon bends left, straightens,

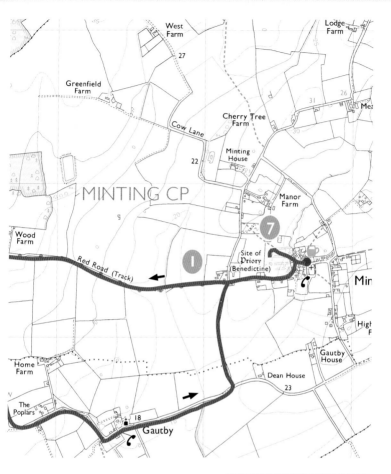

goes left again then straightens once more to reach another open area, also with a 'Red Route' waymark. (We will return here to head back to Gautby and/or Minting.)

3. Keep forward about 100 yards to a footbridge on the right and turn onto the 'White Trail'. From a marker post go left over another footbridge and then essentially follow the 'White Route' as it meanders through the woods. Look out for carved sculptures along the way; one tree-trunk bench has a badger hiding in a hole at its far end! After two sharp

left turns the path runs parallel to the reserve approach road. Beyond a clearing with a woodsman and deer sculptures immediately turn right to join the road opposite the visitor centre.

4.  Turn left through the car park then follow marker posts and a track round to the left back to the 'Red' waymark mentioned in section 3. Now turn right.

5.  At the next clearing (where we joined the 'Red Route' after entering Chambers Wood) veer right back along the outward route from Minting. Retrace your steps to the bend in the track outside the woods. [The shorter walk now returns to Minting the way you came.]

6.  The main route, however, turns right. Follow the track to a road and turn left then left again at the first junction to reach Gautby. Half a mile beyond the church make a third left turn. Finally bear right for the Sebastopol Inn when you again reach Minting village hall.

7.  Some readers may wish to visit the priory site which has a public right of way across it. Just before the Sebastopol Inn turn left at the footpath sign by 'The Green'. Immediately go left again behind a cottage following a walled path to a kissing gate. After passing a pond the right of way bears right across a meadow with obvious earthworks on either side. At the far side is a stile; walk to that and return the way you came.

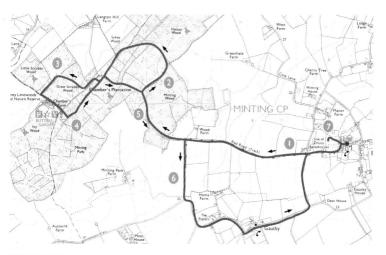

# NEWTON & PICKWORTH

The picturesque stone-built village of Newton lies just off the busy A52 to the east of Grantham. Our walk starts from the Red Lion inn.

On leaving the main road Newton is approached over Sixpenny Hill, a name derived from the payment due at the former toll bar beside the ancient Salter's Way that preceded the modern A52. Locals reckon that, provided you travel due east, Sixpenny Hill is the highest ground between Newton and Russia.

The oldest part of the Red Lion inn dates from the mid 1600s though it is likely an inn was here much earlier. Newton developed as an estate village belonging to the wealthy Welby family of Denton near Grantham, who built Newton House in 1841. The first school was set below the church overlooking the green but in 1874 the Welbys paid for the building of a 'new' one across the road – this is now a private residence. St Botolph's Church is mostly 14th and 15th century and in the Early English style though some fragments of Norman stonework survived an 1867 restoration. The village cross still proudly occupies the green.

Having left the village our walk uses Getton's Lane, initially narrow but broadening into a wide grassy highway that may date from the local enclosures completed around 1769/70. The gentle climb soon gives extensive views over the South Kesteven countryside including the neighbouring parish of Pickworth – reached via an optional extension to the main walk on a DEFRA Conservation permissive footpath. (The access permit to this expires on 31 August 2019.) Later in the walk we follow another tree-lined track called Green Lane.

A visit to Pickworth is recommended for St Andrew's Church which contains some truly remarkable medieval wall paintings – perhaps the best in Lincolnshire. Keyholder details are displayed at the porch. (And even if you don't do the extension anyone interested in old churches should still visit Pickworth afterwards.)

The little hamlet of Haceby has been farmed since at least Roman times, for one of their villas was excavated nearby in 1939. Here also is St Margaret's Church (Grade I listed), one of Lincolnshire's hidden architectural treasures and maintained by the Churches Conservation Trust. The tower base is Norman with a late-13th to mid-14th-century upper section. There is 17th-century graffiti in the porch but the real surprise is inside where there are more medieval paintings over the chancel arch, although they have been partially overpainted with Queen Anne's royal arms – another rarity!

This is a good nature walk too! The route includes roadside wildflower nature reserves and the surrounding woods are home to fallow deer. And red kites have been spotted hereabouts! A look around Newton is recommended too!

NOTES. Walkers are welcome to park at the Red Lion inn. There is some rough ground and strong footwear is recommended.

## THE BASICS

Distances: 4½ miles / 7km or 5¾ miles / 9km or 6½ miles / 10.5 km
Gradient: Easy
Severity: Easy
Approx time to walk: 2 to 3½ hrs
Stiles: Three on main route; none on extension
Maps: OS Landranger 130 (Grantham), Explorer 248 (Bourne & Heckington)
Path description: Country lanes, green lanes, field paths and tracks; one arable field
Start point: Newton (Red Lion Inn) (GR: TF 045361)
Parking: Red Lion inn (NG34 0EE)
Dog friendly: Off leads possible on green lanes
Public toilets: None
Nearest refreshments: Red Lion, Newton

# NEWTON & PICKWORTH WALK

1. From the inn car park turn right uphill and continue round a right-hand bend, then after 150 yards take the track to your left (Getton's Lane). After a mile come to a road and turn right. In 100 yards the extension to Pickworth begins; look for the DEFRA Access Map on the left.

2. If you are not doing the extension then continue to a T-junction and keep ahead. Then see 4 below.

3. Otherwise turn left and walk down the field edge to reach a footbridge. Cross this and bear right for 15 yards, then go left behind and alongside another hedge to the next field corner. (Here you will see a footbridge on your left.) Don't cross this but turn right along a field-edge track and at the field's far corner go left along a short lane to a road. Turn right towards the church and into Pickworth. Two hundred yards beyond St Andrew's turn right and keep right again, into Mill Lane. This will meet with the short cut at a T-junction where you should turn left.

4. After a quarter of a mile turn right along another tree-lined grass track (Green Lane), which continues, eventually over open ground, to meet another road.

5. A second optional extension starts here to Haceby adding less than a mile – there and back! To do this turn left, go round a right-hand bend and across a T-junction into the hamlet – and return the same way.

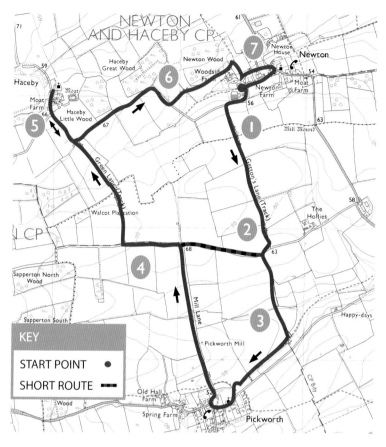

**KEY**

START POINT ●

SHORT ROUTE ▬▬▬

6.  If you are not going to Haceby turn right now. After a right-hand bend look for a signed footpath going left across an arable field. Cross this to a footbridge and kissing gate, then keep forward beside some woods. After a stile, pass a farm and go through a gateway to reach a second stile. Now bear right to a final stile by a gate that gives onto a lane outside the inn.

7.  Turn left to do a 'circular' tour of Newton village. Keep bearing right and you will get back to the Red Lion.

# NORMANBY-LE-WOLD

We really are on the 'roof' of Lincolnshire since we start and end this walk at Normanby-le-Wold, situated on the Viking Way, with the highest point in the entire county (168 metres / 551 feet at grid ref TF 122 965) barely a mile to the north.

Normanby-le-Wold is thus Lincolnshire's highest village and so St Peter's Church is also the county's highest church. It was restored externally in 1868 but the interior is much older than the outward appearance suggests. Once inside its true age becomes apparent, for much of it, especially the south aisle, is medieval. Of special interest are two small carvings. One is curiously (and perhaps uniquely) shaped like a ram's horn and its symbolism – whether religious or secular, or simply a stonemason's 'joke' – has never been convincingly explained. The second is a lifelike representation of a man in agony with toothache. There are some large Victorian paintings at the west end that came here from Burton-on-Trent, Staffordshire in the 1970s; there's another one at Claxby too! Just across the lane stands a Georgian chapel that once served as the Sunday School but is now a farm store.

From Normanby we make the descent of what the author believes is the steepest right of way in Lincolnshire. But before we head downhill there are exceptional views along the crest of the Wolds northwards towards Nettleton Top and south-westwards to Lincoln.

The name Claxby is of Scandinavian origin; it was 'Cleaxbyg' in 1067 and 'Clachesbi' by the time the Domesday Book was compiled in 1086. As you follow the footpath through the village to the church you will pass (on the left) the mound of the Claxby House icehouse, which can be glimpsed again across the meadow (and again on your left) as you leave along the permissive footpath.

Claxby lies peaceful now but has an industrial past for in the 1880s mining began here as the Cretaceous chalk (135 million years old) contains beds of ironstone measuring up to ten feet thick in places. (Mining on a much larger scale took place at nearby Nettleton from 1929 to supply steelworks at Scunthorpe.)

In Claxby we find a rather unusual church for St Mary's has what is known as a nodding

chancel, a feature more noticeable inside than out. If you go inside and look along the nave you will see that the chancel is misaligned. What no one can say is whether this was an error in construction or something deliberate. Some view it as being a reference to Christ's head drooping whilst on the cross.

NOTES. This walk involves a long, steep descent over rough grass; the return climb is gentler but quite rough underfoot in places. Limited parking is possible near Normanby Church; or use verges outside the village.

## THE BASICS

Distance: 4¼ miles / 7 km

Gradient: One very steep descent; one long but gradual ascent

Severity: Moderate to difficult

Approx time to walk: 2½ hrs

Stiles: Four

Maps: OS Landranger 113 (Grimsby), Explorer 282 (Lincolnshire Wolds North)

Path description: Steep grass hillside, country lanes, farm tracks, meadows and open moorland

Start point: Normanby-le-Wold Church (GR: TF 123947)

Parking: Limited parking near Normanby Church (LN7 6ST)

Dog friendly: On leads; there may stock in fields and the route uses public roads

Public toilets: None

Nearest refreshments: None on route. The nearest inns or tearooms are in Nettleton and Tealby

# NORMANBY-LE-WOLD WALK

1. With your back to Normanby Church return down the lane for about 150 yards (a very short bit of the Viking Way) and then take the footpath from the field gate on the left. Keep near the left-hand edge of the meadow, passing Normanby Grange to reach a stile in a hedge. Climb over and pause to admire the views before beginning the steep descent alongside Claxby Wood. At the bottom left-hand corner a stile gives onto a road – the aptly named Normanby Rise!

2. Turn left down the road for some 250 yards and then take the signed path on the right (Boggle Lane). Follow this, ignoring a path branching left, to pass through a gate and over two footbridges. The lane then widens, becomes surfaced and leads into Claxby and to a road junction.

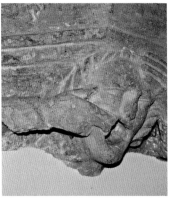

3. Turn left for approximately 200 yards and then go right on an enclosed path beside a white bungalow; this passes close to the icehouse to emerge in a lane near the church. Turn left until just after the church the lane ends at a stile and field gate.

4. A permissive path (not shown on OS maps) now crosses the meadow ahead to reach a kissing gate at a bend of a road. Keep ahead and at the next bend, where the road goes right, keep ahead again into a 'No Through Road'. Just before Claxby House Farm bear left up the signed 'Byway' keeping to a track below some woods. Beyond a gate the track becomes rough underfoot and continues across open moorland. Contour around the hillside to a three-way footpath sign where we rejoin the Viking Way.

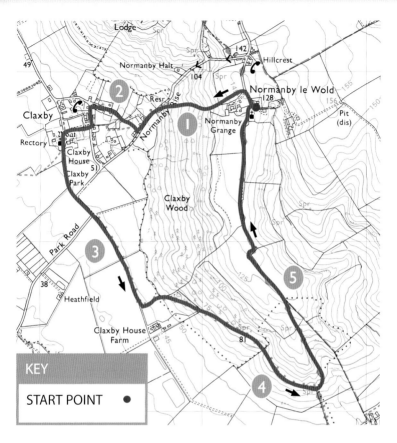

5. Bear left, climbing gently up the side of a shallow valley with rocky outcrops to your left to reach another footpath sign. Continue uphill following Viking Way waymarks, and always with a fence/hedge close on your right. Eventually, with Normanby Grange ahead, look for a stile on the right from which a short, unsurfaced lane heads back to St Peter's Church in Normanby.

# SKILLINGTON

On this walk in south-west Lincolnshire near the Leicestershire border we discover some derring-do adventures in the Swiss Alps and a historic former US World War II airfield.

We begin in Skillington, 'Schellintune' of the Domesday Book, where both inns have unusual names. The early 19th century saw fierce competition for local Parliamentary seats from, amongst others, the local Manners-Tollemache family. They supported the Whigs (whose colour was blue) and with their extensive landholdings could compel innkeepers to change the names of their hostelries. (Buying of votes through hospitality was of course rife too!) Consequently at one time Grantham and the surrounding area had over thirty 'Blue' inns including Skillington's 'Blue Horse'. One of the Manners also became the Marquis of Granby and had strong links with the 21st Lancers, with headquarters in Grantham; the 'Crossed Swords' refers to them.

Saltby airfield was built in 1941 with grass runways but once the USAAF arrived three years later a 6,000-foot runway was built. Douglas C-47s were the main aircraft here and the station's 'hours of glory' were during the D-Day and Arnhem operations in which the Polish Parachute Brigade was also involved. There is a memorial to the Saltby airmen and a more detailed information board at the site where the Union Jack, the Stars and Stripes and the Polish Red and White flags fly. The airfield closed in 1955 and since 1971 has played host to the local gliding club.

Back in Skillington we pass St James's Church. In 1859 a new rector arrived here but 31-year-old Reverend Charles Hudson was also an accomplished mountaineer, indeed one of the best amateurs of Victorian times. Whilst in Zermatt in 1865 rumour came that an Italian team was nearby hoping to make the first ascent of the Matterhorn, so Hudson grabbed the opportunity to join an English party being organised by veteran alpinist Edward Whymper to beat them.

Whymper, Hudson, two others and two local guides set out on 13 July and made it – first! – to the summit the following day. Tragedy struck, however, on their descent when four of the party, including Hudson, fell 4,000 feet to their deaths. Hudson was buried at the Englische Kirke at Zermatt. Whymper recollected the episode in his book Scrambles Amongst the Alps – a somewhat understated title! However, their achievement is commemorated in St James's by two stained glass windows, both depicting the Matterhorn, one donated by Whymper and 'Brother Mountaineers'. St James's is also a lovely church in its own right with much 13th and 14th-century stonework.

NOTES. Please park considerately around the green below Skillington's 1847 Methodist Chapel.

# THE BASICS

Distance: 5¾ miles / 9.5km

Gradient: Only gentle ascents/descents

Severity: Moderate

Approx time to walk: 3 hrs

Stiles: Three

Maps: OS Landranger 130 (Grantham), Explorer 247 (Grantham)

Path description: Village and country lanes, meadows, farm tracks and airfield roads

Start point: Skillington (GR: SK 898257)

Parking: On road at start (NG33 5HB)

Dog friendly: Best on lead throughout

Public toilets: None

Nearest refreshments: Blue Horse or Crossed Swords, Skillington

# SKILLINGTON WALK

1. With your back to the chapel walk down through the village to a T-junction and turn left. After 200 yards take the signed footpath on your right. A short track leads to a gate from which you walk up a meadow to a stile in the middle of the top hedge, then in a second meadow head for another stile in the far left-hand corner. Now keep forward on grass headlands through four fields to a farm road and turn right.

2. At a bend and waymark go left through a hedge to a second waymark a few feet ahead, go through another hedge and turn right to a stile at a road. Now go left for 300 yards to the entrance of Heslin's Barn Farm and turn left onto the farm road. Just beyond the farmhouse a waymark directs you right onto a grass track. At the field corner go left on another track to a concrete road where our route continues almost opposite.

3. On reaching the corner of Stoke Pasture Wood follow the track leftwards, then bear right past Mere Barn Farm to continue on a grass track with a hedge on your left. When the track splits get the hedge on your right (or – as you near a conifer woodland get between the hedge and the trees!). Continue to a three-way footpath sign at a wide track that is the Viking Way.

4. Turn sharp left and follow this track as it loops to the right round the end of Saltby airfield runway then keep forward on concrete airfield roads past a low hangar and some woodland. Where the trees end, at a Viking Way sign pointing left, is a seat, flagpoles and the airfield memorial.

5. Retrace your steps to the low hangar and turn right between it and the woods looking for a waymark post at the end of a grass track; go left along this following it as it bends right and passes a barn. At the next bend (and a waymark post) leave the main track onto a grass one on your left. At the next waymark turn right by a hedge then in the next

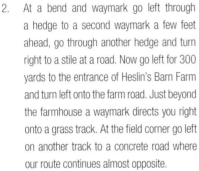

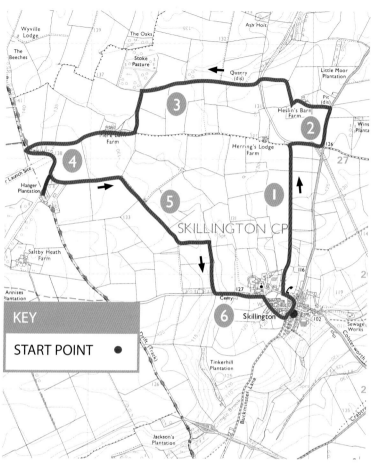

## KEY

**START POINT** ●

field swing right for a few paces, then left, now with a hedge on your right. At the final field corner go right through the hedge and immediately left to a road.

6. Turn left back to Skillington Church. Turn right along Back Lane and at a junction bear left back to the start.

# TEALBY & RISBY

As one of Lincolnshire's prettiest villages Tealby is the starting point for many walks amongst fine Wolds scenery. This short route is no exception and enjoys some of the best local views.

The village has a long history, being recorded as 'Tevelsbi' in the Domesday Book. At that time this prosperous village had fourteen mills powered by local streams. Eventually paper production became an important local industry and the name Papermill Lane survives.

Tealby is famously associated with the Tennyson family, especially Charles Tennyson D'Eyncourt, who was the poet's uncle. Charles had succeeded to the family fortunes instead of Alfred (later Lord) Tennyson's father George and it was Charles who added D'Eyncourt to the family name. He also built Bayon's Manor, a replica medieval castle, in the nearby park. Charles also financed the interior restoration of All Saints' Church in the 1870s. Even so parts of the Norman exterior remain, though noticeably weathered. There are Tennyson family monuments inside and an impressive display of coloured kneelers created by parishioners. Charles reputedly also designed, and certainly paid for, the village school in 1856 – but his 'castle' was demolished in 1965.

On the extension our route to Walesby passes an enclosure for a herd of red deer so look out for them! Risby is renowned too for its flock of rare 'Lincolnshire Longwool' sheep and some of them may be seen as we return towards Tealby.

Walesby's All Saints' Church is one of Lincolnshire's most enigmatic, for centuries isolated on its hilltop site since the medieval village migrated to the valley below. Restored in the 1930s it is now famous in its role as the 'Ramblers' Church' and inside a unique stained glass window depicts Christ with ramblers and cyclists.

The present white rood screen, whilst seeming so very medieval, was actually installed in 1933 though the access stairs are original. The views from the churchyard are some of Lincolnshire's finest, especially northwards to the county's highest Wolds at Normanby (see Walk 14).

We begin along 'The Smootings', dialect for a narrow passage or pathway. The walk follows the Viking Way for most of the return from Risby and also comprises the optional extension to Walesby.

NOTES. Park at the inn by kind permission of the landlord. The optional extension involves some strenuous climbs and descents.

# THE BASICS

Distance: 4 miles / 6.5km or 5¼ miles / 8.5km

Gradient: Some steep ascents and descents – especially on the extension

Severity: Moderate – difficult on extension

Approx time to walk: 2½ or 3 hours

Stiles: Three

Maps: OS Landranger 113 (Grimsby), Explorer 282 (Lincolnshire Wolds North)

Path description: Lanes, farm roads meadows. Some rough, steep ground.

Start point: King's Head, Tealby (GR: TF 156905)

Parking: King's Head, Tealby (LN8 3YA)

Dog friendly: Best on lead throughout

Public toilets: None

Nearest refreshments: Kings Head, Tealby

# TEALBY & RISBY WALK

1. Turn left out of the inn car park and keep ahead at the nearby junction, then in 100 yards bear right into 'The Smootings'. The lane soon reduces to a footpath and leads through to Beck Hill. Turn left uphill and at the main road cross carefully to some steps up into the churchyard. Walk round the tower, leave the churchyard by more steps, turn right and in 20 yards go left up a signposted lane.

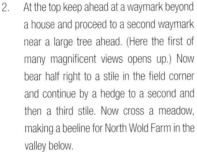

2. At the top keep ahead at a waymark beyond a house and proceed to a second waymark near a large tree ahead. (Here the first of many magnificent views opens up.) Now bear half right to a stile in the field corner and continue by a hedge to a second and then a third stile. Now cross a meadow, making a beeline for North Wold Farm in the valley below.

3. Go through the farmyard and turn right behind a barn onto an uphill track. At a road go left for 300 yards then left again at another track opposite a barn. Follow this (with views now extending to Lincoln) to Risby Manor, staying on the track as it passes round the house and heads downhill to a cattle grid; just below that are two kissing gates, one on either side. (The optional extension to Walesby begins here.)

4. [THE EXTENSION] After the cattle grid turn right and contour along the hillside for 200 yards, then descend steeply to a gate and footbridge in the valley ahead and climb (equally steeply!) up the far side. Near the top, at a waymark, veer left through trees to a gate in a deer fence and keep forward over a field to a handgate leading into Walesby churchyard. Return the same way to Risby.

5. [THE MAIN ROUTE] Turn left – ahead after

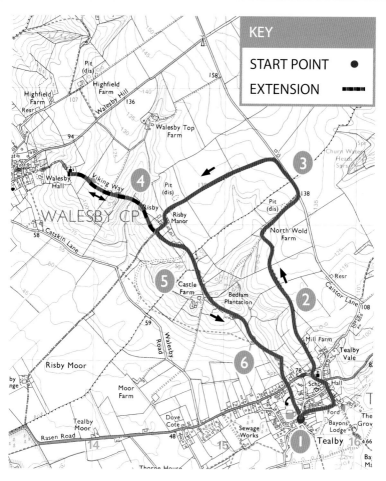

doing the extension – and walk along the top of the field and then by a fence to another kissing gate. Now begin to bear gradually leftwards uphill past a pond to enter some woods at another kissing gate. The path runs just inside the wood boundary to emerge near Castle Farm. Now bear left following a clear downhill path into the valley. When the path appears to split keep to the narrower right-hand branch (there's a boardwalk over a boggy section) until after a metal kissing gate the Viking Way bears off leftwards. Our route keeps ahead here alongside a hedge towards a house seen ahead.

6. Pass to the right of the house and at the road cross onto a continuing path by the small barn opposite. From a kissing gate go down a meadow edge to a road and turn right for the King's Head.

# WAINFLEET

On this walk the countryside around Wainfleet reveals some aspects of surprising and perhaps unexpected history. As we shall see, there's history around every corner.

Wainfleet is one of Lincolnshire's lost ports and in medieval times was a significant one, exporting wool from the Wolds. In those days, of course, the coast was much closer than today. Its decline began in the early 16th century, primarily through the silting of the River Steeping and the growth of Boston, but even 200 years later Daniel Defoe on his Tour Through Great Britain remarked on 'the fens at Wayneflete . . . where the very ditches are navigable'. On leaving Wainfleet the walk follows the River Steeping.

The town's most historically significant building is William of Wayneflete's Magdalen College, seen near the start, founded in 1484 and built of brick much like Tattershall Castle. William was born here as William Patten in 1395 and educated at Winchester and Oxford, thereafter rising rapidly in political and ecclesiastical circles to become the Provost at Eton, Bishop of Winchester and Lord Chancellor to Henry IV. He also founded Magdalen College, Oxford. He died on 11 August 1486.

As we head into the countryside we pass St Mary's Mill; built in the early 19th century, working until 1947 and now a private house.

Because of its remote location Wainfleet St Mary's church might be locked, but clear windows allow a good interior view. Curiously the church interior has five bays in the north aisle but only four in the south with a mixture of Norman, Early English and Perpendicular architectural styles. There is an imposing lychgate too! On our approach we see extensive earthworks of Old Wainfleet in the field beside the track, and beyond the churchyard there are more in a hummocky paddock.

A mile from Old Wainfleet is Crow's Bridge, built circa 1812 by John Rennie, the engineer responsible for the local fen drainage schemes implemented from 1802 onwards. A few yards before the bridge is the site of a Quaker burial ground that surrounded a building here used as a Meeting House (there's an information board).

On both outward and return legs we pass close to Bateman's Brewery, established in 1874 and still a family business whose 'real ales' are nationally famous. The adjacent mill dates from around 1820 and worked until about 1920. It was Bateman's who added the crenellations and weathervane. Incidentally Peter Dolman in his book Lincolnshire Windmills points out that the mill on the Bateman logo has four sails whereas the original had five.

Heading back into Wainfleet we cross the railway, which reached the town in September 1871 and Skegness in 1873. Especially note the signal box; it still contains its original equipment and is now a listed building. We end back in the Market Place with its medieval Buttercross (from which John Wesley preached) and 1899 clock tower.

# THE BASICS

Distance: 5¾ miles / 9.5km
Gradient: Level throughout
Severity: Easy to moderate
Approx time to walk: 3½ hrs
Stiles: Six
Maps: OS Landranger 122 (Skegness), Explorer 274 (Skegness, Alford & Spilsby)
Path description: Field paths, country lanes, grass tracks and riverside footpaths
Start point: Wainfleet Market Place (GR: TF 498589)
Parking: Market Place, Wainfleet (PE24 4BJ)
Dog friendly: Possible off-lead by river and on track beyond Hallgate
Public toilets: In Wainfleet
Nearest refreshments: Choice of inns, cafés and takeaways in Wainfleet. There's a visitor centre and café at the brewery

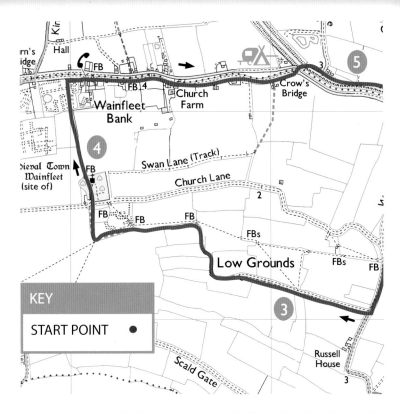

1.    Facing away from the Woolpack Hotel leave the Market Place from the far right-hand corner then go left into Rumbold Lane. (But first visit Bishop Wayneflete's School 100 yards ahead.) When Rumbold Lane bends left take the walled footpath ahead, then cross a small meadow to the railway. Cross this and immediately turn right to follow a winding riverbank path to a stile and gate. Now bear left into Havenside and continue to a road bridge (Salem Bridge).

2.    Cross the river, then the road, and go left along the pavement to a kissing gate on the right beyond the town sign. Walk ahead between some large trees and then veer slightly left to come alongside (and to the right of) a fenced area. Head for a hedge gap with a kissing gate, join a track and follow the field path ahead to reach a road (St Michael's Lane).

3.    Now turn right and at a T-junction – beyond the mill – turn left. At the next junction turn left again and then turn right at the third junction (Hallgate). Beyond a house the surfaced lane becomes a track; follow it through several bends until, after turning sharp right it reaches another road with St Mary's churchyard lychgate opposite.

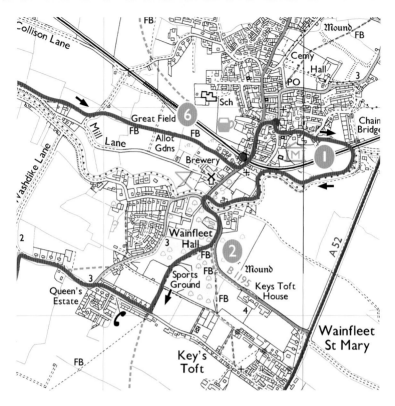

4.  Enter and pass to the left of the tower to a footbridge and stile in the churchyard's back left-hand corner. Walk forward on rough ground by a ditch, zigzag through a hedge gap then on to a second footbridge. Cross the paddock ahead with its Old Wainfleet earthworks, to a stile at a road.

5.  Turn right. In half a mile, pass the Quaker cemetery and reach Crow's Bridge over the River Steeping. Cross over and keep ahead at the first junction. (It's a pleasanter walk along the grassy embankment top.) After 400 yards take the signed footpath on the left which passes behind houses to reach another lane.

6.  Turn left for 75 yards then take the footpath going off to the right. This path crosses two footbridges and passes some houses to reach the main road. Finally turn left over the railway crossing back into Wainfleet.

# WELBOURN

This walk explores the village of Welbourn with its former medieval castle site and its surrounding countryside. We also walk along an abandoned railway and enjoy extensive views from the nearby heath.

Welbourn nestles below the western scarp of the Lincoln Heath and the village surrounds the ring-shaped earthworks of its castle site. This was first recorded in the mid 12th century and was probably first a simple motte-and-bailey layout; the grounds are accessible with information boards for visitors. Much of the moat survives (quite a bit of it still with water) and although any visible trace of the actual buildings has long gone some of the stonework is possibly still nearby – re-used at St Chad's Church. Castle Hill was purchased by the Parish Council in 1998 as a village open-air amenity.

The church stands across the road and, as with most churches, consists of many architectural styles having a 13th-century tower, a 14th-century porch and a 15th-century spire. The last of these has a distinct swelling outline known as 'entasis' – an architectural 'trick' to try to prevent the spire from looking as if it is curving inwards. The gates are a memorial to King George V.

Inside is another memorial to local lad William Robertson, born at Welbourn in 1860. He began work as a gardener's 'boy' but at age seventeen, with little education, joined the army and went to India, where he taught himself five local languages. During his long career he rose to Chief of the General Staff with the rank of field marshal. He died in 1934. Nearby on the green stands a sculpture by Richard Brett of the 'Bell Tree' marking the spot where a bell hung to summon villagers.

Part of the walk follows the former Great Northern railway line heading south from Lincoln. This opened in 1867 and provided a quicker route, via Grantham, from the city to London than that offered by the pre-existing Lincoln–Newark route. It was also a busy freight line

serving the ironstone quarries around Caythorpe. Welbourn had no station of its own but shared with nearby Leadenham where a siding was frequently used by the Royal train following the opening of the Cranwell Air Force College in 1920. Declining services were further reduced under Dr Beeching's railway reforms and the last train ran on 30 October 1965.

NOTES. Welbourn village hall is at the north end of Beck Street. The inn is in the High Street. a little way on from the school. (To learn more visit Welbourn's informative village website.)

# THE BASICS

Distance: 2¾ miles / 4.5km

Gradient: Mostly level but short climbs and descents at the old railway and a longer one onto the heath

Severity: Easy

Approx time to walk: 2 hrs

Stiles: Three

Maps: OS Landranger 121 (Lincoln & Newark), Explorer 272 (Lincoln)

Path description: Village lanes, meadows, old railway track and grassy farm track

Start point: Welbourn village hall (GR: SK 968543)

Parking: Welbourn village hall (LN5 0LZ)

Dog friendly: Off-lead possible in parts

Public toilets: In village hall; if open

Nearest refreshments: Joiner's Arms, Welbourn

# WELBOURN WALK

1. From the car park entrance cross the road to a handgate and walk across the castle site, aiming just right of a seat at the far side where there are some steps leading to a footbridge over the moat. Join High Street and turn left. Next to the school turn right where a footpath sign points down a short track. At the end is a waymark; zigzag left then right here onto a field-edge path leading to the old railway.

2. Go under the bridge and then double back leftwards and up onto the former track bed and bear right. After 200 yards descend to the right (where a bridge is missing), go left and then right back up onto the railway again; continue for a further 300 yards. At the next bridge parapet, above a lane, descend carefully (it's steep!) on the right.

3. Pass under the bridge and follow the road (Dycote Lane) into Welbourn again. When the road swings left look for a footpath sign by a small green and take the path on the right between a fence and a hedge. From a kissing gate keep forward by a wall and then a hedge to another kissing gate on the left. Exit into a lay-by.

4. Turn right and at the end carefully cross the road (A607) onto the signed grass track a few paces to your left and follow it uphill through a dogleg to a waymark below South Barn Farm. (The next section has particularly fine views; the path does, however, follow the spring line where the heathland limestone and underlying clays meet so it may be wet in places!)

5. Turn left, keeping below the hedge, and follow clear field-edge paths to reach a road.

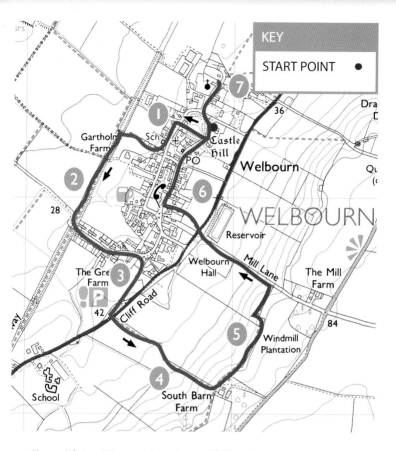

Now go left downhill to meet the main road (A607) again.

6.  Re-cross it to a footpath sign and stile almost opposite. Cross a meadow to a second stile just to the right of a pond, then reach a third stile and a fenced path. This leads to the road (Beck Street) in Welbourn village emerging opposite the 17th-century Manor House. Finally turn right back to the start point.

7.  To visit the church walk past the village hall, first bearing left by the 'Bell Tree' sculpture and then right into North End. Return the same way.

THIS WALK STARTS AND FINISHES AT ONE OF
LINCOLNSHIRE'S FOREMOST NATURE RESERVES – WHISBY
NATURAL WORLD.

The reserve occupies an area that
geologically once formed part of the River
Trent valley where gravel terraces, up to nine
metres thick, were deposited by the river
before the last ice age about 25,000 years
ago. The river's course was blocked and
diverted by the glaciers and it subsequently
maintained its 'new' course once the the ice
had retreated. The gravel and sand deposits
have been extracted industrially since the
1930s, latterly by Lafarge Aggregates, but
since the 1990s the company has worked
in collaboration with the Lincolnshire Wildlife
Trust (LWT) to create the landscaped nature
reserve we see today. The reserve covers
nearly 400 acres and has been leased to the
LWT since 1998.

Tunman Wood extends to about 132 acres and both it and Stocking Wood are recognisable
as ancient woodland habitats because of the wide variety of plant species that they
contain. (In addition to the permissive paths that we use for our walk there are others,
here and in adjacent woods. All of them are part of North Kesteven District Council's
(NKDC) 'Stepping Out' scheme, but not all appear on OS maps. NKDC map leaflets for
these are available at Whisby visitor centre.)

Thorpe-on-the-Hill does indeed stand on a slight rise, though it's not much of a hill really,
with virtually the whole village being within the OS 20-metre (less than 80 feet) contour
line. St Michael's church tower dates from 1722 and although the rest of the church was
rebuilt in 1912 it does retain a Norman window.

Also at Thorpe is the 1909 Memorial Church commemorating local boy John Hunt, whose
short life history is told in Arthur Mee's book Lincolnshire (The King's England). Hunt
worked as a ploughboy but managed to educate himself sufficiently well so that when he
was twenty-one he could enrol at a Wesleyan Methodist college where he trained to be

a missionary. He then followed his calling in Fiji, where he laboured to translate the Bible into Fijian before dying at the early age of thirty-six – as Mee explains, 'from overwork'!

After refreshments at the Whisby Natural World café those with energy to spare – or

renewed – should explore some of the reserve's colour-coded nature trails using a map obtainable from the Visitor Centre. If you can't fit all this into one day remember that the 'Stepping Out' woodland walks and the nature reserve will amply repay visits in every season of the year.

NOTES. Look for the Whisby Natural World signs off the A46 by-pass to the west of Lincoln. There is a small parking fee.

# THE BASICS

Distance: 4¼ miles / 7km

Gradient: Mostly level; very gradual slopes

Severity: Easy

Approx time to walk: 2 to 2½ hrs; plus optional time in the nature reserve

Stiles: None

Maps: OS Landranger 121 (Lincoln & Newark), Explorers 271 (Newark) & 272 (Lincoln)

Path description: Country lanes, reserve, woodland and farm tracks

Start point: Whisby Natural World (GR: SK 911664)

Parking: Whisby Natural World (LN6 9BW)

Dog friendly: Leads compulsory in reserve

Public toilets: At Whisby Natural World

Nearest refreshments: Whisby Natural World visitor centre café

1. Walk towards the car park entrance but just before the road bear right on a path within the reserve beside Thorpe Lake. Where the path divides keep left to come to a kissing gate exiting onto a road. Turn right and almost immediately left at a crossroads. Follow this road (Station Road – there is a pavement) gently uphill to the edge of Thorpe-on-the-Hill village.

2. At the bend where Station Road meets Lincoln Lane take the signed path going right through Home Farm onto a track that bears right downhill (Clay Lane). On reaching a junction, with a 'Stepping Out' waymark and a 'No Horses' sign, turn left and continue to a three-way footpath sign at the next track junction beside Stocking Wood.

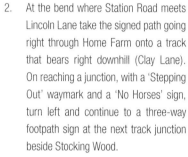

3. Turn right through the trees and you will reach a clearing and track junction, with Tunman Wood ahead. (If you wish to explore the paths within Tunman Wood keep ahead but be sure to return to this point – and then turn right!)

4. Otherwise turn left now. After a few hundred yards the track swings left but when it bears right round the edge of more woods go left from a waymark post along a grass track. At an electricity pole and hedge gap turn left.

5. Ignore a path joining from the left but keep forward to a field corner before cutting through a hedge gap and maintaining your direction towards Thorpe-on-the-Hill, seen ahead. As you near the village go through a metal kissing gate on your right and cross a paddock to a second kissing gate then walk along a hedged footpath to a road.

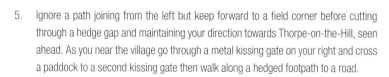

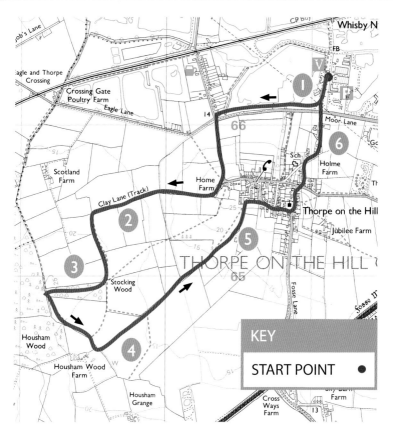

6. Turn right, pass Thorpe Church and at the corner of the churchyard bear left into Fosse Lane. Just beyond the Memorial Church bear right for 50 yards before turning left down Little Thorpe Lane. At the next junction you are back at the Whisby Natural World car park entrance.

# WOODHALL SPA

OUR FINAL 'SEASONAL' WALK EXPLORES SOME OF THE
BEAUTIFUL WOODLANDS SURROUNDING THIS FORMER SPA
VILLAGE WITH THEIR VARIED FLORA AND FAUNA. IT IS
ESPECIALLY COLOURFUL IN THE AUTUMN.

We begin at Royal Square the site of the
former Royal Hotel of 1897 along with its
tennis courts and gardens. It was re-named
the Royal Hydro in 1905 but on 17th August
1943 German bombs destroyed it almost
entirely leaving only today's Mall Hotel still
standing.

Today the former gardens contain the 617
Squadron "Dambusters" memorial, dedicated
on 17th May 1987, with its stylised breached
dam recalling their most famous raid, but
others are listed including that against the
"Tirpitz" in 1944. Nearby is another black
pyramidal memorial to 617 Squadron.

Woodhall Spa's story began in the early 1800's with "entrepreneur" John Parkinson's
fruitless search for coal here. His mines however unexpectedly brought about the
discovery (by the local Squire Thomas Hotchkin) of the mineral waters that made the
village a Victorian and Edwardian spa resort. Once Parkinson abandoned his mine
shafts they quickly filled with water whose beneficial effects on the local's health (and
apparently, that of their horses too) was quickly noticed. Squire Hotchkin had samples
chemically analysed to reveal their higher concentrations of iodine and bromine than any
other known spa. Woodhall's future was thus assured!

Increasing visitor numbers soon created the economic stimulus for a resort, which in
turn was partly responsible for attracting the branch railway line linking Kirkstead and
Horncastle. (Now the Spa Trail and part of the Viking Way - both used on our walk.) The
first local railway was the Great Northern Railway's (GNR) line from Boston to Lincoln
(then part of the main line from London to the north) built in 1848 alongside the River
Witham at Kirkstead. In 1855 this was followed by the 7½-mile Horncastle and Woodhall
Junction Railway, which whilst operated by the GNR remained a separate company until
the railway amalgamation of 1923.

Woodhall Spa's greatest heydays were in the late Victorian and Edwardian eras. Most of the village's larger houses and hotels date between 1885 and 1905. Railway passenger and freight revenue declined however under competition from the increase in motor traffic, passenger trains ceasing in 1954 and goods traffic surviving until 1971. The spa itself declined too but remained open until its sudden, unexpected end came on 21st September 1983 when the wells collapsed.

Towards the end of the walk we pass two Lincolnshire "institutions". The "Kinema", originally a tennis pavilion converted into a cinema in1922 is one of the country's oldest and unique in having the only remaining back projection system still in working order. And nearby is what will always be known to Lincolnshire folk as "The Teahouse in the Woods".

The walk also visits Kirkby Moor Wood and other woodland close to the village's internationally famous golf course.

The final section brings us full circle through the Woodland Trust's "Pine Woods". These were planted around 1811 by John Parkinson to supply pit props for his coal-mining venture. Note the "Old Man of the Woods" carvings.

## THE BASICS

Distance: 4¾ miles / 7.5km

Gradient: Level throughout

Severity: Easy

Approx time to walk: 2 hrs

Stiles: None

Maps: OS Landranger 122 (Skegness & Horncastle), Explorer 273 (Lincolnshire Wolds South)

Path description: Village roads, woodland paths and tracks

Start point: Royal Square, Woodhall Spa (GR TF 193631)

Parking: Royal Square, Woodhall Spa (LN10 6QL)

Dog friendly: Possible off-lead sections in woods

Public toilets: Near junction of Station Road and Spa Road

Nearest refreshments: Tearooms, cafés and inns in Woodhall Spa

# WOODHALL SPA WALK

1. From Royal Square car park turn right and proceed along Station Road into Broadway until you reach the Golf Hotel.

2. In another 80 yards (and across the road from the hotel) take the hedged footpath on the right. At a road keep ahead, passing a cul-de-sac to reach a T-junction. Turn left and in 60 yards take another path signed to the right. At another cul-de-sac follow the continuation path opposite and at the next road go left. Ignoring any side roads continue to the junction with Kirkby Lane. (There's a seat on the corner.)

3. Now turn right. Pass a cemetery, a double bend and the entrance to Ostler's Wood on the right, then shortly afterwards reach a signed path going left into Kirkby Moor Wood. Follow the track, which narrows to a path, to a junction with a waymark. Now turn left, soon bearing right to pass a chalet park. Continue to the B1191 Woodhall–Horncastle road.

4. Turn left (using the pavement) for just over a quarter of a mile, then cross the road to a signed track that crosses the golf course. At a three-way footpath sign turn left, walking until you can glimpse the golf course clubhouse to your left. Go left a few paces then turn right along the tree-lined Spa Trail.

5. At the end turn right through two sets of white gates and then along Coronation Road to pass the Kinema. Keep ahead at the King George Avenue junction and then cross the first footbridge on your left. Walk through the woods to their far end, then turn right. At the road turn left back into Royal Square.

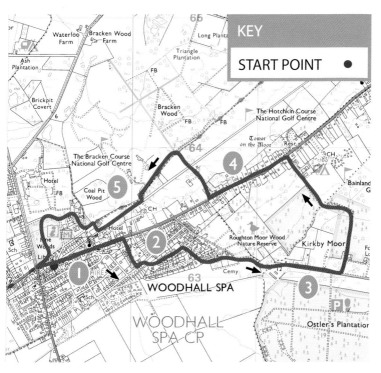

# ABOUT THE AUTHOR

Hugh Marrows is Lincolnshire born and bred. He is married with two grown-up children. His working life was spent as a career civil servant and for many years his job involved considerable travelling throughout Lincolnshire. It is from that time that he first developed an interest in the county's diverse landscape and architecture together with a fascination for its local history and heritage.

With a long-standing love of the outdoors and an interest in photography he came to appreciate over the years the extraordinary visual heritage that Lincolnshire has to offer, including its churches, vernacular buildings and the industrial legacy of its mills, canals and long-lost railways.

He was fortunate to be offered early retirement from his civil service career. This afforded him both the time and the opportunity to pursue his interests more fully and prompted him to turn them to advantage by writing about them – initially for a county magazine – in the hope of encouraging others to explore Lincolnshire for themselves. Before long he found himself writing for local newspapers as well as undertaking freelance work for various publications produced by Lincolnshire County Council.

Over the years this led to him having several books published including a guide to the 'Viking Way' for Lincolnshire County Council, two books devoted entirely to walks on the Wolds – Lincolnshire's own Area of Outstanding Natural Beauty – and volumes of walks spread throughout the county plus one concentrating upon the Grantham Canal.

His other interests include watercolour painting, travel and jazz.

# Wales After 1536

## Towards Modern Wales:
### Revivals, the Industrial Revolution and Social Unrest

Donald Gregory

Gwasg Carreg Gwalch

First published in 1995; new edition: 2018
© text: Donald Gregory estate
Images © Crown copyright (2017) Visit Wales
© publication: Gwasg Carreg Gwalch 2018
,

ISBN: 978-1-84524-212-1
Cover design: Eleri Owen
Published by Gwasg Carreg Gwalch,
12 Iard yr Orsaf, Llanrwst, Wales LL26 0EH
tel: 01492 642031
email: llanrwst@carreg-gwalch.cymru
website: www.carreg-gwalch.cymru

## Acknowledgements

The publishers are grateful to the family of the
deceased author for every co-operation in
launching this new edition.

**Donald Gregory** (1911 – 2006) became a
Radnor youth when his father became
postmaster at Llandrindod. He became familiar
with the remote countryside of moors and hills
and interested in its past and heritage. Later, as
a history student and teacher, his obsession
with understanding and appreciating the past
evolved to cover the whole of Wales. He and his
wife spent decades of their holidays on the
bylanes of Wales, visiting the places where
history comes alive.

*Page 1: Cefn Coed Colliery Museum;
below: Blaenau Ffestiniog slate quarries*

# Contents

# Introduction

## Welsh Hopes and Fears

With the passing of the Act of Union in 1536, Wales became a part of England, the text of the treaty openly speaking of 'annexation'. It was not a cause of uniting two kingdoms – it would be more correct to state that the larger country tried to swallow the smaller one. Henry VIII, however, thought to sugar the pill by explaining to the Welsh that the Act would give them equality with the English and the same opportunities to advance themselves. The inequality arose, of course, from the racist Welsh penal laws passed by Edward I and Henry IV! But it appears that most Welsh people accepted this royal assurance, bearing in mind that the king's own father, a Welshman, had won the Battle of Bosworth and captured the throne of England.

In 1542, six years after the political union of the two countries, a subsequent act of parliament announced the suzerainty of the laws of England at every level of Welsh life. Arrangements were made for the setting up in every Welsh county of local courts of Quarter Sessions, which, meeting four times a year, would be empowered to deal with every breach of the law of England, short of the most serious crimes of robbery and murder, which were to come under the aegis of higher courts. Wales was divided up into four circuits, to be visited twice a year by Judges in Assize. (These so-called Great Sessions were to last until 1830.) Furthermore, this Act of Parliament also insisted that in these courts of law, both Quarter Sessions (presided over by Justices of the Peace) and higher courts (where Judges held sway), only the English language would be tolerated. The Welsh languaged was banned from its own people and in its own country from all legal and administrative usage. It had a devastating and far-reaching effect on the psychology of its speakers.

In consequence the anglicisation of Wales proceeded, increasing the probability that in the course of time the Welsh language might become the language of only the unambitious and the underprivileged.

The intention of government in England after 1536 was clearly to treat Wales in every respect as a part of England, completely ignoring crucial

THE THIRTEEN SHIRES OF
WALES AFTER THE ACT OF UNION, 1536

acknowledged in 1942 with a significant legislation on the language – the Welsh Courts Act – which had allowed Welsh speakers to give evidence in Welsh, the first of many Acts before Welsh was given official status in 2011. Even in 1536, Wales was administered differently to England in spite of all the attempts for complete unity. Traditional values and customs survived in Wales, and the wisdom and justice of the Laws of Hywel Dda have been forever present in radical and social movements; they are finally expressing themselves in the law-making powers that now belong to the Welsh parliament – the Senedd (established in 1997).

differences in culture and in the Welsh pattern of historical development. At the same time this transition seems to have been sufficiently gradual for most Welshmen to be unaware of any significant change, apart from the obvious exclusion of the Welsh language from the courts of law.

In reality, however, the Welsh language remained in use in law courts in Wales through the centuries; this was legally

# The Sixteenth Century

**The Reformation in Wales (1535–1558)**

In the early years of the sixteenth century came the Reformation, the break-away of a considerable part of Europe from the authority of Rome. In the Middle Ages the church had shared power with the Holy Roman Empire, the Emperor for the most part ruling men's bodies while the Pope made himself responsible for their minds. This dichotomy was to be fractured at the beginning of the sixteenth century, but whereas on the mainland of Europe the Reformation was initially caused by the religious teaching of the German monk, Martin Luther, there was an altogether different set of circumstances operating on this side of the Channel. For despite the fact that from the time of John Wycliffe in the fourteenth century there had been growing resentment here of the continuing authority of Rome, what happened in the reign of Henry VIII had at first absolutely nothing at all to do with the religious ideas of Wycliffe and Luther. Indeed Henry so disapproved of the revolutionary religious stand taken by Luther in 1517 that four years later he wrote a thorough denunciation of Luther's Protest, to which the newly-invented printing press was able to give much publicity. So very pleased was the Pope with this opposition to Luther that he rewarded Henry with the title of Defender of the Faith (*Fidei Defensor*), the initials of which (*FD*), readers will hardly need reminding, still appear on our coins.

Between 1521 and 1527 however circumstances caused Henry to change his mind, not indeed about Luther's religious opposition to Rome, but about his own attitude to the authority of the Pope. Having grown tired of his wife, Catherine of Aragon, who had failed to produce a son, Henry wanted a divorce to enable him to marry the niece of the Duke of Norfolk, Anne Boleyn, with whom he had fallen in love. In 1527 Henry's Chancellor, Thomas Wolsey, was given the thankless task of petitioning the Pope for a divorce for his royal master, citing as justification the invalidity of Henry's marriage to Catherine – who, at the time of their marriage nearly a quarter of a century previously, had been the newly-bereaved widow of Henry's

**Cathedral**  ⛪  **monastic sites**  ⬠
**town, village, &c.**  ■

with Rome. Two men, from different backgrounds and with different objects, served the royal will. Thomas Cranmer, already at variance with Rome on religious matters, was made Archbishop of Canterbury in 1533, while Thomas Cromwell became Henry's political henchman. Every year from 1529 Parliament made inroads into papal power; in 1533 the parliamentary veto on all appeals to Rome was followed by the king's order to Cranmer to try his divorce case. The divorce was of course speedily granted, Henry's first marriage to the Spanish Catherine being declared invalid. The king, who had already secretly married Anne Boleyn, at once had her crowned queen. The tie with Rome was thus broken; parliamentary approval came the next year with the passage of the Act of Supremacy, which explicitly stated that the king was the supreme head of the Church of England, to which the Pope's predictable retort was to excommunicate Henry and declare him deposed. Thus the first part of the Reformation – the political part – was brought about here, but any changes in religious beliefs were not at this stage being contemplated. Readers will please bear in mind that the Act of Union,

elder brother, Arthur, who had died in 1502. (In taking this line Henry was conveniently forgetting that Catherine's second marriage had at the time received an official dispensation from the Vatican!) In 1529, after two years of deliberation, Pope Clement VII decided against a divorce for Henry VIII.

In the same year Henry, throwing caution to the winds, called parliament, which thereafter for seven eventful years piecemeal brought about a complete break whereby Wales became joined to England, was to follow the next year, 1536.

Wales thus, on the morrow of the Act of Union, found itself part and parcel of a country which had severed its ties with Roman Catholicism; such changes as took place in religious practice in church thereafter were to affect churches in Wales as much as in England. It would be misleading, however, to give the impression that churchgoers in Wales greatly resented such changes as took place in the services they attended; indeed it is very probable that the changeover in Wales was smoother than it was in England; this was not, however, to be ascribed to any great enthusiasm shown by the Welsh for Henry's volte-face. It has to be remembered that before the Reformation in Wales services were conducted in Latin, of which most worshippers had no knowledge at all. After the passage of the Act of Supremacy Latin was superseded by English, a language which was as incomprehensible to most Welshmen at this time as Latin had been. The substitution of the Protestant prayer book for the Roman Catholic missal made little difference to those who understood neither tongue. The Reformation, thus, could hardly in early days have been expected to stir up much Welsh enthusiasm when it amounted to little more than an English priest reading to a Welsh congregation from an English Bible. When, in 1534, following the passage through parliament of the Act of Supremacy, all the clergy in England and Wales were required to recognise the king as the Supreme Head of the Church of England, only two priests in the whole of Wales refused, and neither of them was a Welshman!

Thomas Cromwell's ambitions for his royal master went far beyond putting him at the head of his own church and thus independent of the spiritual authority of Rome; he fully shared Henry's intention of making himself the powerful ruler of a modern state, and in order to achieve this position of strength he would need greatly to replenish the exchequers of state. Hence Cromwell directed Henry's willing attention to the monasteries, whose assets would be so helpful in financing the powerful nation state which he envisaged. It has to be realised that these monasteries, which had in past centuries

*1. Llanthony Abbey;*
*2. Basingwerk Abbey; 3. Margam Abbey*

served medieval society very well indeed in a wide variety of ways, had by the sixteenth century fallen on bad times and in many cases were already in an advanced state of decay – with, however, many of their secular assets largely unimpaired.

Between 1536 and 1540 all houses of religion in England and Wales were suppressed, their priors and abbots driven from their places, to be severely punished if they resisted the change, or pensioned off if they were lucky. Of the 46 such establishments in Wales dissolved by the king in the 1530s, the best known ones on the eve of their dissolution were the Augustinian priory at Llanthony in the Honddu valley, the Benedictine abbeys at Chepstow and at Usk, and the Cistercian monasteries at Cwm Hir in remotest Radnorshire, Basingwerk, Margam, Neath, *Strata Florida*, Tintern and *Valle Crucis*, while the Benedictine abbey at Ewenni was saved by being incorporated into the Priory there, and the abbey at Brecon became the nucleus of the future cathedral. Some details of the subsequent fate of former abbeys, at Tintern, *Strata Florida* and Llanthony, will be found in a later part of this section of the book, under 'Notes and Illustrations'.

Once the personnel in the monasteries had been dealt with, the lands and wealth were taken over by the royal commissioners, who redistributed these very considerable assets in ways that were most favourable for the advancement of the king's plans for power. There seems to have been virtually no outcry in Wales at what seems to us to have been a policy of ruthless exploitation; there was some Welsh resentment, though not of any real significance, when later in the 1530s much-loved images were destroyed, and time-honoured religious pilgrimages were forbidden.

At the same time that the king was divorcing Catherine of Aragon and was beginning to pursue wider ambitions to make himself a powerful monarch (an ambition much favoured and advanced by Thomas Cromwell), there was also a growing undercurrent of Protestantism in the country, the source of which had sprung from the preaching in the second half of the fourteenth century of John Wycliffe, an Oxford scholar and Master of

*1. Tintern Abbey; 2. Neath Abbey;*
*3. Ewenny Abbey*

Balliol; he had begun by condemning what he saw as the corruption of the Pope, later moving on to deny the validity of some parts of Catholic doctrine before virtually challenging the supreme authority, claimed by the Pope. The spiritual inheritors of Wycliffe's way of thinking in the 1530s took advantage of the opportunity afforded by the king's break with Rome. In 1537 and 1538 these Protestant leanings revealed themselves; in the former year a religious manual, known as the Bishop's Book, written by Thomas Cranmer, the Archbishop of Canterbury, himself a man of Protestant tendencies, was circulated among the clergy. This was followed in 1538 by the placing – and chaining – of a copy of a new English translation of the Bible, based on the work of the Protestant Tyndale in every parish church in the land. This was the so-called Great Bible, that Shakespeare knew. One consequence of this preaching of the Bible was, in the words of G. M. Trevelyan, that 'men could read the Bible and think what they liked in silence'. Henry VIII, for his part, soon sensed the dangers implicit in these acts and quickly put a stop to what to his way of thinking was Protestant heresy.

In 1539 a newly-elected and extremely servile parliament meekly accepted from the king a statement of his own religious views, incorporated in the so-called Six Articles, and proceeded to pass an act which threatened draconian penalties against those who failed to observe its provisions. Amongst these were the enforcement of celibacy among all clergy, and an absolute ban on speaking or writing against transubstantiation. This year, 1539, represented the high water mark of Henry's despotic powers; it was the year in which a man was burned to death for eating meat on a Friday. It was also the year when Thomas Cromwell talked Parliament into accepting the monstrous notion that any royal proclamation was to have the force of law. Cromwell, having loaded his master with despotic powers, himself suffered from their application in 1540, when, arrested on a trumped-up charge, he was speedily beheaded.

In the last five years of Henry's reign, from 1542 to 1547, the king tended to mark time, as he tried to consolidate his position; in one respect at least he showed an unusual impartiality, as he sent to the block both Catholics and Protestants, the former for questioning his claim to religious supremacy, the latter for disagreeing with his theology. At his death in 1547 England and Wales remained Catholic in doctrine, a state of affairs that in Wales, at any rate, was greeted with complete apathy. The time was still in the future when Wales was to become by far the most Protestant part of the United Kingdom.

The widespread apathy in Wales, which had attended most of the religious changes in Henry's reign, became tinged with resentment in the reign of Edward VI, the boy-king who ruled from 1547 to 1553 under the successive Protectorships of the Dukes of Somerset and Northumberland. England became a strictly Protestant country during those six years, when significant changes in doctrine were accompanied by more superficial but much more obvious practical measures. Royal commissioners from London were despatched to all parts, their instructions to destroy chantries, confiscate surviving religious endowments, and even to knock down images, crosses and altars, which reminded extreme Protestants of Roman Catholicism.

Fortunately for those in Wales who treasured their altars and their churchyard crosses, some of the churches that housed these honoured relics, were in remote places, a long, long way from London. As confirmation of the survival of some of these objects readers are advised to visit Partrishow in Gwent (GR 279224). The old church (there is no other building in the neighbourhood) is 4½ miles north-east of Crickhowell, and contains several stone altars, which bear on their tops a number of incised consecration crosses, while in the churchyard still stands in its original height a medieval cross, the king's commissioners having totally failed to find their way to this idyllic spot.

To summarise Protestant activity in Edward's reign, the foundations of the tyrannical government of Henry VIII were successfully undermined when the harsh laws of 1539 were repealed. Thereafter full legislative power was restored to parliament. In 1549 the First Prayer Book of Edward VI, the work of Cranmer, was imposed on the church, to be replaced three years later by the Second Prayer Book, which is basically the same prayer book that is still in use in the Church of England today. In 1553 England and Wales officially embraced Protestantism when Protestant beliefs were defined in the Forty-Two Articles. But in the summer of that year the sickly Edward died, and the crown passed to his half-sister, Mary, daughter of the Roman Catholic, Catherine of Aragon, whom Henry VIII had spurned.

To the English the volte-face of the years of Mary's reign (1553–1558) brought horror or rejoicing according to individual religious beliefs. But to most ordinary Welsh people the apathy with which they had met the many changes they had known since the annexation of their land by England continued as Protestantism was abandoned by Mary's parliament, and Roman Catholicism was restored. Remember that to the Welsh the Roman Catholic missal (which was in use until rejected by Protestants), the Protestant Prayer Book (introduced in Edward VI's reign), and the former Catholic missal restored again by Mary, were written in alien and largely incomprehensible tongues.

The bare bones of Mary's reign are these: she succeeded her half-brother, Edward in 1553; the 37-year-old daughter of Henry VIII, Mary was personally popular, her succession being widely welcomed by the general public until it became clear that she was more sympathetic towards her mother's country, Spain, than she was towards her own. It has to be stressed that Spain, having been of late marvellously enriched by the silver her successful sailors had brought home from the New World, was developing alarming political ambitions in Europe. In 1554 Mary married the Spanish king's son, Philip, who became King of Spain in 1556, when Charles V abdicated from the throne of Spain. Thereafter until Mary's death in 1558 England became virtually a vassal of Spain.

Parliament carried out the Queen's wishes and repealed all the anti-Catholic laws, with the result that the Pope regained his previous spiritual supremacy in Wales and England. Between 1555 and 1558 300 Protestants were burned at the stake in England, including Cranmer, Latimer and Ridley, who perished in Oxford in 1555; in Wales, however, only three Protestants suffered in this way, of whom the most prominent was Robert Farrer, the Bishop of St David's (*Tyddewi*), who met his fate in Carmarthen (*Caerfyrddin*).

Despite the widespread apathy in

Wales towards the various religious changes of these times, there were, of course, among the educated minority a number of devout men of religion (almost all of whom educated at Oxford) who put their religious consciences, be they Catholic or Protestant, before their professional advancement. There seem not to have been any Vicars of Bray in Wales! Two outstanding Protestants were Richard Davies and Rowland Meyrick; the former, of humble birth, the son of a curate in Conwy valley, went to Oxford, where he became attracted to the prevailing revolutionary talk of young Protestants. After leaving the university he became a priest but on Mary's accession in 1553, after being summoned to appear before the Privy Council, was deprived of his living. He then exiled himself and his family to Frankfurt until Mary died. More will be heard of this distinguished priest and scholar in Elizabeth's reign. Roland Meyrick, who, like Davies, became a Protestant at Oxford in 1550, had been made Canon and Precentor of St David's until he was forced out of office by Mary in 1553.

In the other religious camp were three determined and devout Catholics, Morys Clynnog, Morgan Phillips and Gruffydd Robert. Morys Clynnog, born in Clynnog Fawr in 1525, after studying theology at Oxford became Rector of Corwen in 1556; early in 1558 he was appointed Bishop of Bangor, but before he could be consecrated, Queen Mary died and Morys Clynnog fled voluntarily into exile. Morgan Phillips, a son of south Wales, after graduating at Oxford, succeeded Rowland Meyrick as Precentor of St David's in 1553 on Mary's accession. He stayed in St David's until her reign ended, when he fled to the continent. Most important of Welsh Catholics at this time was Gruffydd Robert; born in Caernarfonshire in 1522, he was educated at Oxford and in 1558 was appointed Archdeacon of Anglesey, but had to flee soon afterwards. He was one of the most distinguished Welsh figures in the Renaissance, being a poet, a song-writer and a scholar as well as being a priest. His book on Welsh grammar is regarded as a masterpiece of clear writing, which did a great deal in the Renaissance years to elevate the Welsh language as a medium of educated expression. He was one of the great grammarians of Wales.

## The Elizabethan settlement

With the death of Mary in the summer of 1558, it was all change again; in 11 years the country had known four rulers, a ruthless father and his three children; the father, who had changed his religion solely for political reasons, having been followed by a sickly, underage son whose guardians had made the most of their opportunity to adopt extreme Protestant policies. On Edward's death the pendulum had swung back again, welcoming the Pope back to England and restoring Roman Catholicism here. Five years later, in 1558, when Catholic Mary died, her half-sister Elizabeth, who succeeded her, was faced with the vexed problem of unravelling once and for all, if at all possible, the complicated religious tangle. This, then, was the first problem encountered by the 25-old-year old daughter of Anne Boleyn; however, unlike her half-brother and her half-sister, who had preceded her on the throne, Elizabeth had no strong religious beliefs of her own, a fortunate circumstance which made it possible for her to attempt to secure some sort of compromise. This she was determined at all costs to achieve.

The drastic religious upsets of recent years had been for the most part motivated by fanaticism, which, if it had continued into the new reign, could well have endangered national unity. This danger the young queen quickly realised, causing her from the very beginning of her reign to act with the greatest circumspection. Politically she found herself in a very exposed situation: Spain was clearly in the ascendant, and in order to make herself even more powerful was attempting to enter into an alliance with France, at a time when the heir to the throne of France had recently married Elizabeth's cousin, the Catholic Mary of Scotland, who was next in succession to the throne of England. Elizabeth, on the very morrow of her accession, was presented with the real possibility of future opposition by a hostile alliance between Spain, France and Scotland. Meanwhile, despite the gravity of the international outlook, she had the good sense first to attend to the ever-pressing problems at home, posed by fundamental differences of religious opinion.

Elizabeth's troubles started at her coronation, when only one bishop was prepared to recognise the legitimacy of her succession; hence she was crowned by the

Bishop of Carlisle. The queen thereafter found it politically expedient to take heed of advice proffered by Protestants rather more than she had originally intended. Turning her attention at once to the religious issues that confronted her, she was shrewd enough not to repeat the mistake made by her father, Henry VIII, when he forced parliament to give his personal edicts the force of law; instead Elizabeth arranged for the speedy free election of a new parliament, to which she handed the problem of solving the religious dispute, though of course from time to time she attempted to steer the course of the long debate. Meanwhile the bishops, who had been one and all appointed by the dead Catholic Mary, stood their ground, both in the House of Lords and in the House of Convocation, where Elizabeth made no attempt to stop them from speaking their minds. Gradually but surely, the bishops were worsted in debate by laymen. The settlement, when it emerged, was very much a laymen's settlement, reached only after long and earnest debate. It was not to be imposed by authority. When the bishops resolutely refused to accept the agreed changes, then and only then did the queen act, by replacing them by men very carefully chosen for their moderate, middle of the road views.

The new religious order became law in April 1559, when parliament passed two acts, the first of which was an Act of Supremacy, which for the second time abolished papal authority here; the accompanying legislation, an Act of Uniformity, stated the doctrines and beliefs of the Church of England. The Second Prayer Book of Edward VI was adopted with a number of minor modifications. This new Prayer Book was carefully worded to give as little offence as possible to Roman Catholics who might be wavering. Indeed it contained no specific criticism of Rome. This tactic proved successful insofar as many moderate Catholics did join the Church of England. Politically the settlement was a sensible compromise and it is perhaps significant that in the opening years of the new reign, up to 1565, there was no persecution of Catholics. Indeed in those years only 200 clergy found themselves unable to give the necessary assurances and were deprived of their livings.

What has so far been said about Elizabeth's religious settlement affected everybody in England and Wales; nevertheless some readers may feel that this general account of events has too little direct relevance to Wales. It has however to be remembered that, like it or not, Wales had been subject to the laws of Westminster since 1536. Furthermore – and this may surprise some – at this time, that is to say, at the accession of Elizabeth, few Welshmen showed any dissatisfaction with the new arrangements made for their country's government. A great many Welshmen – those with land and education – were becoming very anglicised and had developed a vested interest in Tudor prosperity. The evil in the Act of Union, which largely arose from the ban on the use of the Welsh language in courts of law at all levels, had not as yet been fully felt.

On the morrow of the 1559 legislation official visitors were appointed to the four dioceses of Wales in order to administer the Oath of Supremacy to all the clergy and to make sure that the new Prayer Book was properly in circulation and in use. Of these official visitors to Wales three men merit particular mention: all three were Welsh, Oxford-educated and worthy representatives of the New Learning. Rowland Meyrick, it has already been seen, when Canon and Precentor of St David's, had been forced into exile by Mary. In 1559 he was appointed Bishop of Bangor. Thomas Young, a Pembrokeshire (*Sir Benfro*) man, and, like Meyrick, a former Precentor at St David's, had also gone into exile in Mary's reign; in January 1560 Elizabeth made him Bishop of St David's, the premier ecclesiastical office in Wales, before elevating him to the see of York in the following year. Third of this distinguished trio was Richard Davies. A man of the Conwy valley, he had in the middle 1550s shown himself so fervent a Protestant in the discharge of his religious duties that he had been hauled up before the Privy Council when Mary became Queen. Richard Davies, who went into exile, was later to play an even more important part in the history of Wales.

In the event nothing much came out of the visitation to Wales; the reasons for the low-key reception seem complex. Most churchgoers had no opinion at all, the English prayer book meaning as little to them as the Latin missal. Of the others, many perhaps only paid lip-service, where they thought that the Elizabethan changes might have as short a life as those that preceded them in Henry VIII's reign, Edward VI's and in Mary's. On the other hand, some will have welcomed with real relief an end to the bickering, while others were probably prepared to say anything to keep the peace. Of religious enthusiasm at this time there was little actual evidence, except in the cases of the handful of devout priests, who refused to toe the line. The most distinguished of these, who have already been referred to in Mary's reign for their stalwart support of the old religion, were Gruffydd Robert, Morys Clynnog and Morgan Phillips, who all chose to go into exile; all three in later years, when the time seemed more propitious, were to play leading roles in planning the return of Roman Catholicism to Wales. In these early years of Elizabeth's reign too, the young queen, in marked contrast to her behaviour in later times, showed real tolerance towards those who disagreed with her in religious matters.

## The struggle for the mind of Wales
Educated Welshmen by this time, whether Protestants or Roman Catholics, whether they lived in Wales or in exile in Europe, realised that the utter apathy of their fellow countrymen towards the drastic religious changes of the sixteenth century could not be overcome until all Welshmen could hear their spiritual leaders talking to them in a language they could all understand. As the English had the very clear intention of reducing the use of Welsh rather than of encouraging it, it was up to the Welsh themselves to take the lead in the matter. On this crying need for books written in Welsh, to be made available in order that ordinary Welsh people might be properly informed about religious matters of great moment, Protestants and Roman Catholics were for once in complete accord, each group believing that if only their message might reach ordinary people in Welsh, they would surely in consequence be able to see the light (as each denomination saw it).

Probably the first Welshman to see the need for religious books to be written in Welsh was William Salesbury, who, born about 1520, probably in Llansannan in Denbighshire, was educated at Maenan Abbey in the Conwy valley (his father came from Llanrwst) before going on to study at Oxford, where he first decided that Wales above all needed the Bible to be translated into Welsh. Meanwhile, in 1551 he published his own Welsh translation of the lessons that were to be read in church; this worthy venture was unfortunately doomed to failure because Salesbury used such archaic and high-falutin' language that few of his hearers could understand what was being said. During Mary's reign, 1553–58 he lay low, thereby escaping official action against him.

In 1561, by which time Elizabeth's new religious order was in place, word went forth from London that the lessons in Welsh churches should be read twice, first in English, then in Welsh; this edict helped to prepare the way for the welcome official announcement two years later of a parliamentary bill, which would arrange for the translation of the Bible and the Prayer Book into Welsh, although the period of three years allowed for this to happen was very over-optimistic.

This salutary parliamentary edict of 1563 was first heeded by Richard Davies, one of the four visitors originally appointed by Elizabeth to see that her religious settlement was being carried out in Wales; appointed Bishop of St Asaph (*Llanelwy*) in 1559, he had been promoted in 1561 to St David's, from which see he wrote to William Salesbury, inviting him to collaborate with him in carrying out the official summons to translate the Bible and the Prayer Book into Welsh. Salesbury gladly accepted the offer and for two years the two scholars seem to have worked in reasonable partnership, completing the translating of the New Testament and the Prayer Book, with Salesbury apparently being chiefly responsible for the former and Davies for the latter.

The Prayer Book was very favourably received, but Salesbury's translation of the New Testament, like his earlier attempt at translating lessons, was largely incomprehensible to most ordinary Welsh people, with whom he seems to have had little real contact. Nevertheless the two men then turned their attention to translating the Old Testament, but, after a while, their efforts came to a full stop and the two scholars parted company. Common report had it that they had quarrelled bitterly over the translation of a single word, but modern scholars however tend to the belief that while serious differences of opinion did occur, financial considerations may have also played a considerable part. Thus this great and vital task was left unfinished, with the result that ordinary Welsh Christians, as will be seen, were to wait another 20 years before being allowed access to the Bible in their own language.

William Salesbury has probably not been given his due by posterity; after all, he had been the first man to realise the great need for a Welsh Bible. It was his misfortune – and that of his fellow Welshmen – that he failed to possess the necessary common touch. Nevertheless he did perform another very useful service to Wales in compiling an English-Welsh dictionary. Sir John Wynn, his contemporary and near neighbour in the Conwy valley, called him 'a Protestant humanist scholar and the chief representative of the Renaissance in Wales'.

Meanwhile, while Bishop Davies and William Salesbury were busy at work with their translation, devoted scholars of the opposite, Roman Catholic persuasion, who were languishing in exile in Italy, were being equally industrious in pursuing their very different goals. Gruffydd Robert, who was probably the most important of Welsh Catholics, had already achieved a reputation for his Welsh scholarship, before being forced into exile. In 1564 he was appointed by the Pope to be Chaplain of the English Hospital in Rome, but soon was promoted to a position of much greater power and potential in Milan, where he stayed for 20 years in the service of the Cardinal Archbishop Borromeo. During these long years of exile he wrote, among other books, a Welsh grammar, on which much of his reputation as an outstanding Welsh scholar was based. Gruffydd Robert was a great Welsh patriot, who, apart from his devotion to the Roman Catholic faith and his desire to see Roman Catholicism restored to his native land, was also a fervent believer in the excellence of the Welsh language as a medium for the spread of Welsh culture.

Morys Clynnog, whose promotion in 1558 to the bishopric of Bangor was only prevented by the death of Queen Mary, was another very influential Welsh figure in Italian exile; in Rome in 1567 he wrote (in Welsh) an important treatise on Roman Catholic doctrine, while further north in the Netherlands, two more Welsh Roman Catholics, Morgan Phillips and Owen Lewis helped to set up in Douai a college for the training of Roman Catholic missionaries, whose future task would be to try to bring back the Roman Catholic faith to England and Wales.

The activities of devout Welsh Roman Catholics like Gruffydd Robert, Morys Clynnog and Morgan Phillips have to be seen as part and parcel of a great Roman Catholic attempt on the continent to restore the fortunes of the Roman Catholic church. By 1540 the Roman Catholic church had realised somewhat belatedly that their own house needed to be put in order before any large-scale attempt could be made to restore the fortunes of Roman Catholicism. In 1546 the Council of Trent was called, with the twofold task assigned to it of cleaning up the church and of deciding ways and means of winning back those countries which had become Protestant.

Contemporary with the deliberations of the Council of Trent was the growth and development of the Society of Jesus – the Jesuits – an order of militant Catholics founded in 1540 by Ignatius of Loyola with the avowed purpose of opposing the further spread of Protestantism. By 1562 the members of the Council of Trent had finished their long years of soul-searching and had made their plans for the future, the instrument devised for the bringing back of back-sliders being the Inquisition. The widespread Catholic revival, which

the Council of Trent set in motion, was known as the counter-reformation. The political champion of this counter-reformation, who was also the most powerful Catholic ruler in Europe, was Philip II of Spain, at a time when the chief champion of Protestantism was Elizabeth; after about 1560 these two countries, champions of two different religious faiths, were on a collision course. Thereafter war between Spain and England seemed inevitable.

The years 1569, 1570 and 1571 were years of great danger for England, years in which discontented Catholic aristocrats here encouraged the Catholic Mary, Queen of Scots to stake an illegal claim to the throne of England. The risings were numerous and sporadic and were easily put down, but they caused Elizabeth to harden her heart against her Catholic subjects. Many a day was thereafter to elapse before religious tolerance returned to this country.

The Pope in 1570 retaliated in the face of Elizabeth's firm stand against Catholic plotters by excommunicating her and relieving all her Catholic subjects from their vows of allegiance to the Queen, who replied characteristically by declaring that in future she would treat all her subjects who remained Catholic as traitors. Four years later, in 1574, Roman Catholic missionaries, trained in Douai by Morgan Phillips, Owen Lewis and others crossed over from the Netherlands; the very first of these was a Welshman, Lewis Barlow, a Pembrokeshire man. In the following years a stream of missionaries followed from Douai, Rome and later from seminaries in Spain. Their efforts were greatly strengthened in 1580, when the Jesuits too sent their representatives here, of whom the best known, and the most saintly, was Edmund Campion. Parliament, thoroughly alarmed by this development, in 1581 passed an act that imposed a fine of £20 (an enormous sum of money in those days) on all who refused to attend their parish church.

As to Wales, there was certainly a marked increase in the amount of Catholic missionary activity in the late 1570s and early 1580s, both in the north and the south of the country, but the rigorous imposition of penal laws and the growing fear of Spain (the Armada sailed in 1588) makes it impossible to quantify Catholic resurgence in Wales. What is known is that in the remaining years of Elizabeth's reign no fewer than 187 recusants, as those Catholics were called, who failed to obey the law, were executed, but readers should not judge one century by the standards of another nor should they forget that between 1555 and 1558 no fewer than 300 Protestants had also been executed by Mary's orders.

During these anxious times of crisis and intolerance in the 1570s and 80s, in the quiet rural parish in Denbighshire of Llanrhaeadr-ym-Mochnant the vicar toiled away in his study month after month, year after year, translating the Bible into Welsh. William Morgan, who had been born in 1545 at Tŷ Mawr, a farmhouse in the Wybrnant valley, near Penmachno, was the son of a tenant of Sir John Wynn of Gwydir in the Conwy valley, in whose house the promising young William was educated, before being sent to Cambridge. Subsequently he held livings at Llanbadarn Fawr and at Welshpool, moving to Llanrhaeadr in 1572. At Cambridge he had been encouraged by his tutor to turn his hand to translating religious books into Welsh; at Llanrhaeadr he found the chance and during his years there, from 1572 to 1587, William Morgan translated the Old Testament and re-translated the New,

turning William Salesbury's stilted version into contemporary Welsh idiom. However, rightly or wrongly, voices began to be raised in the parish against what seemed to his critics to be time-wasting habits, voices which grew so loud that they reached the ears of John Whitgift, the Archbishop of Canterbury, who ordered Morgan to come to London to plead his case. Fortunately for the future of Welsh culture and Welsh Protestantism the Archbishop was wholly convinced and sent Morgan back home, comforted and encouraged, to carry on with his great work, which he finished in 1587.

This Welsh Bible appeared in 1588 – the year, be it remembered, when the Spanish dream of conquering England faded, as the Armada broke up on our inhospitable shore. Certainly Richard Davies and William Salesbury had played very important parts in furthering this great achievement but most of the credit has rightly been given to William Morgan. Indeed there are those who believe that this Welsh Bible of 1588 is the most important book ever to be written in Welsh, the same experts crediting Morgan with having thereby saved the Welsh language. Morgan did for Wales what Shakespeare did for England, and at about the same time; they both rendered respectable the languages in which they wrote. There was however a time-lag of 40 years before ordinary Welsh people could read this Bible as Morgan's translation did not appear in a cheap – and therefore generally available – edition until 1630. Morgan himself was rewarded for his labours by being made Bishop of Llandaff in 1595 and six year later Bishop of St Asaph, where, according to Sir John Wynn's contemporary account, 'he repaired and slated the chancel of the cathedral church, which was a great ruin'.

## The beginnings of
## Nonconformist dissent

No village in Wales today is complete without a Nonconformist chapel, thus presenting a very different picture from that of the sixteenth century, when there was no such place as a chapel of that kind. Nonconformity only began to take root in Wales in the middle of the seventeenth century, when in the short-lived Commonwealth of the 1650s Quakers and Baptists first openly expressed dissent in their places of worship. Methodism, readers are reminded, represents a later mode of dissent, the earliest such chapels in Wales being built in the first quarter of the nineteenth century, following the great

missionary efforts of Howell Harris in the second half of the previous century. However, despite the almost total absence of any Nonconformist activity in the sixteenth century, there was one lone dissenting voice raised in Wales – that of John Penry – crying in the Welsh wilderness; his unique, heroic, and quite ineffectual contribution justifies inclusion here because he was a man of absolute integrity, who burned with a passionate desire to satisfy the spiritual needs of his under-privileged fellow-Welshmen.

John Penry was born in 1563 into a Wales to which Protestantism had only recently come in the trappings of the Church of England, whose priests read from an English Bible to their largely uncomprehending congregations. His home was near Llangamarch, Brecknockshire, and he was educated at Christ College, Brecon and at Peterhouse, Cambridge, where he studied theology. There he came into contact with students whose interest in the revolutionary ideas of the Puritans attracted Penry, who spent most of his university vacations in Northampton, at that time a hotbed of Puritanism. He was entertained there by a Puritan family, the Godleys, whose daughter Eleanor he later married. He graduated in 1584 and after a spell in Oxford returned in 1586 to his home in Wales, where he withdrew for a while to write his first book, a short treatise that was above all an impassioned plea to Elizabeth and her government to right what, according to him, were the many wrongs suffered by his fellow-countrymen. Five hundred copies were printed and circulated in London, where to his chagrin John Penry was almost immediately arrested on the instructions of the Archbishop of Canterbury, John Whitgift.

He appeared before the Court of High Commission to answer charges of slandering the government and committing treason and heresy, whereas in truth all he had had in mind was to draw the attention of the public to the many problems of Wales. He was treated as a naughty boy who knew no better, and sent to prison for 12 days, a sentence which was extended to a month. Penry had gone to prison an innocent, but left it wary and determined in future to watch his every step; one fact he had learned was that the Court of High Commission was able to act quite independently of parliament, to whom Penry had addressed his book.

He at once returned to the attack by writing a second and much more important treatise, which he called his Exhortation to the Governors and People of Wales. Once again he stressed the unhappy state of his country, emphasising his belief that the lawless behaviour of many Welshmen could only be changed if adequate religious teaching became available. He specifically criticised the Church of England in Wales for not preaching the Gospel properly, above all condemning the Welsh bishops and suggesting that Welshmen should take it upon themselves to choose their own ministers. This indeed was fighting talk; with the censuring of the bishops the gauntlet had been thrown down, because to Elizabeth an attack on the bishops was tantamount to an attack on her authority, the bishops in her opinion providing a necessary balance between Church and State. This Exhortation was published by a travelling press, operating from secret locations, which government agents failed to find. This printing press, of which John Penry was probably the manager, produced a steady stream of Puritan pamphlets, of which this one alone took up the cudgels on behalf of Wales.

The year was 1588 and the Armada was soon to beat its way up the Channel; the Exhortation could hardly have appeared at a less opportune time. Nevertheless it was shortly afterwards followed by another such publication, the Supplication, which was actually presented to parliament. Its opening words were these:

Behold the mountains of Wales do now, in the thirty-first year of Queen Elizabeth's reign, call upon heaven and earth to witness that they are weary of the dumb ministers, the non-resident Lord Bishops etc. and they desire to be watered by the dew of Christ's Holy Gospel'.

Accompanying this treatise to Parliament was a note from the author, begging Parliament 'to have poor Wales in remembrance'.

All was in vain. John Penry, who had by then married Eleanor Godley, went into hiding; before long deeming it wise to flee to Scotland, where for two years he stayed with friends, beyond the reach of the authority of England. In 1592 however he took the fatal decision to go back to London, where he attached himself to the Separatists, a Puritan sect, which was the spiritual father of Congregationalism.

Coinciding with this secret return of John Penry to London was the application of an Act of Parliament, passed earlier in the year, designed 'to punish persons obstinately refusing to come to church', an act intended to bring to book the Separatists, many of whose leaders were already in prison. Before long Penry was arrested at an open-air meeting of Separatists and quickly recognised as the author of the Exhortation; he was in consequence charged with being a seditious traitor, who endangered the security of the state and threatened the life of the queen.

On 29 May 1593 Penry was hanged; he was just 30. Mourned by few beyond his wife and their four daughters – Deliverance, Comfort, Safety and Sure Hope – Penry's only aim had been to find ways and means of helping the poor and underprivileged, the wicked and the irreligious in his native Wales. The sad fact, however, was that in his short life no fellow Welshman worked with him in that field. He had been born half a century too soon; all the same let him be remembered and revered for giving his life for his friends.

## Notes and illustrations

### Sequel to the Dissolution of the Monasteries

Earlier mention has been made of the ruinous state of most of the monasteries in the 1530s, when Thomas Cromwell, acting on the orders of his royal master, caused them to be suppressed. Of the monasteries in Wales, Tintern alone had a full complement of monks. The fact that most of these religious houses had for the most part outlived their usefulness, hardly gave the king the right to confiscate their property and to take away their lands. In 1539, by which time most of the forcible transfer of land and prosperity had taken place, parliament stepped in and passed a law which legalised all these expropriations.

The subsequent history of three well-known Welsh religious houses, two Cistercian and one Augustinian, may be of interest to readers.

### i)  Tintern Abbey

Tintern Abbey, especially if the sun is shining, seems an earthly paradise; in a sylvan setting on the bank of the river Wye, 5 miles (8 km) upstream from Chepstow, stands this much-loved ruin, where William Wordsworth once listened to 'the still sad music of humanity'. In the twelfth century, however, when the first Cistercian monks came that way, they decided to settle and to build there because the site was so wild and so remote, and so isolated from the busy haunts of man, which Cistercians always avoided.

After the dissolution the abbey passed into the keeping of the Earl of Worcester, whose family retained possession of the ruins until the Crown moved in and bought Tintern from the family in 1901. In 1875, when the Worcester family still owned Tintern, Kilvert, the Victorian diarist, visited Tintern on a day trip in a coach from Chepstow; he seems to have been the only passenger who bothered to savour the beauty of the abbey ruins and the monastic buildings. He 'climbed to the top of the walls . . . adorned with a perfect wildflower garden of scarlet poppies, white roses, yellow stonecrop and purple mallow, which formed a low hedge along each side of the otherwise undefended footpath'.

It is perhaps difficult today in Tintern to realise that an iron industry had flourished thereabout since probably Roman times, the plentiful supply of wood providing the means of smelting the locally-produced ore. The monks are thought to have successfully organised this manufacture of iron, which survived the dissolution and indeed prospered – in different hands of course – until about 1820. In addition a plaque outside the abbey draws the attention of visitors to the fact that it was in Tintern in 1568 that brass was first made by fusing together copper and zinc.

### ii) **Strata Florida**

Strata Florida, the second Cistercian abbey to be visited, lies 2 miles (3.2 km) north of Tregaron in Dyfed; its situation today, unlike that of Tintern, is nearly as remote and in winter nearly as bleak as it must have been in the twelfth century when it was founded. In its prime the monastery was very prosperous, thanks to the wool trade which had greatly flourished in the expert hands of the monks, and it became a centre of culture and influence.

At the dissolution, the abbey and its precincts were given to the Stedman family, who retained it until the eighteenth century when the male line of the Stedmans died out. It then passed to the family of Richard Stedman's wife, the Powells, which in 1739 built a splendid mansion at Nanteos, 2½ miles (4 km) south-east of Aberystwyth. When the Powells left *Strata Florida* and went to Nanteos, they took with them a certain artifact, which had been entrusted to the monks of *Strata Florida* shortly before the dissolution.

The story goes that Joseph of Arimathea, after the crucifixion of Christ, settled in Glastonbury, bringing with him

*Tintern Abbey*

the wooden cup from which Christ had drunk at the Last Supper. The tradition persisted, and the monks of Glastonbury jealously guarded their precious secret until news of the impending dissolution of Glastonbury reached them, when several of their number carried it over the hills to *Strata Florida* for safe custody. When the Stedmans took over from the monks at *Strata Florida*, they promised to take care of this Holy Grail, 200 years later handing it over to the Powells, who took it with them when they moved from *Strata Florida* to Nanteos. Gradually magic properties were assigned to the blackened piece of olive wood; indeed until the early years of the twentieth century the Powells allowed sick people in their neighbourhood to borrow the cup, on condition that on recovery, when they brought the cup back, they would sign a statement, confirming that they had been restored to health. The last known note is dated 1903. Thereafter presumably the cup stayed with the Powell family, but in 1967 they moved house, it is believed, to a new home in Herefordshire.

One final note: *Strata Florida* today, remotely situated as it is, possesses a modern and admirably-equipped museum on the site.

### iii) Llanthony Priory

This Augustinian ruin is superbly situated in the Honddu valley in Gwent, about 6 miles (9.65 km) north of Llanfihangel Crucornau, on the main road from Abergavenny to Hereford. Visitors are recommended, while in this valley, also to make a small detour to see the little church at Cwm-iou, and, if possible also to savour the unique charm of Partrishow Church, in the next valley to the west, the Grwyne Fawr.

At the dissolution of Llanthony in 1538 the last prior received a small pension and the buildings and the surrounding land were sold by the king to the Chief Justice of Ireland, Nicholas Arnolde; in later years the estate was sold to the Harleys, who kept it until 1790, when it was bought by a Colonel Wood, from Brecon, who turned the Prior's lodgings into a comfortable house for himself and equipped the south tower of the west front as a shooting lodge for his sporting guests.

The history of Llanthony changed direction in 1807, when the new owner was none other than the celebrated poet Walter Savage Landor, he who, on his 75th birthday, referred to 'warming both hands before the fire of life'. In 1807 this friend

## Patrishow Church

*This church was visited in the twelfth century by Archbishop Baldwin and his faithful chaplain, Giraldus Cambrensis; from the steps of the churchyard cross, near the south door, Baldwin invited his audience to join the Third Crusade. Energetic historical enthusiasts may care, after admiring the wonderful screen in the church and studying the churchyard, to walk about a 100 yards/metres down the hill, at the foot of which may still be seen a holy well, without which there would have been no church today.*

*Tradition has it that Issui, a sixth century Christian missionary, who lived in a cell near this well, ministered to the neighbourhood, whose sick he had the power to heal until one day he was murdered. The same tradition insists that thereafter Issui's healing powers were transferred to the well itself, to which in the eleventh century a wealthy leper came and received a miraculous cure for his terrible affliction. Whereupon in gratitude he paid for a church to be built on top of the hill, a church which was dedicated to the martyred Issui, which gradually became simplified into Partrishow, which in Welsh is called Patrisio.*

of Browning and Swinburne paid £20,000 for his estate, which he fondly intended to transform into something unusually splendid. Landor's gifts, however, were poetic rather than practical and in addition he never succeeded in acquiring any understanding of his neighbours in the Honddu valley, or indeed in making any agreement with them. Hence his elaborate schemes all came to nothing and he decamped to Italy, leaving the estate with his mother, who organised it so well that the Landor family still lived there in 1870, when Kilvert (who else?!) paid it two visits.

On the first occasion, early in April the diarist was sorely put out by having to wait while two tourists, who had had the temerity to order dinner before him, finished a leisurely meal. Kilvert, keen readers will have noticed, disliked tourists even more than he did dissenters! The entry in the diary for Tuesday, 5 April 1870 is well worth reading; as is the account of his subsequent visit two months later on Midsummer Day, when his arrival coincided with Mrs Landor's Rent Day,

when all her tenants were being entertained by her to dinner. In the unusual circumstances Kilvert and his party had to make do, we are told, with only bread, butter, cheese, beer and boiled eggs (of which they consumed 20!).

Llanthony today is in the hands of Cadw; the ruins are, of course, well cared for and the Archaeological Department of the University of Cardiff have been allowed every summer since 1978 to carry out scientific digging. Much new and valuable information has been discovered about this medieval priory, and undoubtedly future digs there will yield up many more archaeological secrets.

Meanwhile, Colonel Wood's house is now a comfortable hotel, whose guests have to find their way to their beds up a spiral staircase, while in the cellar which is part of the medieval undercroft, real ale may be obtained, thus making possible a return to the hospitality enjoyed by visitors to the religious houses of the Middle Ages.

## Gruffydd Robert in exile

In the middle of the sixteenth century this most illustrious of Welsh Roman Catholic scholars languished for 20 years

1. *Abbey Cwm Hir*; 2. Strata Florida; 3. Valle Crucis

in Milan, from where he wrote nostalgically:

> although fair the place where we are now, yet I long for many things which were to be had in Wales . . . if you wanted entertainment, you could find a minstrel and his harp to play gentle airs or a singer of sweet ditties to sing to the harp . . . if you wished to hear about the customs of the country, there would be gray-haired old men who would relate every remarkable and worthy deed in the land of Wales since time immemorial . . . as for the vineyards here, although they look beautiful enough, yet a Welshman's heart does not respond to them, as it would to the banks of the Dee or the Vale of Clwyd, or in many other places I could name from St David's to Holyhead . . . my heart would gladden sooner to hear the cuckoo sing in my own country than it would here on hearing the sweet notes of the nightingale...

(from *A Book of Wales*, by Meic Stephens, published by J. M. Dent, 1987)

## Pilgrimage to Tŷ Mawr

For those who like to see their history on the ground as well as to read it in their armchairs, an excursion from Penmachno is suggested; little persuasion should be necessary to make attractive a country walk from there to Tŷ Mawr in the Wybrnant valley. Tŷ Mawr may be approached, it is true, by a number of paths from the Lledr valley, but the walk from Penmachno is recommended because there is a meaningful Christian connection between the two places.

There was a time when pilgrimages were popular pursuits (Chaucer's *Canterbury Tales* will spring to readers' minds); in very early Christian times the most popular goal was Rome, where Peter and Paul died, but Rome, of course, was beyond the reach of most would-be pilgrims. The earliest such pilgrimage in Wales, it seems, was to Bardsey Island (*Ynys Enlli*), which over the years found such favour with the church authorities that three pilgrimages to Bardsey were regarded as equal to one to Rome! Recalling the tradition, another Christian pilgrimage is here suggested, on foot, of course, from Penmachno to Tŷ Mawr, a Christian journey that spans a thousand

*1. The Welsh Bible, 1588; 2. Tŷ Mawr Wybrnant, the birthplace of William Morgan*

years of history. First of all to get to Penmachno, take the A5 westwards from Pentrefoelas; after about 7 miles (11.26 km) turn left on to the B4406, which, after a further 3 miles (4.8 km), leads to Penmachno, a large village, where a car may be left. The church is locked, but a notice in the porch indicates a nearby house where the key may be obtained. In this church will be found four inscribed memorial stones, all taken from Romano-British graves in the neighbourhood, all

dating from the fifth to the early sixth centuries. With one in particular of these stones pilgrims will be especially concerned; first, however, it has to be stressed that Wales is singularly fortunate in possessing a great many of these early Christian memorial stones, which commemorate the lives of Christians, who died long before Augustine brought Christianity to Kent in the late sixth century. Of all these early stones, two only in the whole of Wales bear the exciting Chi-Rho monogram, which is a joining-together of the first two Greek letters in Christ's name; one of these

Chi-Rho stones is here in Penmachno church, its Latin inscription indicating that 'Carausius lies here in this heap of stones'.

With an Ordnance Survey map as an essential companion, now take the western road out of the village and after less than a mile (1.6 km) follow the path through the woods to the right of the road, which, after 2 more miles (3.2 km) of forest trails, leads down to Tŷ Mawr, the farmhouse, where William Morgan was born. This one-time farm is now a museum in the safe custody of the National Trust and, in Jan Morris' appropriate words, a national shrine. Morgan's Welsh Bible, published in 1588, did as much for Wales as the Royal Navy's defeat of the Spanish Armada in the same year did for England.

### Sir John Wynn

John Wynn (1553–1626) of Gwydir in the Conwy valley, succeeded to the extensive Gwydir estate in 1580, thereafter devoting much of his time to adding to the prosperity and affluence of his family, with the result that the Wynns became the most powerful family in northern Wales. After several terms of office as Sheriff, both of Caernarfonshire and of Meirionnydd, he became the Member of Parliament for Caernarfon; in 1606 he was knighted by James I, who three years later made him a baronet.

Posterity however remembers him above all for the fact that he wrote the history of his family, in which an invaluable picture is painted of the social history of north Wales at that time. This *History of the Gwydir Family* is an important piece of contemporary Welsh history, which is now available in an English translation, which the Gomer Press published in 1990.

An indication of the historical value of this family history and its attendant memoirs is provided by an idea Sir John Wynn entertained for the possible reclamation of land in Traeth Mawr, near the modern Porthmadog, which was a part of the Gwydir estate. Readers will find later in this book an account of the eventual successful reclamation of Traeth Mawr at the beginning of the nineteenth century by William Madocks. However, a letter survives in which Sir John Wynn invited Sir Hugh Middleton to take an interest in draining Traeth Mawr, Sir Hugh having recently been successful in winning

*1. Sir John Wynn; 2. Gwydir Castle near Llanrwst*

back from the sea some 2,000 acres in the Isle of Wight.

In this letter to his fellow baronet Sir John Wynn wrote:

> My skill is little, my experience none at all in such matters . . . yet I ever had a desire to further my country in such actions as might be for their profit, and leave a remembrance of my endeavours . . . now seeing it pleased God to bring you into this country, I am to desire you to take a view of the place, not being above a day's journey from you; and if you do see things fit to be undertaken, I am content to adventure a brace of hundred pounds to join you in the work.

Sir John died a few months later.

### In retrospect

Looking back over 400 years and more to the sixteenth century, it can be seen that Wales in that century had been annexed by England, that Welsh people in their public affairs had been prevented from using their own language, and had also had a change of religion foisted upon them. Yet in 1586, when Camden's *Britannia* was published, he could write:

> Mary, Elizabeth and Edward, the children of Henry VIII, although they received not the investiture, yet styled themselves Princes of Wales. For at that time Wales was by the Act of Union so united and incorporated into England that they enjoyed the same laws and privileges.

No matter how superficial that judgement, nevertheless it was true that most Welsh people had come to accept the Act of Union, failing as yet to realise the long-term significance of the banning of the Welsh language from their courts of law. It seems also to be true that by the end of this sixteenth century Wales had, generally speaking, accepted the Reformation. This more or less tacit acceptance by the Welsh of what was an English Reformation arose partly through the general Welsh ignorance of English, which naturally tended to result in Welsh indifference, and partly because the English-trained priests provided the main channel of communication for English ideas to pass into Wales. This continuing stream of English influence through a church system, which was based on Canterbury, was, happily for those Welshmen, who could see the dangerous drift of events, to be splendidly offset by the ever-increasing use in the seventeenth century of the Welsh Book of Common Prayer and of William Morgan's Welsh Bible, which succeeded in preserving for posterity the widespread use of the Welsh language, and with it the means of maintaining an essentially different culture.

1. The Bible translator's memorial at St Asaph; 2. St Asaph cathedral where William Morgan became a bishop; 3. The Bishop's memorial at Llanrhaeadr-ym-Mochnant

# The Seventeenth Century

## The Civil War in Wales and a Cultural Renaissance

Just a hundred years before, many Welshmen will have greeted the new century with some optimism; their country was not yet a part of England but 15 years previously a Welshman, Henry Tudor, having beaten and killed the king of England in battle at Bosworth, had made himself king. Bosworth was regarded in Wales as a great away victory! For a long and bitter quarrel with England had ended, as they saw it, in a great and glorious victory. Henry VII, however, did very little to alter the government of Wales; the six counties of Anglesey, Caernarfon, Meirionnydd, Flint, Cardigan and Carmarthen had since the reign of Edward I been directly ruled from London, but the Marches after 1485 were governed by the newly-revived Council of Marches, based on Ludlow, which acted as a bridge between central authority in London and the people of the Marches. In addition, Henry VII sensibly placed in key positions in Wales Welsh leaders like Sir Rhys ap Thomas, who had won his knighthood on the field of Bosworth.

After 1536, when Parliament passed the Act of Union, which finally made Wales politically a part of England, English ideas spread more rapidly in Wales, one of which was beginning to have considerable social and political consequence. In the Middle Ages the Welsh law of inheritance was known as gavelkind, whereby at a man's death his property was equally divided up between his sons; this traditional way of doing things, which had begun to be ignored by some in the fourteenth century, disintegrated very quickly in the sixteenth, when it was wholly replaced by the rule of inheritance in favour east of Offa's Dyke, that of primogeniture, whereby the eldest son inherited all his late father's estate. Hence in the sixteenth century there grew up in Wales a new rural middle class, whose power was based on land. These 'new' men developed a strong vested interest in the success of the Tudor dynasty, which they served by officiating at the Petty Sessions:

*Ludlow, where the Council of Marches was based*

moreover they sent their sons to be educated at English universities, in order to prepare them eventually to follow in their father's footsteps.

Early on in the new century, in 1603, Elizabeth died, and with her ended the Welsh dynasty of the Tudors; with the succession of James I to the throne, there began a new dynasty, that of the Scottish Stuarts, a change which may well have caused many Welshmen to anticipate the future with some apprehension. The acid test was thought likely to be the way the new king treated the Council of the Marches, which in fact was to continue to exist in Ludlow for another 40 years. Over the years influential and ambitious Welshmen, leaders of the new middle class, had tended to foregather at Ludlow, where they sought to engage the ear of every Englishman, who happened to be the Lord President. Power may have ebbed from Ludlow, but influence continued to flow. James I, not always the wisest of men, on this occasion displayed shrewdness in his treatment of influential Welshmen, who, thus encouraged, transferred their previous allegiance to the old Tudors to the new Stuarts.

The history of the seventeenth century (and it is the history of Wales as well as of England) was bedevilled by the great quarrel between the king and his parliament; thanks to the perspective which the intervening passage of 300 years and more allows, it is possible to see the development of this contest, like the plot of a great drama unfolding itself. Pressure built up quite early in the century in the reign of James I, leading to the call to arms in mid-century and, as the tumultuous century was drawing to its close, a momentous dénouement held the stage in the settlement of 1688.

The quarrel between king and parliament, which 40 years later was to lead to a bitter Civil War, had its beginning in the reign of James I; its causes were manifold, of which two in particular need here to be stressed. Firstly, the prevalent political doctrine at this time in Europe was a belief in the divinity of kings, a view passionately held by James I. Parliament, on the other hand, despite occasional periods of abject subservience to Tudor rulers, gradually but surely, as its members were more and more drawn from the

*Tŷ Aberconwy – a town house in Conwy; Cochwillan hall*

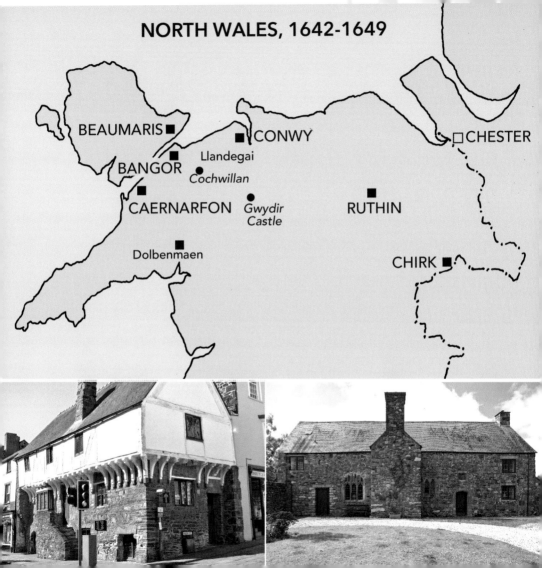

NORTH WALES, 1642-1649

BEAUMARIS

CONWY

□CHESTER

BANGOR

Llandegai

*Cochwillan*

CAERNARFON

*Gwydir Castle*

RUTHIN

Dolbenmaen

CHIRK

merchant middle class, refused to believe that any king of England could interpret the will of God and, in so doing, stood up increasingly for the rights of the king's subjects. This fundamental difference of opinion between king and parliament first assumed serious proportions in the closing years of James I's reign, when a second cause of dissension arose, which concerned the amount of money parliament was prepared to give to the king.

In those far-off days financial responsibility for the carrying-on of government, whether it was for the waging of wars or of paying servants of the Crown, from all-powerful diplomats to common soldiers alike, rested on the shoulders of the monarch, who, in turn, of course, depended upon parliament once a year to vote him the necessary money. James I soon came to realise that his predecessor on the throne, Elizabeth, had left the royal exchequer sparsely furnished – the war with Spain had seen to that! Parliament for its part was perhaps less than understanding of the royal predicament, which became worse during James' reign, as the value of our currency dropped. Europe at the beginning of the seventeenth century was indeed suffering from a very modern economic disease, inflation, which had been made very much worse by the large quantity of silver, brought back to Europe by the Spaniards from their conquests in central America. Parliament, however, ignored, as parliaments sometimes do, basic economic facts, and refused to make an adequate increase in their contribution to the royal exchequer; hence James had to look around for alternative methods of raising money. This, in general terms, was the background against which the great drama of the seventeenth century was played out, a drama in which a Welshman, a product of the new rural middle class previously referred to, was to play a leading part.

## A Welshman in high places

John Williams was born in 1582 in Conwy, the second son of Edward and Mary Williams, his illustrious godfather being Sir John Wynn. On his father's side he was descended from a younger branch of the Gruffydd family of Penrhyn; their fifteenth-century home at Cochwillan, east of the A5 between Llandygái and Bethesda, has miraculously managed to survive. His mother's forebears were none other than the Wynns, whose mansion at Gwydir near Llanrwst in the Conwy valley was likewise built in the fifteenth century. All his life John Williams regarded himself first and foremost as a son of Conwy, within whose historic walls many momentous events in his later life took place.

He was educated at Ruthin Grammar School before in 1598 going up to Cambridge, where on his own admission, he knew more Greek and Latin than he did English, causing him to be the friendly butt of his fellow students for his Welsh turn of speech. After graduating in theology at Cambridge, John Williams was ordained and prepared himself for a successful career in the church, to which his qualifications, his background and his affluence clearly pointed. Meanwhile storm clouds were gathering in the world outside, as the conflict started to take shape between the king and his parliament, between those who favoured a despotic monarchy and those who preferred sovereignty to reside to parliament. As the struggle loomed nearer, James came to rely more and more on the advice of extra-parliamentary noblemen, of whom by far the most influential was

the future Duke of Buckingham, who was in time also to become the close friend and confidant of Charles I.

In 1611, John Williams was invited to preach before James I and so impressed his royal audience that thereafter not only did his career take off in a spectacular fashion but it also began to suggest political advancement too, especially when in 1612 the Lord Chancellor, Lord Ellesmere, the most powerful politician in the land, made Williams his chaplain. Soon the king himself was asking Williams his opinions on matters of state. Religious preferment followed in 1619, with his appointment as Dean of Salisbury, and again in 1620 when Williams became Dean of Westminster, an appointment as lucrative as it was prestigious. The widespread belief that he was developing political ambitions received astonishing confirmation in 1621, when in addition to becoming Bishop of Lincoln, he was also appointed Lord Keeper of the Seal. Thus before his 39th birthday John Williams, despite being a bishop, was already even higher up the political ladder.

The rocket that had ascended so brilliantly into the political sky began to fall back in the last years of James' reign, only to crash to earth soon after Charles succeeded his father in 1625. Within the first months of the new reign, twice the king sought Williams' opinion, twice he counselled moderation, and twice had his counsel ignored. From that time Charles grew to depend more and more on the Duke of Buckingham and a new rising star in the Church of England, William Laud, who like the duke, was a strong believer in the divine right of kings. Before 1625 had ended John Williams had been dismissed from his high office of state. He then retired, for the time being, to his see at Lincoln, where for the next 12 years, until 1637, he lived in the grand manner, entertaining munificently. These were years of immense importance, and although he was of necessity an enforced spectator of national events, he was by no means unaware or unmoved by them.

Crisis followed crisis as the king was forced by his desperate need for money to summon parliament, only to dismiss it, when Members tried to put a brake on royal autocracy. The king, such was his dire need, tried again, but parliament, in whose ranks were numbered men of the calibre of John Hampden and his cousin, Oliver Cromwell, before taking any decision about what money to vote to the royal exchequer, pushed through the Commons in 1628 the Petition of Right; this act, one of the great charters of our liberties, made illegal any royal demand for money unless sanctioned by parliament, and in addition forbade the imprisonment of any citizen without due cause being given. John Williams, staunch supporter of monarchy though he was, wrote urgently to the king from Lincoln, begging him to accept this Petition of Right; the king thought otherwise, dismissed parliament, and from 1629 to 1640 ruled the country without once summoning parliament.

In these long years of arbitrary royal rule the position of William Laud became ever stronger; sensing the rivalry to be expected from John Williams, Laud carefully gathered evidence of what he regarded as Williams' illegal actions over the years, alleging betrayal of state secrets and perjury. Laud's hand was much strengthened in 1633 when Charles made him Archbishop of Canterbury. Finally his dossier on John Williams complete, Laud had him arrested, his fellow bishop be it remembered, and hauled him up before the infamous Court of Star Chamber in

London, where various charges were brought against him. The outcome was that Williams was fined £10,000, suspended from the deanery of Westminster and from the bishopric of Lincoln, and packed off to the Tower of London, where he was to stay until 1640.

Any relief that Laud may have felt after the imprisonment of his rival must have been short-lived because John Williams was to prove as unpleasant a thorn in his side in prison as he had been outside, with the result that in 1639 he was taken from the Tower to face the Court of Star Chamber once again, this time on a charge of libelling the Archbishop of Canterbury. Again Williams was heavily fined before being returned to the Tower of London. Late in the following year, 1640, the king, reduced to desperately straitened circumstance by lack of money, which he required to finance a war against the Scots, had to swallow his pride and summon parliament. At once this parliament released John Williams from prison; this was the Long Parliament whose objective was to get the legal relationship of the king to parliament clearly defined and forever enshrined in statute. To make their task easier, they first ordered the arrest of Laud; the king, thus bereft of his normal source of support, decided, in an attempt to win over public opinion, to summon John Williams to advise him once more. By the end of 1641 his fortunes seemed about to be restored to their former height, when the king made him Archbishop of York. By this preferment Williams was now virtually Head of the Church of England, as Laud was never to leave the Tower, except to be executed in 1645.

Meanwhile great events were being set in train; parliament, under the leadership of John Pym, drew up the Grand Remonstrance, which was then debated at great length and with rising passions. It amounted to a vote of no confidence in the king, which, when put to the vote, was only carried by a meagre majority of 11. The king, much encouraged by the unexpected strength of the parliamentary opposition to Pym, decided on action. On 5 January 1642, Charles went down to Westminster and attempted to arrest the ringleaders, including Pym himself. The Five Members, notified in advance of what was afoot, had made good their escape. This abortive and illegal act on the king's part was the last meeting of king and parliament before the recourse to arms. After this humiliating farce the king left London, to which he never returned, of his own free will. John Williams, in June 1642, went to York to be consecrated Archbishop. Two months later the Royal Standard was raised in Nottingham and the Civil War had begun. When John Williams learned that a party of parliamentary soldiers was approaching his palace, he fled from York and sought the security of the walls of Conwy Castle.

At this climacteric in John Williams' career it is salutary to pause a moment and take stock; he had already achieved the highest positions in two different spheres, in Church and State. To have kept the Great Seal of England and to have become the virtual Head of the Church of England was a remarkable feat indeed, especially for a man who at the outset was a scholar with no obvious inclination for a career that would lead to political or spiritual pre-eminence. And now, in 1642, on the morrow of his consecration as an archbishop, John Williams, having already celebrated his 60th birthday; many men might have looked longingly forward to a life of slippered ease in a well-earned retirement. Instead he stood upon the threshold of a third career: that of a soldier in the service of his royal master.

## The impact of the Civil War

It is necessary at this stage of the unfolding drama to introduce a new character, whose path was to cross that of the archbishop for the next four years. This new character was John Owen; north Wales produced no more unswervingly a loyal supporter of the royal cause. After the lapse of more than 300 years it should be possible today to view the clash between these two leaders of men dispassionately, while still registering dismay that such a clash ever took place. John Owen hailed from the remote and beautiful Pennant valley, west of Snowdon; his family home, Clenennau, lying between Dolbenmaen and Penmorfa. His father had been secretary to Elizabeth's great man of mystery, Sir Francis Walsingham. John succeeded to the family estate in 1626, becoming Sheriff of Caernarfon four years later, when he was only 30.

An up and coming man, he also became Sheriff of Meirionnydd the following year. In the very prime of life, when the Civil War broke out in 1642, John Owen was at once commissioned by the king to raise and train an army in the counties of Gwynedd, Anglesey, Meirionnydd and Caernarfon.

It was in that same year that John Williams returned to Conwy from York; after a brief visit to Oxford, where he pledged his loyalty to the king, Williams, sent back to Conwy, where he attended to the needs of the town and castle. At his own expense he greatly improved the fortifications of the castle, he laid in supplies and he strengthened the garrison. Meanwhile he kept in constant touch with the king, being Charles' chief and most valuable source of information on developments in north Wales and more particularly in Ireland, where a full-blooded rebellion had broken out in 1641. Ormonde had been despatched there by the king to try to contain the outbreak, taking with him an army, in the ranks of which were many Welshmen. By 1643 the Irish rebellion seemed to have quietened down sufficiently for Ormonde to agree to the king's request to send home the Welsh contingent. John Williams made detailed arrangements for the eventual reception of the Welsh soldiers both in Beaumaris and in Conwy, where the returning soldiers were to be fed, reclothed and rearmed for further service in the royal cause nearer home. By the end of 1643, John Williams was ready for anything; he still awaited the arrival of the Welsh soldiers, whose return in fact Ormonde was never to authorise. At any rate Conwy Castle was equipped for all eventualities, prompting Williams before the year was out to ask his royal master to make him its Governor.

John Owen, meanwhile, having duly raised and armed an army in Gwynedd, as the king had ordered, marched as its head into England; he took part in an engagement outside Oxford in May 1643, then in July he commanded a brigade under Prince Rupert at the siege of Bristol, where he was wounded, recovering in time to participate in further fighting at Newbury in September. It was not until

*Conwy Castle*

April 1946 that Owen was back in Caernarfon, where the king promptly made him sheriff again. From that moment John Williams had a rival on the spot; in December of the same year Williams learned to his chagrin that the Governorship of Conwy to which he had aspired had been given to John Owen, along with a knighthood. Spurned as he felt himself to have been, John Williams stayed on in Conwy Castle as the *de facto* Governor until Sir John Owen forcibly but legally expelled the archbishop, who for the time being withdrew to Bangor.

This local quarrel, humiliating as it was for John Williams, was of little consequence compared with the grave decline in the royalist fortunes not many miles away at Chester, to which important base a parliamentary army laid siege in the early summer of 1645. Throughout this fatal year for the king's cause Charles pleaded all in vain for reinforcements to be sent from Ireland; in a forlorn attempt to relieve the siege, Charles led an army against the parliamentary forces that were encamped outside the city walls. The resulting battle at Rowton Moor in September was disastrous for the king. Chester was to hold out for a few more months but finally surrendered to Parliament in May 1646.

After the fall of Chester the first Civil War virtually came to an end because Charles, feeling at the end of his tether, when his own headquarters at Oxford were shortly afterwards besieged, managed to slip out and surrendered to the Scottish army, which by that time had come as far south as Newark – the Scots were the allies of Parliament. John Williams, faced with a new situation after Chester's fall, wrote tactfully to Sir John Owen, hoping that thereby the breach between them might be narrowed; receiving only a dusty answer, he made contact with Mytton, the parliamentary general, who was in the process of systematically reducing those coastal towns in northern Wales that had stood up for the king. It is interesting in this connection to discover that Williams' letter to Mytton drew a reply from none other than Oliver Cromwell (who had baptised Williams); in his letter Cromwell acknowledged himself to be the archbishop's cousin.

In the autumn Mytton's forces, now unexpectedly aided and abetted by Williams and his men, captured Conwy

*Gloddaeth Hall near Llandudno*

town and in November the castle itself, its defender Sir John Owen being allowed to leave and return to his home in the Pennant valley, on certain stringent conditions. John Williams' defection, however, was no isolated affair as many of the gentry in north Wales, feeling that the war had been lost and that ordinary men and women in north Wales had suffered enough, also decided to throw in their lot with the parliamentary forces and so help to bring to a speedy conclusion a sorry chapter in the history of north Wales. Sir John, it must be said, stayed loyal to the king's cause, and somehow managed to escape from a death sentence passed on him in the aftermath. Indeed he lived long enough to welcome the restoration of the monarchy in 1660.

After the parliamentary capture of Conwy in 1646, John Williams went to live at Gloddaeth Hall, which still stands across the water from Conwy, a mile or two (1-3 km) behind Deganwy. There he spent his few remaining years, though it was, while he was staying with his kinsmen in Gwydir Castle that he heard the news of Charles' execution in 1649, news which, some believe, caused him to regret his defection. In March 1650, John Williams died at Gloddaeth and was buried at Llandygái, where a monument on the church wall commemorates him, along with his helmet and spurs.

A scholar, a statesman, a church leader and in his old age a man of action, John Williams was a true son of the Renaissance and one of the greatest Welshmen of his age; in a quieter century he would have been able to devote more of his time to his undoubted love of fine arts, music and architecture. The archbishop was certainly an opportunist but also a man of wise moderation, whose counsels, had they been heeded, might well have guided the storm-tossed ship of state into calmer waters.

Summing up the course of the Civil War in Wales, in the early days in general most people were on the king's side, parliamentary support being restricted to south Pembrokeshire and the areas around Chirk and Ruthin where Sir Thomas Myddleton had his way. In addition to the Welsh gentry and the middle class, who had derived most benefit from the Act of Union, there was also a very considerable contingent of Welsh regular soldiers fighting for the king.

## Wales under the Commonwealth

When Charles I was executed in 1649, the government of England was firmly in the hands of the 60 survivors of the original Long Parliament, known as the Rump. Theirs was the difficult task of ruling Wales, their agents Oliver Cromwell and the army, whose object was to encourage the spread of Puritanism there. Today Wales is thought of as being more Nonconformist than England, and certainly there is a proliferation of Nonconformist chapels up and down the

*1. Derwen cross, near Ruthin, which survived the Puritan's mallet in Wales; 2. A broken cross at St Bride's Major*

country. At the end of the Civil War, however, the Puritan Movement, which in England had provided Oliver Cromwell with such sturdy support, had hardly touched Wales. Evidence of early scattered Nonconformist activity was to be found in Wrexham, which became a Puritan stronghold through Walter Cradoc and Morgan Llwyd; in Radnorshire, where the Baptist voices of Hugh Evans and Vavasor Powell were raised aloft; in the Gower peninsula where the first Baptist chapel in Wales was established by John Miles in 1649; and in Gwent, at Llanfaches, north of Newport, where an independent chapel had been consecrated in 1639 by the former vicar, who had been driven out for his 'Puritanical leanings'. Apart from these rather isolated exceptions there was little enough Puritanism to encourage Cromwell, who early on in the Commonwealth settled some of his time-expired soldiers in Radnorshire, in the hope that they might be successful evangelists. The Rump Parliament, alerted to the extent of the problem by Cromwell, in 1650 passed an Act for the Better Propagation of the Gospel in Wales.

A God-fearing cavalry officer, Colonel Thomas Harrison was named by parliament to see that the provisions of the Act were duly carried out; under him were appointed 70 commissioners, with Colonel John Jones put in charge of north Wales and Colonel Philip Jones in charge of the south. Their task was in the course of the following three years to seek out and to expel unsatisfactory priests and teachers; by 1653, when their work had to end and the Act lapsed, 300 priests and teachers had lost their jobs. This sort of arbitrary action, however conscientiously carried out by soldiers, could hardly fail to produce dissatisfaction and with is quite unsatisfactory results. And so it proved, especially as it gave rise to a new and intractable problem, namely, how to find adequate replacements for those who had been driven out.

In an attempt to solve this problem a system was established whereby a panel of itinerant preachers was enrolled to whom districts were assigned in which they were to preach and teach. Such an arrangement could hardly have succeeded had all the chosen preachers been educated men, but as in many cases zeal seemed their only obvious qualification, some of the consequences were lamentable. Nevertheless among the chosen were some outstanding men, men of the calibre of Morgan Llwyd, who had originally gone to Wrexham to learn at the feet of Walter Cradoc; in the Civil War he had fought for parliament, but thereafter he devoted his life to preaching and writing, and during the 'itinerant preaching experiment' had been responsible for a very large area which included a part of Caernarfonshire.

Another of these preachers was Hugh Evans, a Radnorshire Baptist, who, before being enrolled for itinerant preaching had been successful in making a Baptist connection in Radnorshire. In the same county lived Vavasor Powell, who was probably the best-known and most successful of the itinerant preachers. Radnorshire-born, he had been educated at Oxford; he first became a teacher before feeling the urge to preach. On one occasion, as a young man he had to appear at the Radnorshire Assizes in Presteigne (*Llanandras*) in order to answer a charge of 'disturbing the peace through preaching'! He too had supported Parliament in the Civil War, when he took every opportunity to exercise his power of preaching. Such was the reputation he gained as a public speaker, that in 1650 he was ordered to preach before parliament in London. His subsequent contribution to itinerant preaching was substantial and successful, although, as will be seen later, his enemies remembered his achievements in after years.

However, Cromwell in 1653, discouraged by what seemed to him the failure of the itinerant preachers to supply the needs of Wales and disenchanted with the activities of the Rump, dismissed parliament; this was the famous occasion when the Mace was removed, along with all remaining traces of constitutional action. Oliver Cromwell's impatient dismissal of the Rump Parliament found favour with some extreme Puritans, especially with the sect, known as the Fifth Monarchists, who had some enthusiastic members in Wales; these people expected Christ to return to earth in the near future in order to rule here for a thousand years. Such Puritans became even more whole-hearted in their support for Cromwell, when later that same year, 1653, he indulged in another constitutional experiment by appointing a parliament of 140 upright and God-fearing men (the six representatives chosen to

*Early dissenters' chapels:*
*1. Llanwenarth; 2. The Pales*

speak for Wales were all selected by Vavasor Powell). This strange government, the Rule of the Saints, sometimes known as the Barebones Parliament after the unusual name of one of its members, spent five months in eager, ineffectual chatter before being driven out by Cromwell, to the utter chagrin of extreme Puritans, whose friendly feelings towards Cromwell soon gave way to implacable hatred.

After several more unavailing experiments in government, one of which gave him the welcome title of the Lord Protector, Cromwell chose a simple solution, army rule. The whole country was divided up into ten areas, over each of which presided a Major General, who had at his disposal units of the army to see that his decisions were carried out. Thus England passed under complete and open army rule, which became, not surprisingly, everywhere thoroughly detested. These rigorous years of arbitrary military government did much to prepare the mind of the people for an eventual return to monarchy. Cromwell died in 1658, his son Richard briefly inheriting responsibility for governing the country. He soon called a parliament, which he quickly dismissed before himself resigning.

In 1659 the Rump was recalled; its first act was to abolish the Protectorate. In 1660 it invited the eldest son of the late Charles I to become king, and in May Charles II rode into London, to the joy and relief of the populace. It has too to be said that the news was received with widespread pleasure in Wales, where Charles was proclaimed king at Wrexham. Nevertheless it needs also to be clearly stated that although Nonconformity had as yet made little headway in Wales, such successful beginnings as had been made here and there in the country by Independents (Congregationalists), Baptists and Quakers were to assume great importance and give much needed hope in the dark days of intolerance that were to follow so soon on the restoration of the monarchy. Indication of the wrath to come was provided by the fates of Vavasor Powell, who had to languish in prison from 1661–07, and of Colonel John Jones, one of the commissioners appointed by Parliament in 1650 to weed out unsuitable Welsh priests, who was executed, while John Miles, who had built the first Baptist chapel in Wales at Ilston in the Gower, emigrated with most of his congregation to America.

## The spread of Nonconformity

Many were the flags of welcome put out for the new king, in 1660 in Wales, where the Restoration rewarded successful and orthodox Welshmen, many of whom by this time, having become thoroughly anglicised, had been suitably promoted to posts of high responsibility in church and state. There was, however, a minority of Welshmen who felt no particular wish to cheer or to share in the general jubilation. These odd men out were the Nonconformists, who had become intoxicated by the heady wine of freedom, especially in the early 1650s. These simple people, some of whom, of course, may have been too simplistic, had seen a chance in the brave new world of the Commonwealth to produce a new society, based on the underlying principles of the New Testament. The persecution that later accompanied the implementation of the new, reactionary anti-Puritan laws of the 1660s, after the dream had faded, seems in retrospect to have benefited the Quaker Movement most, because these remarkable people actually seem to have succeeded in thriving on persecution, as will be shown later.

First, readers may like to be reminded

how the Restoration Parliament reacted to the spread of the free religious thinking of the previous decade. From 1661 to 1665 four Acts of Parliament together clearly stated this new position: every member of a municipal council was required to take Holy Communion in his parish church (Corporation Act 161). Every priest had to

swear on oath of allegiance to the Book of Common Prayer and the Thirty-nine Articles, which had been accepted as the embodiment of the Anglican faith (Act of Uniformity 1662); 2,000 clergymen forfeited their livings rather than take the oath. Any people attending a religious meeting of more than four persons, excluding members of a family, were liable to be sent to prison (Conventicle Act 1664; this was the act which put John Bunyan in

Bedford Jail, thus giving him the opportunity to write The Pilgrim's Progress). Finally the Five Mile Act 1665 forbade any former priest who had not taken the required oath to live within 5 miles (8 km) of a town or of his former church. The combined object of all these pieces of legislation was to destroy Puritanism; in the event these laws, though certainly reducing the number of religious dissidents, greatly strengthened the moral fibre of those who could not be forced to toe the line.

This firm sequence of repressive anti-dissident acts of parliament was surprisingly – and only temporarily – interrupted in 1672 by a Declaration of Indulgence made by Charles II (to the vexation of parliament), whereby Christian worshippers who were not members of the Church of England would be allowed to hold services in private houses, provided that these houses were officially licensed for that purpose. Curious readers will have to be satisfied with the brief comment that such tolerance would benefit Roman Catholics as well as Nonconformists, and, at that particular moment Charles II had good reasons for wanting to favour Roman Catholics! As far as Wales was concerned, more than a few private houses were duly registered including – to take examples from only a single county, Radnorshire – a Baptist house in Llandrindod, an Independent one in New Radnor and a Presbyterian house in Beguildy.

This strange politically-inspired intermission of tolerance was of short duration, persecution soon resuming its former course against Nonconformists, until in 1688 the second great revolution of the seventeenth century took place. This so-called Glorious Revolution (glorious possibly because unlike its predecessor it was brought about without any blood-letting) enabled the new Government in 1689 to pass the Toleration Act, whereby complete freedom of worship was granted to all Christians who would subscribe to 36 of the Thirty Nine articles, Roman Catholics and Unitarians alone of non-Anglican groups failing to benefit from the provisions of the Act. This Toleration Act, which attracted some criticism for not going far enough, at least assured the future spread of Nonconformity in Wales, with the removal of all legal barriers to the establishment of denominational places of worship.

The Baptists were probably the first of the Nonconformists sects to organise themselves in Wales; they, along with the Quakers and the Independents (Congregationalists) took advantage of the opportunities provided by the freer conditions of the early years of the Commonwealth. Readers will remember how, following the Act of Parliament in 1650 that concerned itself with the propagation of the Gospel in Wales, two of the energetic itinerant preachers appointed to see that the act's provisions were properly carried out were Baptists, Hugh Evans and Vavasor Powell. Later Baptists, like other dissident groups, suffered in the 1660s from the rigorous laws applied by the Church of England through their Members of Parliament, but after the short-lived Declaration of Indulgence, made by Charles II in 1672, a number of Baptist houses were officially recognised where services could legally be held. After the passage of the Toleration Act in 1689, ushering in a new and more enlightened attitude towards differing Christian sects, considerable Baptist expansion soon took place in Wales, more particularly in the south of the country, where the first Baptist chapel was consecrated in the early 1690s at Llanwenarth, near Abergavenny.

The Independents followed a similar, if rather slower pattern of development; in 1639, as has already been mentioned, the very first Nonconformist community in Wales was established at Llanfaches, near Newport. This Independent chapel however seems to have been an isolated development, arising from the personality of the former Anglican vicar of Llanfaches, whose liberal views caused his parishioners to turn him out. There was certainly some Congregationalist advance in Wales during the Commonwealth, but Congregationalism in Wales only really began to prosper in the freer religious atmosphere that followed the Toleration Act of 1689. The first Congregational chapel was built in 1692 at Rhayader, in the remote northern part of Radnorshire, where Congregationalist worshippers had previously met in a registered private house a few miles to the east in Nantmel. Four years later another Independent chapel was consecrated near Glasbury in south Radnorshire, known as Maes-yr-onnen, while, between these two early places of worship, in the eastern outskirts of what today is Llandrindod a

Congregational chapel was erected in 1715. Caebach still serves the community thereabouts.

The Quakers (originally their enemies' name for them, which, in the course of time, such was their courage and integrity, became an acceptable and respected alternative for their official name of The Society of Friends) were amongst the earliest Nonconformist sects to establish themselves in Wales. In 1654, two Radnorshire Quakers wrote to George Fox, the founder of the movement, to invite him to visit them in central Wales, where their movement was thriving. In 1657, Fox accepted the invitation and was met by a great throng of interested men and women, who, previously advised of his coming, had gathered on Pen-y-bont Common, near Llandegley in Radnorshire, where some stood, while others stayed on horseback to listen to Fox, who spoke to them for three hours. He paid further visits to the district in 1663 and 1666, as the Quaker cause prospered, despite increasing persecution.

In 1673 a farmer died, who had been in the original outdoor congregation in 1657; in his will he left a piece of land nearby, which was to be consecrated as a Quaker burial ground (The Pales) at a time, of course, when Nonconformists were denied burial in consecrated ground. Six years later a Quaker meeting, which was in progress, either in the burial ground or in a building nearby, was raided by the High Sheriff of the county, who arrested all 12 members of the congregation, who were thereafter abused, maltreated, fined and imprisoned. Meanwhile there were many further Quaker conversions in central Wales, the new Quakers meeting in widely-separated safe houses.

In 1681 something unexpected happened, when the wealthy young son of Admiral Penn was expelled from Oxford for being a Quaker; William thereupon emigrated to America, where he bought a piece of land, which he named Pennsylvania in honour of his father and there established a Quaker connection. This soon became a focal point for many Quakers in England, who sought freedom to practise their own religion. Amongst these emigrants were many from Wales, especially from Radnorshire, whose meetings for a while in consequence were much diminished. Quite how serious was the persecution of Quakers in England and Wales at this time can be seen from these

*The earliest surviving Independent chapel in northern Wales: Capel Newydd Nanhoron, Llŷn*

figures: between 1650 and 1688 14,000 suffered imprisonment, of whom 369 died in prison.

Back in Radnorshire in 1717 on a piece of land, which adjoined the Pales' burial ground, a Meeting House was built, which today still caters for the needs of Quakers; it is the oldest such meeting house in Wales, in uninterrupted use. The GR is 138641; it will be found, with the aid of an Ordnance Survey map, near Llandegley, which is on the A44, between Kington and Rhayader.

## Notes and illustrations

### A sturdy Welsh Puritan

Briton Ferry in south Glamorgan was the birthplace in 1590 of John ap Henry, who in early adulthood, finding little prospect of earning his living locally, did what many of his fellow Welshmen did and migrated to London to make his way in the world. It is known that early on he became a servant in a Welsh family in the capital, moving later to a domestic position in the household of Philip, the Earl of Pembroke, the Lord President of the Welsh Council. Later, in 1625, John Henry (the 'ap' seems to have been lost in London) moved into the king's employment at Whitehall, where he became Keeper of the Orchard; his house, which went with the job, was near the much-frequented Garden Steps, where, in addition to his responsibilities as a gardener, he was also required to help all visitors, as they embarked or disembarked. In the seventeenth century, when the river Thames was the main highway of London, the landing places were of considerable importance, none more so than the Garden Steps at Whitehall, which were to loom large in the life of the young Philip.

In 1631 a son was born, who was named Philip, after his father's former employer, the Earl of Pembroke. King Charles I had two sons: the future Charles II, born the previous year in 1630, and James, the future James II, born in 1633, both of whom became the constant playmates of the young Philip Henry, who all his life was to treasure a book given to him in boyhood by the younger brother, the Duke of York.

The gathering clouds of political discord between the king and his parliament gave rise to Civil War in 1642; the very next year Philip Henry, now 12 years old, was entered at Westminster School, where he was to remain for the next four years. School became for the youthful Philip a peaceful oasis in those troubled times; his headmaster, the famous Dr Busby, thought highly of his Welsh pupil, coming to regard him as an outstandingly able scholar. Indeed in 1647 Philip won a scholarship to Christ Church, Oxford, receiving as a leaving present from his father's former employer, the Earl of Pembroke a gift of £10, which in his diary he gratefully acknowledge to be 'a seasonable mercy'.

Going into residence at Christ Church in October 1647, Philip was at once confronted with the need to answer a difficult question, on the answer to which his future career at the university depended. This indeed was the moment of decision; Parliament had won the Civil War and had every intention of rooting out all supporters of the defeated Royalist cause. Hence at the beginning of term all members of the University were compelled to reply to the question: 'Will you submit to Parliament in the present visitation?' Philip managed to placate his interviewer by making this tactful reply. 'I submit', he said, 'as far as I may with a safe conscience and without perjury'.

A year later, shortly before Christmas 1648, he qualified for a vacation in London, where he was able to stay for some weeks with his father, who still lived near the Garden Steps in Whitehall. At the end of

January 1649, while Philip was still at home, his father's employer, Charles I was executed, Philip, a sad witness of the event, commenting thus to his diary:

> The blow I saw given and can truly say with a sad heart; at that instant whereof there was such a groan by the thousands there present as I never heard before and desire I may never hear again.

Back at Christ Church he resumed his studies, first taking his Master's degree before being ordained in the Church of England in 1651. The offer of employment Philip was eagerly waiting for came in September 1653: he was invited to visit Emral Hall in Flintshire, where he would be interviewed by Judge Puleston, who had the gift of the living of Worthenbury. Philip's host Judge Puleston had been a loyal supporter of the Parliamentary cause in the tumultuous times of the 1640s, and as reward for his services had been made a judge after the death of the king in 1649.

Philip, for his part, was most certainly a Royalist up to the time that he went up to Oxford; in the difficult early days of the Commonwealth he seems to have kept to himself any doubts he may have felt about politics and religion. At Emral Hall on the occasion of this all-important interview he met the Judge, whose loyalty to Parliament had never been in doubt and his wife, who not only shared her husband's views but was also a tireless and persuasive advocate of the Parliamentary cause.

The young Philip having enjoyed the hospitality of the Pulestons and been introduced to their five sons, eagerly accepted the Judge's offer to preach in Worthenbury Church and to act as tutor to his five sons, for which he was to get an annual stipend of £60 and receive free board and lodging in Emral Hall, where he would be treated as one of the family.

While Philip Henry was serving his professional apprenticeship as a preacher, great changes were taking place in church and state. The monarchy had been abolished and the republican commonwealth had taken its place, with Oliver Cromwell leading the nation. Parliament ruled supreme. In matters of religion local committees had been set up, which were authorised to appoint parish priests, who in the next few years came to represent just about every possible shade of Protestant opinion.

In Worthenbury, Judge Puleston was very tolerant towards dissent, while Lady Puleston was positively enthusiastic about it. Against this contemporary background of religious experimentation, Philip Henry settled down to fulfil his dual role of parish priest and tutor to the Judge's sons. In 1655, the Judge showed his approval of his protégé by increasing his stipend to £100 per annum; in 1656 the eldest boy, Roger was enrolled in his tutor's old college, Christ Church. From that time there was growing evidence of a widening rift between Philip and Roger, who also fell out with his mother (probably for doctrinal reasons, as Lady Puleston's Puritan tendencies found less and less favour with her eldest son, who was deeply attached to the traditional beliefs of the Church of England). In that same year Philip confided to his diary a deep sense of shame; apparently, in the course of a difference of opinion with Roger, the latter lost his temper and struck his tutor, who retaliated by slapping the young man's face. Later, in 1657 a seemingly anomalous situation arose when Philip, the Rector of Worthenbury, was also ordained as Presbyterian Minister of Prees.

1658 and 1659 were years of doubt and misfortune for Philip Henry. The first blow fell in September when his champion Lady Puleston died; Philip took the funeral service and preached the sermon, later that day lamenting in his diary that 'she was the best friend I had on earth'. The following February Philip moved out from Emral Hall into the Rectory at Worthenbury, which the Judge had had specially built for him. Later that same year the second blow fell, when the Judge himself died; thus the new baronet was Roger, who was a staunch upholder of the Church of England and an implacable enemy of the Rector. The restoration of the monarchy in 1660 brought everything to a head locally in Worthenbury, leading to open hostility between patron and

*The Shire Hall, Presteigne*
*Here in the 1640s (Presteigne at that time being the county town) the leading Radnorshire Baptist, Vavasor Powell appeared to answer a charge; the building seen in the photograph, was erected in 1829.*

priest, between Sir Roger Puleston and his old tutor, whose Nonconformist attitude seemed to increase as his patron's heart hardened against him.

The difficult situation was inflamed by Philip's refusal to read in church from the Book of Common Prayer, to which Sir Roger reacted by refusing to pay Philip's stipend. Philip, after repeating his offence of not reading from the Prayer Book, twice found himself brought up at the Flintshire Assizes, the consequences of which were that he agreed to take an oath of allegiance to King Charles II but refused to submit himself, as required, for reordination. Hence on 26 October 1661 Sir Roger Puleston, acting on instructions from his bishop, had Philip Henry ejected from Worthenbury. In 1662, Parliament legalised this and other similar actions elsewhere by passing the Act of Uniformity. Thus cast out, Philip Henry passed the remaining 35 years of his life, ploughing a very lonely furrow as a staunch and very determined Puritan. Some readers may care to know that two months after this ejection his first son, Matthew was born, who 25 years later became a Presbyterian minister in Chester. This Matthew Henry was to achieve great fame as a leader of Nonconformist thought.

### Lhuyd of the Ashmolean (1660–1709)

Most of the seventeenth century, it has already been seen, was devoted to constitutional issues, which led to serious internal dissension and Civil War, culminating in the temporary abolition of monarchy; the disastrous quarrel broke out again in the second half of the century and only found its solution in the last decade of the century. After the 1688 settlement, however, with its insistence on the future supremacy of Parliament, and the prospect of better times ahead, signs appeared which suggested the possible dawn of a new age, signs which had previously been stunted and delayed by the social and political upheavals earlier in the century. Changes, when they come, do not of course happen suddenly; it is one of the advantages that accrue from studying the past that new developments, new ways of thinking can be seen in their historical context. The future never lies ahead of us, said Confucius, but always comes flying over our heads from behind.

Soon after the restoration of the monarchy in Charles II's reign, at a time when religious bigotry was once again rearing its ugly head, scholars in universities were beginning to realise the virtue of working together in the common interest of acquiring new knowledge, more particularly in connection with scientific ideas. Indeed the growth of modern organised scientific research can be traced back to the early years of Charles II's reign, when the king himself gave his approval and his patronage to the Royal Society, which was founded in 1663; it was the first scientific society in this country and one of the first in Europe.

In a wider sense, however, this Royal Society can be seen to have had its roots in the Renaissance, which had given rise to a new and welcome spirit of enquiry in western Europe. If in London this spirit of enquiry had found belated expression in the Royal Society, in Wales it had already inspired the antiquarian movement, whose foremost and most distinguished contributor, Robert Vaughan of Hengwrt in Meirionnydd, caused it to flourish in the seventeenth century. When he died in 1667, there were on hand other Welshmen ready and able to take on where Vaughan had left off. Such a man was Edward Lhuyd.

*Edward Lhuyd's memorial at Aberystwyth*

Lhuyd was born to Welsh parents near Oswestry in 1660; he was educated at Oswestry Grammar School before going up to Jesus College, Oxford the alma mater for generations of Welshmen past and present. He had already developed a lively interest in heraldry and genealogy, and on arrival at Oxford opted to study geology and botany; with what success is not known because he left the university without taking a degree. In 1684, however, his path crossed that of Elias Ashmole, an antiquary who had spent many years collecting curios; in old age he presented his collection to Oxford University on condition that a suitable museum was built to house his exhibits. The outcome was the Ashmolean Museum, which in fact was the first such public museum in this country; in 1684 Lhuyd was appointed its Assistant Keeper.

Before long the Assistant Keeper was back in Wales, exhaustively collecting on behalf of the museum fossils and plants; something of his enthusiasm and thoroughness can be gauged from the fact that on Snowdon alone he managed to identify 37 plants that were not native to these islands, among them the exceedingly rare Mountain Spiderwort, a white flower with purple-red veins, which thereafter bore his name, *Lloydia serotina*. In 1686, he was back at the Ashmolean in Oxford, busily sorting, collating and preparing his material for his first book, which was published in 1699; this book dealt mainly with fossils, though his remarkable plant findings were listed earlier in the works of others. Edward Lhuyd was already an acknowledged naturalist.

Having, as it were, served his apprenticeship at the Ashmolean as an Assistant, Lhuyd set out upon his life's main work, fortified by his appointment as the Keeper of the Museum. From 1697 to 1701 he was to travel continually on behalf of the museum, his ambitions, archaeological and linguistic. His ultimate goal was to compile an *Archaeologia Britannica* but, as he became more and more immersed in his enthusiastic work in the field, his interest in fossils and bones, in plants and in sites of archaeological importance gradually became subordinated to a greater awareness of the over-riding need to make a full study of all the Celtic languages, their grammar, their vocabularies and their cultures. This all-consuming interest was to involve him in journeys to Ireland and Scotland, to Cornwall and Brittany, as well, of course as innumerable visits to Wales. Over the years vast quantities of future museum exhibits were packed up and sent back to Oxford, rocks and fossils, plants and detailed plans and drawings of archaeological sites, while all the time he continued to soak himself in Celtic languages.

Travel in these largely unvisited places was at this time uncomfortable, difficult and sometimes dangerous, as when Lhuyd saw the inside of a Breton prison, as a suspected spy! Wherever he went, he asked questions and took copious notes, which happily survive and are still of real value. Two examples must suffice to show just how great a debt modern students owe to him for his thoroughness and his insistence on writing down everything of interest which came his way.

Readers in the Llangollen area of north Wales will be familiar with Eliseg's Pillar, which stands in a field, some 2 miles (3.2 km) north of the town, near the ruins of the *Valle Crucis* monastery; it is the oldest (ninth century) and most important field monument of its kind in the whole of Wales. Originally it was a cross, which so impressed the Cistercians when they came to the district to build their monastery that they remembered it in giving it a name. Unfortunately posterity and the elements have together dealt harshly with the monument, but on the credit side, when Edward Lhuyd visited it, the inscription, incised on the shaft, was still mostly visible. Hence, with Lhuyd's help, we may still learn something of the history of the early rulers of Powys.

Further south, in Llanddewi Brefi, 4 miles (6.43 km) south of Tregaron, is one of the most historically interesting churches in Wales, with its association with St David himself, to whom it is dedicated. Today high up on the outside north-west wall of the nave can just be detected an early Christian memorial stone. Less than half of the original Idnert Stone survives, but, when Lhuyd passed that way in the 1690s, it was intact and, of course, he made a copy of the Latin inscription, which had originally marked the churchyard grave of the murdered Idnert, the abbot of the monastery of Llanbadarn Fawr (near Aberystwyth); this inscription, which dates from the seventh century, has the added interest of containing the earliest known reference to St David.

Sometime in 1701 Lhuyd returned to the Ashmolean Museum, where he started the long and arduous task of organising and collating his material, preparatory to setting about the massive task which he had set himself. The first volume of this *Archaeologia Britannica* was eventually published in 1707; it marked the beginning of a new academic approach, that of comparative philology, whereby the grammars, the vocabularies, the syntaxes of the various Celtic languages studied were described, analysed and compared.

This book was the first scientific enquiry into the Celtic languages, and its publication assured its author of the status of an outstanding Celtic scholar. His old university rewarded him with an honorary Master of Arts degree, but in 1708 he received the supreme accolade of scholarship, when he was made a Fellow of the Royal Society.

Anticlimax tragically was to follow because his health broke down; the many hardships which he had had to endure on the many strenuous journeys he had undertaken in distant places and always regardless of the weather, had undermined his ability to resist disease. Asthma, followed by pleurisy, sapped his vitality; furthermore, though he received the highest academic recognition, he continued to exist on a meagre stipend. The resultant poverty, allied with chronic pleurisy, brought about his premature death, in 1709, before his 50th birthday and before any more of the other projected volumes could be written.

To summarise, Edward Lhuyd was a very great Celtic scholar, a pioneer in Celtic philological studies, and a pathfinder to those as yet unborn to whom his studies would point the way to future scientific enquiries into Celtic culture.

## The Centre for Advanced Welsh and Celtic Studies

The Centre for Advanced Welsh and Celtic Studies is a dedicated research institute of the University of Wales, located alongside the National Library of Wales in Aberystwyth. Outside the institute is a bust of Edward Lhuyd, It carries out collaborative research projects into the language, literature and history of Wales and the other Celtic countries. The Centre was established by the University of Wales in 1985, with a well-stocked library which has grown over the years into an invaluable resource for Welsh and Celtic Studies. The 2008 Research Assessment Exercise confirmed their status as an international centre of excellence in Celtic Studies.

Celtic Studies is a wide-ranging academic discipline encompassing the languages, literatures, history and cultures of Wales, Ireland, Scotland, Brittany, Cornwall and the Isle of Man, as well as wide areas of continental Europe and central Asia Minor in ancient times. The origins of the Celtic languages and groups called Celts continue to be matters of considerable debate, questions which are central to their current project on Ancient Britain and the Atlantic Zone. Also highly controversial is the question of a common Celtic culture and identity. Some claim to see essentially Celtic forms of art, music, literature, religion, and even world-view, but the only certain feature uniting the Celtic peoples of today is the common origin of their languages, as first identified by Edward Lhwyd in his *Archaeologia Britannica* in 1707.

Nevertheless, the Celts have certainly made a major contribution to European civilization from the Bronze Age onwards. Their history has been one of marginalization and oppression by imperial powers, but their languages and cultures continue to survive, adapt and develop in the modern era. The poetry of Wales and Ireland is one of the little-known treasures of medieval Europe, and yet both countries have vibrant contemporary literatures too. Although Celtic Studies provides a wealth of unique insights into tradition and cultural heritage, it is not just a backward-looking discipline, but offers essential opportunities for the study and enrichment of modern culture and

planning for the future of our languages and communities.

## A seventeenth-century church

For those who like to envisage past events happening against an actual historical background, like watching a play unfold in front of well-designed scenery on the stage, a visit to a seventeenth-century church is not only a useful visual aid to the understanding of past events, but also a spur to the imagination, without which some studies of the past tend to become too arid and too academic for many readers. In this connection it is as well to remember that there were notable churchmen in Wales at this time as well as dissidents, though the latter seem in after years to have attracted most attention. When, therefore, seeing in the mind's eye religious observances in a seventeenth-century church, think, if you will, of a man like Huw Morus; he hailed from the Ceiriog valley, where an obelisk marks his birthplace at Pont-y-meibion, and he worshipped at Llansilin Church, in southern Denbighshire, in whose churchyard he was buried. Readers of George Borrow may recall that the English traveller in 1854 persuaded the local innkeeper in Llansilin to show him the grave, whereupon the Englishman proceeded to kneel down and kiss the cold stone. Morus, an outstanding poet of his times, was always a devout Anglican, who supported the king's side in the Civil War, but later quarrelled with James II because he the king no longer upheld the Church of England!

A seventeenth-century church happily survives in Radnorshire at Diserth, which lies about 2 miles (3.2 km) south-west of Llandrindod (GR 034583). There is no village, the church and a farm comprising Diserth, which, deriving its name from the Latin *desertum*, indicated a suitable place for a hermitage, which is were St Cewydd, a sixth-century Christian missionary, first established himself. Today's church, dedicated to the same early Christian missionary, stands near the river Ithon; it was built in the Middle Ages on the original site and largely restored in the seventeenth century, but had the great good fortune to escape further restoration in Victorian times, with the happy result that the interior today is very much as it was 300 and more years ago; the box pews are still in place, many of them still bearing the names of their seventeenth-century

*Llanddewibrefi Church stands on a mound, suggesting an earlier Celtic or Bronze Age site. But local legend has it that St David preached so eloquent on this spot that the very ground rose up under him!*

occupants, their arrangement a vivid illustration of the social structure of the time. In addition the triple-decker pulpit also belonged to the seventeenth century, while on the wall can still be faintly seen the royal arms of Charles II.

Bearing in mind the Stuart insistence on the divinity of kings, it is hardly surprising that the ancient royal belief in the king's ability to cure diseased subjects, if they were only allowed to touch the royal person, was popular with the Stuarts. This quaint custom, which seems to have been begun in the twelfth century in the reign of Henry II, was at its most popular in the reign of Charles II, who is reputed to have allowed more than 90,000 sick subjects to touch him in order to be cured of scrofula (an earlier name for tuberculosis). Here in Diserth there survived on a wall of the church, well into the nineteenth century, a proclamation, dated 1683, which informed sick parishioners where they had to go and when, if they wanted to be cured of what was then called 'the king's evil'.

Readers will know how important a part wells have played in the customs and folk-lore of rural Wales; Diserth was no exception and, when Edward Lhuyd visited the district in 1698, he talked with a local woman, who informed him that women still decorated the local well on New Year's Eve with mistletoe, in the sure hope that the New Year might look with favour upon them. This local custom apparently still survived at the beginning of the twentieth century.

*Disserth Church, Radnorshire where the northern side of the churchyard was used as a village playground*

# The Eighteenth Century

### A Revival – Literacy and Religion

At the end of the seventeenth century, a century of religious, social and economic turmoil, there was a need above all for a period of consolidation, especially as England was about to be ruled by a new dynasty from abroad whose members could make no pretence of believing in the divine right of kings, when they had been invited to London by mere human beings! The century that followed in England was politically dull and unexciting; in London, parliament, to whom power had passed in the revolutionary settlement of 1688, needed time to feel its feet. Wales, for its part, may still have lain largely undigested in the belly of England, yet, for the time being, seemed unwilling or unable to kick against its masters. In fact, at this time many leading Welshmen, having allowed themselves to become thoroughly anglicised, probably thought the outlook in the new century very promising in terms of career prospects. Nevertheless, though politically little was stirring in eighteenth-century Wales, in other and equally important spheres of life things were beginning to move. In the course of the century significant educational reforms and even more significant religious changes took place; however, something has first to be said about one very important aspect of Welsh economic life and, when the educational and religious developments have been described, it will be necessary to introduce the reader to some new ideological thinking that spread in Wales towards the end of the century, as revolutionary ideas began to inspire men of action in France.

### Economic

Of all the branches of government into which academics tend to divide up our lives, none is so calculated to raise a yawn as economic; lest readers of this book should agree, let me hasten to reassure them: this economic section is one of the most interesting, as well as being one of the most important parts of this chapter. This is solely because enthusiasts, Ordnance Survey maps in hand, can spend many happy holidays tracing the drovers' roads, for which a great deal of visual evidence survives. Actual stretches of roads, inns, cider houses and groups of Scots pine trees may all be seen in true historical context.

Where there are mountains there are valleys; on mountain slopes sheep graze, while cattle graze down below. From the early years of the Middle Ages sheep and cattle provided Welsh farmers with a livelihood, whenever they were able to get their beasts to market – preferably in the more populous areas of England. The strong black cattle that flourished in Wales were probably the first to plod their long, hard way eastwards, later to be joined by sheep, later still by geese and pigs, and in the eighteenth century by turkeys.

For a long time this passage of cattle eastwards through Wales was probably quite haphazard, but gradually, as the trade grew and prospered, the values of co-operation became obvious. Thereafter, from Anglesey in the north to Pembrokeshire in the south, herds of cattle congregated at pre-arranged places, before starting the long trek together. Resting places were agreed upon, where the drove masters could find suitable and comfortable places to stay, and their assistants adequate if less expensive, bivouacs, where the herds could be fed and watered and when necessary, reshod in conveniently located smithies. Today many a former drovers' inn will be found to have as neighbour a one-time forge.

After the Act of Union this increasingly important drovers' trade became properly organised; as a general rule herds were divided into sections of about 400 cattle, for whose welfare 12 men were responsible. These assistants accompanied their charges on foot, but the drove masters usually rode ponies, and at their side scampered the quite invaluable corgi dogs. It was at this juncture, in the middle of the sixteenth century, that parliament began to legislate in this matter; laws passed in the reigns of Edward VI and Elizabeth required a drove master, who had to be relicensed every year, to be a married man and a houseowner, as well as being at least 30 years old. A century later, Civil War in the 1640s presented a serious threat to the drovers, but towards the end of the century the trade expanded very rapidly, as the gentlemen of England in their country houses discovered that their guests greatly appreciated the 'roast beef of old England' – imported from Wales!

The drove masters, the bosses on horseback, had much to arrange before setting out on their long journey to the east; they had to budget for the expenses that would accrue, the payment for accommodation for themselves in inns, for their assistants in farmhouses or in barns, for fodder and pasture for the herds, and, by no means least, for the re-shoeing of their cattle, which was usually necessary several times in the course of their long trek. These drove masters were often men of substance, and were certainly held in high esteem. Their acquaintance was thought worth cultivating by innkeepers, farmers and blacksmiths. Farmers, anxious to attract attention, often indicated their willingness to provide pasture and accommodation by planting clusters of Scots pine trees at the approach to the farm. The public generally in Wales also came to regard the drove masters as something of an institution, which could be trusted. People with relatives living in England trusted the drovers to deliver letters to them; many went much further and gave them sums of money to be handed over, maybe, to a son in an English university or in an inn of court in London. Often, too, drovers were given money for the repayment of a debt in England. So frequent were these calls made on the drovers that they gradually arranged with safe houses back in Wales to look after the money for them; this happened especially in the eighteenth century when it was more dangerous to travel with money, as highway robbery became a much greater problem. In such cases the drovers would then, once they had sold their cattle in England (and sometimes their ponies too, causing them to have to walk home!), hand over equivalent sums of money to creditors or waiting sons out of the proceeds of their financial transactions. On their return to Wales the drovers would reimburse themselves from their 'safe houses', which in the course of time became private banks, one of the best known of which was the Black Ox at Llandovery.

By the eighteenth century, which was the heyday of the drovers' activities, about 9,000 cattle a year headed east from Anglesey, while as many as 20,000 were thought to leave Pembrokeshire every year

> 1. Ffynnon Eidda – a well on the drovers' route above the Conwy valley; 2. A drovers' bank 10 shillings note; 3. Rhyd-spence – a droving inn on the Radnorshire border

for the English market, some 13,000 of which passed through Herefordshire. In the course of this century the routine of the drovers was considerably affected by the great increase in the number of Nonconformists in Wales, who threatened eternal damnation to those who worked on Sunday. In consequence Sunday became a compulsory day of rest for all drovers and their cattle, necessitating drastic changes in their arrangements. Great apparently was the activity to be observed in many country places on Sunday nights as midnight approached! Penalties exacted against those who failed to heed the Sabbath were very heavy indeed. Also in this second half of this eighteenth century there came into existence the first turnpike roads along which at intervals tollgates were set up, where money had to be paid by those who used the roads. Drovers – and there were many of them – who wanted to escape this extra expense tended to leave the roads and take their herds over hill and dale. By the end of the century, despite these unexpected changes, the drovers' activities had been accepted as economically very necessary; successful drovers became prosperous and important members of society. It was ironical therefore that this widespread acknowledgement of success should have been so suddenly followed by their rapid decline, because in the early years of the nineteenth century the coming of the railways provided a very different and a very much speedier solution to the problem of getting cattle to market. Over the centuries so many cattle were driven from Wales into England on so many different routes that a selection has to be made if the text is to be kept within reasonable limits. Hence it is proposed to deal with five much-used drovers' routes, covering the whole of Wales, in the hope that these outlines and their maps may give a fair general picture of this very important social and economic activity.

## Route 1: From north-west Wales to Wrexham

The herds from Anglesey and Llŷn, having joined up near Pren-teg (not far from where Porthmadog is today), and been marshalled, used to take off for Maentwrog en route for Ffestiniog; next they crossed the moors to Ysbyty Ifan before they reached Pentrefoelas, where they would be joined by more cattle,

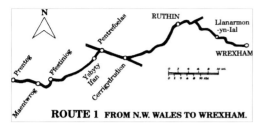

**ROUTE 1** FROM N.W. WALES TO WREXHAM.

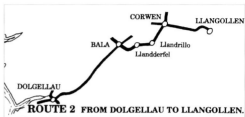

**ROUTE 2** FROM DOLGELLAU TO LLANGOLLEN.

coming there from further north. At Cerrigydrudion, about 6 miles (9.65 km) east of Pentrefoelas, there was usually a very necessary stop for re-shoeing. From there a popular route again lay across moorland, this time to Ruthin, where several drovers' routes met. In fact Ruthin was a drovers' town, where much accommodation was available. There was a popular Drovers' Arms to the north of the town, while 4 miles (6.43 km) to the south on the road to Llanfair Dyffryn Clwyd, there was a hostelry, well-known to the drovers, known as the Three Pigeons. Thereafter the final stage to Wrexham generally passed through Llanarmon-yn-Iâl.

## Route 2: From Dolgellau to Llangollen

The coastal districts to the north-west of Dolgellau were a very important catchment area for cattle; from Dolgellau many cattle were driven inland up the hilly road which led to Bala, roughly corresponding to the modern A494 via Rhyd-y-main. After Bala a much-traversed route lay via Llandderfel, Llandrillo and Cynwyd to Corwen, where a number of drovers' routes met; from Corwen the most straightforward way to Llangollen was similar to the one the A5 takes today.

## Route 3: From Machynlleth to Shrewsbury

From medieval times Machynlleth has been a cattle-grazing centre; even before Owain Glyndŵr in the opening decade of the fifteenth century brought fame to the town (he made it the capital of Wales) Machynlleth held important cattle markets in the spring and autumn. From the town the drovers' route climbed south-east up the Dulas valley to Staylittle, where more cattle joined the drove from

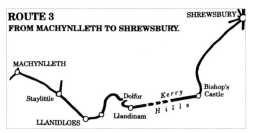

**ROUTE 3**
**FROM MACHYNLLETH TO SHREWSBURY.**

SHREWSBURY

MACHYNLLETH

Staylittle

Dolfor

Kerry

Bishop's Castle

Hills

Llandinam

LLANIDLOES

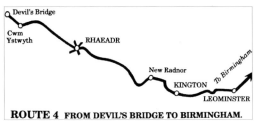

Devil's Bridge

Cwm Ystwyth

RHAEADR

New Radnor

KINGTON

To Birmingham

LEOMINSTER

**ROUTE 4** **FROM DEVIL'S BRIDGE TO BIRMINGHAM.**

Llanbryn-mair, further north. Thus augmented, the herd trudged its way to Llanidloes, which, then as now, was a farming area of some consequence. There was a choice of routes for drovers moving east of Llanidloes, one of which went north-east to Llandinam before turning in an easterly direction, keeping to the south of Newtown (*Y Drenewydd*) and crossing over the Kerry Hills into Shropshire, where a choice of markets from Shrewsbury southwards beckoned to them.

## Route 4: From Devil's Bridge to Birmingham

The area around Devil's Bridge has long been a cattle centre, which necessitated the establishment there of an essential local industry, devoted to providing suitable footwear for the cattle, who migrated from there to the east in great numbers. Many drovers chose to drive their herds eastwards to Cwmystwyth, from where they set out over the hills, thus approaching Rhayader from the north-west. Rhayader, which has been a thriving market town ever since the Middle Ages, was conveniently situated for the drovers, many of whom, after leaving the town in a south-easterly direction more or less anticipated the line of the future A44, through Crossgates and Kington to Leominster, and on to Birmingham.

## Route 5: From Tregaron to the Midlands and London

Further to the south is Tregaron, today, as for centuries, a busy market town, giving access to the most picturesque of all drovers' routes over the Cambrian Mountains to the east of the town. Modern visitors to Tregaron, who want to absorb something of the historical atmosphere of the place, would do well to have a leisurely

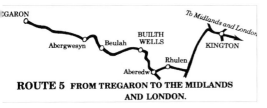

**ROUTE 5** **FROM TREGARON TO THE MIDLANDS AND LONDON.**

meal in the Talbot Arms, in the main square. In this former favourite calling place for drove masters George Borrow stayed in the 1850s, and it was here that he was assured that 'Tregaron is not quite so big as London but is a very good place'. Sheep and cattle from south and south-east of the town for centuries assembled near the Talbot Arms, there to be shod before setting out on the daunting climb up into the mountains to the east.

The road today from Tregaron to Abergwesyn is quite feasible for cars, if care is taken, especially when negotiating the tight bends on the Devil's Staircase; the hills here are remote and beautiful and silent. True lovers of the wild should make the journey at least once, preferably travelling from west to east, as the drovers had to do. After Abergwesyn, the route lay through Beulah and then down to the river Wye at Builth, turning east up the Edw valley, a few miles south of Builth.

Between Aberedw and Kington, if readers want to keep strictly to the way the drovers' went, consult an Ordnance map and make sure to include a stop at the little white-washed church at Rhulen (*Rhiwlen*), before making use of more modern roads to Kington, Leominster and places further east and south. Readers who want to find out more about the drovers and their times are strongly recommended to read *The Drovers' Roads of Wales* by Fay Godwin and Shirley Toulson.

## Educational

General illiteracy had become apparent in Wales towards the end of the sixteenth century, when it became clear that many could not read Bishop Morgan's Welsh Bible. A few years earlier the lone voice of John Penry had been raised in protest against the ignorance and poverty of so many of his fellow countrymen. Nothing much however seems to have been done to improve matters until the early years of the Commonwealth, when in 1650 Parliament passed the Act for the Better Propagation of the Gospel, one result of which was the establishment in Wales of a number of schools for the children of parishes, attached to churches, which helped to maintain them in part from their tithes. The curriculum was mostly devoted to reading, writing and arithmetic and, believe it or believe it not, some Latin, but no Welsh. This absence of Welsh helps to explain the lack of success, which attended this otherwise useful experiment, which was to come to a full-stop, when the status quo was restored by the restoration of the monarchy in 1660.

Twelve years later, in 1672, would-be reformers were given another chance when Charles II unexpectedly proclaimed (for political reasons) a Declaration of Indulgence, which marked the beginning of a short-lived period of toleration, of which a certain ejected London Puritan took full advantage. Thomas Gouge, who had been ejected from St Sepulchre's Church in Southwark, had paid his first visit to Wales in 1671, when, in the course of an illegal preaching tour he had been struck by the large number of destitute and quite illiterate Welsh people. He thereupon took the decision to set up schools in Wales and returned hotfoot to London to appeal for the necessary financial help, which he seems to have done so successfully that in 1674 he established the Welsh Trust. He was to have an important ally in this work, a Welshman, Stephen Hughes, who too had been ejected – from Meidrim in Carmarthenshire. This Stephen Hughes had independently of Gouge for some time been thinking and working along similar lines. He had already translated into Welsh the Catechism, the Book of Psalms and the Book of Common Prayer; indeed, it was on a visit to London to get his translations published that Hughes met Gouge and the fortunate and fruitful partnership was formed.

In the Trust, along with ejected Puritans like Gouge and Hughes were orthodox Anglican priests like Tillotson and Stillingfleet (both destined later to become bishops), as well as Nonconformists like Richard Baxter. Of the outstanding contribution made by Gouge to this movement pride of place must go to his success in building a bridge, at least during the early years, between those who had been thrown out of the Church of England and those who had chosen to stay inside. This Welsh Trust, which enjoyed the financial patronage of the Lord Mayor of London and his Aldermen, seems to have had two main objects, to pay for the publication and the distribution of Welsh Christian literature to the Welsh, and to establish free schools for Welsh children, the so-called charity schools. Stephen Hughes above all showed the way in translating suitable books into Welsh and in supervising their printing and their subsequent distribution, the climax of his achievement coming in 1678, when 1,000 copies of a newly-published edition of Morgan's Bible were given to those in Wales who needed them most. The considerable expense involved in this and other religious publications during these years was jointly borne by Anglicans and Nonconformists.

That this Welsh Trust, with its wholly admirable aims and intentions, lasted for so short a time (it virtually came to an end when Thomas Gouge died in 1681) must above all be attributed to the seemingly illogical obstinacy of most members of the Trust's Board, who, while encouraging Stephen Hughes to feed Welsh minds with books in Welsh, yet steadfastly demanded that all education in their charity schools should be conducted solely in the English language. Reliable facts and figures are not easy to come by, but it seems that at its peak the Trust had 87 schools open in Wales. Gouge's death in 1682 coincided

with the abandonment by Charles II of any tolerance towards Nonconformists; sterner times for minorities lay ahead in the immediate future. All the same, this Welsh Trust did provide a link in an educational chain, which had been forged in the years of the Commonwealth. When at the end of the seventeenth century, a new voluntary educational development took shape, the new men, as will be seen, were able to build upon some of the foundations laid by Thomas Gouge and Stephen Hughes.

When the Society for the Promotion of Christian Knowledge came into being in 1699, it owed a very great deal to the pioneering work of the Welsh Trust, most of whose leaders had vanished from the scene, many of them dying with a quite unmerited sense of failure. Men like Gouge and Hughes laboured long and hard in their cause, their posthumous contribution being of considerable value to the founders of the new movement. The SPCK, however, limited its membership to those who subscribed to the tenets of the Church of England, as there was no place for Nonconformists in their ranks. There were a number of early members with strong Welsh associations, none more outstanding than Sir John Phillipps, a Pembrokeshire landowner, who devoted all his energies and most of his fortune to the cause of the SPCK.

Its aims were implicit in its title, its method to spread Christianity through publishing and distributing suitable religious tracts and books, and to set up, where the need was greatest, basic schools, where a knowledge of Christianity and the ability to read the Bible might be obtained. Its activities were organised on a territorial basis with each district having its own correspondent, who provided a link with headquarters in London. The early work of the SPCK was seriously hampered by a woeful shortage of clergy in Wales, a situation which encouraged pluralism. In these circumstances many a Welsh clergyman, not unreasonably, preferred a living with an adequate stipend east of Offa's Dyke to one which barely guaranteed survival for his family in Wales. In addition, it has to be remembered that a very large number of Anglican livings in Wales were in the hands of secular landlords, some of whom often accepted no obligation to take into account either the spiritual needs of the parishioners or the physical well-being of the priest. To take an extreme example one lay patron, an English duke, obtained £900 per annum from rents in certain parishes in Carmarthenshire, out of which he contributed a mere £70 towards the annual stipends of the six curates, whom he appointed to do what little they could. Thus widespread and growing poverty in many parts of Wales meant that fewer and fewer parishes could be adequately served. In Anne's reign (1702–14) the good queen did something through what became known as Queen Anne's Bounty, to ameliorate conditions for those Welsh priests whose stipends amounted to less than £50 a year.

The SPCK, like its predecessors in educational pioneering in Wales, had to face the language problem; their agreed general principle was to insist on English being the language of instruction, except where common sense suggested otherwise – as in Welsh-speaking areas! The outcome was the widespread use of Welsh in the north of the country, and indeed in other parts where Welsh was in general use, while elsewhere, and particularly in the south-west, English prevailed. In these SPCK schools, 96 of which were set up between 1699 and 1740, all children had to learn to read and to write and to recite the catechism; the boys were also taught arithmetic, while the girls' curriculum concentrated on the imparting of knowledge of such domestic skills as needlework, knitting, spinning and weaving.

The most serious handicap faced by the schools was a shortage of teachers, for whom the basic qualifications were membership of the Church of England and a reasonable familiarity with the three Rs. The SPCK correspondent in Pembrokeshire, the admirable Sir John Philipps, sensing the problem, suggested the setting-up of a training college for teachers, but his appeal fell on deaf ears. At the heart of the problem was lack of money. Indeed the only funds accruing to the schools for their maintenance came from voluntary subscriptions, a few endowments and church collections. The SPCK itself could not afford to contribute money, though it did much to supply books, free of charge, where the need was greatest.

Of the 96 schools, 68 were established by 1715; after 1727 a serious decline set in, which by 1740 had become terminal. While it is difficult to attempt to make an appraisal of these schools, they did at least maintain a certain continuity of educational effort, which was to have beneficial consequences in the long run. Of more long-lasting significance was the SPCK's achievement in continuing to publish books in Welsh for adults. They also founded eight libraries (the first at Carmarthen) where Church of England priests were able to continue their education and widen their knowledge. Above all, it has to be remembered that it was one of the Society's teachers, Griffith Jones, who in later years mounted a most successful campaign against illiteracy in Wales.

Of the many outstanding Welshmen of the eighteenth century none sensed and supplied the needs of his fellow countrymen more accurately than did this Griffith Jones; from small beginnings as a parish priest who also taught in SPCK schools, he set in motion the most important educational movement of the eighteenth century, the circulating schools. The bare bones of his career are these; born in 1683 in Carmarthen, where he went to school, he was ordained, without going to university, in 1708. He became a curate at Laugharne, where he also taught in a SPCK school, later moving to Llandeilo, before being presented in 1716 by Sir John Philipps with the living at Llanddowror, where four years later he married his patron's sister. Griffith Jones was to spend the rest of his life as Vicar of Llanddowror, dying in 1761.

In his early days he had concentrated on being an evangelical preacher, frequently preaching out of his own parish, though always with the permission of the local vicar. By 1730, however, he felt the need for a change of direction and spent more time teaching people to read the Bible. Hence he rented a cottage in Llanddowror, where he organised short courses for would-be teachers; here he enrolled keen young men, who were allowed to join his classes provided that they were members of the Church of England and loyal supporters of George II. To these enthusiasts Jones imparted sufficient basic knowledge of rudimentary methods of teaching to enable his young men to go out into the schools which Griffith Jones was setting up and there teach the children their catechism. These missionary teachers, for such in fact they were, held their classes, wherever a suitable place was available, in church or

*Llanddowror Church*

barn, and in three months equipped the children as best they could. Griffith Jones was ever a realist; he knew that children would not be available in the summer months, when their labour would be required in the fields. Hence these three-monthly courses were organised between September and May, for the children in the daytime and their parents in the evenings, thereby laying the foundations of adult education.

In this, the first home-produced educational programme for Wales, Griffith

Jones placed great emphasis on the use of the Welsh language; for the first time Welsh was insisted upon in all schools, even in the south, where it was certainly a new idea. That these circulating schools succeeded in their limited purpose cannot be denied, the most important single factor in their success being the personality of Griffith Jones himself. He was, however, exceptionally fortunate to enjoy the support of two extremely wealthy people: his patron and brother-in-law, Sir John Philipps, and Bridget Beavan, the heiress wife of the Member of Parliament for Carmarthen. Bridget Beavan's generosity relieved Griffith Jones of any financial worry, enabling him to use all his own money, which mostly came from subscriptions in England, to provide salaries for his teachers. In addition, the SPCK continued to give the movement invaluable assistance by equipping all the circulating schools with books. When Griffith Jones died in 1761, Bridget took over full responsibility for maintaining all the schools; this she continued to do until she died eighteen years later, in which year there were 243 schools. These circulating schools indeed managed to survive well into the nineteenth century.

It is sad to have to report that throughout his long and honourable career, Griffith Jones was subjected to much criticism and abuse from inside the Anglican Church in Wales. In the early years it was the style of his evangelical preaching that got him into trouble, from which he was only saved by the timely intervention on his behalf by Sir John Philipps with the Bishop of St David's. Later, the criticism became deeper and more dangerous; as readers will learn in the next section of this book, the time of the circulating schools was also the time of Methodist enthusiasm in Wales, when men of the calibre of Howell Harris and Daniel Rowland, both from inside the Church of England, were advocating significant changes. Griffith Jones particularly fell foul of his Anglican detractors because of his friendship with John Wesley and George Whitefield.

One final thought; with all their limitations in curriculum, the circulating schools served their times well, as the Welsh people were thereby enabled to become literate at a time when most of their English neighbours remained unable to read and write.

## Religious

As readers will already be aware, no worthwhile account of educational activities in Wales in the eighteenth century is possible that ignores the relevance of religious factors. They will remember too that a great educational stimulus had been provided by the widespread desire to be able to read Bishop Morgan's Bible. As educational standards began to rise in the course of the century, so the awareness of the importance of religion grew, along with the parallel awareness of the failure of many existing churches to satisfy the deep religious cravings of ordinary people.

The Church of England in Wales at this time was at an exceedingly low ebb; very little money was available, priests received utterly inadequate stipends, ignorance was widespread as was pluralism, which was inevitable in the circumstances. All these facts accumulated at a time when enlarged congregations thronged the churches, like hungry beggars clamouring to be fed. In view of these strictures, it is perhaps surprising that the Church in Wales at this time managed to produce a number of remarkable personalities of the calibre of Griffith Jones, Howell Harris, Daniel Rowland and William Williams of Pantycelyn, all of whom interacted on each other to a quite remarkable extent. To illustrate this interaction, it needs to be recorded that it was through listening to advice given by Griffith Jones that Howell Harris first started to teach; that Daniel Rowland became a changed man through hearing Griffith preach; just as William Williams had a similar experience through sitting at Howell Harris' feet. Again the first meeting, which was in 1737, between Daniel Rowland and Howell Harris, had the most significant consequences for the future course religion was to take in Wales. However, although all these four outstanding men remained stalwart members of the Church of England, they were all subjected to much bitter vituperation from their own church leaders, and cannot therefore be regarded as belonging to the Establishment.

As well as there being a rising tide of discontent inside the Anglican church, there was also a powerful ground swell of Puritanism at work; ever since the Commonwealth had encouraged the growth and expression of dissident opinion in Wales, Nonconformity had flourished, first encouraged by the unusual

*Daniel Rowland's statue at Llangeitho*

educated. Among the alumni of these academies, along with Nonconformist Ministers, were men like Howell Harris and William Williams, who were to change the course of religious life in their country, while still remaining in the ranks of the Anglican church. Out of the twin struggles of the emerging Nonconformists and the dissatisfied Anglicans was born the Methodist movement.

Whenever the rise of Methodism in Wales is under discussion, inevitably the name of Howell Harris is the first to be mentioned. That there would eventually have been some breakaway from the Church of England seems most likely, but the actual shape of the Methodist church which finally emerged in Wales in the early years of the nineteenth century would have been markedly different, had not Howell Harris many years before imposed his considerable powers of organisation and his powerful personality upon the course of events.

Howell Harris' father, a joiner, was a Carmarthenshire man, who in 1700 moved to the Talgarth area of Brecknockshire in search of work; two years later he married and of the five children of the marriage, the third boy, Howell, was born in 1714.

climate of freedom, only to be further strengthened after the Restoration of the monarchy in the fires of persecution, and finally to surge ahead after the passage of the Act of Toleration, which enabled dissident sects to worship as they pleased in their own places of worship. During these later days of expansion at the beginning of the eighteenth century, a significant educational development took place, when dissident academies were set up especially in the south-west of Wales, where future religious leaders were to be

Howell's father, a humble man, was a devout Christian, who in his desire to give his son the best education possible, allowed his wife's more prosperous family to pay for his schooling at the academy at Llwyn Llwyd near Hay, in Brecknockshire. Howell stayed there until his father died three years later, when he left, equipped with enough Latin and Greek to enable him to open small schools in the district. If Howell Harris' diaries are to be taken at their face value, he was something of a bad lad until Palm Sunday 1735, when at the age of 21 he underwent a remarkable experience in the parish church at Talgarth, where the vicar called his parishioners to repentance. This experience was to transform his life and later caused him to transform the lives of thousands of his fellow countrymen.

Without more ado Howell started to go round the district, button-holing bystanders as he underlined the vicar's call to repentance. He stayed a teacher for three more years, but after 1735 teaching was a secondary consideration: yesterday's lay-about had become today's reformer. But his elder brother, Joseph, was less than impressed with what was happening, and, thinking to bring his young brother to his senses, pulled the necessary strings and arranged for Howell to take up a place at Oxford in the autumn. Howell, however, allowed his preaching to be interrupted only for a few days while he journeyed to Oxford and cancelled the arrangement, before returning home and resuming his preaching. Things came to a head at Christmas 1735, when he conducted a one-man house-to-house mission in Talgarth, calling all to repentance. From that time local opposition grew and soon hardened into confrontation. Before long the Vicar of Talgarth, whose preaching had started Howell off, clashed with him; he rebuked him and effectively stopped him from becoming an ordinand. At this moment of crisis Howell seems seriously to have considered the idea of going over to the dissenters, but he finally – and, as things turned out, permanently – rejected the notion.

Meanwhile crowds flocked to hear him preach, mostly out-of-doors, presenting Howell with the problem of finding a way of keeping in touch with those he converted. This he did by organising them into small groups, which he called Societies. These early groupings around Talgarth were the first beginnings of what

*Talgarth Church*

was to become the Methodist Movement in Wales. For the first time Howell Harris had revealed a real talent for organising.

Meanwhile readers must be introduced to another who was destined to carry the Methodist banner in Wales. Daniel Rowland was a Cardiganshire man, born in 1713, who was ordained a curate in 1735, the year of Howell Harris' conversion. Daniel Rowland also underwent a remarkable experience, in his case when he heard Griffith Jones preaching in the church at Llanddewi Brefi. Until 1737 the careers of the two reformers ran on parallel lines, but in 1737 Rowland heard Harris preach. The ensuing meeting was of the utmost importance for the reform movement in Wales; they were both driven by a sense of mission to bring sinners to repentance. No Welshman in the eighteenth century had a more compelling voice or a greater gift for moving a congregation than Daniel Rowland. His sermons were immensely powerful, many of his audience being held captive by his ability to frighten them almost out of their wits! He often preached away from his own parish and in unconsecrated places and in so doing incurred the gravest displeasure of the religious establishment, in consequence of which he remained a curate all his life. At this first meeting between the two men in 1737 they at once became friends, each recognising the other as a kindred spirit.

The third member of the great triumvirate of Methodist pioneers in Wales was William Williams, who was younger than Howell Harris but who was educated at the same academy. He had intended to become a doctor but one day chanced to hear Howell Harris preaching in the churchyard at Talgarth, with the immediate result that he opted to be ordained. As he became ever more evangelical he developed his musical powers and indeed became Wales' foremost writer of hymns. The eventual success of the reform movement in Wales rested firmly on the shoulders of these three remarkable men, Howell Harris, Daniel Rowland and William Williams of Pantycelyn.

From 1738, the Methodist Movement in Wales gained substantial momentum, as the partnership of Harris and Rowland began to develop and to bear fruit. By the end of that year 12 societies had been formed in Brecknockshire, four in Monmouthshire, two in Carmarthenshire, and some in Glamorgan and Montgomeryshire, all these counties having been visited and preached in by Howell Harris during the year. In the following year many adherents to the cause came to regard Harris as their leader, especially as the fourth rejection in that year of his plea for ordination gave him the freedom to preach what he liked where he liked and when he liked, whereas Daniel Rowland was at all times subject to the jurisdiction of his religious superiors.

By 1740, the Societies numbered 64; with this remarkable growth members began to clamour for an acknowledged leader who would be able to exercise central control. (At this time Harris' official title was General Superintendent.) To elect such a leader the first meeting of the Welsh Calvinistic Methodist Association met in Carmarthenshire in 1742, when members had to choose between Harris and Rowland. Partisanship, however, became so rife that it was decided for the present to shelve making this necessary decision. Further organisation could not be shelved and at this meeting it was agreed that all Societies should hold monthly meetings, a provision being made to hold District meetings every two months and Quarterly meetings every four months. The idea of holding these tiers of meetings was certainly Howell Harris' brainchild; without his skill, foresight and patience at this critical time little valuable harnessing of the Methodist Movement would have been possible. At this same meeting it was also decided not to break away from the established church, despite the protests of many dissenters who had been converted to the Methodist way of thinking.

In the 1740s the movement was at the

*Pantycelyn, the hearth of William Williams*

crossroads, with both would-be leaders having fervent followings. A rift looked ominously near, especially when Harris withdrew from the leadership contest, clearly indicating that he would not be prepared to serve under Rowland. Howell continued with his preaching but frequently chose to attend Methodist meetings in London, where he became a close friend of John Wesley and George Whitefield. By 1750, Daniel Rowland was the acknowledged leader, while Harris, who had meanwhile married, and moved to Trefeca, near Talgarth, thereafter tended to distance himself from Welsh Methodists, as he became increasingly involved in something exciting that John Wesley told him he had seen at work in America from where Wesley had lately returned. Wesley's path had happened to cross that of the Moravians, whose missionaries from central Europe at this time had established socio-economic communities, where all lived, worked and prayed together. Back in Trefeca in 1752 Howell at once set about imitating the Moravians by setting up what he called the Family. A timely gift of money enabled him to start building at Trefeca straightaway; in the next few years further buildings were erected as new needs arose. When John Wesley came to stay at Trefeca, he described what he saw as a little paradise, where 120 people lived and worked and worshipped together. A full viable communal life was set in motion to which all members of the Family made contributions in labour and in worship. At Trefeca full scope was given to Howell Harris' genius for organisation and from small beginnings no fewer than 60 trades and crafts were practised.

In 1759, he decided that the Family was functioning so successfully that he could afford to leave it for a while; he thereupon joined the Army and saw three years of service in the Seven Years' War against France. On his return to Trefeca in 1762 he received a letter from leading Welsh Methodists, welcoming him back to Wales and expressing the hope that old quarrels might be patched up. The fact that two of the signatories were Daniel Rowland and William Williams caused Howell Harris to bury the hatchet and to resume a round of visits to Societies and Association meetings. What Harris failed to realise, however, was that in his years of isolation at Trefeca big changes had taken place in the Methodist Movement, as a result of which a new generation of impatient, able and persuasive young Methodists had arisen who had no intention of staying indefinitely inside the Church of England. However, in recognition of Howell's past services they reappointed him General Superintendent.

Howell Harris died in 1773, and was buried inside the parish church at Talgarth, where 38 years previously he had first seen the light; Daniel Rowland died in 1790 and William Williams the following year. With the deaths of the three great stalwarts, the old generation had passed away, their place taken by evangelistic and energetic leaders. Furthermore, whereas up to this time the south and central parts of Wales had been the centre of the Movement, Methodism now took firm root in the north where, in 1784, Thomas Charles joined the Bala Society, whose increasing influence soon made Bala the northern headquarters of Methodism. By the end of the century it was clear that the Church of England would not for much longer be a strong enough vessel to contain the spirited membership of Welsh Methodism. Independence came in 1811.

By way of postscript, readers may be interested to know that the Family at Trefeca survived for 50 years after its founder's death; in those years a printing press was established in the community, which did much to publicise Howell Harris' life and achievements. The buildings that had formerly housed the Family became a College, whose function changed over the years. Today it is a lay training centre for Welsh Methodists (the Presbyterian Church of Wales). There is also a memorial chapel to Howell Harris, adjoining which is a museum, a visit to which is recommended to all who for religious or historical reasons find the story of the second half of the eighteenth century in this part of Wales an absorbing one; the museum is open 10 am to 4 pm Monday to Friday, but telephone first (01874 711423).

### Intellectual and imaginative

Of all the seminal events in European history none has had more importance or longer-lasting consequences than the French Revolution, which, starting as an internal quarrel in 1789 between government and people, in a few years broadened out into a European war. The soldiers of France, as they fanned out over Europe, carried with them new ideas that thereafter were to alter the course of history in most countries of Europe in the nineteenth and further afield in the twentieth century. In short, the French Revolution, like the American Revolution, which preceded it by a few years, fundamentally affected the way people thought in succeeding centuries.

With the benefit of hindsight it can be seen that after the years of terror, when horrible excesses took place in the streets of Paris, certain new ideas emerged, of which the most significant were nationalism and liberalism. By the former was meant the right of people of one nationality to rule themselves, while liberalism involved the right of individuals, once national independence had been achieved, to have some say in the way in which they were to be governed.

These then were the consequences but the causes were less complicated; they were rooted in the refusal of a succession of French governments to reform their archaic systems of rigid autocracy and to limit the privileges of the minority in the interests of the down-trodden majority, a necessary change which apparently could not be brought about by constitutional means. Grievances were deep-seated and primarily economic, but, as the eighteenth century wore on, there arose men of ideas, both in France and elsewhere, including Wales, who pointed the way to fundamental change.

In formenting the ideas that touched off revolution in America and France, three Welshmen played prominent parts: Richard Price, David Williams, and Edward Williams, who preferred to be known as Iolo Morganwg. The grievances of the American colonists, which precipitated the American War of Independence in the 1770s, seem to have made a special appeal to Welshmen.

Richard Price (1723–1791), probably the foremost political thinker that Wales has produced, had been educated in several Nonconformist academies in south Wales before going to London, where he became Minister of the Unitarian Church at Stoke Newington; in London he moved in intellectual circles, where he established a strong friendship with the American philosopher Benjamin Franklin, and was elected a Fellow of the Royal Society. In 1776 he wrote 'Observations on the Nature of Civil Liberty', wherein he expounded the need for parliamentary reform and openly advocated the cause of the American colonist, whose war of independence had just begun.

The second Welsh supporter of revolution was David Williams, likewise a Nonconformist minister until he abandoned Christianity for Deism; in 1776, in co-operation with Benjamin Franklin, he produced a Cult of Nature, which Robespierre later used as a template for his own cult of the Supreme Being. In the early years of the revolution Williams was made an honorary citizen of France, arriving in that country in 1792 and leaving on the very day that France declared war on England. Back in London he inflamed the imagination of the third Welsh apologist of revolution, Iolo Morganwg.

In the person of Iolo Morganwg ideas and imagination met; he has at different times been regarded as scholar, folklore collector, druidic poet, traveller, stonemason, revolutionary thinker, romantic myth-maker, forger and charlatan, the emphasis varying from one generation to the next. He was, arguably, the most extraordinary figure in the entire cultural history of Wales. He did make himself into a very considerable scholar, and tried to enliven and enrich our understanding of the past by using his creative drive and vivid imagination.

Trained by his father to follow in his footsteps as a stonemason, in 1770 he left Glamorgan for London, which in the late eighteenth century proved to be a magnet to young Welshmen, who gathered there in search of fame and fortune. There they formed associations of their fellow countrymen, of which the best known was the Honourable Society of Cymmrodorion, whose transactions to this day are of outstanding value to researchers. Iolo became a member, and his rapid acquaintance with Owen Myfyr and William Owen Pughe did much to advance his literary endeavours. First, however, he had to establish himself as a stonemason, which trade provided him with the necessary money and leisure to devote his spare time to further his growing reputation as a writer.

In 1777, he returned to Wales (by foot – he was a prodigious walker), and four years later married. Margaret Roberts was a truly remarkable woman; she was no shrinking violet but gave as good as she got. Somehow she managed to stay loyal to her rather difficult husband. In addition

*Iolo Morganwg*

she had, when she married him, a good deal of money, which was to pass through her husband's fingers with almost unbelievable rapidity. Tiring of being a stonemason, he tried to find other suitable employment, experimenting in strange ventures thanks to his wife's money. Finally funds becoming exhausted, and his debts having accumulated alarmingly, he fled from his creditors, along with his wife and three-year old daughter. The law caught up with him; he was arrested, tried and sent as a debtor to Cardiff prison for a year. There he stayed from 1786 to 1787.

To many men a 40th birthday is something of a landmark; youth is thought past, middle age looms. Iolo might have been forgiven had he felt downhearted, when he passed his 40th birthday in Cardiff gaol, but in fact his year in prison turned out to be one of the most productive in his whole life. After all, his material worries were all over for the time being; his wife and child came to live near the prison, while his father, who saw to the needs of Iolo's family, frequently came to visit him. Meanwhile, Iolo, untrammelled by responsibility, spent the year reading widely and writing prose and poetry in Welsh and English; he conducted an exhaustive correspondence with a number of Welsh scholars and he learned how to play the flute. Much that he wrote in this most unusual sabbatical year was published, with the result that his reputation grew apace, while he recharged his batteries.

Above all, it was in this year that he first perfected a talent for deception; by then, thanks to his previous researches in London and elsewhere, into the poetry of Dafydd ap Gwilym, he knew a very great deal about Wales' foremost medieval poet. Armed with this knowledge, he proceeded to write many poems, in which he imitated so brilliantly the great poet's style that he was able to pass them off as genuine products of the fourteenth-century poet, poems, which he claimed to have discovered in remote and unspecified locations in Glamorgan. Many of these ap Gwilym forgeries which he had made in prison, he sent to London, where they were published in a book, which Iolo edited and to which he added an appendix. The fame which resulted from the success of this book caused the author to abandon his baptismal names and proclaim himself to be Iolo Morganwg.

Fortified by a return to freedom and encouraged by the success that attended the ap Gwilym forgeries, Iolo dreamed another dream in which he planned another but different sort of deception. By 1789 he had conceived the idea of restoring druidism to Wales, announcing his own claim to be the last surviving druid bard. A recurring bout of restlessness, allied with the need to publicise his views on druidism, caused him in 1791 to make a second visit to London, where before long he joined the Society of Gwyneddigion, whose membership was mostly recruited from exiles from north Wales. He found the company very congenial and stimulating, especially as much stress was laid upon the strong literary achievements of the men of Gwynedd, even going as far back as the Middle Ages.

## The Gorsedd at Primrose Hill, London

Iolo Morganwg returned to London in 1791. There he founded the Gorsedd, a community of Welsh bards, at a ceremony on 21 June 1792 at Primrose Hill in London, using 12 stones that Iolo had in his pocket. Primrose Hill is 256 feet (78 m) high, and located on the northern side of Regent's Park, with a wide-angled view of the city, and was the closest hill to where Iolo lived in Soho. He organised the proceedings, which he claimed were based on ancient druidic rites.

It was a fantasy, of course, as scholars have found many of Iolo's works to be. Yet the body of bards he established resonated with the Welsh people. It gave them an institution which esteemed and cherished the language, something which hadn't existed since the Age of the Princes hundreds of years earlier. In 1819, the Gorsedd was formally linked with the Eisteddfod, an act which ultimately led to the National Eisteddfod we know today.

In 2009, a commemorative plaque by Ieuan Rhys and a slate painting by John

*Gorsedd plaque at Primrose Hill, London*

Meirion Morris were unveiled on Primrose Hill to celebrate Iolo Morganwg's contribution and the creation of the Gorsedd of the Bards of the Isle of Britain, the first national institution of modern Wales.

Iolo's philosophy represented a fusion of Christian and Arthurian influences, a romanticism comparable to that of William Blake and the Scottish poet and forger James MacPherson, the revived antiquarian enthusiasm for all things 'Celtic', and such elements of bardic heritage as had genuinely survived among Welsh-language poets. Iolo Morganwg believed – quite correctly as later scholars have proven – that the fact that the culture and heritage of the Celts belonged to the Welsh was a fact which needed emphasising, and he believed that the creation of the Gorsedd was the perfect vehicle to reflect this. His impact on Welsh culture survives to this present day.

Iolo was also an anti-slavery campaigner who tried to avoid everything to do with slavery. His shop in Cowbridge refused to stock slave-grown sugar, and he refused to take subscriptions for his book from Bristol slave merchants.

His bardic name is Welsh for 'Iolo of Glamorgan' (the county's name is spelt 'Morgannwg' in modern Welsh). *Iolo* is the diminutive of 'Iorwerth', a Welsh name often seen as equivalent to 'Edward', although neither name is a translation of the other.

Iolo thereafter burned with a passionate longing to do for Glamorgan what these Gwynedd members were doing for their own part of Wales. If Gwynedd had had splendid cultural traditions back in the Middle Ages, which showed themselves in many a literary reference to early eisteddfodau, then he, Iolo Morgannwg, was fiercely determined to do the same for his much-loved Glamorgan, even if it became necessary to involve himself in another round of literary forgeries. Before long he produced these, only to pass them off to his fellow club members as genuine manuscripts, which, according to him, he had rescued from oblivion in remote corners of Glamorgan valleys.

Iolo's obsession with druidism was greatly increased when he discovered that there were authentic records in north Wales of long-established druid procedures, dating from the Middle Ages, whereby poets and musicians met periodically to compete with each other in poetry and song. These were genuine traditions of medieval eisteddfodau, organised at the local level. At the end of the eighteenth century these surviving but much-diluted observances received a salutary shot in the arm by a very successful eisteddfod, held in Corwen in 1789. This did much to encourage future meetings.

In September 1792, Iolo made a determined effort to give his native Glamorgan at least cultural parity with

Gwynedd. Earlier in the year a volume of Welsh poetry had been published to which Iolo contributed an introduction in which he stressed that contemporary Welsh poets, whose work appeared in the collection, were the true descendants of the ancient druid bards, who had, he said, sung their songs in the valleys of Glamorgan in the Middle Ages. The publication of this book was followed by a remarkable event that took place on Primrose Hill in London on 23 September 1792; to that outdoor meeting Iolo had invited friends to participate in the celebration of the autumn equinox. This was the time when new styles of religious practise were being talked about, especially in France; in devising rituals and ceremonies for this occasion Iolo, though certainly influenced by current developments in France, where revolutionaries were becoming excited about nature worship, was primarily concerned with acquiring for Glamorgan a prominent place in the cultural history of Welsh bards.

*The Gentlemen's Magazine* in October 1792 (quoted by Stuart Piggott in *The Druids*, which is an essential source book for this subject), wrote thus:

This being the day on which the autumn equinox occurred, some Welsh bards resident in London, assembled in congress on Primrose Hill, according to usage. The wonted ceremonies were observed. A circle of stones formed, in the middle of which was the Maen Gorsedd, or Altar, on which a naked sword being placed, all the bards assisted to sheath it.

An accompanying chant and fervent prayers, all written by Iolo, may have caused a few eyebrows to be raised, as references to nature worship smacked at that time of David Williams and Robespierre.

By 1795, Iolo's reputation in literacy circles in London was at its peak, with the publication the previous year of his *Poems Lyrical and Pastoral*; among the subscribers listed were William Wilberforce and George Washington, a tribute to his championship of the down-trodden. It was at this time of triumph that circumstances forced him to turn his steps homewards, to take up again his long-neglected responsibilities towards his family. Valiant woman though his wife was, she could no longer cope with her problems single-handed. Iolo returned to find a state of utter destitution. Somehow a family move was arranged to Cowbridge, where he had to find ways to augment the meagre sums which he was able to earn as a stonemason. He tried his hand at a number of different jobs, which included selling books and groceries, but penury was only staved off by generous gifts of money from anxious friends in London. After 1795 Iolo spent the rest of his life in Wales and, despite his preoccupation with poverty he never ceased to preach the virtues of druidism to his fellow countrymen, stressing in particular two aspects of druidical teaching, nature worship and belief in one god. Before the eighteenth century was out, he had also become a Unitarian, but saw no inconsistency in embracing both faiths. To those who may think druidism and Unitarianism incompatible one can only say that in Iolo's case the common ground between the two creeds was provided by a joint acceptance of monotheism and a love of nature. He played a prominent part in setting up a Unitarian Association in south Wales (1802), for which he wrote the rules and regulations. He was also to write many Unitarian hymns, some of which are still sung in Unitarian chapels in Wales.

The even tenor of life in south Wales was rudely shattered in February 1797 by the news of the French landing in west Pembrokeshire; fine republican sentiments at once died the death as Jemima Nicholas rounded up French soldiers with her pitchfork on the cliffs above Fishguard. This indeed was no time to write poems on liberty; instead even Iolo wrote a recruiting song for the Glamorgan Volunteers! After 1797 Iolo concentrated on preaching druidism and Unitarianism and in helping to stimulate the general acceptance of eisteddfodau, but deteriorating health slowed him down and limited his activities, although in 1820 he did make a significant suggestion, which went unheeded for 120 years. In proposing the formation of a Welsh Academy he was thinking not only of focusing national attention on the need to study every aspect of Welsh history and culture but also of setting up the sort of Folk Museum, which was founded in 1946 in the grounds of St Fagan's Castle, just outside Cardiff, under the expert tutelage of Iorwerth Peate, and survives as the National History Museum.

Posterity tends to take the view that Iolo was outstanding as an antiquary, a Welsh scholar and a poet, despite the forgeries and fabrications and the deceptions practised, for which the excuse, though not the justification, must be his excessive love for all things appertaining to Glamorgan, and his over-dependence on laudanum, which for many years he had taken to relieve the pain of arthritis. His was one of the main influences on Welsh culture in the nineteenth century; he was a great communicator in the Welsh language, both in poetry and prose. Iolo was probably the spiritual father of Welsh nationalism and radicalism, and he turned the eisteddfod into a great national institution.

### Notes and illustrations

### Iolo Morganwg: Two Anecdotes

Readers who may have become interested in the personality of Iolo may care to read of two incidents in which he was involved: the first, when he first visited London as a young man and the second many years later, when he was down on his uppers in Cowbridge: his head may have been 'bloody' but most certainly had remained 'unbowed'!

In his youthful desire to improve his English style he cultivated the acquaintance of a London bookseller, who told him that Dr Johnson was in the habit of visiting the shop on the first day of each month to see what new books were available. Iolo thereupon decided to waylay the great man. As soon as Dr Johnson appeared in the shop, Iolo picked up three English grammar books and, with a deep bow, introduced himself as a poor Welsh workman who wanted to improve his English, and asked him which of the three grammars he would recommend him to buy. Dr Johnson, uncouth as ever, pushed the books back at Iolo, with the ungracious throw-away comment: 'Either of them will do for you, young man'.

Iolo, much offended, answered him back with 'Then, Sir, to make sure of having the best, I will buy them all' and proceeded so to do, ill though he could afford the extravagance.

In time, however, he recovered sufficiently from the humiliation to boast, when consulting one of these books in company, that it was one of the books which Dr Johnson had recommended! Years later, when Iolo came to know Boswell, he told him of this snubbing, only to be informed that if only he had been patient, he would probably have come to enjoy more of the doctor's company thereafter.

Outside a shop in Cowbridge's main shopping street today will be found a wall plaque, which commemorates Iolo's brief career in later years as a shopkeeper. There he sold books, stationery and groceries, and despite little commercial success, he sometimes gladdened the hearts of residents by a certain flair for publicity. On one occasion he had on a stand in his window a book simply entitled *Rights of Man*, which soon attracted the attention of two men, who were thought to be government agents. They entered the shop in triumph, believing the book to be Tom Paine's famous polemic. Having made the purchase, the two men realised too late that the book was none other than the Bible, causing them to call the shopkeeper a cheat and to ask for the return of their money. Iolo refused their demand with these words: 'No, Sir, I am no cheat. You will find in this book the best and dearest rights of man.'

## Traeth Mawr

Readers may remember that early in this book reference was made to Sir John Wynn's unsuccessful attempt to involve Sir Hugh Middleton in trying to drain Traeth Mawr, which was a part of the Gwydir estates. Over the centuries other attempts were made to attempt this formidable task; indeed between 1770 and 1800 about 1,500 acres were reclaimed, until 1798 a large-scale undertaking was planned under the aegis of William Alexander Madocks, who, greatly daring, tried to alter the entire landscape from the bridge at Aberglaslyn to the coast.

First he recovered sufficient land on the west of the Glaslyn estuary to build a town, Tremadog, which is worth studying as a good example of eighteenth-century town planning. From this base in Tremadog he set out to reclaim the rest of the Traeth. He caused to be thrown up a great embankment, on which a road was built, to join the former west side of the Glaslyn river to the east. Completed in 1811, great praise was heaped upon Madocks and extravagant celebrations took place, but before a year had passed the sea had returned and the work was entirely undone. Soon, aided by public

*The Cob at Traeth Mawr, Porthmadog*

subscription and the support of sympathisers like the poet Shelley (who promised £100 but forgot to pay up!) and by Madocks' own fortune, the massive work was safely and satisfactorily carried out. Visitors today would do well, as they drive along the Cob, or better still stand above it and look towards the hills, to venerate Madocks' memory and to reflect that this Fellow of All Soul's College, Oxford shortly afterwards died in Paris and suffered the indignity of a pauper's grave.

## Thomas Pennant

There is no better contemporary picture of eighteenth-century Wales and Welsh people than that afforded by Thomas Pennant's two volumes of travels in Wales in 1778 and 1781 (re-edited by David Kirk: Gwasg Carreg Gwalch, 1998). Pennant (1726–1798), was born near Flint and became widely respected as a traveller and historian, Dr Johnson regarding him as the best travel writer he knew. The following excerpt from the 1781 volume (*A Tour in Wales*) will, it is hoped, send readers hurrying to reach for Pennant's much-neglected volumes:

> near this lake (Llyn Padarn) lived a celebrated personage . . . Margaret Evans of Penllyn . . . she is about ninety

years of age . . . the greatest hunter, shooter and fisher or her time . . . she killed more foxes in one year than all the hunts do in ten . . . rowed stoutly and was queen of the lake . . . fiddled excellently and knew all our old music . . . did not neglect the mechanic arts, for she was a very good joiner and at the age of seventy was the best wrestler in the country . . . Margaret was also blacksmith, shoemaker, boat builder and maker of harps . . . she was under contract to convey the copper ore down the lakes . . . at length she gave her hand to the most effeminate of her admirers, as if predetermined to maintain the superiority which nature had bestowed on her . . .

*Williams Pantycelyn*

## William Williams

It seems right that William Williams, Pantycelyn (1716–1791) should have the last word, as scant justice was done to him in the text, where Howell Harris and Daniel Rowland stole the limelight. Even so Williams was a travelling preacher for more than 50 years, in addition to being Wales' most prolific hymn writer. His reputation, too, has stood the test of time, as one of his hymns is still remembered by thousands of his fellow countrymen every time the Welsh rugby team scores a try, when one and all raise their voices to render *Guide me, O Thou Great Redeemer*!

*Caebach Chapel, Llandrindod*
Situated about a mile (1.6 km) from the centre of Llandrindod, the small, recently refurbished chapel of Caebach, built in 1715, still flies the flag of Congregationalism.

*Trefeca college is to the memory of Howell Harris, who, born in Trefeca, not only went on to sow the seeds of Methodism in Wales but also, here in Trefeca, engineered a remarkable social experiment, a religious-industrial family community that played an important part in Welsh social history in the eighteenth century. Adjoining the chapel is a fascinating museum, which contains along with personal artefacts associated with Howell Harris rare books printed by the Trefeca Press and illuminating accounts of the activities of Harris' social experiment.*

# The Industrial Revolution and Social Unrest in Wales, 1800–1850

## The impact of the Industrial Revolution on Wales

Wales in the eighteenth century summoned up a picture of rural and for the most part poverty-stricken communities, small villages, where a drab and unexciting existence was periodically disturbed by the noisy arrival of the drovers, where parish priests were few and far between, and where ignorance was widespread, although something worthwhile was being attempted by dedicated people to encourage and to make more meaningful the practice of religion and to provide some basic education for both young and old. There was little opportunity for most ordinary men and women to move from one part of the country to another; roads were hardly worthy of the name and transport other than that provided by the horse and Shank's pony was virtually non-existent. As the eighteenth century wore on, however, the simple agricultural economy of Wales was suddenly fractured by industrial activity, brought about by external circumstances.

Vital geographical discoveries, made in previous centuries, had led to the formation of trading companies overseas, which by the early years of this eighteenth century caused a great influx of raw materials into this country. The Treaty of Utrecht in 1713, marking the end of a successful war with France, gave further opportunities to increase trade outside Europe. If these new supplies of goods were to be properly utilised, industrial processes here had to be improved. Hence there was, after Utrecht, a conscious, deliberate attempt to change our methods of production in order to take full advantage not only of the increased supply of raw materials but also of potential export markets.

As things were, all industrial production was on a very small scale and very many industries were home-based: that is, men, women and children worked in their own homes, dealing with raw materials supplied to them by their peripatetic employers. This was the cottage or domestic system, which enabled many families just to make ends meet, albeit often in very bad conditions and for minimal financial return. Such a system was economically unsound and could not possibly cope with the opportunities that the eighteenth century had to offer.

In Wales, from the middle of the eighteenth century, small-scale industrial activity increased and in the last 20 years of the century gained quite extraordinary momentum. In Anglesey, where Parys Mountain was found to be made of solid copper, in Neath and Swansea (*Abertawe*), where this precious copper ore was smelted by charcoal; in the slate quarries of Caernarfonshire and in the woollen mills of Llanidloes in Montgomeryshire, industrial production had been on the increase, but it is to the valleys of Glamorgan and Gwent (then known as Monmouthshire) that the attention of readers is to be directed, and above all to Merthyr Tudful, where an immense coalfield awaited large-scale development and where even more important deposits of iron ore were about to be worked.

In 1759, the first great ironworks was set up at Dowlais, to be followed in 1765 by another at Cyfarthfa. In consequence the output of iron, smelted no longer by charcoal but by the abundant Merthyr coal, quadrupled within thirty years. Thereafter, thanks to these vast natural resources of iron and coal in the valley, Merthyr became the greatest iron and steel manufacturer in the world. By 1801 it had become the largest town in Wales and 30 years later it was found to be bigger than Cardiff, Swansea and Newport put together!

The Industrial Revolution proper really stemmed from the application of steam to industrial processes; at the same time the factory owners built as many small houses as they could to accommodate their workers in the immediate neighbourhood of their premises. These factories were unregulated, wages were low, hours of work long, working conditions downright bad, and the need for hygiene and sanitation totally disregarded. The workers' homes were overcrowded hovels, dark and damp and insanitary; perhaps the worst social evil of all was the ruthless exploitation of child labour in these places.

In the new century industry settled like a plague upon the Welsh countryside with consequences whose significance can hardly be exaggerated. In the new communities, which had been created by the development of factories and the building of workers' homes in the immediate neighbourhood, social problems speedily proliferated, as new and appalling living conditions were suffered by those employed in mills and factories and mines. Before long there began to emerge from the ranks of the workers leaders who suggested remedies for the social evils in their midst, remedies that their employers for a very long time ignored. Then it was that the ideas of thinkers like David Williams – whose *Right of Man* had been discredited when the fires of revolution in France had got out of control and led to a European conflagration – were remembered in the valleys, where they quickened the understanding of the down-trodden and the dispossessed. In the social conflict, which accompanied the settling-in of the factory system, the forces of Capital and Labour crystallised, the divisions becoming the more apparent in Wales, as most of the employers there were Englishmen and most of the workforce hailed from the valleys of Wales.

This then was Wales on the eve of peace in 1815, where victory at Waterloo freed the government from the exigencies of war and allowed it to turn its attention to the infinitely more taxing problems of social organisation and social justice.

## Revolution or Reform: 1815–1831

The 20 years and more of war between France and England at the end of the eighteenth and the beginning of the nineteenth centuries acted as a powerful forcing frame for our industrial system, enabling it, with an enlarged labour force, to cope successfully with the unusually heavy demands made upon it by the prolonged war. As far as Wales was concerned, the factory owners became very rich men, of real substance, while their employees still had to work and live in the same wholly unsatisfactory conditions that had prevailed before the war. With the coming of peace in 1815 the demand for goods suddenly fell off and an economic depression followed, which, subsequent experience has shown us, seems unavoidable after a long war. In

*1. Mynydd Parys copper mine, Amlwch; 2. Sirhowy ironworks; 3. Gadlys ironworks museum, Merthyr Tudful*

1815, as fewer goods were produced and wages were being reduced, parliament, whose power base was still the land, passed a Corn Law, the effect of which was to increase the price of bread. The outlook for the working class in Wales (and, of course, elsewhere in Britain) was bleak in the extreme, with conditions at home and in the factory and mine being quite unsatisfactory, with wages reduced and the price of bread put up.

In London, the government appeared to believe that with Napoleon Bonaparte at last safely out of the way in St Helena and with the ideas of the French Revolution away in cold storage, the future would be untroubled. They seemed unaware of the plight of a great many ordinary people, whose condition on the morrow of peace was probably worse than was that of the peasants of France in 1789. The Government suffered a rude awakening in 1816, when it found its authority challenged by a riot in the capital, to which parliament replied by passing an act to suspend Habeas Corpus, making it legal to keep a suspect in prison without bringing him to immediate trial. It was to protest against this particular instance of corking the bottle too tightly

that a large number of radicals assembled in Manchester in August 1819; a peaceful and lawful demonstration turned into a shambles when the yeomanry was ordered to charge. Parliament then panicked and passed the Six Acts, one of which forbade the holding of public meetings.

To return to Wales, so straitened were the circumstances even of those in employment that most of the strikes and riots in the post-war period were organised to protest against the reduction of wages. Social grievances in those years became so intolerable that observers of the scene thought wholesale and drastic changes had to come, either by bloody revolution, as in France, or by parliamentary reform, which in the political climate after 1815 seemed most unlikely. It was a Welsh factory owner, the enlightened Robert Owen, who openly expressed the opinion that a social revolution would be necessary if the workers were to receive an adequate share of the profits of industry.

Robert Owen was not overstating his case, as can be seen from the increase in the number of acts of almost barbaric violence that occurred in Wales in the 1820s. Many of these extremists, desperate men, were known as Scotch Cattle; they organised themselves into groups, who, operating in the coal and iron fields, intimidated those who opposed them. As hunger grew, so did the number of recruits for these groups. Before long the situation threatened to get out of hand. A food riot that broke out in Nant-y-glo in 1822 speedily merged into a local war; eventually the leaders were arrested and sent to prison. The considerable bloodshed that year can be seen in retrospect as a prelude to the greater riot in Merthyr Tudful in 1831.

Before that ominous and momentous outbreak in Merthyr took place, there was some evidence coming out of London of a change of attitude, if not an actual sign of a move towards reform. Briefly the situation was this. Back in 1799 and 1800 parliament, mindful of the excesses that had occurred in France, took fright and passed the Combination Acts, the effect of which was to make illegal any attempt made by workers to band together. When peace came in 1815, Francis Place, an unemployed radical, took up the cudgels on behalf of the workers but, having failed to move public opinion to take an action, in 1824, he successfully won over a Member of Parliament, Joseph Hume. Hume managed to persuade parliament to repeal what, after all, had been a piece of war-time legislation. Ignorance and indifference rather than a change of heart probably underlay this parliamentary action, but the consequence was that from that day trade unions have at all times been legal. News of the repeal of the Combination Acts was most welcome to Welsh workers, but, perhaps surprisingly, spread dismay in the ranks of those who had hitherto championed the workers' cause. Nonconformist leaders who had for years stood up and condemned the greed of factory owners and actively supported the workers, while continuing their support, had resolutely set their hearts against the formation of trade unions.

It was wholly appropriate that the first large-scale protest against the social evils of the factory system should have taken place in Merthyr Tudful, where all the pains of rapid industrialisation were most keenly felt. The spark that caused the conflagration had been supplied at Cyfarthfa ironworks, where the workers' wages were being reduced. The background to this protest in Merthyr, however, was the political upheaval that was going on in London, where the Reform Bill was being passed in the House of Commons only to be rejected by the then powerful House of Lords. In Merthyr a large political demonstration had been planned on a hill above the town where, amongst other topics, the need for parliamentary reform and the extension of the franchise were passionately debated; eventually the meeting broke up into groups, one of which, largely composed of miners and ironworkers, hurried down to the town, waving their banners which called for Reform. Amid growing excitement the group raided the debtors' court, where they took possession of goods which had been confiscated by the magistrates and gave them back to their former owners. They shouted Reform, but many of the rioters wanted Revolution, when units of the Argyll and Sutherland Highlanders marched to the scene, in response to an urgent summons by the frightened magistrates. The bitter fighting that followed lasted for several days before the Regular army gained the upper hand. About 20 lives were lost in the fighting, which came to an end when 18 men were arrested. These included Lewis Lewis, the chief spokesman of the men, and a 23 year-old miner, Richard Lewis, also known as Dic Penderyn, who was generally believed to have taken no part in the fighting. Strikes in sympathy were called in the valleys as the trials took place. Many of the men were convicted and transported to Australia, but the young Dic Penderyn was executed in Cardiff; in life he may have played at most a minor role, but in death he became a focal point for future dissent, contributing far more in death than he could ever have thought to achieve in life.

Three weeks later, in answer to further acts of official repression, branches of trade unions were formed in the valley, causing employers to lock out trade union members, who were forced to disband their unions when their food supplies ran out. Nevertheless this Merthyr Riot in 1831 greatly assisted the social education of the underdogs and prepared them for even sterner encounters with authority when Chartism later became the burning issue.

### The spread of unrest 1831–1834
Throughout the 1820s serious social unrest spread in England and Wales, as successive governments goaded malcontents to greater endeavours; in 1831, as had already been seen, a political

demonstration in Merthyr Tudful, which was aimed at furthering the cause of parliamentary reform, let to dangerous violence in the streets. Clearly parliament, which represented only the propertied and landed classes, would have to act with unusual and uncharacteristic speed and determination if widespread trouble was to be avoided.

It was not only in the United Kingdom, however, that talk of revolution was in the air; in July 1830 reform had gained the victory in France, when the illiberal King Charles was replaced by a constitutional ruler, Louse Philippe. A month later the Belgians rose in revolt – and proclaimed their independence from Holland, while, another month later still, talk of the need of revolutionary change was being expressed in parts of Germany, in Poland and in Italy. Men and women in western Europe had dared to remember ideas that had been bandied about in Paris 40 years before.

News of these events on the mainland of Europe further inspired would-be radical reformers at home, who came seriously to consider abandoning the quest for parliamentary reform in favour of more direct ways of achieving political

*Dic Penderyn memorial plaque*

change. There was a real chance of revolution here in the autumn of 1831, with angry meetings taking place up and down the country, with peasants burning hay-ricks and with workers, especially in the north, going on strike. The last chance of avoiding bloody revolution seemed to depend upon the ability of parliament to put through really fundamental reforms.

From March 1831 to June 1832 England lived on a knife-edge; in that March a bill was proposed in Parliament, which, among other provisions, abolished pocket boroughs, of which 160 had survived. With these extra seats available new towns became parliamentary constituencies. At the same time the right to vote was given to men, living in towns, whose rent for their houses was above a certain minimum. As Parliament debated these measures, a great many people, in their excitement at the proposed changes, failed for a while to realise that, however significant and beneficial the suggested changes might prove to be, they in no way alleviated the grievances of the rapidly-increasing number of underdogs in society. When this Reform Bill painfully passed its second reading in the House of Commons – by a solitary vote – the Prime Minister resigned and called an election to give the country the chance to express approval of the bill. He succeeded in his ploy and the new parliament quickly passed the Reform Bill, but at this time it has to be remembered that for a bill to become law it had also to be accepted by the House of Lords, as well as by the Commons. In September 1831, the House of Lords rejected the bill; whereupon the House of Commons at once passed it again and again sent it back to the Lords for their decision. This impasse was overcome by the prime minister's acumen in asking the king to make as many new peers as would be necessary to see the bill through the Lords. The trick worked and the House of Lords, rather than see its privileges shared by newcomers, proceeded to accept the Reform Bill, which became the law of the land in June 1832.

The main achievement of this very necessary and long overdue piece of legislation was the enfranchisement of the middle class; this act may have done little to help the underprivileged, yet had done enough to fill with alarm those who were fearful of any change which might affect the status quo in society. The victor of Waterloo and former prime minister, the Duke of Wellington, wrote:

> The revolution is made, that is to say, that power is transferred from one section of society, the gentlemen of England, professing the faith of the Church of England, to another class of society, the shopkeepers, being dissenters from the church, and many of them atheists.

William Wordsworth, who at the fall of the Bastille 40 years before, had been moved to exclaim, 'Bliss is it in this dawn to be alive', in 1832 talked of leaving the country 'on account of the impending ruin to be apprehended from the Reform Bill'.

Working-class leaders, meanwhile,

watched suspiciously as the reformed parliament set about governing the country; in their eyes the government was on probation.They were deemed to have failed in 1834, when they tackled the problems of poverty, which were everywhere acute but nowhere worse than in the coalfields of north-eastern Wales and in the newly-industrialised valleys of Glamorgan and Monmouthshire. The Poor Law Act of 1834 stated that in future no able-bodied man who lost his job would be eligible for outdoor relief. Instead the unemployed would have to live in one of the new workhouses, which the Government was to build in the wake of this act, workhouses, where they would have to work for their keep in conditions, deliberately made less attractive than those to be found in factory and mine. The working class felt itself betrayed by the middle class, many of whose members for their part disliked having to contribute in taxes for the upkeep of these workhouses.

In that same year, 1834, Robert Owen, the enlightened Welsh factory owner, formed a trade union (trade unions had been legal once the Combination Act had been repealed in 1824). His aim in setting up this Grand National Consolidated Trade Union was to encourage all workers to join for their mutual advantage. Shortly afterwards some agricultural labourers in the Dorset village of Tolpuddle, having formed a branch of Owen's union, found themselves under arrest. They were charged, not with being members of a union, but with 'swearing illegal oaths', their prosecutors taking advantage of an obsolete but unrepealed act, passed in 1797 for the special purpose of dealing with a naval mutiny in wartime. The six leaders were found guilty and transported to Australia. This appalling act of official injustice, along with the rigours of the workhouses imposed on the unemployed, together turned the workers into would-be revolutionaries.

## The Chartists

Early Chartist agitators in England were to find eager adherents in Wales in the aftermath of the Merthyr riots of 1831; after Merthyr thoughts of reform in the workers' minds gave place to wild dreams of revolution. Fuel was added to their sense of injustice when the Reform Act of 1832 failed to give them the vote and the Poor Law Act two years later decreed that when they lost their jobs, they should go

to the workhouse. Workers with grievances such as these, along with their many middle-class sympathisers, were thereafter searching for a banner under which they might enlist. The English Chartists were to supply this need. When in addition further proof of the Government's repressiveness was forthcoming in the scandalous treatment meted out to the Tolpuddle labourers who had dared to form a trade union branch (ten years after parliament had made trade unions legal!) a great many men in England and Wales – and not all of them members of the working class – decided to nail their colours to the mast.

In 1836 some London artisans, led by William Lovett, formed the London Working Men's Association and proceeded to draw up a charter of their aims and aspirations. Similar associations were formed in other towns in the Midlands and in the north, which in a year or two combined to form a national association. So very critical were many contemporary reports of these so-called revolutionaries that it would be as well to find out what their charter consisted of. To begin with, every man should have the vote; and parliament should be elected every year, the voting to which should be in secret. Constituencies should contain an equal number of voters, while members of parliament should be paid. Finally, men should no longer have to own property in order to qualify to stand as candidates for parliament. Such demands were reasonable, if Utopian, in the political climate of the 1830s. The methods advocated in different parts of the country, however, differed very widely. In some parts the Chartists preferred a moderate, constitutional approach, while elsewhere, as in those parts of Wales where social grievances were at their most bitter, violent solutions were frequently sought. The Chartist movement, it has to be said, suffered greatly in the public mind from this disparity of methods advocated. The first Chartist group to be formed in Wales was at Carmarthen, its champion none other than the middle-class lawyer, Hugh Williams, of whom more will be said when the Rebecca Riots are under consideration. In general, Welsh Nonconformity was on the side of the Chartists: not, of course, because they agreed with violent methods,

*1. Soldiers fire on the Chartists' march at Newport; 2. Llanidloes; 3. Rebecca riots*

but rather because the avowed aims of the Chartists were held to be in accordance with Christian principles.

The critical year for the Chartists in Wales was 1839, when a bitter riot broke out in Llanidloes, a small but important wool-weaving town in Montgomeryshire, only to be followed later in the year by a tragic farce in Newport. It was also the year in which Rebecca and her daughters first gave public expression to their pent-up rage.

As a prelude to what was to come in Llanidloes, it has to be noted that a few months before the rioting began, Henry Hetherington, the national Treasurer of the London Working Men's Association, had paid the town a visit. News of this official Chartist interest in the plight of the distant wool-weavers in Llanidloes caused some alarm in official quarters, where the government, already alerted to the intended march of Chartists to London, planned to send a squad of London policemen to Llanidloes to reinforce the local forces of law and order. Arrangements were also made to hold military forces at readiness, to be drafted into central Wales, in the event of civil unrest taking place. Certainly the wool-weavers of Llanidloes lived and worked in such deplorable conditions and for such low wages that their poverty was thought to be far worst of any industrial district in the whole of Wales. With tension high both in the ranks of the magistrates and of the workers, one small incident was sufficient to touch off a very ugly riot. One day in April a London constable, lately arrived in the town, saw fit to arrest a wool-weaver who was walking through the town on the way to his vegetable garden with a garden spade over his shoulder. From such seemingly trivial incidents are riots made. Furious fellow-wool-weavers, alerted and alarmed by this stupid act of arrogant officialdom, took immediate retribution when they imprisoned three of the London policemen in the Trewythen Arms Hotel. The magistrates thereupon called in the soldiery and five days of intermittent skirmishing followed between the rioting wool-weavers and units of the militia, by whom authority was eventually restored. Of the 40 wool-weavers arrested 32 were to find themselves on trial at the next Montgomeryshire Assizes, their offence: 'drilling and marching in unauthorised groups'; their punishment: transportation to the other side of the world, from which fate not even the freely-given services of the lawyer, Hugh Williams, were able to save them.

Meanwhile in England the Chartist plan to march peacefully to London, where they wanted to present their charter and an accompanying petition to parliament, finally came to fruition in July 1839, when a petition, bearing more than a million signatures, was duly carried into the House of Commons, where the charter was debated and rejected. This setback tended to encourage the more extreme elements in the movement, especially in Wales, where the anger and resentment that followed the harsh punishment received by the Llanidloes Chartists, helped to swell the number of recruits to the Chartist ranks. Momentum was added, by the failure of peaceful protest in London, to the plan in south Wales to adopt more violent policies in the autumn of that year. Preparations were soon in hand to organise and to arm a military-style march down the valleys to Newport; the capture of Newport by the Chartists was intended to be followed up with a further attack on Monmouth, with the avowed object of freeing from prison

*Chartists' bridge memorial, Blackwood*

Henry Vincent, who was the Chartist movement's most successful orator.

As summer gave place to autumn in 1839, all the talk in the well-patronised public houses in the valleys north and north-west of Newport was of the forthcoming march. Many people must have known about the coming 'secret' march, as conspirators foregathered in local public-houses, especially in Blackwood, Blaina and Bryn-mawr, in Nant-y-glo, Pontypool and Tredegar. The acknowledged leader of this Chartist enterprise was John Frost, a former magistrate and mayor of Newport. who organised the march, the basic idea of which caught the Welsh imagination. Many passed under John Frost's spell, including men as eccentric and as different as Zephaniah Williams, who was a publican, and William Price from Pontypridd, a fiery and unorthodox general practitioner, who had for the time being switched his interest in druidism to Chartism. He began to assume a dominant place in the movement, after making a long and eloquent appeal in Welsh to an enthusiastic public meeting in Blackwood. The contribution he was called upon to make to the common armoury, hidden away in the caves above the valley, was 'seven pieces of cannon'. In the event Price took no active part in the march, but more will be written about this truly remarkable character in the Notes that follow, where there will also be more information about the later life of John Frost.

In all, several thousand men were drilled and armed and mobilised for the Newport march; most of them came from the coalmines and the ironworks. They were organised into three parties, which were to march separately towards Newport, the eastern column under William Jones of Pontypool, the central one led by Zephaniah Williams, the other in the west under the command of the leader, John Frost. The overall plan was for the three columns to meet at the agreed time at the Welsh Oak public house, in the outskirts of Newport, from where a unified attack would be mounted against the town. The arms carried by the marchers ranged from billhooks and pikes to swords and old guns. When they left their points of muster on 4 November the weather was already wild and windy, but in the course of the day the conditions became appalling. The nearer the three parties drew to Newport, the more dishevelled and the less disciplined they became, with many men much the worse for drink. All the same Frost's party met Williams' party at the Welsh Oak, though William Jones and his men never made the rendezvous. Next morning, 5 November, Frost led the leading party of several hundred men into

Newport, where they found it ominously quiet everywhere, with the streets quite empty and the windows of the houses carefully shuttered against any attack. Frost halted his men in the middle of the town, outside the Westgate Hotel, which the mayor had made his headquarters; at his side 30 soldiers and some special constables. A solitary shot rang out before Chartist hatchets broke down the front door, allowing Frost's men to burst into the hotel. Hand-to-hand fighting ensued, while other soldiers from the open windows of the hotel fired their muskets at those Chartists who were standing about outside. It was all over in a quarter of an hour, the hapless attackers escaping as best they could along side-streets before seeking the security of the hills. The bodies of the dead were laid out in the square, which sympathetic citizens in after years renamed John Frost Square. Many failed to make good their escape and were arrested. At the next Monmouthshire Assizes, eight leaders, including John Frost, were sentenced to death, all of them subsequently reprieved and sent to Australia for life. The march was a fiasco and a humiliating failure; the conspirators went back home, with their heads bowed;

their bitter grievances, unresolved, were left to fester.

Three years later the Chartists tried for a second time to interest the government in their Charter, and for a second time they failed. A general strike was then called, but nothing came of it except a marked increase in official repression, which resulted in 1,500 arrests being made. Of that number 79 were transported to Australia. In 1843, the flame of Chartism briefly flickered for the last time in Wales, when a secret branch was established in Merthyr Tudful, whose members agreed to make weekly contributions to help in the purchase of a cache of firearms. Chartism might thereafter have been expected gradually to have faded from view, but for a general tendency in Europe in the 1840s among the intelligentsia who had survived repression to think once again in terms of revolution.

Hence in London the Chartists, for the third and last time in 1848, that brave year of revolutions, once more produced the Charter, accompanied by a petition of mammoth proportions, but public opinion seemed no longer to be interested. The government rejected it with contempt, this time not even deeming it necessary to make any arrests. This indeed seemed to be the very end of Chartism. In the short view this may have been true, as Chartism had been defeated by a revival in trade and by a start being made in vital social reform. If a longer view be taken, however, it will appear that the Chartists had succeeded, by their repeated willingness to agitate, in bringing forward the time when certain important changes would be made, such as the repeal of the Corn Laws and the passing through parliament of acts, which began to regulate conditions in the mines and began to make the government responsible for public health. Politically the Chartists did fail to achieve their aim of getting the working man the right to vote. On the other hand five of the six demands in their charter (all save the annual calling of parliament) passed into law after the 1860s, when the Liberal party, who represented the middle class, made these demands a part of their own policy.

By the middle of the nineteenth century, despite the seeming failure of Chartism, the ordinary man, in England and in Wales, was slowly fighting his way to the surface. He was coming of age, even though he did not get the right to vote until 1867, if he lived in a town, or later still until 1884, if he worked on the land.

## Rural unrest and the Rebecca Riots, 1839–43

The rioting associated with the Rebecca movement and the Chartists went on at the same time, both providing outlets for the expression of social grievances; indeed in Wales men like Hugh Williams were engaged in both activities. Nevertheless, in two important respects there were real differences between the two uprisings; to start with, the Rebecca riots were confined to Wales, and to a relatively small part of Wales, while the Chartists were openly militant in industrial areas both in England and in Wales. The other difference is far more significant, in that, while Chartism was a working class activity, the Rebecca movement was very much a middle class affair, although it is true that over the years many farm labourers certainly enrolled under the Rebecca banner. Hugh Williams, who was a great driving force, was a solicitor, and he received much help and encouragement from others with a similar social status to his own, like magistrates and Nonconformist ministers. The bulk of the followers of Rebecca, however, were farmers and tenant farmers, men who, as will be seen, suffered much from the imposition of tolls on the turnpike roads; they were also members of a class who much resented having to pay in their taxes for the upkeep of workhouses which the 1834 Poor Law caused to be built.

Agriculture in Wales had not experienced the benefits that an agricultural revolution had brought to some parts of England; an economic depression in the 20s and the 30s had produced general unrest in rural areas at a time when there was an influx of population, the effect of which was a serious food shortage. Poverty in Wales was everywhere rife. In addition the land was of poor quality and depended upon frequent applications of lime to make it produce reasonable crops. Since the middle of the eighteenth century many limekilns had been built, mainly in coastal areas, to which the farmers brought their carts to collect the essential lime, travelling along new roads which the turnpike trusts had built from the coasts up into the hills. Herein was to lie the most obvious grievance felt by the farming community. On average a farmer had to

*Rebecca memorial, Efail-wen*

pay up to three shillings for a load of lime when he collected it from the kiln, but on the journey the tolls imposed at the various tollgates were on average double that amount. Glaring injustice though the imposition of such tolls may seem to be, the existence of these tollgates should not be held to be solely responsible for the ensuing riots. The gates acted as visible reminders of their grievances; the real cause of the riots was the poverty, which seemed as real to the middle as it did to the working class.

The Rebecca movement was uniquely Welsh; it made a great appeal to Welsh imaginativeness and it was wrapped in mysterious secrecy, so much so that to this day not all its secrets have been divulged; no one knows for certain the identity of the leader, even though the finger of probability is pointed at Hugh Williams. Protected by a passionately loyal countryside these would-be leaders of rural insurrection elected one of their number as leader, to whom the soubriquet of Rebecca was given. Many of the conspirators were probably Nonconformists, and all who could read were very familiar with the Bible, where in Chapter 24 of Genesis an account is given of how Abraham chose Rebecca as a suitable wife for Isaac; her family, greatly approving of Rebecca's selection, said, in verse 60: 'Thou art our sister, be thou the mother of thousands and millions and let thy seed possess the gate of those who hate them.' Before long reports were being circulated of the so-called daughters of Rebecca, riding on horseback with blackened faces in the midnight hour, all of them male, though many of them wore female attire; thus arrayed they struck terror into the hearts of those whose job it was to hold the tollgates on the turnpike roads.

The Rebecca Riots began in earnest in 1842, but a preliminary skirmish in 1839 proved to be a useful rehearsal for the daughters of Rebecca. In January 1839 the trustees of the Carmarthenshire Turnpike Trust at Whitland decided to erect four extra tollgates on important lime-carrying roads from a lime kiln south of Narberth up into the hills to the north and north-east of the town. Early in May two of these gates were in place at Efail-wen and at Maes-gwyn. Tension had been rising for some time in west Wales; indeed there had even been an attempt in January to set fire to the newly built workhouse in Narberth, and in April, the fires of resentment were further fuelled by news of what was happening up in Llanidloes.

The daughters of Rebecca went into action for the first time in May, when they destroyed the week-old toll-gate at Efail-wen (and went on to burn down the toll-house too). A week later a new gate was in position, which was duly destroyed early in June. Soon the new gate at Maesgwyn was attacked and put out of action. A challenge had been thrown down to the powers that be, which was answered by the despatch from Brecon of a squad of soldiers to keep the peace. At the end of July the local magistrates decided that there was no real need for the four extra gates, which had been sanctioned in January. With the revoking of this order peace was restored to the district. The first round had been won by Rebecca. Thereafter there were no more attacks on tollgates for three and a half years until the winter months of 1842, when real trouble began.

Despite a more than satisfactory harvest, which followed a hot, dry summer, social stresses apparently could no longer be contained; a new gate erected near St Clears gave the signal for the renewal of Rebecca hostilities, and on a more ferocious scale than before. The gate at St Clears was at once destroyed, and as speedily rebuilt before the daughters of Rebecca destroyed it for the second time, and for good measure went on to destroy another gate the same night. To cope with this emergency special constables were enrolled but all to no avail as they received individual warnings from Rebecca about what would happen to them if they were to do their duty. Marines were then brought in from Pembroke Dock. Meanwhile gates were being attacked as far away as on turnpike roads around Haverfordwest and Fishguard. Readers who would like to read a full and authoritative account of the tumultuous events of 1842 and 1843 are recommended to read David Williams' book *The Rebecca Riots*. Many rioters were arrested and many received savage sentences, but still Rebecca rode. As summer lapsed into autumn, reports came in of serious clashes west of Carmarthen.

The final sequence of events was played out far away from west Wales, when in the following autumn, 1843, Rebecca rode for the last time, into the remote regions of north Radnorshire, where the six approach roads into Rhayader were equipped with six tollgates. Here the daughters of Rebecca set out on a campaign to clear the tollgates from the roads; after some initial successful skirmishing the climax to the campaign came early in November, when 50 Rebecca rioters, armed and on foot, marched in three separate parties into the middle of the town, where they joined forces and together destroyed a gate, before marching on with military precision to four other gates, which they in turn burned down, despite the efforts made to stop them by a Metropolitan Police sergeant, sent down from London, at the head of a squad of special constables. A month later the remaining operational gate was similarly treated, but this action proved to be the very last instance of Rebecca violence. The Rebecca riots were suddenly over.

At the time when the Rebecca riots in Rhayader had started, the government in London, at last listening to the advice that reached their ears from various sources in Wales and in particular taking notice of suggestions put to them by the sympathetic Times correspondent in Wales, set a Commission of Enquiry. This Commission started its work in the autumn in Carmarthen, where it took evidence from all interested parties; this peripatetic commission, which spent 35 days actually conducting interviews in all the trouble spots, finished its work in Rhayader. In March 1844, the Commission presented its report to parliament, which acted with commendable speed in passing an act which became law in August, whereby in general terms the whole system of tollgates and turnpike roads was overhauled and reformed. In so doing the main demands of the daughters of Rebecca were met; as they disbanded their forces, they were able to claim a very considerable victory. The long struggle, brutal as it had sometimes become, seemed to have served its purpose.

Full justice to the Rebecca movement will not have been done, however, if only its practical success in getting the turnpike and toll-gate system reformed is highlighted; the secrecy that attended all its activities may have prevented some of their other efforts from receiving much publicity. Suffice it to say that some of the leaders of the movement constituted themselves into an unofficial but effectual Watch Committee, which threatened with dire punishment certain named individuals who had fathered illegitimate children without making adequate provision for the upbringing of their off-spring, while other well-established members of society, who were known to have maltreated their wives, were left in no doubt about the consequences if they continued with their cruelty.

In addition to the success enjoyed by the daughters of Rebecca in alleviating a particular grievance, one other fact needs to be stressed for the part it played in relieving social pressures in the countryside of west Wales at this time, and that is the swift development in the middle of the century of the railway system up the valleys, which provided an invaluable safety-valve for the over-populated rural areas, whose unemployed were thus able to find jobs in the rapidly expanding industries down below.

## Wales in mid-century

The last sections have concentrated on the problems and growing grievances of those Welshmen who lived and worked in the coal and ironfields of north-east Wales and in the newly-industrialised valleys of the south and west, along with their agricultural hinterland. Little has been said about the rest of the country, where life was being lived at a less demanding speed, although here too the yeast was beginning to rise. Between 1801 and 1851, the population of Wales doubled. Whereas at the beginning of the nineteenth century most people claimed, however tenuously, an association with the Church of England, by mid-century an astonishing change had come about, as in the 1851 census 80% of the population admitted to being Nonconformist. In 1801, the Baptists and Independents (Congregationalists) had been the torch-bearers of Nonconformity, with the Unitarians beginning to catch up, but ten years later Welsh Methodists at long last declared themselves free of the Established Church, and started a separate independent existence. In the following four decades so successful did these spiritual descendant of Howell Harris become that by 1851 they had supplanted the Baptists as the Nonconformist church with the greatest number of adherents. By this time the Nonconformist churches were producing outstandingly able leaders in public life, men of the calibre of Henry Richard and Samuel Roberts. Meanwhile, while Congregationalists of this quality were spearheading social reform movements, at the grass-roots level up and down the country Methodist ministers were taking upon their shoulders the burdens of the people they served, identifying with the hardship and the social injustice suffered at this time by so many men and women.

As the next great landmark in Welsh history is strictly speaking beyond the terms of reference of this book, only a passing comment will be made here about the General Election of 1868, when the working class of Wales, enfranchised the previous year, helped to elect 21 Liberal Members of Parliament, perhaps the most distinguished of whom was Henry Richard, who was to represent Merthyr Tudful for the next 20 years.

### Notes and illustrations

It is perhaps not altogether surprising that so dramatic a period of Welsh history as the Chartist agitation should have thrown up such dramatic characters as Hugh Williams, John Frost and William Price. The indulgence of readers is sought for this addendum, which is being made use of solely for the purpose of drawing attention to these eccentric contributors to the story of Wales.

### Hugh Williams
Mention has already been made of the part Hugh Williams played in the Chartist agitation of Wales and of his deep involvement in the Rebecca movement, of which in all probability he was the actual leader. Hugh was born in Machynlleth in 1796, of middle class parentage; he qualified as a solicitor and practised in Carmarthen, where he married a woman 25 years older than himself, a woman of great wealth and property. His younger brother, who was also a solicitor, practising in London, invited Hugh to the capital, where he was introduced to the leaders of the London Working Men's Association, whose treasurer, Henry Hetherington, became a firm friend. Through Hugh's influence Hetherington visited Wales, where he vigorously campaigned on behalf of the Chartist cause; readers may remember that Hugh Williams unsuccessfully defended the Llanidloes wool-weavers after their abortive riot in 1839. Apart from his leadership of the Rebecca movement, where he displayed remarkable powers of oratory in pleading the cause, he also took an active part in the Anti-Corn Law league, of which the leading figure was Richard Cobden, who had married Hugh's sister. Cobden's children were often known to refer to their mother's brother as 'wicked

Uncle Hugh'! His philandering was well-known!

In 1851, the excitement of Rebecca and Chartism well behind him, he was made Recorder of St Clears, where ten years later, in 1861, his wife died, aged 90. Two months later, at 65, Hugh remarried, his second wife his junior and by 39 years! They moved to Ferryside, where Hugh died in 1874, aged 77, the proud father of four children by his second wife.

## John Frost

Of the Chartists convicted after the abortive attack on Newport and sentenced to transportation to the far side of the world, most died in captivity, but their leader, their General, whose beliefs had caused him to abandon his successful career as a draper, a magistrate and a mayor, was eventually pardoned after serving 14 years in Tasmania. In 1854 he came home to Newport, where he was welcomed by former Chartist sympathisers, who had come to the station in a horse-drawn cart, suitably decorated with flowers. Stalwarts among them took out the horses from the shafts, and then donned the harness themselves and proceeded to pull the triumphant hero,

*John Frost*

now 70 years of age, through the streets of the town. John Frost died more than 23 years later, in 1877, at the ripe age of 93.

## William Price

Of the charismatic characters already described, Hugh Williams supplied the leadership and the oratory, and John Frost the idealism; the third man, William Price, was quite different. He was certainly no leader and no orator, through he did sometimes speak persuasively in public, mostly in courts of law, while it would stretch credulity too far to call him an idealist, rather than a crank. A strong case may, however, be made for regarding him as the outstanding Welsh eccentric of the nineteenth century, as well as being in his own odd way a very good friend to the underprivileged and the downtrodden. William Price was a doctor, both physician and surgeon, who practised at various times in his very long career at Caerphilly, Pontypridd, Treforest, Nantgarw and at Llantrisant, where in 1893 he died, aged 93.

The physical appearance of this most striking of anti-establishment figures, whose patients were mostly miners and farm labourers, matched the strangeness of his way of life. He was a man of above average height, with a very prominent nose and fierce, staring eyes; his beard was long, as were the black plaits of hair at the back of his head. In his dress he favoured red, white and green; over a white tunic, which he was reputed to change every day, he wore a striking red jerkin, his trousers were of some green material and over his head of black hair he often wore the skin of a fox, whose paws lay on his forehead,

*William Price's statue, Llantrisant*

as its brush dangled down his back between his plaits.

His views on hygiene were quite modern, even though their application was often extraordinary; for instance, he was so obsessed with cleanliness that he always refused to wear any socks, despite the fact that he was in the habit of walking great distances and always visited his patients, many of whom lived many a mile up the valley, on foot. Further evidence of this trait is furnished by his absolute insistence of washing all coins, handed over to him as fees, before making sure that he also washed his own hands. It is perhaps not surprising that he was also a vegetarian, though his reasoning was unusual: as he believed that animal passions might possess those who ate animal flesh! He never owned a watch, claiming that a good doctor had no need to know the time but called upon his patients when they sent for him. In addition, he preferred to make his visits at night because he believed that his patients had greater need of him then, as sick people generally felt worse at night. He had no time at all for man-made institutions, whether they were churches or courts of law. He was at loggerheads with the law all through his life, while he made no secret of his aversion to all churches and, above all, chapels. Marriage he utterly rejected, preferring the pleasures that free love dispensed.

During the 1820s and 30s, Dr Price spent much of his leisure time acquainting himself with early religions, as a result of which he became fascinated by everything to do with the druids. As he became more and more involved in druid affairs, he managed to convince himself that he was descended from ancient druids and indeed in time he went on to claim to be an Archdruid. As he became disappointed with the lukewarm interest local residents took in his druidism, he became fired with enthusiasm for something else, which had a similar appeal for him. He had for some time nursed a yearning for republicanism, which the political conditions of the 1830s tended to encourage; this new political awareness he now felt the need to inculcate in others. The stark social stresses of the time affected the lives of a great many Welshmen in the valleys. With Chartist developments in south Wales he was in complete sympathy, Chartism becoming for him a more than worthwhile additional interest to druidism. As he healed the sick he talked about Chartism and succeeded thereby in winning many converts among his patients. In after-years Price defended his absence from the march on Newport by disclosing that at the eleventh hour he had been warned not to participate as the soldiers had been given specific orders to shoot the 'one with the long hair'. True or false, he regarded discretion as the better part of valour and went underground. Despite his absence from the ranks of insurrection, Price thought it wise to stay in hiding, as a warrant had been issued for his arrest. Soon he shaved off his beard and disguised himself as a woman, his long plaited hair coming to his assistance. At the dockside in Cardiff he was helped up the gangway of a coastal ship, bound for Liverpool, by the police inspector, who had been sent to the docks to arrest the wanted man! The sea journey was interrupted by a 48 hour stop in Milford Haven, where William Price made a short call on shore, from which he returned to the ship with considerable speed when someone penetrated his disguise. The rest of the journey was uneventful and, after disembarking at Liverpool, he took a train to London, where he rejoiced to see, pinned to a post, the offer of a reward of £100 for his capture, dead or alive! He then crossed to France, where he stayed until the following summer, when, believing that all danger was past, he quietly went home to Wales.

Soon he was able to ease himself back into his practice but he soon gave proof that he had no intention of changing his opinions. Apparently he formed the habit of holding Chartist meetings in his own home on Sunday afternoons, but the attendance never exceeded 30 and, according to local gossip more time was spent in talking about druidism than about Chartism. Nevertheless he became, on his daily sick visits, more and more concerned about the miners' grievances and did all he could to publicise their misfortune; whenever they went on strike, he openly identified with them, frequently speaking up at their meetings on behalf of his patients and friends.

However, his greatest collision with the law still lay many years ahead of him in extreme old age, but as this contest did not take place until 1884 no detailed account can possibly be justified here; it may well be that the appetites of some readers may be whetted to find out more when they learn that in that year William Price succeeded in getting cremation legalised in the most bizarre circumstances. Nature tends to break the mould in which a Dr Price was cast!

Those who would like to know more about William Price are recommended on their next visit to the superb museum at St Fagans, just west of Cardiff, to investigate the medicine section of the Gallery of Material Culture, where objects relating to

William Price's medical practice are on view. Then, if time allows, a further visit is suggested, to Llantrisant, about four miles north-west of St Fagans, where in the Bull Ring may be seen a life-sized bronze statue, whose inscription reads:

*Dr William Price – (1800-1893).*
*Surgeon, Chartist,*
*Self-styled Druid.*

## Henry Richard

Henry Richard was born in Tregaron in 1812. He was an Independent minister in London and was elected Liberal Member of Parliament for Merthyr and Aberdare in 1868, remaining as an MP until his sudden death in 1888. But it was as Secretary of the Peace Society for almost 40 years, from 1848 till 1884, that Henry Richard came to international recognition.

Known as 'the Apostle of Peace,' he worked tirelessly to secure peace in the world. He arranged a series of major peace conferences in European capitals and, following the armistice of the Crimean War, he went to Paris to persuade the authorities discussing the 1856 Treaty of Paris to include a clause of arbitration which served as an important precedent

*Henry Richard's statue, Tregaron*

leading to the establishment of The Hague Tribunal in 1899.

## Thomas Ellis

Thomas Ellis MP for Meirionnydd (1886-99) became a chief Liberal whip and a leader of Welsh life at the end of that century. He was a radical, devoted to bring justice and fairness to the question of land and its tenants in Wales and self government for his country. He devoted much time to educational matters and was largely instrumental in securing the appointment of the royal commission on land in Wales, and the promotion of measures for the disestablishment of the Church of England in Wales.

### Keir Hardie

Born in Lanark, the illegitimate son of a domestic servant and a miner who wanted nothing to do with him, Keir Hardie became the first working class socialist MP and the first leader of the Labour Party in the UK parliament. Yet when he passed away not one word of tribute was paid to him in the House of Commons. No representatives from any other political party appear to have attended his funeral in Glasgow. Newspaper tributes were hostile and unforgiving, with one saying he was one of the most hated men of his time.

Keir Hardie died virtually penniless and a public appeal had to be launched to help his family.

He became MP for Merthyr Tudful in 1900 and made a secret electoral pact with the Liberal Party and, as a result, 29 Labour MPs were elected in 1906. The parliamentary Labour Party was formed

*Thomas Ellis's statue, Bala; Keir Hardie*

and Keir Hardie became its first leader. He resigned after suffering a health breakdown in 1908 but continued to support causes such as votes for women and peace between the working classes of Europe during the First World War.

### Blaenafon World Heritage Site

Blaenaon is well-known for the unique and exciting experience of going underground at Big Pit: National Mining Museum. This is the most popular attraction within the Blaenafon World Heritage Site. The museum is based around the former Big Pit Colliery, which was sunk in about 1860 and closed in 1980. The site opened as a museum in 1983 and is now known around the world, especially after winning the Gulbenkian Prize for Museum of the Year in 2005.

A visit to Big Pit includes a 300 ft (90 m) descent into the old colliery, where a former coalminer will take you on a fascinating and personal tour with the sights, sounds and smells of the mine creating an impression of what working life was like at the coalface.

Above ground there is an exciting 20-minute audio-visual presentation describing the daily toil of miners and the changing methods of coalmining through time.

The museum also includes historic buildings linked to the coal industry, including a blacksmith's forge, stables, miners' canteen, explosives magazine and winding house. Perhaps the most fascinating are the Pithead Baths, which were voted Wales's best national treasure in a 2007 BBC television programme. You can see the intact showers and locker rooms, along with artefacts and exhibition displays that provide an understanding of the daily life of a coalminer.

As part of the National Museum of Wales, admission to Big Pit is free.

There are other attractions in this high valley – as you walk through the Industrial Landscape you may find remnants of the area's industrial past. If you stroll around the town you will meet friendly locals who love the area - many of whom have ancestors that helped build this community through the iron and coal industries. Since the year 2000 the Blaenafon Industrial Landscape has been on the list of World Heritage Sites and it therefore ranks alongside places like the Pyramids and the Great Wall of China. To fully appreciate Blaenafon's story we need to travel back in time some 200 years, back to the early days of the industrial revolution when the Ironworks at Blaenafon was one of the most important producers of iron in the world. If you were able to explore the landscape back then you would have seen that it was rapidly being transformed by human industrial activity – people were scarring it by mining, carving it up with their tramroads, canals and railways and burying it under tips. However, as the iron industry went slowly into decline so this industrial landscape became neglected and largely forgotten. Over time plants started to grow on the barren spoil heaps and gradually other wildlife began to return.

Today the Forgotten Landscapes are a rich mosaic of geological features, industrial relics and nationally important wildlife habitats.

Blaenafon Ironworks, the setting for the award-winning BBC television series *Coal House*, is the most significant feature within the Blaenafon Industrial Landscape. The ironworks, which commenced production in 1789, is the best preserved blast furnace complex of its period and type in the world and is one of the most important monuments to have survived from the early part of the industrial revolution. Blaenafon Ironworks is historically significant as during the early nineteenth century the ironworks was one of the most important producers of iron in the world.

Today you can view the extensive remains of the blast furnaces, the cast houses and the impressively restored Water Balance Tower. Through exhibitions, advanced interpretation features and reconstructions, you can learn about the international significance of the iron industry and the scientific processes involved in the production of iron. A fascinating insight into the social history of industrial Britain can be gained by glimpsing into the past at the reconstructed company shop and the refurbished workers' cottages, at Stack Square and Engine Row.

Managed by Cadw Welsh Historic Monuments, the site has been carefully restored and now, offering free admission, the Blaenafon Ironworks is receiving record visitor numbers.

No two visits to Blaenafon need be the same – there are events throughout the year as well as exhibitions, talks and walks to join. Information is available at the Blaenafon World Heritage Centre or get in touch by emailing Blaenavon.tic @torfaen.gov.uk.

**Wales, the First Industrial Nation**
The Industrial Revolution of the late eighteenth and nineteenth centuries was largely fuelled by the minerals and rocks hidden beneath the mountains and valleys of Wales. In the north of the country,

*1. Big Pit National Museum, Blaenafon; 2. Blaenafon ironworks; 3. Six Bells mining disaster memorial*

Anglesey copper, Gwynedd slate and Flintshire iron, lead and coal were extracted. Thousands of people from across rural Wales, the rest of Britain and further afield flocked to find work in the south Wales valleys' great iron, steel, copper, tinplate and coal industries and the ports along the Severn estuary.

A new society emerged where vast fortunes were made by a few powerful industrialists but where the rapidly expanding workforce endured hard work and poverty. Wales changed dramatically from an agricultural to an industrial society. This gave rise to the development of workers' unity and the birth of trade unionism which influenced the development of socialism around the world.

Times have changed. The huge slate quarries are now mainly tourist attractions. The coalfields are exhausted and the great furnaces have grown cold. Wales' world domination in heavy industry has gone forever. Though most of the scars have disappeared and the valleys have become green once more, that period of heroic industry and associated human endeavour can still be traced through the reminders left in the landscape.

*National Mining Memorial, Senghennydd*

## The National Waterfront Museum, Swansea

Situated on Swansea's historic waterfront, the museum successfully blends modern architecture, Victorian dockside buildings and state of the art technology. The museum tells the dramatic story of South Wales' outstanding and complex industrial and maritime history – which led to Wales being referred to as the 'First Industrial Nation'. Here, you can find out what life was like in those days of rapid industrialisation, take a virtual look inside homes and factories and learn about the great iron, steel, copper, tinplate and coal industries.

## The Pierhead Building, Cardiff

By 1890 Cardiff was the most important coal port in the world. The 1896 Pierhead Building, designed for the Bute Dock Company, was the nerve centre for a network of coal shipping businesses linking railways and ships. Today, it stands amidst the modern buildings of the reborn Cardiff Bay as an iconic reminder of south Wales' great industrial past.

*Rhondda Heritage Park*

## Rhondda Heritage Park, Trehafod

A living testament to the mining communities of the world famous Rhondda valleys, Rhondda Heritage Park offers an insight into the rich culture and character of the area in an entertaining and educational environment for all ages. In the lamp room visitors don helmets for the thrilling trip to the 'pit bottom', the site's special underground experience conducted by former miners.

## Cyfarthfa Castle, Merthyr Tudful

This impressive castellated mansion, commissioned by ironmaster William Crawshay II in 1824, demonstrated the emergence of the captains of industry as leading figures in a new industrial society. The castle overlooked Crawshay's ironworks, at that time one of the largest in the world.

### Aberdulais Tin Works and Waterfall, Neath

This National Trust visitor centre is next to the thundering Aberdulais Falls where the water powered the wheels of industry from the manufacture of copper in 1584 to the later tinplate works. Nowadays the power is captured by a unique hydro-electric scheme. The waterwheel is a major feature of the site and is the largest of its kind in Europe.

*National Woollen Museum*

### National Woollen Museum, Dre-fach Felindre, Teifi valley

Wool was historically the most impotant and widespread of Wales' industries. The picturesque village of Dre-fach Felindre in the Teifi valley was once the centre of a thriving woollen industry, earning the nickname 'The Huddersfield of Wales'. The Museum is located in the historic former Cambrian Mills, where visitors can follow the process from fleece to fabric and see the restored mill buildings and historic machinery.

### National Slate Museum, Llanberis

The Museum is sited in the Victorian workshops of Gilfach Ddu, built in the

*National Slate Museum*

*The huge slate tips at Blaenau Ffestiniog*

shadow of Elidir Mountain, site of the vast Dinorwig Quarry. The workshops and buildings are designed as though quarrymen and engineers have just put down their tools and left for home. An array of talks and demonstrations, including slate-splitting, gives a real insight into quarry life.

### Llechwedd Visitor Centre, Blaenau Ffestiniog

Buried deep under the mountains of Snowdonia lies the extraordinary story of the slate industry. It was a way of life which built communities and defines generations of families in north Wales. The Deep Mine Tour explores the living history of Welsh Slate throughout the 1800s; the Quarry Explorer is an off-road adventures into the heart of Llechwedd mountain, and Our Slate Workshops offer slate-splitting demonstrations in the workshops and also a chance for the visitor to try their hand at splitting.

## Welsh place names

Abergavenny *Y Fenni*
Anglesey *Môn*
Beguildy *Bugeildy*
Brecon *Aberhonddu*
Briton Ferry *Llansawel*
Builth Wells *Llanfair-ym-Muallt*
Cardigan *Aberteifi*
Carmarthen *Caerfyrddin*
Chepstow *Cas-gwent*
Conwy valley *Dyffryn Conwy*
Crickhowell *Crucywel*
Cwm Hir Abbey *Abaty Cwm Hir*
Devil's Bridge *Pontarfynach*
Fishguard *Abergwaun*
Glasbury *Y Clas-ar-Wy*
Gower *Gŵyr*
Haverfordwest *Hwlffordd*
Hay *Y Gelli Gandryll*
Llandegley *Llandeglau*
Llandovery *Llanymddyfri*
Llanthony *Llanddewi Nant Hodni*
Merioneth *Meirionnydd*
Milford Haven *Aberdaugleddau*
Neath *Castell-nedd*
New Radnor *Maesyfed*
Newtown *Y Drenewydd*
Patrishow *Patrisio*
Pembrokeshire *Sir Benfro*
Radnorshire *Sir Faesyfed*
Rhayader *Rhaeadr*
Rhulen *Rhiwlen*
Snowdon *Yr Wyddfa*
Snowdonia *Eryri*
St Clears *Sanclêr*
*Strata Florida Ystrad Fflur*
Tintern Abbey *Abaty Tyndyrn*

Usk *Brynbuga*
*Valle Crucis* Abbey *Abaty Glyn-y-groes*
Welshpool *Trallwng*
Whitland *Hendy-gwyn ar Daf*
Wrexham *Wrecsam*
Wye river *afon Gwy*

By the same author:

Wales Before 1066 – a guide (New edition)
Wales Before 1536 – a guide (New edition)
Radnorshire – A Historical Guide
Country Churchyards in Wales